# Psychology 12/13

*Forty-Third Edition*

## EDITOR

**William Buskist**
*Auburn University*

William Buskist is the Distinguished Professor in the Teaching of Psychology at Auburn University and a Faculty Fellow at Auburn's Biggio Center for the Enhancement of Teaching and Learning. He is a past president of the Society for the Teaching of Psychology (Division 2 of the American Psychological Association) and a member of the National Institute on the Teaching of Psychology (NITOP) planning committee. He is published widely in the teaching of psychology and has received several teaching awards, including the Charles L. Brewer Distinguished Teaching of Psychology Award from the American Psychological Foundation, the Robert S. Daniel award from the Society for the Teaching of Psychology, the Fred S. Keller Behavioral Education Award from Division 25 (Behavior Analysis), and The Gerald and Emily Leischuck Presidential Award for Excellence in Teaching from Auburn University. He is a Fellow of APA (Divisions 1: General Psychology, 52: International Psychology, and 2) and the Association for Psychological Science.

ANNUAL EDITIONS: PSYCHOLOGY, FORTY-THIRD EDITION

Published by McGraw-Hill, a business unit of The McGraw-Hill Companies, Inc., 1221 Avenue of the Americas, New York, NY 10020. Copyright © 2013 by The McGraw-Hill Companies, Inc. All rights reserved. Printed in the United States of America. Previous edition(s) © 2012, 2011, 2010, and 2009. No part of this publication may be reproduced or distributed in any form or by any means, or stored in a database or retrieval system, without the prior written consent of The McGraw-Hill Companies, Inc., including, but not limited to, in any network or other electronic storage or transmission, or broadcast for distance learning.

Some ancillaries, including electronic and print components, may not be available to customers outside the United States.

This book is printed on acid-free paper.

Annual Editions® is a registered trademark of the McGraw-Hill Companies, Inc.
Annual Editions is published by the **Contemporary Learning Series** group within the McGraw-Hill Higher Education division.

1 2 3 4 5 6 7 8 9 0 QDB/QDB 1 0 9 8 7 6 5 4 3 2

ISBN: 978-0-07-8051128
MHID: 0-07-8051126
ISSN: 0272-3794

Managing Editor: *Larry Loeppke*
Developmental Editor: *Jade Benedict*
Permissions Coordinator: *Rita Hingtgen*
Senior Marketing Communications Specialist: *Mark Klein*
Senior Project Manager: *Joyce Watters*
Design Coordinator: *Margarite Reynolds*
Cover Designer: *Studio Montage, St. Louis, Missouri*
Buyer: *Susan K. Culbertson*
Media Project Manager: *Sridevi Palani*

Compositor: Laserwords Private Limited
Cover Image Credits: © ColorBlind Images/Blend Images LLC (inset); © Greg Wright/Alamy (background)

# Editors/Academic Advisory Board

Members of the Academic Advisory Board are instrumental in the final selection of articles for each edition of ANNUAL EDITIONS. Their review of articles for content, level, and appropriateness provides critical direction to the editors and staff. We think that you will find their careful consideration well reflected in this volume.

## ANNUAL EDITIONS: Psychology 12/13
43rd Edition

### EDITOR

**William Buskist**
*Auburn University*

## ACADEMIC ADVISORY BOARD MEMBERS

# Editors/Academic Advisory Board continued

# Preface

In publishing ANNUAL EDITIONS we recognize the enormous role played by the magazines, newspapers, and journals of the public press in providing current, first-rate educational information in a broad spectrum of interest areas. Many of these articles are appropriate for students, researchers, and professionals seeking accurate, current material to help bridge the gap between principles and theories and the real world. These articles, however, become more useful for study when those of lasting value are carefully collected, organized, indexed, and reproduced in a low-cost format, that provides easy and permanent access when the material is needed. That is the role played by ANNUAL EDITIONS.

Scientific psychology is barely 130 years old. In 1879, Wilhelm Wundt, a German scientist, founded the first research laboratory in psychology and became the first person to claim the title of a psychologist. With the crudest of methodology, at least by modern standards, Wundt searched for the basic elements of human consciousness. From these humble beginnings, Wundt probably could not have possibly imagined the mushrooming of psychology into what it has become today—a vital and healthy science that serves as the basis for psychological practice in just about every corner of the world. Each year, psychological science and practice is studied by millions of students across the globe. And each year, thousands of young men and women graduate with PhDs in psychology and begin careers in which they conduct research, apply their knowledge in the world of business and industry, practice psychology to improve the human condition, or engage some combination of these.

Indeed, there is no aspect of human behavior, thought, or emotion that psychological scientists and practitioners leave unexamined—the entire spectrum of human nature is fair game. After all, human nature is the most complex and fascinating subject matter in all science, and to understand it, even its most basic and mundane elements must be thoroughly examined.

Unlike in Wundt's time, when no psychological journals existed, today there are literally hundreds of thousands of science reports in hundreds of journals each year. Also, unlike in Wundt's time, the scientific methodology and instruments are as complex as they are technical, and it often takes advance study in psychology to even begin to understand many of these articles. For this reason, McGraw-Hill publishes its *Annual Editions*—an anthology of current, clearly written, and highly understandable articles about psychology. The editorial staff at McGraw-Hill has designed *Annual Editions: Psychology 12/13* to meet the needs of lay people and students who are curious about psychological science and its applications. *Annual Editions: Psychology 12/13* provides a large selection of readable, informative articles primarily from popular magazines and newspapers. Most of these articles are written by journalists, but many are authored by psychologists. We have also provided a large number of credible website addresses for you to browse in order to expand your study of psychology even further.

We selected those articles for this volume that are representative of current research and thinking in psychology. They provide clear examples of the types of research and issues discussed in most introductory psychology classes. As in any science, some of the topics discussed in this collection are revolutionary; others confirm things that we already know. Some articles invite speculation about social and personal issues; others encourage careful thought about potential misuse of research findings. Your teacher will expect that you will read assigned articles carefully and critically, so that you will better understand how psychologists view their subject matter and what issues loom large on the horizon in need of further study.

We assume that you will find this collection of articles helpful to you in your study of psychology and useful.

Please look at the organization of this anthology and compare it to the organization of your course syllabus and textbook. By examining the topic guide provided after the table of contents, you can identify those articles that best match any particular unit of study in your course. Your instructor may provide some help in this task or assign articles to supplement the text. As you read the articles, try to connect their contents with the principles you are learning about in your text and classroom lectures. Some of the articles will help you better understand a specific area of psychology, and others will help you connect and integrate information from diverse research areas in psychological science and practice. Both of these strategies are key to learning about psychology. After all, it is only through careful study and thoughtful integration of research findings from many studies that we are able to discover and apply new knowledge.

William Buskist
*Editor*

# The Annual Editions Series

## VOLUMES AVAILABLE

Adolescent Psychology

Aging

American Foreign Policy

American Government

Anthropology

Archaeology

Assessment and Evaluation

Business Ethics

Child Growth and Development

Comparative Politics

Criminal Justice

Developing World

Drugs, Society, and Behavior

Dying, Death, and Bereavement

Early Childhood Education

Economics

Educating Children with Exceptionalities

Education

Educational Psychology

Entrepreneurship

Environment

The Family

Gender

Geography

Global Issues

Health

Homeland Security

Human Development

Human Resources

Human Sexualities

International Business

Management

Marketing

Mass Media

Microbiology

Multicultural Education

Nursing

Nutrition

Physical Anthropology

Psychology

Race and Ethnic Relations

Social Problems

Sociology

State and Local Government

Sustainability

Technologies, Social Media, and Society

United States History, Volume 1

United States History, Volume 2

Urban Society

Violence and Terrorism

Western Civilization, Volume 1

World History, Volume 1

World History, Volume 2

World Politics

# Contents

# UNIT 1
## The Science of Psychology

# UNIT 2
## Biological Bases of Behavior

The concepts in bold italics are developed in the article. For further expansion, please refer to the Topic Guide.

# UNIT 3
## Perceptual Processes

The concepts in bold italics are developed in the article. For further expansion, please refer to the Topic Guide.

# UNIT 4
## Learning

# UNIT 5
## Cognitive Processes

The concepts in bold italics are developed in the article. For further expansion, please refer to the Topic Guide.

# UNIT 6
# Emotion and Motivation

# UNIT 7
# Development

The concepts in bold italics are developed in the article. For further expansion, please refer to the Topic Guide.

# UNIT 8
## Personality Processes

# UNIT 9
## Social Processes

The concepts in bold italics are developed in the article. For further expansion, please refer to the Topic Guide.

# UNIT 10
## Psychological Disorders

The concepts in bold italics are developed in the article. For further expansion, please refer to the Topic Guide.

# UNIT 11
## Psychological Treatments

The concepts in bold italics are developed in the article. For further expansion, please refer to the Topic Guide.

# Correlation Guide

The *Annual Editions* series provides students with convenient, inexpensive access to current, carefully selected articles from the public press. **Annual Editions: Psychology 12/13** is an easy-to-use reader that presents articles on important topics such as *development, motivation, psychological disorders,* and many more. For more information on *Annual Editions* and other *McGraw-Hill Contemporary Learning Series* titles, visit www.mhhe.com/cls.

This convenient guide matches the units in **Annual Editions: Psychology 12/13** with the corresponding chapters in three of our best-selling McGraw-Hill Psychology textbooks by Feldman, Lahey, and Feist/Rosenberg.

| Annual Editions: Psychology 12/13 | Psychology and Your Life, 2/e by Feldman | Psychology: An Introduction, 11/e by Lahey | Psychology, 2/e by Feist/ Rosenberg |
|---|---|---|---|
| **Unit 1:** The Science of Psychology | **Chapter 1:** Introduction to Psychology<br><br>**Chapter 10:** Psychological Disorders | **Chapter 1:** Introduction to Psychology | **Chapter 1:** Introduction to Psychology |
| **Unit 2:** Biological Bases of Behavior | **Chapter 2:** Neuroscience and Behavior | **Chapter 3:** Biological Foundations in Behavior | **Chapter 2:** The Biology of Behavior |
| **Unit 3:** Perceptual Processes | **Chapter 3:** Sensation and Perception<br><br>**Chapter 4:** States of Consciousness | **Chapter 5:** Sensation and Perception | **Chapter 4:** Sensing and Perceiving our World |
| **Unit 4:** Learning | **Chapter 5:** Learning<br><br>**Chapter 6:** Thinking, Memory, Cognition, and Language | **Chapter 7:** Basic Principles of Learning<br><br>**Chapter 9:** Cognition, Language, and Intelligence | **Chapter 8:** Learning |
| **Unit 5:** Cognitive Processes | **Chapter 6:** Thinking, Memory, Cognition, and Language | **Chapter 9:** Cognition, Language, and Intelligence | **Chapter 9:** Language and Thought<br><br>**Chapter 10:** Intelligence, Problem Solving, and Creativity |
| **Unit 6:** Emotion and Motivation | **Chapter 7:** Motivation and Emotion | **Chapter 11:** Motivation and Emotion | **Chapter 11:** Motivation and Emotion |
| **Unit 7:** Development | **Chapter 8:** Development | **Chapter 10:** Developmental Psychology | **Chapter 5:** Human Development |
| **Unit 8:** Personality Processes | **Chapter 9:** Personality and Individual Differences | **Chapter 12:** Personality | **Chapter 13:** Personality: The Uniqueness of the Individual |
| **Unit 9:** Social Processes | **Chapter 2:** Social Psychology | **Chapter 16:** Social Psychology | **Chapter 14:** Social Behavior |
| **Unit 10:** Psychological Disorders | **Chapter 10:** Psychological Disorders | **Chapter 14:** Abnormal Behavior | **Chapter 15:** Psychological Disorders |
| **Unit 11:** Psychological Treatments | **Chapter 11:** Treatment of Psychological Disorders | **Chapter 15:** Therapies | **Chapter 16:** Treatment of Psychological Disorders |

# Topic Guide

This topic guide suggests how the selections in this book relate to the subjects covered in your course. You may want to use the topics listed on these pages to search the Web more easily.

On the following pages a number of websites have been gathered specifically for this book. They are arranged to reflect the units of this Annual Editions reader. You can link to these sites by going to www.mhhe.com/cls.

**All the articles that relate to each topic are listed below the bold-faced term.**

# Internet References

The following Internet sites have been selected to support the articles found in this reader. These sites were available at the time of publication. However, because websites often change their structure and content, the information listed may no longer be available. We invite you to visit www.mhhe.com/cls for easy access to these sites.

# Annual Editions: Psychology 12/13

## General Sources

### APA Resources for the Public
www.apa.org/topics/index.aspx

Use the site map or search engine to access APA Monitor, the American Psychological Association magazine, APA books on a wide range of topics, PsychINFO—an electronic database of abstracts on scholarly journals, and the HelpCenter.

### Health Information Resources
www.health.gov/nhic/Pubs/tollfree.htm

This site supplies a long list of toll-free numbers that provide health-related information. None offer diagnosis and treatment, but some do offer recorded information; others provide personalized counseling, referrals, and/or written materials.

### Mental Help Net
mentalhelp.net

This comprehensive guide to mental health online features thousands of individual resources. Information on mental disorders and professional resources in psychology, psychiatry, and social work is presented.

### Psychology: Online Resource Central
www.psych-central.com

Thousands of psychology resources are currently indexed at this site. Psychology disciplines, conditions and disorders, and self-development are among the most useful bits of information located at this site.

### School Psychology Resources Online
www.schoolpsychology.net

Numerous sites on special conditions, disorders, and disabilities, as well as other data ranging from assessment/evaluation to research, are available on this resource page for psychologists, parents, and educators.

### Social Psychology Network
www.socialpsychology.org

The Social Psychology Network is the most comprehensive source of social psychology information on the Internet, including resources, programs, and research.

## UNIT 1: The Science of Psychology

### American Psychological Association
www.apa.org

This site is the home page for APA, the largest organization of professional psychologists in the United States. This site will give you access to all of APA's resources on the net, including news updates, publications, and topical information.

### Association for Psychological Science
www.psychologicalscience.org

This site is the home page for APS, which is a large national organization of scientifically-oriented psychologists. It features up-to-date news items on the science of psychology as well as descriptions of APS activities and events.

## UNIT 2: Biological Bases of Behavior

### Behavioral Genetics
www.ornl.gov/sci/techresources/Human_Genome/project/about.shtml

This government-backed website provides helpful and interesting Information on the Human Genome Project.

### Institute for Behavioral Genetics
ibgwww.colorado.edu/index.html

Dedicated to conducting and facilitating research on the genetic and environmental bases of individual differences in behavior, this University of Colorado site provides links to genetic sites, statistical sites as well as to search engines.

### Serendip
serendip.brynmawr.edu/serendip

Serendip, which is organized into 10 subject areas (e.g., brain and behavior, complex systems, genes and behavior, science and culture, and science education), contains interactive exhibits, articles, links to other resources, and a forum area.

### Society for Neuroscience
www.sfn.org

This site is the home page for the Society of Neuroscience and contains information and links to the most recent research and theory regarding biological bases of behavior.

## UNIT 3: Perceptual Processes

### Five Senses Home Page
www.sedl.org/scimath/pasopartners/senses/welcome.html

This site provides information about human sensory systems for school teachers, but much of the information is interesting and may be useful to you in your study of perception at the college level.

### Visual and Optical Illusions
dragon.uml.edu/psych/illusion.html

This site hosts a wide range of compelling visual illusions.

## UNIT 4: Learning

### Classical Conditioning
http://psychology.about.com/od/behavioralpsychology/a/classcond.htm

This site provides a thorough overview of the basic principles of classical conditioning.

### Operant Conditioning
psychology.about.com/od/behavioralpsychology/a/introopcond.htm

This site provides basic information about the principles of operant conditioning.

### Social Learning Theory
teachnet.edb.utexas.edu/~lynda_abbott/Social.html

This site provides an overview of the fundamentals of modern social learning theory.

# Internet References

## UNIT 5: Cognitive Processes

### American Association for Artificial Intelligence (AAAI)
www.aaai.org/AITopics/index.html

This AAAI site provides a good starting point to learn about artificial intelligence (AI)—what artificial intelligence is and what AI scientists do.

### Cognition and Thinking
www.simplypsychology.pwp.blueyonder.co.uk/cognitive.html

This useful site provides an introduction and overview to the basic principles of cognition, including background on some of this field's early leaders.

### Cognitive Science Society
http://cognitivesciencesociety.org/index.html

This website brings together scientists from all fields of study that are related to advancing cognitive science including psychology, anthropology, linguistics, education, neuroscience, philosophy, and artificial intelligence.

## UNIT 6: Emotion and Motivation

### Emotion
www.psychology.org/links/Environment_Behavior_Relationships/Emotion

This site contains brief descriptions and links to Web articles on all facets of emotion.

### Mind Tools
www.helpguide.org/mental/stress_management_relief_coping.htm

Useful information on stress management can be found at this website.

### Motivation
www.edpsycinteractive.org/topics/motivation/motivate.html

This site provides an abundance of information on psychological research on motivation.

## UNIT 7: Development

### Developmental Psychology
psychology.about.com/od/developmentalpsychology/Developmental_Psychology.htm

This site presents a very good overview of development, especially in childhood. It also contains many helpful links to websites on related issues.

### Puberty and Adolescence
www.nlm.nih.gov/medlineplus/ency/article/001950.htm

This site provides a brief, but compelling overview of puberty and adolescence.

### Social Psychology of Aging
www.trinity.edu/MKEARL/gersopsy.html

This site presents information the social psychology of the aging process and an overview of the challenges faced by older adults.

## UNIT 8: Personality Processes

### Great Ideas in Personality
www.personalityresearch.org

This site provides links to discussions of the major ideas and issues in the psychological study of personality.

### The Personality Project
personality-project.org/personality.html

This personality project (by William Revelle) is meant to guide those interested in personality theory and research to the current personality research literature.

## UNIT 9: Social Processes

### Nonverbal Behavior and Nonverbal Communication
www3.usal.es/~nonverbal

This website has a detailed listing of nonverbal behavior and nonverbal communication sites, including the work of historical and current researchers.

### The Social Psychology Network
www.socialpsychology.org

This site is the "one-stop shopping center" for information on social psychology. It contains hundreds of links to social psychology on the Web.

## UNIT 10: Psychological Disorders

### American Association of Suicidology
www.suicidology.org

The American Association of Suicidology is a nonprofit organization dedicated to the understanding and prevention of suicide. This site is designed as a resource to anyone concerned about suicide.

### Ask NOAH About: Mental Health
www.noah-health.org/en/mental

Information about child and adolescent family problems, mental conditions and disorders, suicide prevention, and much more is available here.

### Mental Health Net Disorders and Treatments
www.mentalhelp.net

Presented on this site are links to psychological disorders, which include anxiety, panic, phobic disorders, schizophrenia, and violent/self-destructive behaviors.

### National Clearinghouse for Alcohol and Drug Information
ncadi.samhsa.gov

Information on drug and alcohol facts that might relate to adolescence and the issues of peer pressure and youth culture is presented here. Resources, referrals, research and statistics, databases, and related Net links are available.

### National Women's Health Resource Center (NWHRC)
www.healthywomen.org

NWHRC's site contains links to resources related to women's substance abuse and mental illnesses.

## UNIT 11: Psychological Treatments

### Abraham A. Brill Library
www.psychoanalysis.org/resources-library.html

Containing data on tens of thousands of books, periodicals, and reprints in psychoanalysis and related fields, the Abraham A. Brill Library has holdings that span the literature of psychoanalysis from its beginning to the present day.

# Internet References

## The C.G. Jung Page
www.cgjungpage.org

Dedicated to the work of Carl Jung, this is a comprehensive resource, with links to Jungian psychology, news and opinions, reference materials, graduate programs, dreams, multilingual sites, and related Jungian themes.

## Knowledge Exchange Network (KEN)
mentalhealth.about.com/library/2010/inf/blrc9.htm

Information about mental health (prevention, treatment, and rehabilitation services) is available via toll-free telephone services, an electronic bulletin board, and publications.

## NetPsychology
netpsych.com/index.htm

This site explores the uses of the Internet to deliver mental health services. This is a basic cybertherapy resource site.

## Sigmund Freud and the Freud Archives
http://users.rcn.com/brill/freudarc.html

Internet resources related to Sigmund Freud, which include a collection of libraries, museums, and biographical materials, as well as the Brill Library archives, can be found here.

# UNIT 1

# The Science of Psychology

## Unit Selections

## Learning Outcomes

*After reading this Unit, you should be able to:*

- Explain the ways in which psychological science depends on neuroscience research to understand behavior, thought, and emotion.

- Understand the brain's role in everyday life.

- Distinguish between science and pseudoscience.

- Explain the historical role of psychology within the U.S. Army.

- How psychologists are using positive psychology to improve the mental health of U.S. soldiers.

- Outline the historical foundations of psychology.

- Explain the challenges and threats to psychology's core foundation as an academic discipline.

- Discuss the importance of cultural-scientific foundation of psychology in terms of its role in helping psychology remain a strong academic discipline.

## Student Website
www.mhhe.com/cls

## Internet References

**American Psychological Association**
   www.apa.org
**Association for Psychological Science**
   www.psychologicalscience.org

Contemporary psychology is defined as the science of mental activity and behavior. This definition reflects the two parent disciplines from which psychology emerged: philosophy and biology. Compared to its parents, psychology is very much a new discipline. Some aspects of modern psychology are especially biological, such as neuroscience, perception, psychophysics, and behavioral genetics. In fact, many of our recent advances in understanding thinking and behavior emanate from neuroscience.

Modern psychology encompasses the full spectrum of human action, thought, and emotion. There is no aspect of human life that does not fall under psychology's purview. In fact, if you can think of a behavior, then you can bet that there is a branch of psychology that focuses on the study of that behavior. From home life, to the workplace, to the athletic field, to the church, synagogue, and mosque, psychologists seek to understand the causes of our behaviors and our thoughts. Some psychologists work to understand these behaviors simply for the sake of advancing new knowledge. Other psychologists take this new knowledge and apply it to improving the quality of everyday life. Still other psychologists focus exclusively on the most challenging problems facing the world today—war, hunger, poverty, sexual and other forms of abuse, drug and alcohol addiction, environmental change and global warming, and so on.

Psychologists work in a varied settings. Many psychologists are academics, teaching and conducting psychological research on college and university campuses. Others work in applied settings such as hospitals, mental health clinics, industry, and schools. Other psychologists work primarily in private practice in which they see clients for personal therapy and counseling sessions. Despite this diversity of settings, all psychologists share a keen interest in understanding and explaining human action and thought.

All psychologists receive rigorous training in their respective subfields of psychology. Undergraduates who are interested in becoming professional psychologists apply for and attend graduate school to receive specialized training. Some of these students earn their master's degree in psychology while others go on to complete their PhD. For some subfields of psychology, such as clinical psychology, individuals must obtain a license to practice psychology. In this case, in addition to completing the graduate degree, the individual must also complete an

© Don Farrall/Getty Images

internship in which he or she receives advanced and closely supervised training in the specialty.

Psychology is an incredibly diverse discipline that offers valuable insights into work, play, suffering, and love. It addresses many fascinating issues, dilemmas, and questions. This unit offers you a glimpse at some of the pressing challenges that face psychologists in their work today and offers considerable insight into what you can expect from your study of psychology.

# The Future of Psychology:
## *Connecting Mind to Brain*

LISA FELDMAN BARRETT

*Physical concepts are free creations of the human mind, and are not, however it may seem, uniquely determined by the external world.*
— Einstein & Infeld (1938, p. 33)

*The cardinal passions of our life, anger, love, fear, hate, hope, and the most comprehensive divisions of our intellectual activity, to remember, expect, think, know, dream , with the broadest genera of aesthetic feeling, joy, sorrow, pleasure, pain, are the only facts of a subjective order which this vocabulary deigns to note by special words.*
— James (1890, p. 195)

From its inception in the early 18th century (as an amalgam of philosophy, neurology, and physiology), psychology has always been in a bit of an identity crisis, trying to be both a social and a natural science.[1] Psychologists attempt to bridge the social and natural worlds using the conceptual tools of their time. Throughout our history, the link between the two has felt less like a solid footbridge and more like a tightrope requiring lightness of foot and a really strong safety net. Mind–brain, and relatedly, behavior–brain, correspondence continue to be central issues in psychology, and they remain the largest challenge in 21st-century psychology.

The difficulty in linking the human mind to behavior on the one hand and to the brain on the other is rooted, ironically enough, in the way the human brain itself works. Human brains categorize continuously, effortlessly, and relentlessly. Categorization plays a fundamental role in every human activity, including science. Categorizing functions like a chisel, dividing up the sensory world into figure and ground, leading us to attend to certain features and to ignore others. Via the process of categorization, the brain transforms only some sensory stimulation into information. Only some of the wavelengths of light striking our retinas are transformed into seen objects, and only some of the changes in air pressure registered in our ears are heard as words or music. To categorize something is to render it meaningful. It then becomes possible to make reasonable inferences about that thing, to predict what to do with it, and to communicate our experience of it to others. There are ongoing debates about how categorization works, but the fact that it works is not in question.

The brain's compulsion to categorize presents certain unavoidable challenges to what can be learned about the natural world from human observation. Psychologists know that people don't contribute to their perceptions of the world in a neutral way. Human brains do not dispassionately look upon the world and carve nature at its joints. We make self-interested observations about the world in all manner of speaking. And what holds true for people in general certainly holds for scientists in particular. Scientists are active perceivers, and like all perceivers, we see the world from a particular point of view (that is not always shared by other scientists). We parse the world into bits and pieces using the conceptual tools that are available at a particular point in time and with a particular goal in mind (often inextricably linked to said conceptual tools). This is not a failing of the scientific method perse—it is a natural consequence of how the human brain sees and hears and feels . . . and does science.

An example of how categorization shapes science comes from the study of genetics. When molecular biologists first began to study the units of inheritance, they (inspired by Mendel) searched for and found *genes*: bits of DNA that make the proteins needed to constitute the human body. Yet, only a small proportion of human DNA (somewhere between 2% to 5%, depending on which paper you read) are genes; the rest of the stuff (that does not directly produce proteins) was labeled "junk" on the assumption that it was largely irrelevant to the biological understanding of life. As it turns out, however, "junk DNA" has some rather important functions, including regulating gene expression (i.e., turning on and off protein production) in a contextually sensitive fashion (for a generally accessible review, see Gibbs, 2003). Scientists have discovered that much of what makes us human and makes one person different from another lurks in this junk. The result has been nothing short of a revolution in molecular genetics. Genes do not, in and of themselves, provide a sufficient recipe for life. The unit of selection is not the gene, but the individual, who, for the purposes of molecular genetics, can be thought of as a bundle of genes that are turned on and off by the rest of our DNA that regulates the epigenetic context. And, the more they learned about junk DNA, the more scientists realized that it is not so easy to define what is a gene and what is not. Some molecular geneticists now try to avoid the word "gene" altogether. Instead they use the more mechanistic term *transcriptional unit.*

In this article, I argue that perhaps psychology needs to reconsider its vocabulary of categories. Like any young science, psychology has been practicing a very sophisticated form of phenomenology, observing the psychological world using categories derived from our own experiences. We then use common sense words to name these categories, leading us to reify them as entities. We then search for the counterparts of these categories within the brain. These two practices—carving and naming—have a far-reaching consequence: Psychology may more or less accept the Kantian idea that the knowledge stored in a human brain contributes to thoughts, feelings, memories, and perceptions in a top-down fashion, but at the same time we accept without question that *emotions, thoughts, memories, the self,* and the other psychological categories in folk psychology reflect the basic building blocks of the mind. We do this in much the same way that Aristotle assumed that fire, earth, air, and water were the basic elements of the material universe; as if the categories themselves are not constructed out of something else more basic. In our causal explanations, psychologists talk about psychological facts as if they are physical facts.

But what if psychological facts are not physical facts? What if the phenomena we want to explain—emotions, cognitions, the self, behaviors—are not just the subject matter of the human mind, but are also the creations of that mind? What if the boundaries for these categories are not respected in the very brain that creates them?

Such a state of things might lead some scientists to conclude that psychological categories are not real, or that psychology as a science can be dispensed with. That all scientists need to do is understand the brain. But nothing can be farther from the truth. The main point I make in this article is that, in psychology, we simultaneously take our phenomenology too seriously and not seriously enough: too seriously when trying to understand how the mind corresponds to the brain and not seriously enough when we want to understand psychological phenomena as real and scientifically valuable, even in the face of spectacular and unrelenting progress in neuroscience. Changing this state of affairs is a central task for the future.

# The Metaphysics of What Exists
## Scientific Ontology

The vocabulary of categories in any field of science segregates the phenomena to be explained and in so doing makes them real. Yet not all categories are real in the same way.

Natural sciences like physics deal with scientific categories that are assumed to be *observer independent* (they are real in the natural sense and can be discovered by humans). These kinds of categories function like an archaeologist's chisel—we need a mind to discover and experience instances of these categories, but they do not depend on our minds for their existence. In 2007, I discovered that philosopher John Searle (in writing

about social institutions and social power; Searle, 1995) called these *ontologically objective categories* or "brute facts." They are also called natural kind categories. At times, human experience can lull scientists into using the wrong categories at first (e.g., genes and junk DNA), but the phenomena themselves (e.g., DNA, RNA, proteins, and so on) exist outside of human experience and can have a corrective influence on which categories are used. Here, the presumption is that the scientific method takes us on what can seem like a long, slow, carnival ride toward discovering and explaining the material world.

Social sciences like sociology or economics deal with categories that are *observer dependent* (and are real because they are invented and shared by humans). Observer-dependent categories function like a sculptor's chisel—they constitute what is real and what is not. Searle calls these ontologically subjective categories because they exist only by virtue of collective intentionality (which is a fancy way of saying that they are real by virtue of the fact that everybody largely agrees on their content). Humans create observer-dependent categories to serve some function. Their validity, and their very existence, in fact, comes from consensual agreement. Little pieces of paper have value to procure goods not because of their molecular structure, but because we all agree that they do, and these little pieces of paper would cease to have value if many people changed their mind (and refused to accept them in lieu of material goods). Only certain types of pair bonds between humans are defined as "marriages" and confer real social and monetary benefits. People are citizens of the same country (e.g., Canada, Yugoslavia, or the Soviet Union) only as long as they all agree that the country exists and this membership becomes part of a person's identity and often confers social and economic advantage.[2] Searle calls these *ontologically subjective categories* because they exist only by virtue of collective intentionality (which is a fancy way of saying that they are real by virtue of the fact that everybody largely agrees on their content). We might also think of them as nominal kind categories,[3] as artifact categories, or as cognitive tools for getting along and getting ahead.

Psychology, in walking a tightrope between the social world and the natural world, tries to map observer-dependent categories to observer-independent categories. The trick, of course, is to be clear about which is which and to never mistake one for the other. Once psychology more successfully distinguishes between the two, I predict that we will be left with the more tractable but never simple task of understanding how to map mind and behavior to the human brain.

Beginning in 1992, I began to craft the position that emotion categories labeled as *anger* and *sadness* and *fear* are mistakenly assumed to be observer independent, when in fact they are dependent on human (particularly Western) perceivers for their existence. I published the first sketch of these ideas about a decade later (Barrett, 2005, 2006b), spurred on by my discovery of the *emotion paradox:* In the blink of an eye, perceivers experience anger or sadness or fear and see these emotions in other people (and in animals, or even simple moving shapes) as effortlessly as they read words on a page,[4] yet perceiver-independent measurements of faces, voices, bodies, and brains do not clearly and consistently reveal evidence of these categories

(Barrett, 2006a; Barrett & Wager, 2006; also see Barrett, Lindquist, et al., 2007). Some studies of cardiovascular measurements, electromyographic activity of facial muscles, acoustical analyses of vocal cues, and blood-flow changes within the brain are consistent with the traditional idea that emotions are observer-independent categories, but the larger body of evidence disconfirms their status as ontologically objective entities. There is not a complete absence of statistical regularities across these measures during the events that we name as the same emotion (e.g., *anger*), but the variance observed within any single category is not all that different from the variability across different categories.

One solution to the emotion paradox suggests that *anger, sadness, fear,* and so on are observer-dependent psychological categories and that instances of these emotions live in the head of the perceiver (Barrett, 2006b). This is not to say that emotions exist only in the head of the perceiver. Rather, it is more correct to say that they cannot exist without a perceiver. I experience myself as angry or I see your face as angry or I experience the rat's behavior as angry, but anger does not exist independent of someone's perception of it. Without a perceiver, there are only internal sensations and a stream of physical actions.

In 2007, based largely on neuroanatomical grounds, I extended this line of reasoning, arguing that the categories labeled as *emotion* and *cognition* are not observer-dependent categories (Duncan & Barrett, 2007; for a similar view, see Pessoa, 2008). *Thinking* (e.g., sensing and categorizing an object, or deliberating on an object) is experienced as a fundamentally different sort of mental activity than *feeling* (i.e., representing how the object influences one's internal state). As a result, psychologists have believed for some time that cognitions and emotions are separate and distinctive processes in the mind that interact like the bit and parts of a machine. But the brain does not really respect these categories, and thus mental states cannot be said to be categorically one or the other. Nor can behavior be caused by their interaction.

In this article, I am extending this reasoning even further by proposing that many—perhaps even the majority—of the categories with modern psychological currency are like money, marriage, nationality, or any of the ontologically subjective categories that Searle writes about. The complex psychological categories we refer to as *thoughts, memories, emotions,* and *beliefs,* or *automatic processing, controlled processing,* or *the self,* and so on, are observer dependent. They are collections of mental states that are products of the brain, but they do not correspond to brain organization in a one-to-one fashion. These categories exist because a group of people agreed (for phenomenological and social reasons) that this is a functional way to parse the ongoing mental activity that is realized in the brain. Some of the categories are cross-culturally stable (because they function to address certain universal human concerns that stem from living in large, complex groups), whereas others are culturally relative. The distinction between categories like *emotion* and *cognition,* for example, is relative and can vary with cultural context (e.g., Wikan, 1990), thus calling into question the fact that they are universal, observer-independent categories of the mind.

Even the most basic categories in psychology appear to be observer dependent. Take, for example, *behaviors* (which are intentional, bounded events) and *actions* (which are descriptions of physical movements). People easily and effortlessly see behaviors in other people and in nonhuman animals. We typically believe that behaviors exist independent of an observer, and that they are detected, but not created, by the human brain. But this is not quite true. Behaviors are actions with a meaning that is inferred by an observer. Social psychology has accumulated a large and nuanced body of research on how people come to see the physical actions of others as meaningful behaviors by inferring the causes for those actions (usually by imputing an intention to the actor; for a review, see Gilbert, 1998; Vallacher & Wegner, 1987). People and animals are constantly moving and doing things—that is, they are constantly engaging in a flow of actions. A perceiver automatically and effortlessly partitions continuous movements into recognizable, meaningful, discrete behavioral acts using category knowledge about people and animals (Vallacher & Wegner, 1987). In emotion research, a rat that kicks up bedding at a threat is said to be *defensive treading* or in a state of *fear*. Similarly, a rat in a small spare box who becomes still (except for respiration) in response to a tone that sometimes predicts an electric shock is said to be *freezing* or in a state of *fear*. Two very different actions are referred to as the same behavior if the same intention is inferred. But a freezing rat might also be referred to as vigilant—in an alert, behavioral stance that allows a martialing of attentional resources to quickly learn more about a stimulus when its predictive value is uncertain (cf. Barrett, Lindquist, et al., 2007). The category used depends on the inference made by the observer.

The same point can be made about situations. Physical surroundings exist separately from observers, but situations do not (for a discussion, see Barrett, 2006c).

A similar point can even be made about what are typically assumed to be the observer-independent phenomena measured during functional magnetic resonance functional imaging. Areas of the brain that show increased activity during *cognition, perception,* or *emotion* (or whatever the researcher is interested in measuring) are assumed to reflect changes in blood flow caused by neuronal firing at those locations. But just as behavioral scientists separate the variance in a measured behavior into *effect* (i.e., the measured variance of interest) and *error* (i.e., the measured variance that is not of interest), so do cognitive neuroscientists routinely separate blood oxygen level dependent changes into *signal* (the strong changes that they believe to be task dependent) and *noise* (the weaker changes that they don't care about). This separation is guided by the neuropsychological assumption that psychological functions are localized to modules in particular brain areas, like islands on a topographical map, because lesions in particular areas appear to disrupt specific psychological functions. In recent years, however, it has become clear (using multivariate voxel pattern analysis procedures) that the so-called noise carries meaningful psychological information (e.g., Haynes & Rees, 2006; Kay, Naselaris, Prenger, & Gallant, 2008; Norman, Polyn, Detre, & Haxby, 2006), just as junk DNA is not junk at all. This turn of events makes brain mapping less like cartography (mapping stationary masses of land) and more like meteorology (mapping changing weather patterns or "brainstorms").

Let me be clear about what I am saying here—it is a brute fact that the brain contains neurons that fire to create mental states or cause actions and this occurs independent of human experience and measurement. It is not a brute fact, however, that this neuronal activity can be easily classified as *automatic processing* or *controlled processing;* that some "islands" in the brain realize *cognitions* whereas others realize *emotion;* or even that *the self,* or *goals,* or *memories* live in specific parts of the brain (whether in a local or distributed specific, unchanging network). We use categories to separate ongoing mental activity into discrete mental states (such as, in this culture, *anger,* an *attitude,* a *memory,* or *self-esteem*), to classify a stream of physical movements into behaviors (such as *lying, stealing,* or *joking*), or to classify parts of the physical surroundings as situations. These categories come from and constitute human experience. The category instances are real, but they derive their reality from the human mind (in the context of other human minds). Mental activity is classified this way for reasons having to do with collective intentionality, communication, and even self-regulation, but not because this is the best way to understand how the brain mechanistically creates the mind and behavior. *Emotion* and *cognition* make up the Western psychological and social reality, and they must be explained by the brute fact of how the human brain works, but emotion and cognition are not mechanisms that are necessarily respected by the human brain or categories that are required by the human brain. Brain states are observer-independent facts. The existence of mental states is also an observer-independent fact. *Cognitions, emotions, memories, self-esteem, beliefs,* and so on are not observer-dependent events, however. They are categories that have been formed and named by the human mind to represent and explain the human mind.

## *What's in a Name?*

Words are powerful in science. When dealing with observer-independent categories, words set the ground rules for what to look for in the world. To the extent that scientists understand and use the word in a similar way, they agree on what to search for. They assume, for the moment, that genetic material really is segregated into genes and junk, and they then go about searching for the deep properties that ground these categories in the material world, with the hope either that they are right or that their observations will lead them to formulate better, more accurate categories. When dealing with observer-dependent categories that populate psychology, however, words are ontologically powerful. They set the ground rules for what exists.

Words can also be dangerous. They present scientists with a Faustian bargain. We need words to do the work of science, but words can lead us to mistake observer-dependent categories (or nominal kinds) for observer-independent categories (or natural kinds). By naming both defensive treading and freezing as *fear,* for example, scientists are lulled into thinking these behaviors share a deep property, and they will spend years searching for it, even when it may not exist. This is because a word doesn't only name a category, it also encourages a very basic form of essentialism that Paul Bloom (2004) argues is already present in how

people think about the events and objects in their everyday lives. A word functions like an "essence placeholder" that encourages people to engage in psychological essentialism—it convinces the perceiver that there is some deep reality to the category in the material world (Medin & Ortony, 1989). This is true even in young children (e.g., Xu, Cote, & Baker, 2005). William James (1890) described the danger of referring to psychological categories with words when he wrote, "Whenever we have made a word . . . to denote a certain group of phenomena, we are prone to suppose a substantive entity existing beyond the phenomena, of which the word shall be the name" (p. 195). In psychology's active and ongoing attempt to knit the social and natural worlds together into one seamless universe, words cause us to take phenomenology inspired categories—Western categories no less—and search for years (often in vain) for the specific brain areas, genes, hormones, or some other biological product that they correspond to. Then we end up arguing about whether the amygdala is the brain locus of *fear,* whether dopamine is the hormone for *reward,* or whether the serotonin transporter gene (5-HTTLPR) is the cause of *depression.*

## Forward into the Past

Thus far, I have suggested that psychology is populated by a set of observer-dependent categories that do not directly correspond (in a one-to-one fashion) to the observer-independent facts of neurons firing in the brain. If this claim is true, then psychology's current vocabulary of phenomenologically grounded categories won't interface very well with neuroscience to effectively weave social and natural sciences together into one cozy blanket and solve the problem of mind–brain (or behavior–brain) correspondence. Psychology may need a different set of psychological categories—categories that more closely describe the brain's activities in creating the mind and causing action. That being said, if emotion, cognition, memory, the self, and so on, exist—they are real by virtue of the fact that everyone within a culture experiences them, talks about them, uses them as reasons for actions—then they cannot be discarded or ontologically reduced to (or merely redefined as nothing but) neurons firing. Psychology must explain the existence of cognition and emotion because they are part of the world that we (in the Western hemisphere) live in (even if they are a part that we, ourselves, created).[5] Can psychology both describe what emotions and cognitions (or whatever the mental categories within a given cultural context) are and also explain how they are caused? I think the answer is yes. And as with most things psychological, the answer begins with William James.

Over a century ago, William James wrote about the psychologist's fallacy. "The great snare of the psychologist," James wrote, "is the confusion of his own standpoint with that of the mental fact about which he is making his report" (James, 1890, p. 196). This is pretty much the same thing as saying that psychologists confuse observer-dependent (or ontologically subjective) distinctions with observer-independent (or ontologically objective) ones. The solution to the psychologist's fallacy, according to James, is to take a psychological constructionist approach. "A science of the relations of mind and brain," James wrote, "must show how the elementary ingredients of the former correspond to the elementary functions of the latter" (James, 1890, p. 28).

Psychological constructionist models of the mind were developed in early years of psychology and have appeared consistently throughout the history of our science, although they have tended not to dominate (for a review, see Gendron & Barrett, in press). They are grounded in the assumption that experienced psychological states are not the elemental units of the mind or the brain, just as fire, water, air, and earth are not the basic elements of the universe. Instead, psychological states are products that emerge from the interplay of more basic, all-purpose components. The importance of distinguishing between the function of a mechanism (or process) and the products that it creates (what the functions are in the service of or what they allow to emerge) is inherent to a psychological constructionist approach. The contents of a psychological state reveal nothing about the processes that realize it, in much the same way that a loaf of bread does not reveal the ingredients that constitute it.

# A Recipe for Psychology in the 21st Century

The modern constructionist approach that I envision for psychology in the 21st century is grounded in a simple observation. Every moment of waking life, the human brain realizes mental states and actions by combining three sources of stimulation: sensory stimulation made available by and captured from the world outside the skin (the exteroceptive sensory array of light, vibrations, chemicals, etc.), sensory signals captured from within the body that holds the brain (somatovisceral stimulation, also called the interoceptive sensory array or the *internal milieu*), and prior experience that the brain makes available by the reactivation and reinhibition of sensory and motor neurons (i.e., memory). These three sources—sensations from the world, sensations from the body, and prior experience—are continually available, and they form three of the fundamental aspects of all mental life. Different combinations and weights of these three ingredients (plus others) produce the myriad of mental events that constitute the mind. Depending on the focus of attention and proclivities of the scientist, this stream of brain activity is parsed into discrete psychological moments that we call by different names: *feeling, thinking, remembering,* or even *seeing.*

*Perception* is the name for psychological moments in which the focus is on understanding what externally driven sensations refer to in the world. Researchers who are interested in understanding perception ("What is the object?") and behavior ("How do I act on it?") might ask how sensory stimulation from the body and prior experience with an external sensory array keep track of and impart meaning to the immediate sensations of light, air, vibrations, chemicals, and so on. Said another way, scientists are asking how the brain makes predictions about the meaning of the current sensory array from the world (Bar, 2007; Barrett & Bar, 2009), allowing us to know our relation to the immediate surroundings in a moment-to-moment way and act accordingly.

*Cognition* is the name for psychological moments in which the focus is on understanding how prior experiences are reinstated in the brain. When a person experiences the act of remembering, this mental activity is called *memory*. When they do not, it is called *thinking*. When the mental activity refers to the future, it is called *imagining*. And this mental activity provides a sense of self that continues through time. Researchers who are interested in understanding cognition ("How is the past reconstituted?") typically ask how prior instances of sensory stimulation from the world, and from the body, are encoded and associatively recombined or reinstated for future use.

*Emotion* is the name for psychological moments in which the focus is on understanding what the internal sensations from the body represent. Researchers who are interested in understanding emotion experience ("How do I feel?") examine how sensory information from the world and prior experience in the form of conceptual knowledge about emotion together create a context for what internal bodily sensations stand for in psychological terms.[6] Together, these three sources of input create the mental states named with emotion words. These conceptualized states are the mental tools that the human brain uses to regulate itself and the body's internal state either directly or by acting on the world. This last piece is essentially a restatement of the model of emotion that I proposed in Barrett (2006b).

This very general description of mental life can be developed into a psychological constructionist approach that consists of five principles: (a) the mind is realized by the continual interplay of more basic primitives that can be described in psychological terms; (b) all mental states (however categorized) can be mapped to these more basic psychological primitives; (c) these basic psychological primitives correspond closely to distributed networks in the brain; (d) the mind is more like a set of recipes than like a machine; and (e) mental events are probabilistically, not mechanistically, causal.

## *Principle 1: Psychological Primitives*

The basic processes that constitute complex psychological categories can be described as psychologically primitive (to borrow a phrase from Ortony & Turner, 1990), meaning that they are psychologically irreducible and cannot be redescribed as anything else psychological. These psychological primitives are the ingredients in a recipe that produces a psychological moment—what we call an emotion, or memory, or thought, and so on—although they are not specific to any one kind of moment. Unlike the culturally relative complex psychological categories that they realize, psychological primitives might be universal to all human beings. (This is not the same as proposing that there are broad, general laws for psychology or for domains of psychology like emotion or memory.) It might be possible to describe the operations that the brain is performing to create psychological primitives, but these operations would be identified in terms of the psychological primitives that they constitute.

Although identifying specific psychological primitives is beyond the scope of this article, elsewhere, my lab and I nominated three phenomena as psychological primitives. One psychological primitive might be what has been termed valuation, salience, or affect (producing a change in a person's internal physical state that can be consciously experienced as pleasant or unpleasant, and arousing to some degree). Another might be categorization (determining what something is, why it is, and what to do about it). And a third might be a matrix consisting of different sources of attention (where attention is defined as anything that can change the rate of neuronal firing; for discussion, see Barrett, 2006b; Barrett, Tugade, & Engle, 2004; Duncan & Barrett, 2007).[7] And of course there are other psychological primitives.

## Principle 2: An Ontology of Levels, Not Kinds

Complex psychological categories refer to the contents of the mind that can be redescribed as the psychological primitives that are themselves the products of neuronal firing. What psychology needs in the 21st century is a toolbox filled with categories for representing both the products and the processes at the various levels. Like David Marr's (1982) famous computational framework for vision (which has been oft-discussed in mind–brain correspondence; e.g., Mitchell, 2006; Ochsner & Lieberman, 2001), the categories at each level of the scientific ontology capture something different from what their component parts capture, and each must be described in its own terms and with its own vocabulary.[8] Unlike Marr's framework, as well as other recent treatments of mind–brain correspondence that explicitly discuss the need for a multilevel approach, it is assumed here that each level of the ontology must stand in relation to (and help set the boundaries for) the other levels. That is, there must be an explicit accounting (i.e., a mapping) of how categories at each level relate to one another. One such ontology of categories to describe mind–brain correspondence is suggested in Table 1 and is discussed as Principle 3.

## Principle 3: Networks, Not Locations

At the top of the ontology, complex psychological categories, such as *anger*, correspond to a collection of brain states that can be summarized as a broadly distributed *neural reference space*. A *neural reference space*, according to neuroscientist Gerald Edelman, refers to the neuronal workspace that implements the brain states that correspond to a class of mental events. A specific instance of a category (e.g., a specific instance of *anger*) corresponds to a brain state within this neural reference space. The individual brain states transcend anatomical boundaries and are coded as a flexible, distributed assembly of neurons. For example, the brain states corresponding to two different instances of *anger* may not be stable across people or even within a person over time.

Each mental state can be redescribed as a combination of psychological primitives. In this ontology, psychological primitives are functional abstractions for brain networks that contribute to the formation of neuronal assemblies that make up each brain state. They are psychologically based, network-level descriptions.[9] These networks are distributed across brain areas. They are not necessarily segregated (meaning that they can partially overlap). Each network exists within a context of connections to other networks, all of which run in parallel, each shaping the activity in the others.

### Table 1 Mind–Brain Correspondence

| Psychology | Example | Brain |
|---|---|---|
| Complex psychological category | Emotion (e.g., anger, sadness, fear, etc.), cognition (i.e., thoughts, memories and beliefs), the self | Neural reference space |
| Psychological primitive | Core affect, categorization, executive attention | Distributed network |
| Momentary mental state | Specific instance of anger | Neural assembly |

All psychological states (including behaviors) emerge from the interplay of networks that work together, influencing and constraining one another in a sort of tug-of-war as they create the mind. From instance to instance, networks might be differentially constituted, configured, and recruited. This means that instances of a complex psychological category (e.g., different instances of *anger*) will be constituted as different neuronal assemblies within a person at different times (which means that there is considerable intraindividual variability in addition to interindividual and cultural variability). It also means that phenomena that bear no subjective resemblance would be constituted from many of the same brain areas.

This scientific ontology has a family resemblance to other discussions of how psychology might map to brain function (e.g., Henson, 2005; Price & Friston, 2005). Like these other scientific ontologies, this one takes its inspiration from a number of notable neuroscience findings that together appear to constitute something of a paradigm shift in the field of cognitive neuroscience away from attempting to localize psychological functions to one spot or in a segregated network and toward more distributed approaches to understanding how the brain constitutes mental content. Specifically, the proposed ontology is consistent with: (a) research on large-scale distributed networks in the human brain (e.g., Friston, 2002; Fuster, 2006; Mesulam, 1998; Seeley et al., 2007); (b) neuroanatomical evidence of pervasive feedback connections within the primate brain (e.g., Barbas, 2007) that are further enhanced in the human brain, as well as evidence on the functional importance of this feedback (e.g., Ghuman, Bar, Dobbins, & Schnyer, 2008); (c) population-based coding and multivoxel pattern analysis, in which information is contained in spatial patterns of neuronal activity (e.g., Haynes & Rees, 2006; Kay et al., 2008; Norman et al., 2006); (d) studies that demonstrate considerable degeneracy in brain processing (the idea being that there are multiple neuronal assemblies that can produce the same output; cf. Edelman 1987; Noppeney, Friston, & Price, 2004); (e) evidence that psychological states require temporally synchronized neuronal firing across different brain areas (e.g., Axmacher, Mormanna, Fernández, Elgera, & Fell, 2006; Dan Glauser & Scherer, 2008) so that the local field potentials that are associated with neuronal synchronization are strongly correlated to the hemodynamic signals that are measured in functional neuroimaging (Niessing et al., 2005); and (f) the idea that a single neuron can code for more than one feature, depending on the assembly it is a part of (i.e., even individual neurons in the primary visual cortex might not be "feature detectors" in the strict sense of the term; e.g., Basole, White, & Fitzpatrick, 2003). By combining these novel approaches, it becomes clear that psychological states are emergent phenomena that result from a complex system of dynamically interacting neurons within the human brain at multiple levels of description. Neither the complex psychological categories nor the psychological primitives that realize them correspond to particular locations in the brain per se, and thus do not reconcile well with the kind of localization approach to brain function that was inspired by neuropsychology, remained popular in neuroscience throughout much of the 20th century, and continues to prevail today.[10]

The scientific ontology proposed here is also distinct from other scientific ontologies in three important ways. First, and perhaps most important, it deals with the existence of two domains of reality (one that is subjective and one that is objective) and their relation to one another.

Second, it helps solve the puzzle of why different sorts of behavioral tasks are associated with similar patterns of neural activity. For example, the so-called "default network" (which includes the ventral medial prefrontal cortex, dorsomedial prefrontal cortex, posterior cingulate and retrosplenial cortex, inferior parietal cortex, and at times, medial temporal structures like the hippocampus and lateral temporal cortex) shows increased activity not only during the spontaneous, highly associative "default" mental activity that is without an external stimulus, but also when one remembers the autobiographical past, envisions the future, or infers mental states in others; during self-referential processing and moral decision making; while imagining fictitious experiences (Buckner, Andrews-Hanna, & Schacter, 2008); during scene construction and contextual framing (Bar, 2007); and during the experience and perception of emotion (Barrett & Lindquist, 2008; Kober et al, 2008; Wager et al., 2008). Many functions have been proposed for this circuitry, but one approach is to ask what all these tasks have in common: They associatively recombine bits and pieces of stored, prior experience to construct episodic projection or mental simulation. Sometimes this process constructs a memory of the past. Sometimes it constructs an imagined future. Sometimes it constructs the present in a manner that is reminiscent of Edelman's notion of the "remembered present." When constructing the present, this circuitry's more general purpose might be to perform a meaning analysis of sensory input both from the body and from the world to indicate what those sensations stand for. When working together as a functional network, this circuitry's more general purpose may be to impart meaning to the current sensory array based on prior, episodic experience. It allows the brain to predict what the current sensory information means based on that last time something like it was encountered and to formulate an appropriate response. A similar view is discussed in Bar (2007), who suggested that this circuitry functions to connect sensory input with memory to create predictions about what the sensory input refers to.

Finally, this psychological constructionist ontology also unifies a number of smaller scientific paradoxes with one solution. For example, it helps us to understand how perceptual memory can influence declarative memory tasks (even though implicit and explicit memory are supposed to be mechanistically different; e.g., Voss, Baym, & Paller, 2008), as well as how the same subjective feeling of remembering (Phelps & Sharot, 2008) or mental imagery (Kosslyn, Thompson, Sukel, & Alpert, 2005) can be produced in different ways (or, as discussed in Principle 4, with different recipes).

## Principle 4: Recipes, Not Machines

In the psychological constructionist ontology proposed here, the metaphor for the mind in the 21st century is not a machine, but a recipe book. Psychological primitives are not separate, interacting bits and pieces of the mind that have no causal relation to one another like the cogs and wheels of a machine. Instead, they are more like the basic ingredients in a well-stocked pantry that can be used to make any number of different recipes (which make the mental states that people experience and give names to).[11] The products of the various recipes are not universal, although they are not infinitely variable or arbitrary either (e.g., bread can be baked with or without eggs, but you need some kind of grain to make bread what it is). The recipes are not universal. The recipe for *anger* will differ from instance to instance (with a context) within a person, and even if there is a modal recipe, it might differ across persons within a particular cultural context, as well as across cultural contexts. At the psychological level, however, the ingredients that make up the recipes might be universal (although how they function in conjunction with one another might not be). And as with all recipes, the amount of each ingredient is only one factor that is important to making the end product what it is. The process of combining ingredients is also important (e.g., are the dry ingredients added to the wet or vice versa, and are they whipped in, stirred in, or cut in?). As a result, it is not enough to just identify what the ingredients are, but also how they coordinate and shape one another during the process of construction.

The recipe analogy also helps us to see the scientific utility of distinguishing between complex psychological categories, psychological primitives, and neuronal firing, and to understand the relation between them. The category *bread* differs for a food critic, a chef, and a chemist. The job of a food critic is to communicate about bread. Food critics don't need to know the recipe for two different breads to describe which one has the preferred flavor and texture for a particular meal. That being said, it helps a food critic to know the recipe to explain why a particular bread tastes better for a particular meal. Also, it is more efficient (and less costly in both the economic and caloric sense) to change the taste of bread by modifying the recipe than by slathering a slice in butter and jam. A chef must know the recipe for bread to make one (e.g., a chef must know that flour and water are key ingredients, and that one must add yeast for bread to rise), but he or she need not know that flour and water interact to produce an interconnected network of coiled proteins (called *gluten*) that trap and hold the gases made by the yeast when bread is baking. That being said, every good chef knows that it helps to have some knowledge of chemistry, otherwise experimenting with changing the recipe can feel like shots in the dark. In a similar way, scientists must understand that the category *anger* differs for the social scientist, the psychologist, and the neuroscientist, but each of them would be better off knowing something about the category at the other levels of analysis.

## Principle 5: Probabilistic Causation, Not Linear Causation

If mental events are constructed like recipes, then *goals* or *anger* or *memories* or *attitudes* do not cause *behavior* in the typical mechanistic way that psychologists now think about causation, where "Psychological Process A" localized in "Brain Area 1" causes the separate and distinct "Psychological Process B" localized in "Brain Area 2", and so on. Instead a psychological-construction approach conceives of mental causation differently. Saying "anger caused aggressive behavior" might translate into the claim that a constructed mental state corresponding to "Brain State A at Time 1" (categorized as anger) increases the probability of occurrence of a second constructed mental state corresponding to "Brain State B at Time 2" ("slamming one's fist against the table"). This is similar to what connectionist modelers like Spivey (2007) and computational neuroscientists like O'Reilly and Munakata (2000) might argue. Alternatively, saying that "anger causes aggressive behavior" might translate into one brain state that is being constructed over time but, for reasons having to do with inferred intention, is experienced as two separate mental events (anger on the one hand, and the behavior of slamming one's fist against the table on the other). Your internal bodily sensations might be categorizing this as *anger* because you experience these sensations in conjunction with your goals being blocked, and you clench your fingers to strike a table because you perform this action as you attend to a desire to cause harm. The point is that your subjective parsing of neuronal responses across space and time may not correspond to discrete bursts of neuronal activity. Either way, to say that "a person pounds a table because he is angry" is to give a reason for a behavior. Reasons are not causes for behavior and therefore do not constitute an explanation of it (for a discussion, see Searle, 2007).

Either option points to the implication that psychologists must abandon the linear logic of an experiment as a metaphor for how the mind works. In the classic experiment, we present a participant (be it a human or some nonhuman animal) with some sensory stimulation (i.e., a stimulus) that provokes some brain activity, and then we measure some response. Correspondingly, psychological models of the mind (and brain) almost always follow a similar ordering (stimulus → organism → response). The relevant neurons are presumed to generally lie quiet until stimulated by a source from the external world. Scientists talk about independent variables because we assume that they exist separate from the participant.

In real life, however, there are no independent variables. Our brains (not an experimenter) help to determine what is a stimulus and what is not, in part by predicting what will be important in the future (Bar, 2007). Said another way, the current state of the human brain makes some sensory stimulation into *information* and relegates the rest to the psychologically impotent category of "background noise." In this way, sensory stimulation only modulates preexisting neuronal activity,

but does not cause it outright (Llinas, Ribary, Contreras, & Pedroarena, 1998), and our brain contributes to every mental moment whether we experience a sense of agency or not (and usually we do not). This means that the simple linear models of psychological phenomena that psychologists often construct (stimulus → organism → response) may not really offer true explanations of psychological events.

The implication, then, is that mental events are not independent of one another. They occur in a context of what came before and what is predicted in the future. This kind of model building is easy for a human brain to accomplish, but difficult for a human mind to discover, because we have a tendency to think about ingredients in separate and sequential rather than emergent terms (e.g., Hegarty, 1992).

## Losing Your Mind?

If complex categories such as *emotions, memories, goals,* and *the self* are collections of mental states that are created from a more basic set of psychological ingredients, it might be tempting to assume that psychology can dispense with the complex categories altogether. After all, a complex psychological category like *anger* will not easily support the accumulation of knowledge about how anger is caused if varieties of anger are constituted by many different recipes. This was certainly William James's position when describing his constructionist approach: "Having the goose which lays the golden eggs, the description of each egg already laid is a minor matter" (James, 1890, p. 449). When it came to emotion, James was both a constructionist and a material reductionist. He espoused a token–token identity model of emotion, in which every instance of emotion that feels different can be ontologically reduced to a distinctive physical state, even when they are all members of the same common-sense category. (This approach stands in contrast to a type–type identity model in which every kind of emotion can be reduced to one and only one type of physical state.) Like James, some scientists believe that once we understand how such psychological events are implemented in the brain, we won't need a science of psychology at all. Mental states will be reduced to brain states, and psychology will disappear.

But even William James can be wrong. In the constructionist account proposed here, a process should not be confused with the mental content it produces, but neither can it replace the need for describing that content. Said another way, the kind of material reductionism that James advocated should be avoided if for no other than the very pragmatic reason that complex psychological categories are the targets of explanation in psychology. You have to know what you are explaining in order to have something to explain. You have to be able to identify it and describe it well. A scientific approach to understanding any psychological phenomenon requires both description ("What is it?") and explanation ("How was it constructed or made?").

But the more important reason to avoid material reduction is that the various phenomena we are discussing (complex psychological categories, psychological primitives, and neuronal firing) each exist at different levels of scientific inquiry and do not exist at others. Complex psychological categories like *cognition*

9

(*memories, beliefs, imaginings, thoughts*), emotions (*anger, fear, happiness*), and other varieties of psychological categories (*the self, attitudes,* and so on) are phenomena that fall squarely in the social science camp. They dwell at the boundary between sociology and anthropology on the one hand, and psychology on the other. Being observer-dependent categories that exist by virtue of collective intention (a group of human minds agree that anger exists and so it does), they are phenomenological distinctions. To understand them is to understand the nature, causes, and functions of these phenomenological distinctions (or the distinctions between whatever categories exist in your cultural context). They may not correspond to the brute facts of neuronal firing, but they are real in a relational way. If I categorize my mental state as a *thought* (instead of a *feeling*) and communicate this to you, you will understand something about the degree to which I feel responsible for that state and the degree to which I feel compelled to act on it, as long as you belong to a culture where the emotion–cognition distinction exists (because in some cultures it does not). Furthermore, from a descriptive standpoint, we have to understand the function of these categories, both for the collective (which could be a dyad or a group of people) and for the individual. They can be epistemologically objective (i.e., studied with the methods of science) because they exist by consensus (in fact, consensus equals recognition in the science of emotion). And these categories may even have a biologically constructive quality of their own. As many neuroscientists have pointed out, humans are not born with the genetic material to provide a sufficient blueprint for the synaptic complexity that characterizes our brains. Instead, our genetic make up requires plasticity. Evolution has endowed us with the capacity to shape the microstructure of our own brains, perhaps in part via the complex categories that we transmit to one another as we create the social and cultural context. From this standpoint, psychological construction can also be understood in relation to social construction and neuroconstruction approaches.

At the other end of the continuum, there are brain states that are made up of collections of neurons firing with some frequency. Brain states are phenomena that fall squarely in the natural science camp. Brain states are observer independent—they do not require the mind they create to recognize them. In realizing the mind, they change from moment to moment within a person, and they certainly vary across people. But understanding how a neuron fires is not the same as understanding why it fires, and the latter question cannot be answered without appealing to something psychological.

In between are psychological primitives—the basic ingredients of the mind that are informed by both the categories above and below them. They are not completely observer independent, but neither are they free from the objective fact of the workings of the brain. Psychological primitives are caused by physical and chemical processes in the brain, but understanding these causes alone will never provide a sufficient scientific understanding of what psychological primitives are. They, too, have content that must be described for a complete understanding of what they are. That being said, when discussing psychological primitives, the structure of the brain cannot be ignored either. Psychological primitives will not necessarily replace complex psychological categories in the science of psychology, although sometimes they should. Whether complex psychological categories can be ontologically reduced to psychological primitives depends on the question that a scientist is trying to answer.

As a result of all this, it is possible to causally reduce complex psychological events to brain states and psychological primitives to distributed neuronal activity (what Searle, 1992, calls *causal reduction*) without redefining the mental in terms of the physical (what Searle calls *ontological reduction*). Just as knowing that a car is made of atoms (or quarks) will not help a mechanic understand what happens when the motor stops working (Searle's example), the firing of neurons alone is not sufficient for a scientific understanding of why a book is enjoyable, whether you enjoyed the book the last time you read it, why you like to read, or what joy feels like.

Now, it may be possible that the scientific need for psychological primitives is merely the result of the rudimentary state of neuroscience methods, and that even these psychological categories can be dispensed with once we have methods that can better measure cortical columns, which are (by conventional accounts) the smallest unit of functional specialization in the cortex (whose size is measured in microns).[12] It is possible that once we can measure columns in a human cortex while it is realizing some psychological moment (e.g., see Kamitani & Tong, 2005), "what" may finally correspond to "where" (i.e., process might correspond to one specific place in the brain), and it will be possible to ontologically reduce psychological primitives into the functioning of these units.[13]

But I suspect this will not happen, for four reasons. First of all, there is some debate over whether columns are, in fact, the most basic functional units of cortical organization. Dendrites and axons of the neurons within a column extend beyond those columns (DeFilipe et al., 2007; Douglas & Martin, 2007), which suggests that the functional units of the cortex may be somewhat larger than a column itself. Second, a single neuron within a column can participate in a number of different neuronal assemblies, depending on the frequency and timing of its firing (Izhikevich, Desai, Walcott, & Hoppensteadt, 2003), which suggests that a given neuron can potentially participate in a variety of different psychological primitives (meaning it is selective, rather than specific, for a function). Third, recent evidence suggests that specific neurons do not necessarily code for single features of a stimulus. A recent study in ferrets suggests that individual neurons (when participating in neuronal assemblies) appear to respond to more than one type of sensory cue, even in primary sensory areas where receptive fields for neurons are supposed to be well defined (as in primary visual cortex or V1; Basole et al., 2003). In addition, a recent study with rats demonstrates that there is a functional remapping of cells in the nucleus accumbens (part of the ventral striatum)—sometimes they code for reward and other times for threat, depending on the context (Reynolds & Berridge, 2008).

Finally, and perhaps most controversially, it may be a bit of an overstatement to assume that all humans have exactly the same nervous system. Human brains continue to expand at a rapid rate after birth (Clancy, Darlington, & Finlay, 2001), with most of the size increase being due to changes in connectivity with other neurons (Schoenemann, Sheehan, & Glotzer, 2005; for a review, see Schoenemann, 2006; but see Schenker, Desgouttes, & Semendeferi, 2005), including an increase in the size dendritic trees and density of dendritic spines (Mai & Ashwell, 2004). This means that although all humans may have the same brain at a gross anatomical level, the connections between neurons are exceptionally plastic and responsive to experience and environmental influence, producing considerable variability in brains at the micro level. The implication is that the neuronal networks that constitute psychological primitives will be molded by experience or epigenetic influences and that they may not be isometric across people.

If these kinds of findings forecast the future of neuroscience, then they suggest even more strongly that psychological primitives may be the best categories for consistently describing what the brain is doing when it realizes the mind. If one accepts this reasoning, then psychology will never disappear in the face of neuroscience.

# Conclusions

As a science of the mind, psychology is equipped with the ability to analyze how being human affects the process of doing science. We are in a better position than most to see how scientists make unintentionally biased observations of the world and have the capacity to correct for this all too common mistake. For the last century, psychology has largely used phenomenological categories to ground our scientific investigations into the mind and behavior. These categories influence the questions we ask, the experiments we design, and the interpretation of our data. We have spent the last century differentiating among psychological phenomena, improving on their labels, and searching for their correspondence in the natural world (i.e., locations in the brain).

Science always begins with common-sense categories. As I mentioned at the outset of this article, Aristotle assumed that fire, earth, air, and water were the basic elements of matter because these are the substances that he experienced. When modern physicists first looked at the world to discover the building blocks of matter, they saw discrete particles, like atoms. Later they identified parts of atoms, like electrons, protons, and neutrons. Then it was discovered that electrons were not really physical particles at all but that they are instead more like probabilistic energy states. Eventually physicists proposed the existence of something even smaller—particles they could not see and had to create new names for (e.g., quarks and leptons). Now, amidst much debate, many physicists believe that the universe is constituted of little strings vibrating in various modes across 11 different dimensions.

Time and space are experienced as separate phenomena and were once used by physicists to guide questions about the material universe. That is, until Einstein changed the terms of the questions entirely with his theories of relativity. We now know that time and space are not rigidly independent categories—they are different ways of experiencing the same phenomenon. Psychology, of course, has studied time and space as subjective experiences for many years. Perhaps we should start approaching *emotion* and *cognition* in the same way.

This is not to say that psychology's work in the 20th century was all for naught. All the work describing psychological categories delineates the phenomena to be explained, even if the categories themselves don't do the actual explaining. A major task of 21st-century psychology, however, is to link description to explanation.

In this article, I have argued that psychology has a crucial role in understanding how the observer-dependent mental phenomena (our human way of parsing the ongoing stream of consciousness into distinct psychological events) are created by a set of observer-independent neural phenomena. To accomplish this, psychology will need a major revision of concepts and framework. Specifically, in the psychology that I envision, we will have a hierarchy of categories: complex psychological categories that are observer-dependent and refer to collections of mental states that correspond to broadly distributed neural reference spaces in the brain; psychological primitives or building blocks of the mind that correspond to distributed networks and that combine to make various mental states; and the (more or less) observer-independent categories describing the anatomy and dynamics of the brain.

The psychological science that I envision for the 21st century is not purely a social constructionist science. Instead, I am suggesting that psychology is a young science, and, like any young science, we must divest ourselves of the assumption that human experience reveals the way the world (in this case, the brain) works. That being said, phenomenology has a place in psychology, even if it is not a causal place in the way that we typically understand cause. Complex psychological categories may be the targets of explanation, but this does not completely strip them of their scientific utility.

When it comes to understanding mind–brain correspondence, perhaps the empiricists, the rationalists, and the Kantians were all a little bit correct. Knowledge about the human mind is achieved from data captured by observing the natural world but not independently of our conceptual understanding of what those data mean for a human living in large, complex groups of other humans. Believing that a psychological phenomenon exists and is real can, in a certain sense, make it so.

# Notes

1. Of course, psychology is not now, nor has it ever been, a unified discipline with a single approach to science. It encompasses many different topics, methods, and assumptions, as well as much diversity in its level of interest toward and treatment of the brain.

2. If enough people withdraw this agreement, the country splinters into two or more new countries. If people cannot agree to disagree, as is the case of those living in Quebec, which is still a province in Canada (the country where I am from), then the country remains intact.

3. A nominal kind is a category, denoted by a word, that is a combination of more fundamental properties (Frawley, 1992).

4. People don't always agree with each other in these perceptions, but that is a different story.

5. The same point can be made about other mental categories that exist in other cultural contexts.

6. Researchers who are interested in emotion perception ("Is the rat fearful?", "Is my dog sad?", "Is my friend angry?") focus their attention more like perception researchers, by asking how the perceiver's bodily sensations and prior knowledge create the momentary experience of another creature's behavior as emotional.

7. There are a number of different sources of attention in the human brain, which neuroanatomist Marcel Mesulam (2000) refers to as an attentional matrix. In my reading of the neuroanatomy, this matrix is made up of at least five interconnected sources that can apply attention to a sensory neuron: (a) sensory stimulation from the world (what scientists term a bottom-up or sensory-driven or exogenous source of attention), (b) projections from lateral prefrontal cortex (what scientists term a top-down or goal-directed or endogenous source of attention), (c) projections from association areas that are involved with encoding prior experience (what might be called a memory-based source of attention), (d) projections from limbic areas and paralimbic cortex (which I have called an affective source of attention); and (e) projections from the ascending arousal systems. The lateral prefrontal cortex, the nuclei that originate the ascending arousal systems in the brainstem and forebrain, and the selected thalamic nuclei all receive projections from affective circuitry and, in a way, can be considered indirect avenues for affective attention.

8. Marr's abstract *computational level* of analysis specifies what processes do, without specifying how they do it. His *algorithmic middle level* provides a description of the logical steps that are needed to implement the computational level. The most basic *implementation level* of analysis specifies how to build something to carry out the sequence of steps outlined by the algorithms.

9. Flour, stock, and butter are the basic ingredients of gravy, but flour and butter are first mixed together first to prepare a roux, which is then mixed into the stock to give a gravy its silkiness. So, a roux would not be considered a basic ingredient of the recipe, but it is a necessary stage or step for gravy without lumps. Similarly, large-scale brain networks contribute to circuits that have different levels of complexity and stand in relation to the network in a hierarchical fashion.

10. Even Brodmann, the originator of the much relied on Brodmann areas of cortical topography, did not believe in the idea that psychological functions are localized to specific, discrete brain areas. In 1909, in describing his views on function–location correspondence, he wrote, "one cannot think of their taking place in any other way than through an infinitely complex and involved interaction and cooperation of numerous elementary activities [. . .] we are dealing with a physiological process extending widely over the whole cortical surface and not a localised function within a specific region" (Brodmann, 1909/1994, p. 255).

11. The metaphor of a recipe works for describing any emergent phenomenon, such as the interplay of genes and epigenetic factors that together produce observed phenotypic behaviors (Bateson, 1976).

12. Neurons with common functional properties lay stacked in a column, from white matter to cortical surface (Mountcastle, 1997). Minicolumns are between 25 and 80 μm (about 11 neurons wide; Buldyrev et al., 2000) and columns (also called hypercolumns or macrocolumns) are aggregates of minicolumns ranging in size from about 300–900 mm wide (Goldman & Nauta, 1977; Mountcastle, 1997). Columns vary in width, neuron makeup, as well as density and connectivity across species (Elston, 2007), with humans having the greatest connectivity between neurons both within a column and across columns.

13. I do not mean to imply that the cortex alone is important to psychology; it goes without saying that subcortical areas are important.

# References

Axmacher, N., Mormanna, F., Fernández, G., Elgera, C.E., & Fell, J. (2006). Memory formation by neuronal synchronization. *Brain Research Reviews, 52,* 170–182.

Bar, M. (2007). The proactive brain: Using analogies and associations to generate predictions. *Trends in Cognitive Sciences, 11,* 280–289.

Barbas, H. (2007). Specialized elements of orbitofrontal cortex in primates. *Annals of the New York Academy of Sciences, 1121,* 10–32.

Barrett, L.F. (2005). Feeling is perceiving: Core affect and conceptualization in the experience of emotion. In L.F. Barrett, P.M. Niedenthal, & P. Winkielman (Eds.), *Emotions: Conscious and unconscious* (pp. 255–284). New York: Guilford.

Barrett, L.F. (2006a). Emotions as natural kinds? *Perspectives on Psychological Science, 1,* 28–58.

Barrett, L.F. (2006b). Solving the emotion paradox: Categorization and the experience of emotion. *Personality and Social Psychology Review, 10,* 20–46.

Barrett, L.F. (2006c). Valence as a basic building block of emotional life. *Journal of Research in Personality, 40,* 35–55.

Barrett, L.F., & Bar, M. (2009). See it with feeling: Affective predictions in the human brain. *Philosophical Transactions of the Royal Society of London: Series B. Biological Sciences, 364,* 1325–1334.

Barrett, L.F., & Lindquist, K.A. (2008). *The emotion enigma.* Unpublished manuscript, Boston College.

Barrett, L.F., Lindquist, K., Bliss-Moreau, E., Duncan, S., Gendron, M., Mize, J., & Brennan, L. (2007). Of mice and men: Natural kinds of emotion in the mammalian brain? *Perspectives on Psychological Science, 2,* 297–312.

Barrett, L.F., Mesquita, B., Ochsner, K.N., & Gross, J.J. (2007). The experience of emotion. *Annual Review of Psychology, 58,* 373–403.

Barrett, L.F., Tugade, M.M., & Engle, R.W. (2004). Individual differences in working memory capacity and dual-process theories of the mind. *Psychological Bulletin, 130,* 553–573.

Barrett, L.F., & Wager, T.D. (2006). The structure of emotion: Evidence from the neuroimaging of emotion. *Current Directions in Psychological Science, 15,* 79–85.

Basole, A., White, L.E., & Fitzpatrick, D. (2003). Mapping multiple features in the population response of visual cortex. *Nature, 423,* 986–990.

Bateson, P. (1976). Specificity and the origins of behaviour. In J. Rosenblatt, R.A. Hinde, & C. Beer (Eds.), *Advances in the study of behavior* (Vol. 6, pp. 1–20). New York: Academic Press.

Bloom, P. (2004). *Descartes' baby: How the science of child development explains what makes us human.* New York: Basic.

Brodmann, K. (1994). *Localization in the cerebral cortex.* (L.J. Garey, Trans.). London: Smith-Gordon. (Original work published 1909)

Buckner, R.L., Andrews-Hanna, J.R., & Schacter, D.L. (2008). The brain's default network: Anatomy, function, and relevance to disease. *Annals of the New York Academy of Sciences, 1124,* 1–38.

Buldyrev, S.V., Cruz, L., Gomez-Isla, T., Gomez-Tortosa, E., Havlin, S., Le, R., et al. (2000). Description of microcolumnar ensembles in association cortex and their disruption in Alzheimer and Lewy body dementias. *Proceedings of the National Academy of Sciences, USA, 97,* 5039–5043.

Clancy, B., Darlington, R.B., & Finlay, B.L. (2001). Translating developmental time across mammalian species. *Neuroscience, 105,* 7–17.

Dan Glauser, E.S., & Scherer, K.R. (2008). Neuronal processes involved in subjective feeling emergence: Oscillatory activity during an emotional monitoring task. *Brain Topography, 20,* 224–231.

DeFelipe, J., Alonso-Nanclares, L., Arellano, J., Ballesteros-Yanez, I., Benavides-Piccione, R., & Munoz, A. (2007). Specializations of cortical microstructure of humans. In J.H. Kass & T.M. Preuss (Eds.), *Evolution of nervous systems: A comprehensive reference* (Vol. 4, pp. 168–190). New York: Elsevier.

Douglas, R.J., & Martin, K.A.C. (2007). Mapping the matrix: The ways of neocortex. *Neuron, 56,* 226–238.

Duncan, S., & Barrett, L.F. (2007). Affect as a form of cognition: A neurobiological analysis. *Cognition and Emotion, 21,* 1184–1211.

Edelman, G.M. (1987). Neural Darwinism: *The theory of neuronal group selection.* New York: Basic.

Einstein, A., & Infeld, L. (1938). *Evolution of physics.* Cambridge, United Kingdom: Cambridge University Press.

Elston, G.N. (2007). Specialization of the neocortical pyramidal cell during primate evolution. In J.H. Kass & T.M. Preuss (Eds.), *Evolution of nervous systems: A comprehensive reference* (Vol. 4, pp. 191–242). New York: Elsevier.

Frawley, W. (1992). *Linguistic semantics.* New York: Erlbaum.

Friston, K.J. (2002). Beyond phrenology: What can neuroimaging tell us about distributed circuitry? *Annual Review of Neuroscience, 25,* 221–250.

Fuster, J.M. (2006). The cognit: A network model of cortical representation. *International Journal of Psychophysiology, 60,* 125–132.

Gendron, M., & Barrett, L.F. (in press). Reconstructing the past: A century of ideas about emotion in psychology. *Emotion Review.*

Ghuman, A., Bar, M., Dobbins, I.G., & Schnyer, D. (2008). The effects of priming on frontal-temporal communication. *Proceedings of the National Academy of Science, 105,* 8405–8409.

Gibbs, W.W. (2003). The unseen genome: Gems among the junk. *Scientific American, 289,* 47–53.

Goldman, P.S., & Nauta, W.J. (1977). Columnar distribution of cortico-cortical fibers in the frontal association, limbic, and motor cortex of the developing rhesus monkey. *Brain Research, 122,* 393–413.

Haynes, J.D., & Rees, G. (2006). Decoding mental states from brain activity in humans. *Nature Reviews Neuroscience, 7,* 523–534.

Hegarty, M. (1992). Mental animation: Inferring motion from static displays of mechanical systems. *Journal of Experimental Psychology: Learning, Memory, and Cognition, 18,* 1084–1102.

Henson, R. (2005). What can functional neuroimaging tell the experimental psychologist? *Quarterly Journal of Experimental Psychology, 58A,* 193–233.

Izhikevich, E.M., Desai, N.S., Walcott, E.C., & Hoppensteadt, F.C. (2003). Bursts as a unit of neural information: Selective communication via resonance. *Trends in Neurosciences, 26,* 161–167.

James, W. (1890). *The principles of psychology.* New York: Holt.

Kamitani, Y., & Tong, F. (2005). Decoding the visual and subjective contents of the human brain. *Nature Neuroscience, 8,* 679–685.

Kay, K.N., Naselaris, T., Prenger, R.J., & Gallant, J.L. (2008). Identifying natural images from human brain activity. *Nature, 452,* 352–355.

Kober, H., Barrett, L.F., Joseph, J., Bliss-Moreau, E., Lindquist, K.A., & Wager, T.D. (2008). Functional grouping and cortical-subcortical interactions in emotion: A meta-analysis of neuroimaging studies. *NeuroImage, 42,* 998–1031.

Kosslyn, S.M., Thompson, W.L., Sukel, K.E., & Alpert, N.M. (2005). Two types of image generation: Evidence from PET. *Cognitive, Affective, and Behavioral Neuroscience, 5,* 41–53.

Llinas, R., Ribary, U., Contreras, D., & Pedroarena, C. (1998). The neuronal basis for consciousness. *Philosophical Transactions of the Royal Society of London, Series B: Biological Sciences, 353,* 1841–1849.

Mai, J.K., & Ashwell, K.W.S. (2004). Fetal development of the nervous system. In G. Paxinos & J.K. Mai (Eds.), *The human nervous system* (Vol. 1, pp. 49–94). New York: Elsevier.

Marr, D. (1982). *Vision: A computational investigation into the human representation and processing of visual information.* New York: Freeman.

Medin, D., & Ortony, A. (1989). Psychological essentialism. In S. Vosniadou & A. Ortony (Eds.), *Similarity and analogical reasoning* (pp. 179–195). New York: Cambridge University Press.

Mesulam, M.M. (1998). From sensation to cognition. *Brain, 121,* 1013–1052.

Mesulam, M.M. (2000). Behavioral neuroanatomy: Large-scale networks, association cortex, frontal syndromes, the limbic system, and hemispheric specializations. In M.M. Mesulam (Ed.), *Principles of behavioral and cognitive neurology* (2nd ed., pp. 1–120). New York: Oxford University Press.

Mitchell, J.P. (2006). Mentalizing and Marr: An information processing approach to the study of social cognition. *Brain Research, 1079,* 66–75.

Mountcastle, V.B. (1997). The columnar organization of the neocortex. *Brain, 120,* 701–722.

Niessing, J., Ebisch, B., Schmidt, K.E., Niesseng, M., Singer, W., & Galsuke, R.A.W. (2005). Hemodynamic signals correlate rightly with synchronized gamma oscillations. *Science, 309,* 948–951.

Noppeney, U., Friston, K.J., & Price, C.J. (2004). Degenerate neuronal systems sustaining cognitive functions. *Journal of Anatomy, 205,* 433–442.

Norman, K.A., Polyn, S.M., Detre, G.J., & Haxby, J.V. (2006). Beyond mind-reading: Multi-voxel pattern analysis of fMRI data. *Trends in Cognitive Sciences, 10,* 424–430.

Ochsner, K.N., & Lieberman, M.D. (2001). The emergence of social cognitive neuroscience. *American Psychologist, 56,* 717–734.

O'Reilly, R.C., & Munakata, J.A. (2000). *Computational explorations in cognitive neuroscience: Understanding the mind by simulating the brain.* Cambridge, MA: MIT Press.

Ortony, A., & Turner, T.J. (1990). What's basic about basic emotions? *Psychological Review, 97,* 315–331.

Pessoa, L. (2008). On the relationship between emotion and cognition. *Nature Reviews Neuroscience, 2,* 148–158.

Phelps, E.A., & Sharot, T. (2008). How (and why) emotion enhances the subjective sense of recollection. *Current Directions in Psychological Science, 17,* 147–152.

Price, C.J., & Friston, K.J. (2005). Functional ontologies for cognition: The systematic definition of structure and function. *Cognitive Neuropsychology, 22,* 262–275.

Reynolds, S.M., & Berridge, K.C. (2008). Emotional environments return the valence of appetitive versus fearful functions in nucleus accumbens. *Nature Neuroscience, 11,* 423–425.

Schenker, N.M., Desgouttes, A.M., & Semendeferi, K. (2005). Neural connectivity and cortical substrates of cognition in hominoids. *Journal of Human Evolution, 49,* 547–569.

Schoenemann, P.T. (2006). Evolution of the size and function of the human brain. *Annual Review of Anthropology, 35,* 379–406.

Schoenemann, P.T., Sheehan, M.J., & Glotzer, L.D. (2005). Prefrontal white matter volume is disproportionately larger in humans than in other primates. *Nature Neuroscience, 8,* 242–252.

Searle, J.R. (1992). *The rediscovery of the mind.* Cambridge, MA: MIT Press.

Searle, J.R. (1995). *The construction of social reality.* New York: Free Press.

Searle, J.R. (2007). *Freedom and neurobiology: Reflections on free will, language, and political power.* New York: Columbia University Press.

Seeley, W.W., Menon, V., Schatzberg, A.F., Keller, J., Glover, G.H., Kenna, H., et al. (2007). Dissociable intrinsic connectivity networks for salience processing and executive control. *Journal of Neuroscience, 27,* 2349–2356.

Spivey, M. (2007). *The continuity of mind.* New York: Oxford University Press.

Vallacher, R.R., & Wegner, D.M. (1987). What do people think they're doing? Action identification and human behavior. *Psychological Review, 94,* 3–15.

Voss, J.L., Baym, C.L, & Paller, K.A. (2008). Accurate forced-choice recognition without awareness of memory retrieval. *Learning and Memory, 15,* 454–459.

Wager, T.D., Barrett, L.F., Bliss-Moreau, E., Lindquist, K., Duncan, S., Kober, H., et al. (2008). The neuroimaging of emotion. In M. Lewis, J.M. Haviland-Jones, & L.F. Barrett (Eds.), *The handbook of emotion* (3rd ed., pp. 249–271). New York: Guilford.

Wikan, U. (1990). *Managing turbulent hearts: A Balinese formula for living.* Chicago: University of Chicago Press.

Xu, F., Cote, M., & Baker, A. (2005). Labeling guides object individuation in 12-month-old infants. *Psychological Science, 316,* 372–377.

## Critical Thinking

1. In what important ways does neuroscience contribute to our understanding of psychology and how people act, think, and feel?

2. What is the brain's role in everyday life?

Address correspondence to **LISA FELDMAN BARRETT**, Department of Psychology, Boston College, Chestnut Hill, MA 02467; e-mail: barretli@bc.edu.

**Acknowledgments**—The ideas contained in this essay were developed, in part, from discussions with many colleagues over the past several years. I especially thank Mahzarin Banaji, Moshe Bar, Larry Barsalou, Brad Dickerson, Dave DeSteno, James Gross, Dae-Shik Kim, Kristen Lindquist, Batja Mesquita, and Wendy Wood. Many thanks again to Moshe, Batja, Kristen, and Dave and also to Jerry Clore, Jennifer Fugate, Paul Gade, Yang-Ming Huang, Kevin Quinn, Debbie Prentice, Mike Ross, and Maya Tamir, who commented on an earlier draft of this article. Preparation of this manuscript was supported by the National Institutes of Health Director's Pioneer Award (DP1OD003312), a National Institute of Mental Health's Independent Scientist Research Award (K02 MH001981), grants from the National Institute of Aging (AG030311) and the National Science Foundation (BCS 0721260, BCS 0527440), a contract with the Army Research Institute (W91WAW-08-C-0018), and by a James McKeen Cattell Award and a Sabbatical Fellowship from the American Philosophical Society. The views, opinions, and/ or findings contained in this article are solely those of the author and should not be construed as an official Department of the Army or Department of Defense position, policy, or decision.

# The 10 Commandments of Helping Students Distinguish Science from Pseudoscience in Psychology

SCOTT O. LILIENFELD

*"Professor Schlockenmeister, I know that we have to learn about visual perception in your course, but aren't we going to learn anything about extra-sensory perception? My high school psychology teacher told us that there was really good scientific evidence for it."*

*"Dr. Glopelstein, you've taught us a lot about intelligence in your course. But when are you going to discuss the research showing that playing Mozart to infants increases their I.Q. scores?"*

*"Mr. Fleikenzugle, you keep talking about schools of psychotherapy, like psychoanalysis, behavior therapy, and client-centered therapy. But how come you've never said a word about sensory-motor integration therapy? My mother, who's an occupational therapist, tells me that it's a miracle cure for attention-deficit disorder."*

## The Pseudoscience of Popular Psychology

If you're like most introductory psychology instructors, these sorts of questions probably sound awfully familiar. There's a good reason: much of the popular psychology "knowledge" that our students bring to their classes consists of scant more than pseudoscience. Moreover, our students are often fascinated by dubious claims on the fringes of scientific knowledge: extra-sensory perception, psychokinesis, channeling, out-of-body experiences, subliminal persuasion, astrology, biorhythms, "truth serum," the lunar lunacy effect, hypnotic age regression, multiple personality disorder, alien abduction reports, hand-writing analysis, rebirthing therapy, and untested herbal remedies for depression, to name but a few. Of course, because some of these claims may eventually be shown to contain a core of truth, we should not dismiss them out of hand. Nevertheless,

what is troubling about these claims is the glaring discrepancy between many individuals' beliefs in them and the meager scientific evidence on their behalf.

Yet many introductory psychology instructors accord minimal attention to potentially pseudoscientific topics in their courses, perhaps because they believe that these topics are of, at best, marginal relevance to psychological science. Moreover, many introductory psychology textbooks barely mention these topics. After all, there is already more than enough to cover in psychology courses, so why tack on material of doubtful scientific status? Furthermore, some instructors may fear that by devoting attention to questionable claims they will end up sending students the unintended message that these claims are scientifically credible.

## Benefits of Teaching Students to Distinguish Science from Pseudoscience

So why should we teach psychology students to distinguish science from pseudoscience? As personality theorist George Kelly (1955) noted, an effective understanding of a construct requires an appreciation of both of its poles. For example, we cannot grasp fully the concept of "cold" unless we have experienced heat. Similarly, students may not grasp fully the concept of scientific thinking without an understanding of pseudoscientific beliefs, namely those that at first blush appear scientific but are not.

Moreover, by addressing these topics, instructors can capitalize on a valuable opportunity to impart critical thinking skills, such as distinguishing correlation from causation and recognizing the need for control groups, by challenging students' misconceptions regarding popular psychology. Although many students find these skills to be "dry" or even deadly dull when presented in the abstract, they often enjoy acquiring these skills in the context of lively and controversial topics (e.g., extrasensory perception) that stimulate their interest. Students often learn about such topics from various popular psychology sources that they seek out in everyday life, such as magazine articles, Internet sites, and television programs.

Indeed, for many beginning students, "psychology" is virtually synonymous with popular psychology. Yet because so much of popular psychology consists of myths and urban legends, such as most people use only 10 percent of their brains, expressing anger is usually better than holding it in, opposites attract in interpersonal relationships, high self-esteem is necessary for psychological health, people with schizophrenia have more than one personality, among a plethora of others, many students probably emerge from psychology courses with the same misconceptions with which they entered. As a consequence, they often depart college incapable of distinguishing the wheat from the chaff in popular psychology.

Teaching students to distinguish science from pseudoscience can prove immensely rewarding. Foremost among these rewards is producing discerning consumers of the popular psychology literature. Indeed, research evidence supports the efficacy of teaching psychology courses on pseudoscience and the paranormal. For example, Morier and Keeports (1994) reported that undergraduates enrolled in a "Science and Pseudoscience" seminar demonstrated a statistically significant reduction in paranormal beliefs relative to a quasi-control group of students enrolled in a psychology and law class over the same time period (see also Dougherty, 2004). They replicated this effect over a 2-year period with two sections of the course. Wesp and Montgomery (1998) found that a course on the objective examination of paranormal claims resulted in a statistically significant improvement in the evaluation of reasoning flaws in scientific articles. Specifically, students in this course were better able to identify logical errors in articles and provide rival explanations for research findings.

## The 10 Commandments

Nevertheless, teaching students to distinguish science from pseudoscience brings more than its share of challenges and potential pitfalls. In my introductory psychology course (in which I emphasize strongly the distinction between science and pseudoscience in psychology) and in my advanced undergraduate seminar, "Science and Pseudoscience in Psychology," I have learned a number of valuable lessons (by first making just about every mistake about which I'll warn you).

In the following section, I summarize these teaching tips, which I refer to as the "10 Commandments" of teaching psychology students to distinguish science from pseudoscience. To avoid being accused of failing to separate Church from State, I have worded all of these injunctions in the positive rather than the negative to distinguish them from the (only slightly better known) biblical 10 Commandments. I urge readers of this column to inscribe these commandments on impressive stone tablets to be mounted outside of all psychology departments.

## First Commandment

*Thou shalt delineate the features that distinguish science from pseudoscience.* It's important to communicate to students that the differences between science and pseudoscience, although not absolute or clear-cut, are neither arbitrary nor subjective. Instead, philosophers of science (e.g., Bunge, 1984) have identified a constellation of features or "warning signs" that characterize most pseudoscientific disciplines. Among these warning signs are:

- A tendency to invoke ad hoc hypotheses, which can be thought of as "escape hatches" or loopholes, as a means of immunizing claims from falsification.
- An absence of self-correction and an accompanying intellectual stagnation.
- An emphasis on confirmation rather than refutation.
- A tendency to place the burden of proof on skeptics, not proponents, of claims.
- Excessive reliance on anecdotal and testimonial evidence to substantiate claims.
- Evasion of the scrutiny afforded by peer review.
- Absence of "connectivity" (Stanovich, 1997), that is, a failure to build on existing scientific knowledge.
- Use of impressive-sounding jargon whose primary purpose is to lend claims a facade of scientific respectability.
- An absence of boundary conditions (Hines, 2003), that is, a failure to specify the settings under which claims do not hold.

Teachers should explain to students that none of these warning signs is by itself sufficient to indicate that a discipline is pseudoscientific. Nevertheless, the more of these warning signs a discipline exhibits, the more suspect it should become.

## Second Commandment

*Thou shalt distinguish skepticism from cynicism.* One danger of teaching students to distinguish science from pseudoscience is that we can inadvertently produce students reflexively dismissive of any claim that appears implausible. Skepticism, which is the proper mental set of the scientist, implies two seemingly contradictory attitudes (Sagan, 1995): an openness to claims combined with a willingness to subject these claims to incisive scrutiny. As space engineer James Oberg (see Sagan, 1995) reminded us, we must keep our minds open but not so open that our brains fall out. In contrast, cynicism implies close-mindedness. I recall being chastised by a prominent skeptic for encouraging researchers to keep an open mind regarding the efficacy of a novel psychotherapy whose rationale struck him as farfetched. However, if we foreclose the possibility that our preexisting beliefs are erroneous, we are behaving unscientifically. Skepticism entails a willingness to entertain novel claims; cynicism does not.

# Third Commandment

*Thou shalt distinguish methodological skepticism from philosophical skepticism.* When encouraging students to think critically, we must distinguish between two forms of skepticism: (1) an approach that subjects all knowledge claims to scrutiny with the goal of sorting out true from false claims, namely methodological (scientific) skepticism, and (2) an approach that denies the possibility of knowledge, namely philosophical skepticism. When explaining to students that scientific knowledge is inherently tentative and open to revision, some students may mistakenly conclude that genuine knowledge is impossible. This view, which is popular in certain postmodernist circles, neglects to distinguish knowledge claims that are more certain from those that are less certain. Although absolute certainty is probably unattainable in science, some scientific claims, such as Darwin's theory of natural selection, have been extremely well corroborated, whereas others, such as the theory underpinning astrological horoscopes, have been convincingly refuted. Still others, such as cognitive dissonance theory, are scientifically controversial. Hence, there is a continuum of confidence in scientific claims; some have acquired virtual factual status whereas others have been resoundingly falsified. The fact that methodological skepticism does not yield completely certain answers to scientific questions and that such answers could in principle be overturned by new evidence does not imply that knowledge is impossible, only that this knowledge is provisional. Nor does it imply that the answers generated by controlled scientific investigation are no better than other answers, such as those generated by intuition (see Myers, 2002).

# Fourth Commandment

*Thou shalt distinguish pseudoscientific claims from claims that are merely false.* All scientists, even the best ones, make mistakes. Sir Isaac Newton, for example, flirted with bizarre alchemical hypotheses throughout much of his otherwise distinguished scientific career (Gleick, 2003). Students need to understand that the key difference between science and pseudoscience lies not in their content (i.e., whether claims are factually correct or incorrect) but in their approach to evidence. Science, at least when it operates properly, seeks out contradictory information and—assuming that this evidence is replicable and of high quality—eventually incorporates such information into its corpus of knowledge. In contrast, pseudoscience tends to avoid contradictory information (or manages to find a way to reinterpret this information as consistent with its claims) and thereby fails to foster the self-correction that is essential to scientific progress. For example, astrology has changed remarkably little over the past 2,500 years despite overwhelmingly negative evidence (Hines, 2003).

# Fifth Commandment

*Thou shalt distinguish science from scientists.* Although the scientific method is a prescription for avoiding confirmatory bias (Lilienfeld, 2002), this point does not imply that scientists are free of biases. Nor does it imply that all or even most scientists are open to evidence that challenges their cherished beliefs. Scientists can be just as pigheaded and dogmatic in their beliefs as anyone else. Instead, this point implies that good scientists strive to become aware of their biases and to counteract them as much as possible by implementing safeguards against error (e.g., double-blind control groups) imposed by the scientific method. Students need to understand that the scientific method is a toolbox of skills that scientists have developed to prevent themselves from confirming their own biases.

# Sixth Commandment

*Thou shalt explain the cognitive underpinnings of pseudoscientific beliefs.* Instructors should emphasize that we are all prone to cognitive illusions (Piatelli-Palmarini, 1994), and that such illusions can be subjectively compelling and difficult to resist. For example, class demonstrations illustrating that many or most of us can fall prey to false memories (e.g., Roediger & McDermott, 1995) can help students to see that the psychological processes that lead to erroneous beliefs are pervasive. Moreover, it is important to point out to students that the heuristics (mental shortcuts) that can produce false beliefs, such as representativeness, availability, and anchoring (Tversky & Kahneman, 1974), are basically adaptive and help us to make sense of a complex and confusing world. Hence, most pseudoscientific beliefs are cut from the same cloth as accurate beliefs. By underscoring these points, instructors can minimize the odds that students who embrace pseudoscientific beliefs will feel foolish when confronted with evidence that contradicts their beliefs.

# Seventh Commandment

*Thou shalt remember that pseudoscientific beliefs serve important motivational functions.* Many paranormal claims, such as those concerning extrasensory perception, out-of-body experiences, and astrology, appeal to believers' deep-seated needs for hope and wonder, as well as their needs for a sense of control over the often uncontrollable realities of life and death. Most believers in the paranormal are searching for answers to profound existential questions, such as "Is there a soul?" and "Is there life after death?" As psychologist Barry Beyerstein (1999) noted (in a play on P.T. Barnum's famous quip), "there's a seeker born every minute" (p. 60). Therefore, in presenting students with scientific evidence that challenges their paranormal beliefs, we should not be surprised when many of them become defensive. In turn, defensiveness can engender an unwillingness to consider contrary evidence.

One of the two best means of lessening this defensiveness (the second is the Eighth Commandment) is to gently challenge students' beliefs with sympathy and compassion, and with the understanding that students who are emotionally committed to paranormal beliefs will find these beliefs difficult to question, let alone relinquish. Ridiculing these beliefs can produce reactance (Brehm, 1966) and reinforce students' stereotypes of science teachers as close-minded and dismissive. In some cases, teachers who have an exceptionally good rapport with their class can make headway by challenging students' beliefs with good-natured humor (e.g., "I'd like to ask all of you who believe in psychokinesis to please raise my hand"). However, teachers must ensure that such humor is not perceived as demeaning or condescending.

## Eighth Commandment

*Thou shalt expose students to examples of good science as well as to examples of pseudoscience.* In our classes, it is critical not merely to debunk inaccurate claims but to expose students to accurate claims. We must be careful not merely to take away students' questionable knowledge, but to give them legitimate knowledge in return. In doing so, we can make it easier for students to swallow the bitter pill of surrendering their cherished beliefs in the paranormal. Students need to understand that many genuine scientific findings are at least as fascinating as are many scientifically dubious paranormal claims. In my own teaching, I have found it useful to intersperse pseudoscientific information with information that is equally remarkable but true, such as lucid dreaming, eidetic imagery, subliminal perception (as opposed to subliminal persuasion, which is far more scientifically dubious), extraordinary feats of human memory (Neisser & Hyman, 2000), and appropriate clinical uses of hypnosis (as opposed to the scientifically unsupported use of hypnosis for memory recovery; see Lynn, Lock, Myers, & Payne, 1997). In addition, we should bear in mind the late paleontologist Stephen Jay Gould's (1996) point that exposing a falsehood necessarily affirms a truth. As a consequence, it is essential not only to point out false information to students, but also to direct them to true information. For example, when explaining why claims regarding biorhythms are baseless (see Hines, 2003), it is helpful to introduce students to claims regarding circadian rhythms, which, although often confused with biorhythms, are supported by rigorous scientific research.

## Ninth Commandment

*Thou shalt be consistent in one's intellectual standards.* One error that I have sometimes observed among skeptics, including psychology instructors who teach critical thinking courses, is to adopt two sets of intellectual standards: one for claims that they find plausible and a second for claims that they do not. The late psychologist Paul Meehl (1973) pointed out that this inconsistency amounts to "shifting the standards of evidential rigor depending on whose ox is being gored" (p. 264). For example, I know one educator who is a vocal proponent of the movement to develop lists of empirically supported therapies, that is, psychological treatments that have been shown to be efficacious in controlled studies. In this domain, he is careful to draw on the research literature to buttress his assertions regarding which psychotherapies are efficacious and which are not. Yet he is dismissive of the research evidence for the efficacy of electroconvulsive therapy (ECT) for depression, even though this evidence derives from controlled studies that are every bit

as rigorous as those conducted for the psychotherapies that he espouses. When I pointed out this inconsistency to him, he denied emphatically that he was adhering to a double standard. It eventually became apparent to me that he was casting aside the evidence for ECT's efficacy merely because this treatment struck him as grossly implausible. Why on earth, he probably wondered, should inducing an epileptoid seizure by administering electricity to the brain alleviate depression? But because surface plausibility is a highly fallible barometer of the validity of truth claims, we must remain open to evidence that challenges our intuitive preconceptions and encourage our students to do so as well.

## Tenth Commandment

*Thou shalt distinguish pseudoscientific claims from purely metaphysical religious claims.* My final commandment is likely to be the most controversial, especially for skeptics who maintain that both pseudoscientific and religious beliefs are irrational. To appreciate the difference between these two sets of beliefs, we must distinguish pseudoscience from metaphysics. Unlike pseudoscientific claims, metaphysical claims (Popper, 1959) cannot be tested empirically and therefore lie outside the boundaries of science. In the domain of religion, these include claims regarding the existence of God, the soul, and the afterlife, none of which can be refuted by any conceivable body of scientific evidence. Nevertheless, certain religious or quasi-religious beliefs, such as those involving "intelligent design" theory, which is the newest incarnation of creationism (see Miller, 2000), the Shroud of Turin, and weeping statues of Mother Mary, are indeed testable and hence suitable for critical analysis alongside of other questionable naturalistic beliefs. By conflating pseudoscientific beliefs with religious beliefs that are strictly metaphysical, instructors risk (a) needlessly alienating a sizeable proportion of their students, many of whom may be profoundly religious; and (b) (paradoxically) undermining students' critical thinking skills, which require a clear understanding of the difference between testable and untestable claims.

## Conclusion

Adherence to the Ten Commandments can allow psychology educators to assist students with the crucial goal of distinguishing science from pseudoscience. If approached with care, sensitivity, and a clear understanding of the differences between skepticism and cynicism, methodological and philosophical skepticism, the scientific method and the scientists who use it, and pseudoscience and metaphysics, incorporating pseudoscience and fringe science into psychology courses can be richly rewarding for teachers and students alike. In a world in which the media, self-help industry, and Internet are disseminating psychological pseudoscience at an ever-increasing pace, the critical thinking skills needed to distinguish science from pseudoscience should be considered mandatory for all psychology students.

# References

Beyerstein, B. L. (1999). Pseudoscience and the brain: Tuners and tonics for aspiring superhumans. In S. D. Sala (Ed.), *Mind myths: Exploring popular assumptions about the mind and brain* (pp. 59–82). Chichester, England: John Wiley.

Brehm, J. (1966). *A theory of psychological reactance.* New York: Academic Press.

Bunge, M. (1984, Fall). What is pseudoscience? *Skeptical Inquirer, 9,* 36–46.

Dougherty, M. J. (2004). Educating believers: Research demonstrates that courses in skepticism can effectively decrease belief in the paranormal. *Skeptic, 10*(4), 31–35.

Gilovich, T. (1991). *How we know what isn't so: The fallibility of human reason in everyday life.* New York: Free Press.

Gleick, J. (2003). *Isaac Newton.* New York: Pantheon Books.

Gould, S. J. (1996, May). Keynote address, *"Science in the age of (mis)information."* Talk presented at the Convention of the Committee for the Scientific Investigation of Claims of the Paranormal, Buffalo, New York.

Hines, T. (2003). Pseudoscience and the paranormal: A critical examination of the evidence. Buffalo, NY: Prometheus.

Kelly, G. A. (1955). *The psychology of personal constructs, Vols. 1 and 2.* New York: Norton.

Lilienfeld, S. O. (2002). When worlds collide: Social science, politics, and the Rind et al. child sexual abuse meta-analysis. *American Psychologist, 57,* 176–88.

Lilienfeld, S. O., Lohr, M., & Morier, D. (2001). The teaching of courses in the science and pseudoscience of psychology. *Teaching of Psychology, 28,* 182–191.

Lilienfeld, S. O., Lynn, S. J., & Lohr, J. M. (2003). *Science and pseudoscience in clinical psychology.* New York: Guilford.

Lynn, S. J., Lock, T. G., Myers, B., & Payne, D. G. (1997). Recalling the unrecallable: Should hypnosis be used to recover memories in psychotherapy? *Current Directions in Psychological Science, 6,* 79–83.

Meehl, P. E. (1973). *Psychodiagnosis: Selected papers.* Minneapolis, MN: University of Minnesota Press.

Miller, K. (2000). *Finding Darwin's God: A scientist's search for common ground between God and evolution.* New York: Cliff Street Books.

Morier, D., & Keeports, D. (1994). Normal science and the paranormal: The effect of a scientific method course on students' beliefs in the paranormal. *Research in Higher Education, 35,* 443–453.

Myers, D. G. (2002). *Intuition: Its powers and perils.* New Haven: Yale University Press.

Neisser, U., & Hyman, I. E. (2000). *Memory observed: Remembering in natural contexts.* New York: Worth Publishers.

Piatelli-Palmarini, M. (1994). *Inevitable illusions: How mistakes of reason rule our minds.* New York: John Wiley & Sons.

Popper, K. R. (1959). *The logic of scientific discovery.* New York: Basic Books.

Roediger, H. L., & McDermott, K. B. (1995). Creating false memories: Remembering words not presented in lists. *Journal of Experimental Psychology: Learning, Memory, and Cognition, 21,* 803–814.

Ruscio, J. (2002). *Clear thinking with psychology: Separating sense from nonsense.* Pacific Grove, CA: Wadsworth.

Sagan, C. (1995). *The demon-haunted world: Science as a candle in the dark.* New York: Random House.

Shermer, M. (2002). *Why people believe weird things: Pseudoscience, superstition, and other confusions of our time.* New York: Owl Books.

Stanovich, K. (1997). *How to think straight about psychology* (4th ed.). New York: HarperCollins.

Tversky, A., & Kahneman, D. (1974). Judgment under uncertainty: Heuristics and biases. *Science, 185,* 1124–1131.

Wesp, R., & Montgomery, K. (1998). Developing critical thinking through the study of paranormal phenomena. *Teaching of Psychology, 25,* 275–278.

# Critical Thinking

1. In what key ways does pseudoscience differ from real science?

2. How accurate is the popular media in its portrayal of psychology?

3. What suggestions do you have for critically reading the popular literature in psychology?

# Comprehensive Soldier Fitness and the Future of Psychology

MARTIN E. P. SELIGMAN AND RAYMOND D. FOWLER

*Whom shall I send? And who will go for us?*
*And I said, "Here am I. Send me!"*

—Isaiah 6:8

The history of American psychology has been shaped by national need. This has been true of both the science of psychology and the practice of psychology. In this article, we look at past turning points and then describe why we believe that the Comprehensive Soldier Fitness (CSF) program is another such turning point.

In the past century, psychologists were among the first professionals to offer assistance to the nation. The work of psychologists in World Wars I and II helped to improve the effectiveness of the military, and it made enduring changes in psychology's identity and in the public recognition and acceptance of psychology.

Psychology in the United States was first recognized as an independent discipline in 1892 with the establishment of the American Psychological Association (APA). It began as a research–academic discipline with little interest in applications, and for the most part it remained so in its early years, with some notable exceptions. For example, two of the founders of American psychology were William James, who treated mentally ill patients with psychotherapy and medication, and Lightner Witmer, who established the first psychological clinic at the University of Pennsylvania in 1896 and is viewed as the founder of clinical psychology. But the first big leap into the application of psychology took place in the context of World War I.

In 1917, as war raged through Europe and American involvement seemed imminent, Robert Yerkes, a 40-year-old Yale professor of biopsychology and president of APA, proposed that APA help to create within the U.S. Army a psychology unit to select recruits and determine their duties. In a letter to the APA Council of Representatives, Yerkes (1918) wrote, "Our knowledge and our methods are of importance to the military service of our country, and it is our duty to cooperate to the fullest extent and immediately toward the increased efficiency of our Army and Navy" (p. 191).

A detailed plan was approved by the National Research Council and submitted to the Surgeon General of the Army. A unit was quickly established under the overall direction of Yerkes, who was commissioned a major. One group developed two new intelligence tests, the Army Alpha and the Army Beta, and administered them to more than 2 million soldiers. A second group interviewed and classified 3,500,000 soldiers and developed proficiency tests for military specialties.

The response of APA members to Yerkes's call for service was immediate. Although APA then had fewer than 300 members, Yerkes was able to compile a list of 150 psychologists who were willing to serve as civilian or uniformed psychological examiners, 24 of whom were available for service within a week. By the end of the war, several hundred psychologists were overseeing the work of several thousand men in personnel units throughout the military.

The effects of the program extended far beyond the military. Psychology, as a scientific and applied discipline, gained the recognition and support of the public, and psychological and educational testing centers were established in colleges and universities and in business and industry.

After the armistice, some of the participants in the Army program remained in military service to work in the 43 Army rehabilitation hospitals that had been established. Others left the service to develop tests for business and industry, but most returned to academic positions. Among those who served in the program were people who became the nation's leading psychologists, including J. R. Angell, E. K. Strong, E. G. Boring, Lewis Terman, E. L. Thorndike, L. L. Thurstone, and John B. Watson.

The attention given to psychology, and the increased number of academic programs, brought about a rapid increase in the number of psychologists. In the years following World War I, APA's membership grew tenfold, from approximately 300 members to 3,000. Doctoral production rose rapidly through the 1920s, and by the end of the decade, at least 35 universities had established doctoral programs, most of which included programs in applied psychology.

In 1939, as war again ravaged Europe, 50 psychologists met together to celebrate the 20th anniversary of their demobilization as members of the Army's Committee on Classification of Personnel. The meeting was attended by a representative from the Army Adjutant General's office, who drew attention to the worsening situation in Europe. Yerkes, representing APA, and Walter Bingham, representing APA's practitioner counterpart, began working to establish psychologists' roles in the coming war. Bingham was commissioned as a colonel, appointed chief psychologist for the Army, and given responsibility for personnel classification.

Yerkes, still vigorous as he approached retirement age but too old for military service, spent his time contacting high-level officials in the government and military to promote a broader role for psychology to include treatment, enhancement of morale, and training of military psychologists. By early 1941, he had drafted a comprehensive plan for the military that also aimed to transform the role of professional psychology. Yerkes wrote,

> Psychology must stand as a basic science for such universally desirable expert services as the guidance and safeguarding of an individual's growth and development, education and occupational choice, social adjustments, achievement and maintenance of balance, poise and effectiveness, contentment, happiness, and usefulness. (Yerkes, 1941, quoted in Capshew, 1999, p. 50)

Just six months after Pearl Harbor, there were over 100 psychologists working in Washington, DC. At the request of the Selective Service, a list of 2,300 psychologists qualified to help local draft boards determine the mental capacity of registrants was compiled, and efforts were made to ensure that some 1,500 psychologists eligible for the draft were placed in positions where their background and training could be utilized. Soon, hundreds of psychologists were spread throughout the military and in government agencies.

Personnel psychology in the military thrived in the war years, as it had in World War I. As psychologists developed many new tests of achievement, knowledge, and aptitude, the Army established the largest and most diversified testing program in history. Millions of tests were administered; for example, The Army General Classification Test (AGCT) was administered to 9 million men, one seventh of the U.S. male population.

At the start of World War II, clinical psychology, as opposed to personnel psychology, had little recognition in the military, and not much more in the wider world. Later in the war, psychologists began to serve in mental illness settings in the military, primarily because of the actions of psychiatrist William C. Menninger, newly appointed chief of neuropsychiatry. An acute shortage of psychiatrists led to the appointment of a chief clinical psychologist, the commissioning of 250 men who had experience in clinical psychology, and the establishment of permanent divisions of clinical psychology in the military services. By the end of the war, clinical psychology had become a full-fledged mental health profession, and the election in 1946 of Carl Rogers as the first clinical psychologist to be APA president confirmed its new status.

Building a productive relationship between psychology and the military was not without problems, but as the war drew to a close, both seemed pleased with the partnership. Surveys indicated that psychologists were more satisfied with their utilization in the military than were physicists, chemists, and geologists. And the military demonstrated its appreciation of the work of psychologists by continuing to recruit them: Demand for psychologists exceeded supply throughout the war (Napoli, 1981, p. 105). The Navy representative on the National Defense Research Committee said, "I believe that the application of psychology in selecting and training men, and in guiding the design of weapons so they would fit men, did more to help win this war than any other single intellectual activity" (Smith, 1948, quoted in Napoli, 1981, p 105). Psychology's contribution received praise from senior military officers and from the Army's chief psychiatrist, William C. Menninger, who foresaw a continuing role for psychologists in clinical work (Napoli, 1981, p. 106).

In 1946, the Veterans Administration, faced with an estimated 40,000 war casualties, launched a major program to fund training for new clinical psychologists. Subsequently, the National Institute of Mental Health and the U.S. Public Health Service provided millions of dollars in training and research grants to psychology graduate programs. The military services, especially the Navy, continued to fund psychological research. In the first 30 years after World War II, the federal government spent over $1.2 billion on psychological research, and over half of the members of APA received some government support (Napoli, 1981, p. 137).

Federal support through the military helped to build psychology into a major scientific discipline and profession and APA into the largest doctoral-level scientific society in the world. There are now approximately 3,000 psychologists in the Department of Veterans Affairs (VA) and over 1,500 serving in the military. And psychologists, with their research and applied work, continue to provide services to a wide spectrum of American society.

## The Current National Need

The first author (Martin E. P. Seligman) was initially visited by Colonel Jill Chambers in August 2008 to discuss the problems of returning warriors, and this led to a meeting with U.S. Army Chief of Staff General George W. Casey Jr. and his advisers in the Pentagon in early December 2008. They outlined two sets of national needs and asked what psychology's response could be.

One national need was the unprecedented rates of posttraumatic stress disorder (PTSD), depression, suicide, and divorce among military personnel. Two facts stood out about this need: (a) The Army and the VA system were expending huge resources to treat these clinical issues, but their question was not how to provide more treatment but rather how to prevent these problems. (b) Related to this question was the identification of who was most at risk for PTSD: The Millennium Cohort Study found that the bottom 15% in mental and physical fitness accounted for 58% of the cases of PTSD (LeardMann, Smith, Smith, Wells, & Ryan, 2009). The other national need was for a resilient fighting force in our small, all-volunteer Army that would be capable of meeting the challenge of the persistent warfare and repeated redeployments that loom in the Army's future.

Seligman responded by suggesting that the human response to high adversity, such as combat, is normally distributed: On the left of the distribution are the minority who collapse—exhibiting what is called variously PTSD, depression, or anxiety. In the middle are the great majority who are resilient; they return to their normal level of functioning after a brief period of disruption. On the right-hand side of the distribution are those who grow: people who after adversity attain a higher level of functioning than they began with or, in other words, exhibit posttraumatic growth. The aim of any prevention program, Seligman suggested, should be to move the entire distribution toward growth. This aim would lower PTSD, increase resilience, and increase the number of people who grow.

Other important ideas, as well as a concrete plan, emerged from this meeting. The former Surgeon General of the United States, Richard Carmona, advised that civilian medicine was perversely incentivized: Of the $2 trillion the United States spends annually on health care, 75% goes into chronic disease and end-of-life care. In contrast, Army medicine is rationally incentivized—its mission is to produce health, not cure disease, and by producing health preventively, it will reduce later disease. This could be a model for civilian medicine.

The Surgeon General of the Army, Lieutenant General Eric Schoomaker, suggested constructively to General Casey that the program should not be part of his Medical Corps. Moving it from medicine to education and training would help remove any stigma and be much more in line with a universal training purpose. Seligman said that his model for preventive training was positive education: The Penn Resilience Program teaches teachers the skills of resilience and positive psychology, and the teachers then embed these skills into the teaching of their students. This reliably produces less depression and anxiety among the students (Seligman, Ernst, Gillham, Reivich, & Linkins, 2009). General Casey said that this model fits the Army's training process well: The teachers of the Army are the drill sergeants, and they would become the teachers of resilience and positive psychology. He further hoped that a successful demonstration of the effects of resilience training in soldiers and their families would provide a model for the civilian education of young people.

General Casey then set the new plan for Comprehensive Soldier Fitness into motion: It was assigned to education and training, under Brigadier General Rhonda Cornum, not to medicine. The four components detailed in this special issue of the *American Psychologist* were fleshed out over the next three months: creating the Global Assessment Tool (GAT); creating self-improvement courses for the emotional, social, family, and spiritual fitness dimensions measured on the GAT; beginning to provide resilience training and positive psychology training throughout the Army; and beginning to identify and train master resilience trainers from Army personnel and civilian psychologists. These four components have involved dozens of psychologists over the past two years. We have worked in test creation and validation, in course creation, in writing and refining resilience and positive psychology training materials, and in serving as data analysts, as research designers, and as the trainers and facilitators of live courses with Army personnel. Of critical interest is the Soldier Fitness Tracker (Fravell, Nasser, & Cornum, 2011, this issue). This powerful platform creates an unprecedented, hypermassive database in which psychological variables, medical variables, and performance variables are merged. All of these activities continue as we write, in active collaboration with our peers from the Army.

# Future Opportunities

We can only speculate about what the future may hold. The validation of the GAT, the effects of the fitness courses, the effects of resilience and positive psychology training, and the efficacy of the master resilience trainers will all be carefully measured by the Army over the months and years to come. We underscore the importance of delineating the four dimensions of psychological "fitness": emotional, social, family, and spiritual (Cornum, Matthews, & Seligman, 2011, this issue). These are the capacities that underpin human flourishing not only in the Army but in schools, corporations, and communities, and the building of these fitnesses may help define the role of the practicing psychologist of the future. The Army will rigorously ask whether building these fitnesses decreases rates of PTSD, depression, and anxiety; improves performance and morale; improves mental and physical well-being; and helps soldiers and their families in the successful transition back to civilian employment.

If the results are positive, we hope to see expanded collaboration between the military and psychology in creating an Army that is just as psychologically fit as it is physically fit. Among the future possibilities are the following:

- Training of all ranks of soldiers and of civilian employees of the Army in resilience and positive psychology
- Parallel training offered for all family members of soldiers
- Mobile training units for resilience training in far-flung outposts
- Comprehensive Military Fitness: the training of *all* the armed services and their employees in the techniques of resilience and positive psychology
- Expanded online and in-person courses for the military in emotional, social, family, and spiritual fitness
- One million soldiers taking the GAT is an unprecedented database for the prospective longitudinal study of the effects of psychological variables on physical health, mental health, and performance. The Soldier Fitness Tracker is the backbone of this longitudinal study, and we predict that this database will become a national treasure for psychological and medical research.

The use of resilience training and positive psychology in the Army is consciously intended as a model for civilian use. The bulk of health care costs in civilian medicine go not to building health but rather to treating illness. The Army's emphasis on building psychological fitness preventively is intended to be a model for the future of medicine generally. Imagine that building emotional, social, family, and spiritual fitness among young soldiers noticeably reduces morbidity, mortality, and mental illness, offers a betters prognosis when illness strikes, and cuts down on treatment costs. We should know whether this is the case in the next decade. If the CSF program turns out to work, it should—in any rational system—revolutionize the balance between treatment and prevention and radically reform how civilian health care is provided.

The implications for public education and for the corporation may be just as sweeping. Positive education claims that teaching young people the skills of emotional fitness along with teaching the traditional goals of education will enable youth to perform better at school and to perform better later in the workplace. And, more important, perhaps these young people will enjoy lives that have more positive emotion, engagement, and meaning and better relationships. All of these claims will be directly tested prospectively in the CSF program: The resilience training and the fitness courses offered are almost exact parallels of the courses we use in positive education (Seligman et al., 2009). If it turns out that soldiers given this training perform better in their jobs, are more engaged, have more meaning in their lives, enjoy better relationships, and have more fruitful employment when they return to civilian society, this will ground a new model for our public schools. Again we will know whether this is so within the next decade.

# Objections

We are not unmindful of those segments of American society, including some psychologists, who look askance on working with the military in any way.

The task of the military is to provide the capability of defending the nation from threat. Revulsion toward war is understandable, but it is not the military that sets the nation's policies on war and peace. The military carries out the policies that emerge from our democratic form of government. Withholding professional and scientific support for the people who provide the nation's defense is, we believe, simply wrong. Psychologists are as diverse in their views as any other group of citizens, but the American Psychological Association has, for six decades, been solid in its support on behalf of the men and women who serve in our armed forces.

Here, in unvarnished form, are three of the objections that might be raised to working with the military, and our responses:

- Psychology should devote its scarce resources to helping those who are suffering, not those who are well.

Positive psychology seeks to broaden the scope of psychological science and practice. It seeks to build more positive emotion, engagement, and meaning and better relationships among all people, and it has developed new interventions to do just that. It is a supplement, not a replacement, for the science and practice of relieving suffering. We believe that soldiers with PTSD, depression, anxiety, and other disorders should continue to receive the best of treatments. We are also mindful, however, that the known treatments are of limited effectiveness (Seligman, 1993, 2006). The CSF program will not subtract from the treatment resources; rather it is a preventive program that will likely reduce the need for them by effectively preventing suffering.

- Psychology should do no harm: Aiding the military will make people who kill for a living feel better about killing and help them do a better job of it.

If we had discovered a way of preventing malaria—mosquito netting, draining swamps, quinine—and our soldiers were fighting in a malaria-infested theater, would these voices also counsel withholding our discoveries? We would not withhold our help: The balance of good done by building the physical and mental fitness of our soldiers far outweighs any harm that might be done. The alleged harm—making healthier killers or helping them to feel better—turns also on the final objection.

- Psychology should not aid the foreign policy of the United States.

Three ideologies have arisen in the past century that have sought to overthrow democracy by force: fascism, communism, and jihadist Islam. It should be noted that without a strong military and the will to use force responsibly in self-defense, our victories would not have happened, and defense against current and future threats would be impossible. Psychology materially aided in the defeat of the first two threats, and in doing so it carved out its identity. We are proud to aid our military in defending and protecting our nation right now, and we will be proud to help our soldiers and their families into the peace that will follow.

# References

Capshew, J. H. (1999). *Psychologists on the march: Science, practice, and professional identity in America, 1929–1969.* Cambridge, England: Cambridge University Press. doi:10.1017/CBO9780511572944

Cornum, R., Matthews, M., & Seligman, M. (2011). Comprehensive Soldier Fitness: Building resilience in a challenging institutional context. *American Psychologist, 66,* 4–9. doi:10.1037/a0021420

Fravell, M., Nasser, K., & Cornum, R. (2011). The Soldier Fitness Tracker: Global delivery of Comprehensive Soldier Fitness. *American Psychologist, 66,* 73–76. doi:10.1037/a0021632

LeardMann, C. A., Smith, T. C., Smith, B., Wells, T. S., & Ryan, M. A. K. (2009). Baseline self reported functional health and vulnerability to post-traumatic stress disorder after combat deployment: Prospective US military cohort study. *British Medical Journal, 338,* 1–9. doi:10.1136/bmj.b1273

Napoli, D. S. (1981). *Architects of adjustment: The history of the psychological profession in the United States.* Port Washington, NY: Kennikat Press.

Seligman, M. E. P. (1993). *What you can change and what you can't.* New York, NY: Knopf.

Seligman, M. E. P. (2006). Afterword: Breaking the 65 percent barrier. In M. Csikszentmihalyi & I. Selega (Eds.), *A life worth living: Contributions to positive psychology* (pp. 230–236). New York, NY: Oxford University Press.

Seligman, M. E. P., Ernst, R. M., Gillham, J., Reivich, K., & Linkins, M. (2009). Positive education: Positive psychology and classroom interventions. *Oxford Review of Education, 35,* 293–311. doi:10.1080/03054980902934563

Smith, L. P. (1948). Foreword. In C. Bray (Ed.), *Psychology and military proficiency: A history of the Applied Psychology Panel of the National Defense Research Committee.* Princeton, NJ: Princeton University Press.

Yerkes, R. M. (1918). Psychology in relation to the war. *Psychological Review, 25,* 85–115. doi:10.1037/h0069904

Yerkes, R. M. (1941). Psychology and defense. *Proceedings of the American Philosophical Society, 84,* 527–542.

# Critical Thinking

1. Historically, what role has psychology played in the armed services? How is this role changing today?

2. What is positive psychology and what role might it play in helping combat veterans readjust to life after war?

# Is Psychology Losing Its Foundations?*

Donald A. Dewsbury

Much has been written about the increasing diversity of psychology, with greater attention given to such perspectives as racial, gender, sexual preference, and international matters, as well as the proliferation of specialties in psychology. Although these trends are important and beneficial to psychology, I also see a homogenization of the field. The focus on psychology as a science and profession and as a means of promoting health, education, and human welfare, as promulgated by the American Psychological Association (APA) appears to me to be incomplete. There are parts of psychology that do not fit readily into any of these cubbyholes and they are being squeezed out. These are the academic, nonscientific parts that provide the basic foundation for all of psychology's other efforts. Neglected parts of psychology concern issues related to the humanities including philosophy, theory, history, literature, the arts, and religions.

It is difficult to provide a name for these approaches. Earlier, I called these the "Academic, Non-Science Psychologists" (Dewsbury, 2000), a term is both cumbersome and negative. The terms "human sciences" and "humanistic psychology" have been co-opted elsewhere. Perhaps the German *Geisteswissenschaften,* that refers to inquiry in the human or social sciences and that are different in kind from the natural sciences *(Naturwissenschaften)* fits best. For convenience, here I will use the term "cultural sciences" to refer to the fields of interest, although, according to many definitions of science, these may not be sciences at all.

In no way do I wish to disparage psychology as a science, practice, and service to humanity. I merely suggest that there is an important, albeit small, part of psychology that is left out with such conceptualizations; it is these other parts of psychology that I address here.

Whatever they are called, I believe that these fields have been an integral part of psychology at least from its beginning as an independent discipline and that they have an important foundational role in today's psychology. I explore recent developments at the levels of society in general, universities, and psychology itself because one needs to understand that they occur in the context of broader cultural influences. I am surely not the first to write about these issues. Indeed, I may be late to the game. Nevertheless, I hope to provide a useful overview of the current situation as I view it.

## In Society

Many authors have bemoaned the anti-intellectualism, or dumbing down, of American culture during the 20th century. It seems as though every generation bemoans the state of contemporary culture and disturbing trends therein. That noted, at least by some measures, there appear to be some disturbing trends in today's culture that do not bode well for the future of values of traditional learning.

### *Dumbing Down American Culture*

One can take one's choice among the many voices reflecting upon the decline of American culture. Hofstadter (1962), for example, traced the history of anti-intellectualism in America. He saw patterns of cyclical fluctuation over time under the influence of such factors as evangelical religion, exaggerated egalitarianism, American practical pragmatism, and the McCarthy era. In *BAD or, the Dumbing of America,* Fussell (1991) addressed the manner in which today's American culture is becoming increasingly dumb or "bad." He documented the trends in virtually all aspects of society from advertising to the arts:

> Instead of the Greening of America, we can now speak of the Dumbing of America—or, as Christopher Lasch has put it, the Spread of Stupefaction. It is hardly news anymore that the schools have failed to produce even a half-educated population. Only 42% of 17-year-old students in American high schools can understand a newspaper editorial, even in our dumbest papers (p. 194).

As the collective attention span is decreasing, in part because of the immediacy of modern technology in TV and the Internet, detailed analyses are replaced by sound bites. The art of conversation is getting lost. The penetrating analyses that used to characterize the intermission features of Saturday Metropolitan Opera broadcasts have been replaced by the cult of personality. My local public radio station is moving from classical music to an all-talk format. The *New York Times* is selling WQXR. The *Ann Arbor News* has folded.

Jacoby (2008) analyzed a trend toward "junk thought," an uncritical acceptance of pseudoscience and pronouncements

---

*Based on presidential address to Division 1, the Society for General Psychology, Toronto, Ontario, Canada, August, 2009.

about phenomena without adequate critical evaluation. Berman (2006) pointed to "the dramatic drop in levels of literacy and overall intellectual awareness" (p. xi). He summarized these factors as internal barbarism of the sort he believes "were crucial to the collapse of Rome and . . . lie at the heart of the American crisis as well" (p. xi).

The mass media have been dumbed down. "In short, the politicized tabloid-news style of Rupert Murdoch has gained ascendancy and the traditional news media is in eclipse" (Welch, 2008, p. 195). This may be termed the "USATodayification" of culture after the shift from newspapers emphasizing text to the dumbed-down visuals and simplicity of *U.S.A. Today*. Jacoby (2008) saw a loss of "middlebrow culture" when there was a belief in self-education, effort, books, and aspiration to the classics in the arts and literature. The Book of the Month Club, Great Books, and other sources were valued even by those not a part of high-brow culture.

## Causes

According to Jacoby (2008), the three main spurs to anti-intellectualism in the past 40 years have been the mass media, the failure of the American school system, and fundamentalist religion. Media present sound bites, rapid visual images, and photographs emphasizing graphics instead of detailed text. She (Jacoby, 2008, p. 260) noted that "all newspapers have aging, declining readerships, and de-emphasizing arts coverage while beefing up coverage of popular video and digital culture—both in print and online editions—is seen as a strategy for attracting younger readers."

Regarding school systems, Jacoby added that demands have been lowered. The teaching of the arts has been reduced. Children's videos indoctrinate them to mass culture at an early age and the schools do little to counteract this. Parents are relieved of parental duties to pursue adult interests, such as they are, while the children are amused.

Fundamentalist religion provides a strong anti-intellectual current, as it provides an escape from rational, secular analysis into the supernatural and from empiricism to faith-based belief. This leads to support for abstinence only in sex education, banning of stem-cell research, prayer in the schools, rejection of abortion on religious grounds, creationism and intelligent design theories, and objections to gay marriage. There are many devout Americans who adopt centrist positions and see little or no conflict between religion and science. It is the extreme fundamentalists whose values impair secular analysis on the bases of reason, not faith. Jacoby (2008, p. 206) summarized a 2003 survey by *The Economist* concluding that "Europeans consider religion the strangest and most disturbing feature of American exceptionalism. They worry that fundamentalists are hijacking the country. They find it extraordinary that three times as many Americans believe in the virgin birth as in evolution." One can only hope that some progress has been made since this survey was completed.

## Possible Solutions

Although some progress is possible, and may indeed be in its early stages, these broad trends may be nearly irreversible.

Fusell (1991) presented a pessimistic picture. He saw little hope of redemption. To escape would require that we should, among other things,

> make C, not B, the average grade again, reinstall Latin in the high schools, . . . teach a generation to sneer at advertising and to treat astrology with contempt . . . persuade educated people that criticism is their main business; speak and write English and other languages with some taste and subtlety . . . produce intelligent movies . . . start a few sophisticated newspapers . . . improve the literacy of public signs and the taste of public sculpture; . . . and develop public TV into a medium free of all commerce (pp. 200–201).

Such changes would not come easily.

# In Universities

Universities are subject to pressures from financial and other considerations. They often institute business-like models of administration.

## Goals and Purposes

An important goal of universities is the instruction of students but one can question what kind of instruction is appropriate. For a traditionalist, "the job of higher education is not to instruct students in popular culture but to expose them to something better" (Jacoby, 2008, p. 314).

The primary *intellectual* goals of universities are "the fundamental search to discover and to order knowledge and ideas" (Engell & Dangerfield, 2005, p. 24) and the ethical application of knowledge The former pair may be the definitive ones in colleges of arts and sciences. Many academics view the "fundamental search to discover and order knowledge and ideas" to be the main noninstructional purpose of the university and the primary goal of their professional lives. I will argue that, at least in psychology, discovery has been emphasized at the expense of the ordering of knowledge and ideas.

Many state legislatures and university boards are controlled by lawyers and businessmen used to running organizations according to efficient, bottom-line models. Many faculty members, by contrast, regard the demands of an efficient business as fundamentally at odds with provision of a balanced liberal education. In the words of Moore (2006),

> I wonder if a university in a business mode truly understands the values and motivation of ordinary faculty who conduct research for its own sake . . . it's time for us to shove the pendulum of history in the other direction for a while, from quantitative to qualitative considerations, from top-down management to bottom-up organization, and toward the recognition of The Academy as an ideal (p. 3G).

To take one example, on December 7, 2007 the Board of Governors of the State University System of Florida approved a measure that would require universities to set goals and sign compacts for performance in meeting them, including the improvement of graduation rates (Stripling, 2007). "If a university failed to produce an agreed upon number of graduates in a master's program, for instance, the board would reserve the right to kill the program or strip the university of its authority to approve new master's programs." Neither the intellectual goals nor the quality of education was mentioned. The message is clear: the objective was to produce graduates. One might imagine passing students to meet a quota. The university becomes like a factory working at a piece rate. The goal is production, not education.

## The Impact of Financial Pressures

Universities have changed in ways that reflect these values and pressures. Regrettably, this is not an entirely new phenomenon. In 1918 sociologist and economist Thorstein Veblen (Veblen, 1918, p. 190) wrote in *The Higher Learning in America: A Memorandum on the Conduct of Universities by Business Men* that "the ideals of scholarship are yielding ground, in an uncertain and varying degree, before the pressure of businesslike exigencies." However, the pace seems to be accelerating.

The Bayh-Dole act passed in by the U. S. Congress (1980) allowed inventions developed in universities to be licensed to private firms, thereby bringing in substantial cash infusions to the universities. Administrators and scientists have been placed in situations of a conflict of interest between dispassionate research and the pursuit of funding and thus in ethically untenable situations that have endangered the pursuit of truth (Washburn, 2005). Past-president of Harvard University, Derek Bok (Bok, 2003) saw both benefits (profits and incentives) and costs (undermining academic standards, damaging the academic community, and risks to reputation) to such commercialization.

Mark Rudd, a protest leader in 1968 at Columbia University was quoted as writing of "expecting the Ivy Tower on the hill,– a place where committed scholars would search for truth in a world that desperately needed help. Instead I found a huge corporation that made money from real estate, government research contracts, and student fees; teachers who cared only for advancement in their narrow areas of study" (Jacoby, 2008, p. 143). Greenberg (2007b) wrote that "the ivory tower is papered with contracts, patents, and business plans, and the pathways to academic laboratories, if not paved with gold, are strewn with stock options–and ethical pitfalls" (p. 257). Elsewhere, he (Greenberg, 2007a) nicely satirized the power of greed in the administrative career of his fictional character, Grant Swinger.

In an effort to train students for jobs, educational breadth erodes in favor of specialization. Many traditional academic requirements have been abandoned (Jacoby, 2008; Kaufmann, 1995). Material that might engender broad perspectives of the world and the student's place therein is discouraged as not pertaining to an economic payoff. Why then are so many seeking higher education? Higher education has, at least traditionally, entailed the life of the mind. Today, although some (e.g., Engell & Dangerfield, 2005) would question the evidence, a university education is viewed by many, perhaps most, students, as a path to higher income. According to a survey from the Higher Education Research Institute at UCLA, from the late 1960s to the late 1990s there was a total reversal in reasons freshman had entered college. Making more money and getting a better job became dominant; such goals as developing values and a broad social vision decreased comparably (Engell & Dangerfield, 2005). Students demand entertainment as much as education. Today's textbooks are beautifully illustrated but dumbed down compared to the books of a few decades ago.

The function of the university is shifting from education to training:

> . . . in an educational world now subsumed under business values, students show up—with administrative blessing—believing that they are consumers buying a product. Within this context, a faculty member who actually attempts to enforce the tradition of the humanities as an uplifting and transformative experience, who challenges his charges to think hard about complex issues, will provoke negative evaluations (Berman, 2006, p. 122).

## Prestige

Administrators want to get their universities ranked high in the media's annual published ratings. Many seek a finish in the "top 10." These rankings are based substantially on such factors as research publications and grants. Greenberg (2007b) put it well:

> The academic arms race giddily accelerates. In Ponzi-scheme fashion, it inflames the pursuit of money for constructing research facilities needed to attract high-salaried scientific superstars who can win government grants to perform research that will bring glory and more money to the university. Academe's pernicious enthrallment by the rating system of *U. S. News & World Report* is a disgrace of modern higher education (p. 278).

University administrators become highly sensitive to financial concerns, filling seats, and recruitment data, which in turn affect prestige ratings.

Twenty-five percent of a university's ranking reflects the ratings of university presidents. There is a temptation to inflate the rating of one's own institution. For the 2010 rankings the University of Florida president placed his institution among just nine schools rated as "distinguished." Few others would rank it that high. Surely, he was not the only president to inflate the rankings of his or her school. On the other hand, a group of university presidents has agreed not to provide any such ratings (Crabbe, 2009).

## The Reward Systems

It should be no surprise that administrators selectively reward those who are productive on their chosen metrics. A typical job advertisement might state that the successful candidate is expected to establish a research program, attract talented students, and attract extramural funding.

Perhaps in response, there has been a great increase in reports of academic cheating and fraud in recent years (e.g., Broad & Wade, 1982; Greenberg, 2007b; Swazey, Anderson, & Louis, 1993; Woodward & Goodstein, 1996). It is not completely clear whether this is real or a result of better monitoring and reporting. Given the pressures on faculty members it would not be surprising it this favored increased fraud and corruption.

## The Humanities in a Corporate-Driven University

Power among university programs can be viewed as distributed according to three economic criteria: the promise of money, knowledge of money, and as a source of money (Engell & Dangerfield, 2005). The humanities do not rank high on any of these. This has created pressures to favor those programs with visible payoffs over those that might be even more significant in fostering understanding of the world around us. With the introduction of business-like metrics departments are placed in competition with one another for finite resources whose distribution is, at least in part, a function of money and related payoffs relevant to business (Donoghue, 2008, p. 134).

Economic hard times have been difficult for universities and especially so for humanities programs in universities (Cohen, 2009; Jaschik, 2009a). "Across the country, schools looking to trim their budgets are targeting programs in history, foreign languages, and journalism or are combining disciples like philosophy, religion, and political science into one pared-down department" (Washburn, 2005, p. 215). As a result, the percentage of faculty positions devoted to the humanities relative to the natural and social sciences has decreased during the 20th century (Jaschik, 2006). From 1970 to 1994 the proportions of undergraduate majors in such fields as health professions, public administration, and business grew rapidly as English, foreign languages, philosophy, and history declined. Faculty salaries are lower for the humanities than other fields. Scores on the SAT tests tend to be lower for humanities students than for other disciplines (Engell & Danger-field, 2005).

## Solutions?

Many authors simply bemoan the loss of breadth that comes from a liberal education. We might ask if something can be done. Donoghue (2008) noted that many accept the implicit assumption that specialized education provides the best basis for graduates to obtain jobs and perform well; that might be challenged. Are there data to support this conclusion? Perhaps a broader education will, in the long-run, actually produce better and more productive workers as they gain a broader perspective on the world and become better prepared for the changes that will occur during their careers. Although it may be difficult, this question may be open to empirical study. To take one example, according to Pinello (2009):

> some years ago, a survey was sent to law-school deans (the "presidents" of law schools). One of the questions on the survey was what majors the deans recommended students have in college in order to prepare effectively for law school. The four majors most frequently recommended by law-school deans were (in alphabetical order) English (sometimes called literature), history, philosophy, and political science (sometimes called government).

Donoghue's other suggestion was that humanistically oriented academicians learn more about how universities actually

work and embed themselves in the process. This goes counter to the approach of many who prefer to remain in our ivory towers and not become soiled by the dirty activities below. However, this may be an unrealistic approach. It may be necessary to become more knowledgeable and more active in minimizing corporate driven trends.

Bok (2006) recognized that we could not retrace the whole history of commercialization. Rather, we need to set limits and draw lines. University leaders are responsible for this and Bok outlined roles for trustees, the faculty, and government. He wrote that

> universities are approaching a critical juncture. They can try hard to create and enforce more effective limits on commercialization. Or, they can temporize, compromise, rationalize, and continue the gradual slide into habits that could alter their character in ways detrimental to their teaching, research, and standing in the community (p. 206).

## Psychology

The pressures that prevail in society at large, and in universities in particular, trickle down to affect academic psychology departments as well. Just as purely intellectual efforts are being downplayed in society and universities are being increasingly run like businesses, so psychology and psychology departments are undergoing related changes. We live in an age of specialists with regard to the topics of interest, but the specialties, at least in much of academic psychology, have coalesced around a narrow range of approaches.

Psychology has become incredibly diversified with regard to subdisciplines and content matter. Today it is viewed not as a unified discipline but as a collection of psychological sciences (e.g., Koch, 1993). In another sense psychology is becoming less diverse. Some psychologists are engaged in worthwhile practice and serving the public interest. I am not concerned with these worthy attempts here. The rest of psychology is becoming focused on application of a set of relatively narrow research principles that bind them methodologically if not in the subject matter of concern. Cronbach (1957) characterized two disciplines of psychology, correlational and experimental, but saw a common labor. I suggest that, in today's context, such commonalities are worth emphasizing. One can argue that we have two cultures (e.g., Kimble, 1984) but, overall a strong empiricism rules both. Thus, there appears to be some degree of unification of goals and approaches even as the approaches are applied in different ways to different subject matter. Psychologists have produced some research that has enlightened out-understanding of many specific problems. I have no problem with empiricism per se; only with nondirected and seemingly goalless empiricism.

Psychology was not always divorced from its foundations. Consider the putative founders of psychology as a discipline, Wilhelm Wundt and William James. Wundt is generally regarded as the first to establish experimental psychology as a discipline. However, he did not believe that all problems of concern to psychologists could be dealt with in the laboratory.

He saw two main branches (e.g., Blumenthal, 1975). Wundt viewed laboratory methods as appropriate for addressing problems of basic processes and cultural methods for other aspects. In essence, some problems, he thought, required the methods of his Völkerpsychologie, which included such fields as the arts, mythologies, and legal and moral systems. William James, who is generally credited with introducing experimental methods to American psychology, also believed that they had limitations. It was the exploration of mental states, especially his own, that most fascinated James and he saw no way to explore these effectively in the laboratory (Bjork, 1988; Evans, 1990; Taylor, 1991).

## Psychological Literature

There seems to be a dissatisfaction for many with the character of the published scientific literature produced in psychology journals. Bevan (1991) expressed a general dissatisfaction with the output and invoked the forest-trees sentiment, noting that

> the character of psychology is increasingly manifest in the rapid proliferation of narrowly focused and compulsively insular camps, a proliferation that seemingly knows no limits. We persevere in looking at small questions instead of large ones and our view of the forest is forever obscured by the trees (p. 475).

Seminara and Peters (1958), writing of perceptions of psychology from abroad, provided a comment from an unnamed Canadian psychologist that

> There is a tendency to be lacking in ideas. Large scale, carefully controlled, and excellently designed studies often seem to lack a purpose in that no clear hypotheses are being tested. One has the feeling that having erected the 'research machinery,' the psychologists sometimes do not know what to do with it (p. 239).

A German psychologist commented that "American psychologists spend a lot of time and money and discover many empirical facts. Most of these facts are not very interesting or significant" (p. 239). The authors added that "on the whole, we are seen as being open-minded, congenial, and enthusiastic, but lacking in general culture and seeming 'too much like businessmen'" (p. 239).

In essence, much of psychological writing seems to reflect what Koch (1981) called "ameaningful thought." The approach "regards knowledge as the result of "processing" rather than discovery. It presumes that knowledge is an almost automatic result of a gimmickry, an assembly line, a 'methodology'" (p. 259).

## Fragmentation and the Unification of Psychology

Many bemoan the fragmentation and lack of unification of psychology (e.g., Henriques, 2003; Staats, 1981, 1983, 1999; Sternberg, 2005; Yanchar & Slife, 1997). This has been an issue in psychology for many years (e.g., Dunlap, 1938; Samelson, 1988). Altman (1987) wrote of the entrepreneurial pressures that have affected universities and psychology in recent years and stressed the centrifugal aspects of psychology's development since 1960. Increasingly, psychologists have a primary identification not with the broad organization of the APA but with smaller, specialized societies.

Arthur Staats has been a leader in the efforts toward unification. According to Staats (1981, p. 239),

> Our field is constructed of small islands of knowledge organized in ways that make no connections with the many other existing islands of knowledge. Moreover, separatism involves the absence of expectation or demand that such connections should occur. (p. 239)

Staats added that "the growth of unrelated knowledge is such that without the benefit of organizing principles, we are being inundated and drowned by our own scientific products" (Staats, 1981, p. 254).

Some (e.g., Bower, 1993) disagree with both Staats's historical analyses and his goal; they see the fragmentation of psychology as a healthy sign. Of course, Koch (e.g., 1993) long argued that psychology is not a coherent discipline at all; he preferred the term *"the psychological studies"* (p. 902, italics in the original).

I tend to side with those who believe that psychology probably never will be truly unified but nevertheless I think that may be possible to develop at least a few integrative principles underlying the diverse aspects of psychology. Research needs to be conducted with attention to broader and more significant questions than is often the case. If there is any chance of effecting these changes, it is likely to be, at least in part, through those who step back from the grind of research papers and grant applications to attempt some kind of overview—precisely the kind of psychologists who are being squeezed out of today's psychology.

## Our Reward Structure

The reward structure in psychology, as elsewhere in universities, is such as to foster narrow specialization and a lack of integration (see also Yanchar & Slife, 1997). If one peruses advertisements for academic positions, one finds many for the specialty areas of psychology such as cognitive psychology, social psychology, and behavioral neuroscience. What are rare are jobs for general psychologists, historians of psychology, philosophers of psychology, and the like. When there is an opening in my department, for example, the debate centers about which of our specialty areas will get the line, not about whether there should be a truly integrative choice.

Annual evaluations and considerations for promotion and tenure, at least at major universities, consider teaching and service but are largely based on research accomplishments. In general that means publications, which are more often counted than read albeit with some attention to journal impact factors, and grant support. The newest guidelines and procedures for tenure and promotion in my department state that because the department is scientifically oriented, research and scholarship are the most important of the three areas of evaluation. This is typical (see Jaschik, 2009b). I have chaired my college's tenure and promotion committee and I can confirm that these pressures come, at least in part, from above the department level and operate across a range of departments. Psychology departments, like others in the natural and social sciences, tend to go along for the ride without protest. In the humanities, in contrast to psychology and the various sciences, faculties are generally rewarded for their books more than grants and articles. There appears to be little tolerance for such faculty members in psychology.

Let me provide a personal example. The first part of my faculty career was devoted to comparative psychology. I ran an active laboratory with numerous graduate students, published many papers, and had 25 consecutive years of grant support, although with relatively small grants, from the National Science Foundation. I was generally ranked at or near the top of the departmental faculty. Later, with the concurrence of my department chair, I decided to switch my efforts to work in the history of psychology. I believe that my work in this field made me more visible and had greater impact than that of my earlier phase. Of course, that is debatable. However, my rankings fell to the middle of the pack. In 1 year I published two books; a statement in my annual letter of evaluation indicated that I had not published enough. At that stage of my career, this was a frustration, rather than a devastating blow, although it had some impact on merit raises.

The messages are clear for younger faculty seeking jobs, tenure, and promotion: stay in your laboratory, do not try to integrate findings, publish research reports, get grants, produce students, do not contribute to service, and keep your students in the laboratory rather than in course work. Is it any wonder that we are producing the kind of psychology that we have today? Yanchar and Slife (1997) reviewed various proposals for dealing with this situation. I offer my own, modest suggestion near the end of this article.

Today, it is difficult to organize a psychology colloquium series. Most faculty and students have little interest in learning more about areas other than those with direct, short-term interest to their own career objectives. If it does not help them in writing grants and papers, what good is it? The result is that we have area seminars in a series of small fiefdoms that, together are called departments but which, in reality are, at best, federations of semi-independent states.

## Graduate Education

These pressures spill over to affect patterns of graduate education in psychology. It is no accident that, in many departments, the only common core courses shared widely among students in different areas are those in statistics and methodology. It is issues of methodology that characterize our infatuation with experimentation to the detriment of integration.

Altman (1987) noted that graduate students no longer are required to obtain the breadth of coursework required of their predecessors. Rather,

research became more central to graduate education, and coursework outside of a student's specialty area became less valued and simply more of a hurdle to overcome. And, with the increasing sophistication of specialty areas, students were less and less *educated*; instead they were vocationally and technically *trained* in a narrow band of research and methodology (p. 1065, italics in original).

Benjamin (2001) provided a historical survey of the issue of a core curriculum in graduate education in psychology. The core courses rarely have been designed to question the prevailing methods and searching for change. Rather, they are training courses indoctrinating the novices into how research is to be done.

Even these substantive core courses have been disappearing. This was not always the case. As a graduate student at Michigan in the 1960s I was required to take core courses in 10 different areas of psychology; the requirements are much looser today. At the University of Florida we used to have six required fields for coursework. Over the years, this requirement has eroded under pressure from faculty members to get their graduate students into the laboratory as early and as much as possible. These changes are not atypical. Many other universities have loosened requirements for course breadth in graduate education in favor of early specialization, increased numbers of publications by the students and, yes, increased research productivity in the laboratory of the faculty mentor.

It is discouraging, however, that, in a survey of graduate catalogs and the National Research Council rankings, Benjamin (2001) found an inverse relationship between departments' research reputations and the breadth of courses required. Perhaps it is not surprising that, at least in the short run, those students presumably spending the most time in the laboratory rather than in courses attain the best research reputations. The deck was stacked.

The psychologists trained in today's programs will, in later years, teach introductory psychology, evaluate candidates from a variety of areas for hiring, promotion, and tenure, serve on grant review boards, and become involved in organizations like the APA. However, many will lack any substantive background whatsoever that prepares them for understanding the broad range of psychological approaches.

Benjamin and Baker (2009, p. 98) put it well:

Losing the common core, as loosely defined as it was, was part of the philosophy of specialization that focused entirely on the trees while losing sight of the importance of the forest. Psychological science does not seem to have a big-picture view of the world. The entire philosophy of reductionism stakes its belief in a future in which all of the minutiae from myriad studies will somehow coalesce into a meaningful whole that ultimately answers the bigger questions. Yet history shows that science doesn't work that way.

In a classic article, historian Stephen Brush (1974) asked "Should the History of Science be Rated X?" Essentially, Brush argued that the indoctrination of students in preparation for careers as traditional scientists might actually be hindered by exposing them to recent scholarship in the history of science. This scholarship challenges some of the dogmas concerning the nature of science. Brush wrote tongue-in-cheek, but his article contains a lesson for psychology. If the goal of graduate training in psychology is to produce graduates with strong publication records, good fellowship prospects, and high placement potential in today's competitive job market, perhaps the present trends make sense. However, this may be short-sighted and work, in the long run, to the detriment of the field. The narrowly trained psychologist typically mines a narrow vein exploiting it with publications in a field related to that of the student's mentor. However, if there is one thing we know about the field, it is that psychology will change in a few years. Each vein currently being mined will dry up and new approaches will be necessary. Who will be better prepared to deal with the new realities—the narrow specialist or the student who sacrificed some productivity in the interest of breadth of perspective? It would be foolish to fully neglect the realities of the marketplace so that graduates go jobless. However, I believe that if we retain some of the breadth that has traditionally been included in graduate programs we can foster scientific productivity, albeit slightly reduced, while graduating more broadly competent psychologists.

## How Cultural Scientific Approaches Might Help

If we are to provide some general principles of psychology we will need both researchers who understand the broad contexts of their work and those specializing in synthesis and integration. Integration and perspective can be achieved in a number of ways including, for example, the history of the field (e.g., Benjamin & Baker, 2009) and theoretical psychology (Kukla, 1989; Slife & Williams, 1997). Lacking this effort, psychology will continue to both explode in diverse directions and remain mired in its methodological morass.

Psychologists have been accused of "physics envy" in their rush to imitate the methodology of that science. However, physics departments are staffed with both experimental and theoretical physicists; there is little that is parallel in today's psychology departments. As noted by Staats (1999, p. 7), "in the unified sciences, resources are also provided for the tasks of weaving diverse and unrelated findings into a generally meaningful, compact parsimonious interrelated, systematic, and substantially consensual body."

The kind of effort required to search for general principles is most likely to succeed if knowledge from outside of psychology, including the humanities, is brought to bear and to help focus psychologists on questions that really matter. As noted by Perloff (2004), "research and theorizing in psychology, as well as in other behavioral and social sciences, will be enhanced, enriched, and made more practical and useful if the variables and constructs therein are broadened and deepened by the words, the expressions, and the observations found in poetry, literature, plays, narratives, and in the arts broadly speaking, media which are more sensitive to the nuances and subtleties in behavior than are those contained more conventionally in psychology" (p. 411). Perloff then went on to provide 16 examples of such benefits.

## The American Psychological Association

The parts of psychology that are most endangered in the present environment are precisely those most closely tied to the humanities. Using the APA division structure as a guide, one might identify general psychology (Division 1), aesthetics, creativity, and the arts (10), theoretical and philosophical psychology (24), history of psychology (26), and the psychology of religion (36) as fields that fall within the category of cultural sciences (see Dewsbury, 2000). One could quibble with inclusion or exclusion of some divisions but they would seem to have a common thread. Perhaps Division 2 (Teaching) fits in some, though surely not all, of the matters I discuss. I intend this list to be useful mainly in defining the areas to which I refer and that I believe are especially endangered. I hope that it conveys the kind of work I am including as the cultural sciences.

The APA bylaws begin by stating that "The objects of the American Psychological Association shall be to advance psychology as a science and profession and as a means of promoting health, education and human welfare by the encouragement of psychology." They go on to provide a liberal interpretation of this statement in supporting "encouragement of psychology in all its branches in the broadest and most liberal manner." However, in practice, the effects of this orientation are clear. There is no obvious home for these divisions within the APA. The APA is organized into four directorates: Education, Practice, Public Interest, and Science. Although there are some overlaps of the orphan fields with all of these, no directorate is really responsible for the welfare of the cultural science approaches. The Association for Psychological Sciences (APS) is no better in this respect (Dewsbury, 2000).

In the opening scene of the classic comedy move *Animal House*, Omega house, the leading fraternity on campus hosts a pledge drive. Two less-than-promising freshman, at least by Omega values, enter. Within a few minutes they are ushered into a separate room with foreign students, handicapped, and other freshman regarded as inconsistent with Omega ideals. One can't help that the cultural science divisions in APA are regarded in a somewhat similar manner.

The problem for these cultural science approaches within the APA is that they are both a small and shrinking part of the larger organization. All five of the primary divisions named have lost membership in recent years. The five divisions combined represented about 11% of the memberships held in 1989 compared to 4.6% today. The bulk of the loss has been in Division 1, which is now just 35% of its 1989 self. These are not the only divisions to suffer losses but the impact may be greater where divisions are already small.

The future is not bright. As is true throughout much of the APA, the age structure of these divisions is discouraging. The mean age of members in all five divisions is over 60; that of Division 26 is 69.6. Forty-five percent of the members of Division 26 are age 70 or older! The APA in general shows a similar trend but the fact is that younger psychologists are not being attracted to the APA in general and these areas of psychology in particular. I believe that there are a number of reasons for this, chief among them are the reward structure for faculty members in our colleges and universities. The problems within the APA are indicative of what is happening in psychology at large. However, the organization could be made more hospitable to these groups.

# Proposed Actions

At this point I have three possible actions to suggest. They concern the APA, graduate education, and interaction between departments and higher administrations.

## The APA

The APA should provide some kind of representation for the cultural-scientific part of psychology. Given the size of these divisions, it would be difficult to justify a full directorate comparable to the four already in place. However, some smaller unit, either within or outside of the current directorates, should be established. This would provide a voice for these smaller, but important, parts of psychology.

## Graduate Education

If some integration of psychological principles is to be achieved, we will need appropriate infrastructure, personnel, and support systems for those working to develop them. If we are to have psychologists with the breadth of vision to accomplish this, we will need to reverse the current trend and broaden again the requirements for graduate education in psychology. Students will need to be educated as to why this is being done. Faculty members will need to see its importance. Further, we will need to encourage those few students who want to follow a path to concentrate on the cultural scientific approach. Of course, that can only happen if there is some prospect of jobs for such graduates.

We should restore some breadth to a core curriculum in graduate programs in psychology even for those students who wish to work primarily in specialty areas. We should challenge assumptions that specialized training provides better preparation for future psychologists than broader psychological education. We might even be able to collect data test this assumption with respect to prominence in the field beyond the first few years following graduate school.

## The Reward Structure

I believe that psychology departments need to make a sacrifice to maintain the character of the field. My proposal is consistent with the approach taken by Halpern et al. (1998) and Myers and Waller (1999). Halpern et al. proposed a multidimensional definition of scholarship in psychology. One of the five parts in their definition is the integration of knowledge, including "review articles and books, meta-analyses, and well crafted texts that bring diverse findings together to enhance knowledge" (p. 1295). They noted that "new knowledge, represented in the category of original research, is of limited usefulness if not integrated into a larger body of concepts and facts" (p. 1295). Not all faculty members will excel in all categories, and faculty ought to emphasize what they do best. Myers and Waller (1999) also supported the proposal of "flexible loads" and noted that the field "needs people who will help us see the contours of the

whole forest by integrating research findings into a big picture story and perhaps challenging our preconceptions" (p. 358).

Departments need to hire some psychologists who concentrate on history, theory, teaching, cultural ties, and the like. This ought to be easy for liberal arts colleges and those where the departments are evaluated based on effective teaching. In addition, however, I propose that each research department in universities with about 20 or more full-time positions hire at least 1–3 psychologists who will be evaluated differently than the rest of the department. Their job descriptions and the bases for their promotion and tenure will be clear, but different from those for the rest of the department. If they are designated teachers, they will be evaluated on their teaching. If they work in general psychology, the history of psychology, the philosophy of psychology, and related fields, they will be evaluated on their work in those fields. They will not be expected to get grants, publish in journals that are regarded as "high-impact," or even have the most graduate students working with them. They will, however, to be expected to work as hard and be as effective in their fields as their colleagues do in grant getting, publishing in more visible journals, and filling their laboratories with graduate students who will find difficulty in getting jobs similar to those of their mentors. These accomplishments will need to be demonstrated. The teachers may have to teach more courses, have lines of students outside their doors, supervise the local chapter of Psi Chi, and so forth These colleagues may write books rather than scores of journal articles. I am not proposing a privileged class to ride on the backs of their hardworking researchers. Rather, I suggest a group to be evaluated as strictly as their colleagues but using a different metric.

The problem, of course, is that this proposal will, in all likelihood, not be popular with university administrators; this is the sacrifice. Consistent with the first two sections of this article, they have pressures put upon them and, in turn, put pressure on departments to maximize grant getting and the overhead money that comes with the grants. They control the purse strings. They want to see high publication rates in prestigious journals so that their college and university can rise in the annual ratings published in the media.

I believe that it is the responsibility of departments to educate these administrators to realize that, while psychology is a field of science, practice, and service, it is more than that. If we lose the cultural-scientific foundation of the field, we lose the heart and soul of the field. Departments will have to be evaluated based on their whole output, not just the ones presently used. Tenure-and-promotion committees will need to be educated to the multiple dimensions of psychology. Some of these criteria are already in force for departments in the humanities. The committees need to be told that evaluating psychologists requires a set of flexible criteria to reflect the complexity of psychology as a discipline. Psychology as a field cannot be pigeon holed into one or the other divisions of the college, such as natural science, social science, and humanities. We are all of those things. Psychology is a wonderfully complex discipline in need of rebuilding its basic foundations.

# References

Altman, I. (1987). Centripetal and centrifugal trends in psychology. *American Psychologist, 42,* 1058–1069.

Benjamin, L. T., Jr. (2001). American psychology's struggles with its curriculum: Should a thousand flowers bloom? *American Psychologist, 56,* 735–742.

Benjamin, L. T., Jr., & Baker, D. B. (2009). Recapturing a context for psychology: The role of history. *Perspectives on Psychological Science, 4,* 97–98.

Berman, M. (2006). *The twilight of American culture.* New York: Norton.

Bevan, W. (1991). Contemporary psychology: At tour inside the onion. *American Psychologist, 46,* 475–483.

Bjork, D. W. (1988). *William James: The center of his vision.* New York: Columbia University Press.

Blumenthal, A. (1975). A reappraisal of Wilhelm Wundt. *American Psychologist, 30,* 1081–1088.

Bok, D. (2003). *Universities in the marketplace: The commercialization if higher education.* Princeton, NJ: Princeton University Press.

Bower, G. H. (1993). The fragmentation of psychology? *American Psychologist, 48,* 905–907.

Broad, W., & Wade, N. (1982). *Betrayers of truth: Fraud and deceit in the halls of science.* New York: Simon & Schuster.

Brush, S. G. (1974). Should the history of psychology be rated X? *Science, 183,* 1164–1172.

Cohen, P. (2009). *In tougher times, the humanities must justify their worth.* Retrieved from http://nytimes.com/2009/02/25/books/25human.html

Crabbe, N. (2009, June 17). Playing the college ratings game. *Gainesville Sun, 1A, 5A.*

Cronbach, L. J. (1957). The two disciplines of scientific psychology. *American Psychologist, 12,* 671–684.

Dewsbury, D. A. (2000). The marginalization of academic, non-scientific psychology in the American Psychological Association. *The General Psychologist, 35,* 96–97.

Donoghue, F. (2008). *The last professors: The corporate university and the fate of the humanities.* New York: Fordham University Press.

Dunlap, K. (1938). *The impending dismemberment of psychology.* Manuscript of address to the National Institute of Psychology, Columbus, OH, September 7, Columbus, OH. Box M565, Knight Dunlap Papers, Archives of the History of American Psychology, Akron, OH.

Engell, J., & Dangerfield, A. (2005). *Saving higher education in the age of money.* Charlottesville, VA: University of Virginia Press.

Evans, R. B. (1990). William James, *The Principles of Psychology,* and experimental psychology. *American Journal of Psychology, 103,* 433–447.

Fussell, P. (1991). *BAD or, the dumbing of America.* New York: Simon & Schuster.

Greenberg, D. S. (2007a). On the road to academic greatness–a parable. *Science, 317,* 1328–1329.

Greenberg, D. S. (2007b), *Science for sale: The perils, rewards, and delusions of campus capitalism.* Chicago. IL: University of Chicago Press.

Halpern, D. F., Smothergill, D. W., Allen, M., Baker, S., Baum, C, Best, D., . . . Weaver, K. A. (1998). Scholarship in psychology: A paradigm for the twenty-first century. *American Psychologist, 53,* 1292–1297.

Henriques, G. (2003). The tree of knowledge system and the theoretical unification of psychology. *Review of General Psychology, 7,* 159–182.

Hofstadter, R. (1962). *Anti-intellectualism in American life.* New York: Knopf.

Jacoby, S. (2008). *The age of American unreason.* New York: Pantheon.

Jaschik, S. (2006). *The rise of the social sciences.* Retrieved from http://insidehighered.com/news/2006/08/21/disciplines

Jaschik, S. (2009a). *The state of the humanities.* Retrieved from http://insidehighered.com/news/2009/01/07/humanities

Jaschik, S. (2009b). *What counts for tenure.* Retrieved from http://insidehighered.com/news/2009/07/20/polisci

Kaufmann, W. (1995). *The future of the humanities: Teaching art, religion, philosophy, literature, and history.* New Brunswick, NJ: Transaction.

Kimble, G. A. (1984). Psychology's two cultures. *American Psychologist, 39,* 833–839.

Koch, S. (1981). The nature and limits of psychological knowledge: Lessons of a century of qua "science." *American Psychologist, 36,* 257–269.

Koch, S. (1993). "Psychology" of "the psychological studies"? *American Psychologist, 48,* 902–904.

Kukla, A. (1989). Nonempirical issues in psychology. *American Psychologist, 44,* 785–794.

Moore, J. H. (2006, October 15). In the business of education, is quantity more important than quality? *Gainesville Sun,* (p. 3G).

Myers, D. G., & Waller, J. E. (1999). Reflections on scholarship from the liberal arts academy. *American Psychologist, 54,* 358–361.

Perloff, R. (2004). Beyond psychology: Literature and the arts as supplements for understanding, predicting, and controlling behavior: Thinking outside the box. *Journal of Business Ethics, 52,* 411–417.

Pinello, D. R. (2009). *Advice for getting into law school.* Retrieved from http://danpinello.com/LawSch.htm

Samelson, F. (1988, June). *The "impending dismemberment of psychology" and its miraculous rescue, 1930–45.* Paper presented at meetings of the Cheiron Society, Princeton, NJ.

Seminara, J. L., & Peters, G. A. (1959). American psychology: As seen from abroad. *American Psychologist, 14,* 238–239.

Slife, B. D., & Williams, R. N. (1997). Toward a theoretical psychology: Should a subdiscipline be formally recognized? *American Psychologist, 52,* 117–129.

Staats, A. W. (1981). Paradigmatic behaviorism, unified theory, unified theory construction methods, and the Zeitgiest of separation. *American Psychologist, 36,* 239–256.

Staats, A. W. (1983). *Psychology's crisis of disunity: Philosophy and method for a unified science.* New York: Praeger.

Staats, A. W. (1999). Unifying psychology requires new infrastructure, theory, method, and a research agenda. *Review of General Psychology, 3,* 3–13.

Sternberg, R. J. (2005). *Unity in psychology: Possibility or pipedream?* Washington, DC: American Psychological Association.

Stripling, J. (2007, December 7). BOG OKs school accountability plan. *Gainesville Sun.* http://gainesville.com/article/20071207/NEWS/712070321

Swazey, J. P., Anderson, M. S., & Louis, K. S. (1993). Ethical problems in academic research. *American Scientist, 81,* 542–553.

Taylor, E. (1991). William James and the humanistic tradition. *Journal of Humanistic Psychology, 31,* 56–74.

Veblen, T. (1918). *The higher learning in America: A memorandum on the conduct of universities by business men.* New York: B. W. Heubsch.

Washburn, J. (2005). *University, Inc.: The corporate corruption of American higher education.* New York: Basic Books.

Welch, B. (2008). *State of confusion: Political manipulation and the assault on the American mind.* New York: St. Martin's Press.

Woodward, J., & Goodstein, D. (1996). Conduct, misconduct and the structure of science. *American Scientist, 84,* 479–490.

Yanchar, S. C, & Slife, B. D. (1997). Pursuing unity in a fragmented psychology: Problems and prospects. *Review of General Psychology, 1,* 235–255.

## Critical Thinking

1. Describe the role of psychology's historical roots in shaping psychology into the vibrant field it is today.

2. What pressures are forcing psychology to abandon these important roots and what might psychology's future be like if these roots are abandoned?

# UNIT 2

# Biological Bases of Behavior

## Unit Selections

5. **The Left Brain Knows What the Right Hand Is Doing,** Michael Price
6. **The Brain's (Dark Energy),** Marcus E. Raichle
7. **Phantom Pain and the Brain,** Sadie F. Dingfelder
8. **Reflections on Mirror Neurons,** Temma Ehrenfeld

## Learning Outcomes

*After reading this Unit, you should be able to:*

- Understand and explain brain lateralization.

- Describe how brain lateralization influence common human traits.

- Explain the brain's default mode network.

- Summarize the connection between the default mode network and human disorders as well as the human capacity for planning.

- Understand the brain's role in phantom pain.

- Describe mirror neurons and explain their role in influencing observational behavior and communication.

## Student Website

www.mhhe.com/cls

## Internet References

**Behavioral Genetics**
 www.ornl.gov/sci/techresources/Human_Genome/project/about.shtml
**Institute for Behavioral Genetics**
 ibgwww.colorado.edu/index.html
**Serendip**
 serendip.brynmawr.edu/serendip
**Society for Neuroscience**
 www.sfn.org

As a child, Angelina vowed she did not want to turn out like either of her parents. Angelina's mother was passive and acquiescent about her father's drinking. When her dad was drunk, her mom always called his boss to report that her father was "sick" and then acted as if there was nothing wrong at home. Angelina's childhood was a nightmare. Her father's behavior was erratic and unpredictable. If he drank just a little bit, most often he was happy. If he drank a lot, which was usually the case, he frequently but not always became belligerent.

Despite vowing not to become like her father, as an adult Angelina found herself in the alcohol rehabilitation unit of a large hospital. Angelina's employer could no longer tolerate her on-the-job mistakes or her unexplained absences from work. Angelina's supervisor therefore referred her to the clinic for help. As Angelina pondered her fate, she wondered whether her genes preordained her to follow in her father's inebriated footsteps or whether the stress of her childhood had brought her to this point in her life. After all, being the child of an alcoholic is difficult.

Psychologists are concerned with discovering the causes of human behavior. Once the cause is known, treatments for problematic behaviors can be developed. In fact, certain behaviors might even be prevented when the cause is identified early enough. But for Angelina, prevention was too late. One of the paths to understanding human behavior is the task of understanding its biological underpinnings. Genes and chromosomes, the body's chemistry (as found in hormones, neurotransmitters, and enzymes), and the nervous system comprised of the brain, spinal cord, nerve cells, and other parts are all implicated in human behavior.

Physiological psychologists and neuroscientists examine the role of biology in behavior. These psychologists often utilize one of a handful of techniques to understand the biology–behavior connection. Animal studies involving manipulation, stimulation, or destruction of certain parts of the brain offer one method of

© Royalty-Free/CORBIS

study, but these studies remain controversial with animal rights activists. There is also an alternative technique available that involves the examination of unfortunate individuals born with malfunctioning brains or those whose brains are damaged later by accidents or disease. We can also use animal models to understand genetics. By studying an individual's behavior in comparison to both natural and adoptive parents, or by studying identical twins reared together or apart, we also can begin to understand the role of genetics and the environment in human behavior.

The articles in this unit are designed to familiarize you with the knowledge psychologists have gleaned by using these techniques to study the biological processes involved in human behavior. Each article should interest you and make you a bit more curious about the role of biology in the psychological functioning of human beings.

# The Left Brain Knows What the Right Hand Is Doing

**New research explores how brain lateralization influences our lives.**

MICHAEL PRICE

Browse through a list of history's most famous left-handers and you are likely to see Albert Einstein's name. You may even see people tying Einstein's genius to his left-handedness. The problem is, Einstein's left-handedness is a myth. Myriad photos show him writing on a chalkboard with his right hand, for example.

But handedness has its roots in the brain—right-handed people have left-hemisphere-dominant brains and vice versa—and the lefties who claim Einstein weren't all that far off. While he was certainly right-handed, autopsies suggest his brain didn't reflect the typical left-side dominance in language and speech areas. His brain's hemispheres were more symmetrical—a trait typical of left-handers and the ambidextrous.

By comparison, 95 percent of righties have brains that strictly divvy up tasks: The left hemisphere almost exclusively handles language and speech, the right handles emotion and image processing—but only about 20 percent of lefties have brains that divide up these duties so rigidly.

Brain hemisphere specialist Michael Corballis, PhD, a psychologist at the University of Auckland in New Zealand, points out that having the hemispheres manage different tasks might increase the brain's efficiency.

"There's an advantage to cerebral dominance because it localizes function to one hemisphere," he says. "Otherwise, information has to cross back and forth across the corpus callosum, and that can sometimes cause problems."

A strongly symmetrical brain, like Einstein's, leaves people open to mental dysfunction, but it also paves the way for creative thinking. Researchers are exploring these unusually balanced brains and finding out why that's the case.

## Righties Rule

About 90 percent of people are right-handed, says Corballis. The remaining 10 percent are either left-handed or some degree of ambidextrous, though people with "true" ambidexterity—i.e., no dominant hand at all—only make up about 1 percent of the population.

That means the vast majority of people on this planet have strongly lateralized brains. That's probably no accident, Corballis says. Early in human history, and possibly even in our pre-human ancestors, evolution delegated different cognitive responsibilities to the brain's two hemispheres, he posits. It would be inefficient for both sides to, for example, process a person's speech when one hemisphere can do that just fine on its own. That frees up the other hemisphere to do something else, such as sort out the speech's emotional content.

Researchers used to think that minor brain damage early in development caused left-handedness, he notes.

"But if that's true, that's probably the minority of cases," Corballis says. There are just too many lefties for brain damage to be the major culprit, "so we look to genetics."

In 2007, geneticists identified a gene on chromosome 2, LRRTM1, that seems to be present in most lefties (*Molecular Psychiatry,* Vol. 12, No. 12). The gene has also been linked to schizophrenia, which fits with earlier research showing that people with schizophrenia are significantly more likely to be left-handed or ambidextrous.

Less-lateralized brains may also be linked to lower IQ scores, suggests a study by Corballis, published in *Neuropsychologia* (Vol. 46, No. 1). The study found that left-handers and right-handers had similar IQ scores, but people who identify as ambidextrous had slightly lower scores, especially in arithmetic, memory and reasoning.

These results dovetail with Corballis's previous findings that ambidextrous people also rate higher on a "magical ideation" scale, which measures people's propensity to, for example, think that people on television are talking directly to them or that they can sense when people are talking about them (*Laterality,* Vol. 7, No. 11).

The link among these three findings—the slight propensity for schizophrenia, lower IQ scores and magical ideation—may suggest that the brain is more likely to encounter faulty neuronal connections when the information it's processing has to shuttle back and forth between hemispheres, says Corballis.

# Lateral of the Sexes

One curious fact about handedness is that men appear to be ever so slightly more prone to left-handedness than women. Over the past few decades, a number of studies have turned up this peculiarity, but there was nothing concrete, nothing consistent. But a recently published meta-analysis in September's *Psychological Bulletin* (Vol. 134, No. 5) seems to prove the point.

In their analysis of 144 handedness and brain laterality studies—accounting for a total of nearly 1.8 million individuals—University of Oxford psychologists Marietta Papadatou-Pastou, PhD, and Maryanne Martin, PhD, found that males are about 2 percent more likely to be left-handed than females. In other words, they note in the paper, if exactly 10 percent of a population's women were left-handed, then around 12 percent of men would be, too.

Interestingly, they found that in places such as Japan and Mexico, with high levels of "cultural masculinity," which is associated with highly differentiated social roles for men and women, there was an even stronger correlation between males and left-handedness. This suggests a cultural dimension of handedness, the authors point out.

So what else might account for the sex difference? One answer might be basic morphology. Some studies, the researchers note, have found that left-handed and ambidextrous people have larger corpus callosums—brain regions that connect the two hemispheres—than right-handed people, which might be linked to differences in brain development between men and women.

Another possibility Papadatou-Pastou and Martin suggest is testosterone. One theory holds that testosterone accelerates right hemisphere growth in the brain, which could lead to more cases of right hemisphere dominance and, consequently, more left-handedness, although this idea is debated.

There may also be a genetic component. No one has discovered a smoking gene or genes for left-handedness, but if it turns out to be linked to the X chromosome and recessive, like red-green colorblindness, it would make sense for more males to be left-handed.

It's even possible that all of these factors play some role in males' penchant for left-handedness, say Papadatou-Pastou and Martin.

—M. Price

Research suggests that there might be a big advantage to a less constrained brain: It might lead to less constrained thinking.

For years, anecdotal evidence has suggested that lefties might think more creatively than right-handers, and recent research supports this link. A 2007 paper in *Journal of Mental and Nervous Disease* (Vol. 195, No. 10) found that musicians, painters and writers were significantly more likely to be left-handed than control participants.

Corballis has a theory as to why: Just as information is prone to errors as it traverses between brain hemispheres, it's also more likely to encounter novel solutions. Righties might dismiss an idea as too radical, but nonrighties might be willing to entertain the thought nonetheless, and develop a solution that a right-hander's brain would skip right over.

"It's good to have a few people in any society who think outside the square," Corballis says.

Left-handers are taking that creativity straight to the bank, too, says Christopher Ruebeck, PhD, an economist at Lafayette College in Easton, PA. In a study published in *Laterality*, he found that lefties earn slightly more money than their right-handed peers who work at the same jobs. These results were most pronounced in left-handed college-educated men, Ruebeck says, who, on average, earn 15 percent more than righties. In fields where creative thinking is valuable, lefties might get the edge and earn more accordingly.

"Left-handed men seem to get a higher return on their education," he says.

The study found this effect in men but not in women, Ruebeck adds, though he's unsure why that might be. And because his study is one of only a few that have looked into this area so far, he cautions against overgeneralizing these results; at the moment, it remains an interesting correlation.

Also, equating left-handedness with creativity glosses over the fact that 20 percent of left-handed people do have strongly lateralized brains and are probably no more creative than right-handers. The idea of lefties as creative types "probably refers to the subgroup of [left-handers] who lack clear dominance in the hemispheres," Corballis says.

So what's the final verdict? Well, in a way, the human condition itself might be summed up as the balance between the brain's asymmetries and symmetries—rationality versus creativity, novel ideas versus traditional solutions.

"The asymmetrical brain might even represent science and the symmetrical brain, religion," Corballis speculates. "An exaggeration, no doubt, but it's fun to think along these lines."

# Ambidexterous Payback

"That poses an evolutionary question," Corballis says. "If this [right-handed] gene is so advantageous, why are there still left-handers?"

# Critical Thinking

1. What is brain lateralization?
2. How important is brain lateralization in influencing common human traits?

# The Brain's (Dark Energy)

Brain regions active when our minds wander may hold a key to understanding neurological disorders and even consciousness itself.

MARCUS E. RAICHLE

Imagine you are almost dozing in a lounge chair outside, with a magazine on your lap. Suddenly, a fly lands on your arm. You grab the magazine and swat at the insect. What was going on in your brain after the fly landed? And what was going on just before? Many neuroscientists have long assumed that much of the neural activity inside your head when at rest matches your subdued, somnolent mood. In this view, the activity in the resting brain represents nothing more than random noise, akin to the snowy pattern on the television screen when a station is not broadcasting. Then, when the fly alights on your forearm, the brain focuses on the conscious task of squashing the bug. But recent analysis produced by neuroimaging technologies has revealed something quite remarkable: a great deal of meaningful activity is occurring in the brain when a person is sitting back and doing nothing at all.

It turns out that when your mind is at rest—when you are daydreaming quietly in a chair, say, asleep in a bed or anesthetized for surgery—dispersed brain areas are chattering away to one another. And the energy consumed by this ever active messaging, known as the brain's default mode, is about 20 times that used by the brain when it responds consciously to a pesky fly or another outside stimulus. Indeed, most things we do consciously, be it sitting down to eat dinner or making a speech, mark a departure from the baseline activity of the brain default mode.

Key to an understanding of the brain's default mode has been the discovery of a heretofore unrecognized brain system

that has been dubbed the brain's default mode network (DMN). The exact role of the DMN in organizing neural activity is still under study, but it may orchestrate the way the brain organizes memories and various systems that need preparation for future events: the brain's motor system has to be revved and ready when you feel the tickle of a fly on your arm. The DMN may play a critical role in synchronizing all parts of the brain so that, like racers in a track competition, they are all in the proper "set" mode when the starting gun goes off. If the DMN does prepare the brain for conscious activity, investigations of its behavior may provide clues to the nature of conscious experience. Neuroscientists have reason to suspect, moreover, that disruptions to the DMN may underlie simple mental errors as well as a range of complex brain disorders, from Alzheimer's disease to depression.

## Probing Dark Energy

The idea that the brain could be constantly busy is not new. An early proponent of that notion was Hans Berger, inventor of the familiar electroencephalogram, which records electrical activity in the brain with a set of wavy lines on a graph. In seminal papers on his findings, published in 1929, Berger deduced from the ceaseless electrical oscillations detected by the device that "we have to assume that the central nervous system is always, and not only during wakefulness, in a state of considerable activity."

But his ideas about how the brain functions were largely ignored, even after noninvasive imaging methods became a fixture in neuroscience laboratories. First, in the late 1970s, came positron-emission tomography (PET), which measures glucose metabolism, blood flow and oxygen uptake as a proxy for the extent of neuronal activity, followed in 1992 by functional magnetic resonance imaging (fMRI), which gauges brain oxygenation for the same purpose. These technologies are more than capable of assaying brain activity, whether focused or not, but the design of most studies inadvertently led to the impression that most brain areas stay pretty quiet until called on to carry out some specific task.

Typically neuroscientists who run imaging experiments are trying to pinpoint the brain regions that give rise to a given

## Key Concepts

- Neuroscientists have long thought that the brain's circuits are turned off when a person is at rest.
- Imaging experiments, however, have shown that there is a persistent level of background activity.
- This default mode, as it is called, may be critical in planning future actions.
- Miswiring of brain regions involved in the default mode may lead to disorders ranging from Alzheimer's to schizophrenia.

perception or behavior. The best study designs for defining such regions simply compare brain activity during two related conditions. If researchers wanted to see which brain areas are important during reading words aloud (the "test" condition) as opposed to viewing the same words silently (the "control" condition), for instance, they would look for differences in images of those two conditions. And to see those differences clearly, they would essentially subtract the pixels in the passive-reading images from those in the vocal image; activity of neurons in the areas that remain "lit up" would be assumed to be the ones necessary for reading aloud. Any of what is called intrinsic activity, the constant background activity, would be left on the cutting-room floor. Representing data in this way makes it easy to envision areas of the brain being "turned on," during a given behavior, as if they were inactive until needed by a particular task.

Over the years, however, our group, and others, became curious about what was happening when someone was simply resting and just letting the mind wander. This interest arose from a set of hints from various studies that suggested the extent of this behind-the-scenes activity.

One clue came from mere visual inspections of the images. The pictures showed that areas in many regions of the brain were quite busy in both the test and the control conditions. In part because of this shared background "noise," differentiating a task from the control state by looking at the separate raw images is difficult if not impossible and can be achieved only by applying sophisticated computerized image analysis.

Further analyses indicated that performing a particular task increases the brain's energy consumption by less than 5 percent of the underlying baseline activity. A large fraction of the overall activity—from 60 to 80 percent of all energy used by the brain—occurs in circuits unrelated to any external event. With a nod to our astronomer colleagues, our group came to call this intrinsic

activity the brain's dark energy, a reference to the unseen energy that also represents the mass of most of the universe.

The question of the existence of neural dark energy also arose when observing just how little information from the senses actually reaches the brain's internal processing areas. Visual information, for instance, degrades significantly as it passes from the eye to the visual cortex.

Of the virtually unlimited information available in the world around us, the equivalent of 10 billion bits per second arrives on the retina at the back of the eye. Because the optic nerve attached to the retina has only a million output connections, just six million bits per second can leave the retina, and only 10,000 bits per second make it to the visual cortex.

After further processing, visual information feeds into the brain regions responsible for forming our conscious perception. Surprisingly, the amount of information constituting that conscious perception is less than 100 bits per second. Such a thin stream of data probably could not produce a perception if that were all the brain took into account; the intrinsic activity must play a role.

Yet another indication of the brain's intrinsic processing power comes from counting the number of synapses, the contact points between neurons. In the visual cortex, the number of synapses devoted to incoming visual information is less than 10 percent of those present. Thus, the vast majority must represent internal connections among neurons in that brain region.

## Discovering the Default Mode

These hints of the brain's inner life were well established. But some understanding was needed of the physiology of the brain's intrinsic activity—and how it might influence perception and behavior. Happily, a chance and puzzling observation made during PET studies, later corroborated with fMRI, set us on a path to discovering the DMN.

In the mid-1990s we noticed quite by accident that, surprisingly, certain brain regions experienced a *decreased* level of activity from the baseline resting state when subjects carried out some task. These areas—in particular, a section of the medial parietal cortex (a region near the middle of the brain involved with remembering personal events in one's life, among other things)—registered this drop when other areas were engaged in

## Brains at Rest

Noninvasive methods, such as positron-emission tomography and functional magnetic resonance imaging, did not initially capture signs of background activity in the brain when a subject was doing nothing and so provided an inaccurate picture of neural activity.

### Old View

Brain scans originally seemed to suggest that most neurons were quiet until needed for some activity, such as reading, at which point the brain fired up and expended energy on the signaling needed for the task.

### New View

In recent years additional neuroimaging experiments have shown that the brain maintains a high level of activity even when nominally "at rest." In fact, reading or other routine tasks require minimal additional energy, no more than a 5 percent increment, over what is already being consumed when in this highly active baseline state.

## A Clue to the New View

Researchers have known for some time that only a trickle of information from the virtually infinite flood in the surrounding environment reaches the brain's processing centers. Although six million bits are transmitted through the optic nerve, for instance, only 10,000 bits make it to the brain's visual-processing area, and only a few hundred are involved in formulating a conscious perception—too little to generate a meaningful perception on their own. The finding suggested that the brain probably makes constant predictions about the outside environment in anticipation of paltry sensory inputs reaching it from the outside world.

carrying out a defined task such as reading aloud. Befuddled, we labeled the area showing the most depression MMPA, for "medial mystery parietal area."

A series of PET experiments then confirmed that the brain is far from idling when not engaged in a conscious activity. In fact, the MMPA as well as most other areas remains constantly active until the brain focuses on some novel task, at which time some areas of intrinsic activity decrease. At first, our studies met with some skepticism. In 1998 we even had a paper on such findings rejected because one referee suggested that the reported decrease in activity was an error in our data. The circuits, the reviewer asserted, were actually being switched on at rest and switched off during the task. Other researchers, however, reproduced our results for both the medial parietal cortex—and the medial prefrontal cortex (involved with imagining what other people are thinking as well as aspects of our emotional state). Both areas are now considered major hubs of the DMN.

The discovery of the DMN provided us with a new way of considering the brain's intrinsic activity. Until these publications, neurophysiologists had never thought of these regions as a system in the way we think of the visual or motor system—as a set of discrete areas that communicate with one another to get a job done. The idea that the brain might exhibit such internal activity across multiple regions while at rest had escaped the neuroimaging establishment. Did the DMN alone exhibit this property, or did it exist more generally throughout the brain? A surprising finding in the way we understand and analyze fMRI provided the opening we needed to answer such questions.

The fMRI signal is usually referred to as the blood oxygen level-dependent, or BOLD, signal because the imaging method relies on changes in the level of oxygen in the human brain induced by alterations in blood flow. The BOLD signal from any area of the brain, when observed in a state of quiet repose, fluctuates slowly with cycles occurring roughly every 10 seconds. Fluctuations this slow were considered to be mere noise, and so the data detected by the scanner were simply eliminated to better resolve the brain activity for the particular task being imaged.

The wisdom of discarding the low-frequency signals came into question in 1995, when Bharat Biswal and his colleagues at the Medical College of Wisconsin observed that even while a subject remained motionless, the "noise" in the area of the brain that controls right-hand movement fluctuated in unison with similar activity in the area on the opposite side of the brain associated with left-hand movement. In the early 2000s Michael Greicius and his co-workers at Stanford University found the same synchronized fluctuations in the DMN in a resting subject.

Because of the rapidly accelerating interest in the DMN's role in brain function, the finding by the Greicius group stimulated a flurry of activity in laboratories worldwide, including ours, in which *all* of the noise, the intrinsic activity of the major brain systems, was mapped. These remarkable patterns of activity appeared even under general anesthesia and during light sleep, a suggestion that they were a fundamental facet of brain functioning and not merely noise.

It became clear from this work that the DMN is responsible for only a part, albeit a critical part, of the overall intrinsic activity—and the notion of a default mode of brain function extends to all brain systems. In our lab, discovery of a generalized default mode

came from first examining research on brain electrical activity known as slow cortical potentials (SCPs), in which groups of neurons fire every 10 seconds or so. Our research determined that the spontaneous fluctuations observed in the BOLD images were identical to SCPs: the same activity detected with different sensing methods.

We then went on to examine the purpose of SCPs as they relate to other neural electrical signals. As Berger first showed and countless others have since confirmed, brain signaling consists of a broad spectrum of frequencies, ranging from the low-frequency SCPs through activity in excess of 100 cycles per second. One of the great challenges in neuroscience is to understand how the different frequency signals interact.

It turns out that SCPs have an influential role. Both our own work and that of others demonstrate that electrical activity at frequencies above that of the SCPs synchronizes with the oscillations, or phases, of the SCPs. As observed recently by Matias Palva and his colleagues at the University of Helsinki, the rising phase of an SCP produces an increase in the activity of signals at other frequencies.

The symphony orchestra provides an apt metaphor, with its integrated tapestry of sound arising from multiple instruments playing to the same rhythm. The SCPs are the equivalent of the conductor's baton. Instead of keeping time for a collection of musical instruments, these signals coordinate access that each brain system requires to the vast storehouse of memories and other information needed for survival in a complex, ever changing world. The SCPs ensure that the right computations occur in a coordinated fashion at exactly the correct moment.

But the brain is more complex than a symphony orchestra. Each specialized brain system—one that controls visual activity, another that actuates muscles—exhibits its own pattern of SCPs. Chaos is averted because all systems are not created equal. Electrical signaling from some brain areas takes precedence over others. At the top of this hierarchy resides the DMN, which acts as an über-conductor to ensure that the cacophony

---

# A Brain Controller
# The Default Mode Network

A collaborating group of brain regions known as the default mode network (DMN) appears to account for much of the activity that occurs when the mind is unfocused and to have a key role in mental functioning.

## Command Station

The DMN consists of several widely separated brain areas.

## Orchestrator of the Self

The DMN is thought to behave something like an orchestra conductor, issuing timing signals, much as a conductor waves a baton, to coordinate activity among different brain regions. This cuing—among the visual auditory parts of the cortex, for instance—probably ensures that all regions of the brain are ready to react in concert to stimuli.

of competing signals from one system do not interfere with those from another. This organizational structure is not surprising, because the brain is not a free-for-all among independent systems but a federation of interdependent components.

At the same time, this intricate internal activity must sometimes give way to the demands of the outside world. To make this accommodation, SCPs in the DMN diminish when vigilance is required because of novel or unexpected sensory inputs: you suddenly realize that you promised to pick up a carton of milk on the drive home from work. The internal SCP messaging revives once the need for focused attention dwindles. The brain continuously wrestles with the need to balance planned responses and the immediate needs of the moment.

## Consciousness and Disease

The ups and downs of the DMN may provide insight into some of the brain's deepest mysteries. It has already furnished scientists with fascinating insights into the nature of attention, a fundamental component of conscious activity. In 2008 a multinational team of researchers reported that by watching the DMN, they could tell up to 30 seconds before a subject in a scanner was about to commit an error in a computer test. A mistake would occur if, at that time, the default network took over and activity in areas involved with focused concentration abated.

And in years to come, the brain's dark energy may provide clues to the nature of consciousness. As most neuroscientists acknowledge, our conscious interactions with the world are just a small part of the brain's activity. What goes on below the level of awareness—the brain's dark energy, for one—is critical in providing the context for what we experience in the small window of conscious awareness.

Beyond offering a glimpse of the behind-the-scenes events that underlie everyday experience, study of the brain's dark energy may provide new leads for understanding major neurological maladies. Mental gymnastics or intricate movements will not be required to complete the exercise. A subject need only remain still within the scanner while the DMN and other hubs of dark energy whir silently through their paces.

Already this type of research has shed new light on disease. Brain-imaging studies have found altered connections among brains cells in the DMN regions of patients with Alzheimer's, depression, autism and even schizophrenia. Alzheimer's, in fact, may one day be characterized as a disease of the DMN. A projection of the brain regions affected by Alzheimer's fits neatly over a map of the areas that make up the DMN. Such patterns may not only serve as biological markers for diagnosis but may also provide deeper insights into causes of the disease and treatment strategies.

Looking ahead, investigators must now try to glean how coordinated activity among and within brain systems operates at the level of the individual cells and how the DMN causes chemical and electrical signals to be transmitted through brain circuits. New theories will then be needed to integrate data on

## Miswired Circuits
## Disease and the Network

The default mode network overlaps areas involved with major brain disorders, suggesting that damage to the network may be involved. Discerning precisely which aspects of the network are affected by Alzheimer's, depression and other disorders may lead to new diagnostics and treatments.

### Alzheimer's

Brain areas that atrophy in Alzheimer's overlap very closely with major centers of the DMN.

### Depression

Patients exhibit decreased connections between one area of the DMN and regions involved with emotion.

### Schizophrenia

Many regions of the DMN demonstrate increased levels of signaling. The importance of this finding is still being investigated.

cells, circuits and entire neural systems to produce a broader picture of how the brain's default mode of function serves as a master organizer of its dark energy. Over time neural dark energy may ultimately be revealed as the very essence of what makes us tick.

## Critical Thinking

1. What is the brain's default mode network and why is it important?

2. What role does the brain's default mode network play in everyday life?

**MARCUS E. RAICHLE** is professor of radiology and neurology at the Washington University School of Medicine in St. Louis. For many years Raichle has led a team that investigates human brain function using positron-emission tomography and functional magnetic resonance imaging. He was elected to the Institute of Medicine in 1992 and to the National Academy of Sciences in 1996.

## More to Explore

**Spontaneous Fluctuations in Brain Activity Observed with Functional Magnetic Resonance Imaging.** Michael D. Fox and Marcus E. Raichle in *Nature Reviews Neuroscience,* Vol. 8, pages 700–711; September 2007.

**Disease and the Brain's Dark Energy.** Dongyang Zhang and Marcus E. Raichle in *Nature Reviews Neurology,* Vol. 6, pages 15–18; January 2010.

**Two Views of Brain Function.** Marcus E. Raichle in *Trends in Cognitive Science* (in press).

# Phantom Pain and the Brain

**An actual touch, or an imaginary one? It's all the same to (some parts of) your brain.**

SADIE F. DINGFELDER

Scientists have long conceptualized the part of the brain known as the primary somatosensory cortex (S1) as where it first registers touch sensations. Prick your finger and S1 springs into action, sending raw information about the injury's location to higher brain areas for further interpretation, according to most neuroscience textbooks.

Those textbooks may need new editions. S1 doesn't simply catalogue physical sensations: It also registers sensory illusions that are generated elsewhere in the brain, according to a recent study in *PLOS Biology* (Vol. 4, No. 3, pages 459–466). In fact, as far as S1 is concerned, there's no difference between a real or imaginary touch, says lead author Felix Blankenburg, PhD, a neuroscience researcher at University College London (UCL). Other researchers, including David Ress, PhD, a neuroscience professor at Brown University, are finding similar results in S1's cousin, the primary visual cortex.

Together, the research paints a picture of a deeply integrated brain, one that begins making sense of information at the earliest stages of perception, says Ress.

"You use a lot of your brain to make a visual decision," he says. "The whole system is probably used as an integrated whole in order to create visual consciousness."

## Tactile Illusions

Tap people's arms rapidly at the wrist and then at the elbow, and they will feel a phantom tap right in the middle, as if a rabbit were hopping the arm's length. Blankenburg and his colleagues, including Jon Driver, PhD, director of the Cognitive Neuroscience Institute at UCL, harnessed this phenomenon, known as the cutaneous rabbit illusion, to see how tactile illusions play out in the brain.

The researchers strapped electrodes to the arm of 10 adult participants, placing the electrodes at three points between each participant's elbow and wrist. While the participants lay in a functional magnetic resonance imaging (fMRI) machine, the researchers delivered pulses to the electrodes. In one condition, participants experienced real sensations hopping up their arms, as experimenters activated the three electrodes in succession. In another condition, participants only thought they felt the sensation

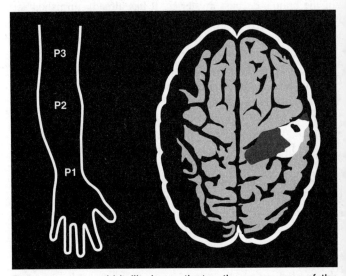

The cutaneous rabbit illusion activates the same area of the brain that would respond if that body site (P2) had actually been touched.

hopping up their arms, as researchers delivered pulses first to the electrode near their wrist and then to one by their elbow.

Participants reported feeling the illusory touch and the real one equally strongly, and their brains agreed—the S1 area registered both sensations at the same location in the brain and with a similar amount of neural activity.

"This is quite remarkable because traditionally we thought S1 formed a map of the body that faithfully represents the actual touch on the skin, but our results suggest this is not always the case," says study author Christian Ruff, PhD, a psychology and neuroscience researcher at UCL. Instead, S1 seems to be representing what we feel—not what is actually there, he adds.

Where is S1 getting its false information? One possibility is that higher areas of the somatosensory cortex, the ones that would integrate information about the time and location of a tap on the skin, also register raw sensory information and then force their interpretation on S1, says Ress, who also studies perception.

In fact, while S1 showed no differences in activation during real and imagined touch, the right premotor cortex showed increased activation during the illusory touch, and that area may be at least part of the illusion's source, Ruff observes.

"It could be that signals from higher-level brain structures can influence the primary sensory cortex via neural feedback connections," Ruff notes.

## Visual Mistakes

Researchers who study an entirely different sense—vision—are coming to similar conclusions. Scientists traditionally claim that the primary visual cortex, or V1, registers sensory information and then kicks it to higher-level areas for processing. A study published in a 2003 issue of *Nature Neuroscience* (Vol. 6, No. 4, pages 414–420) suggests otherwise.

The study's four adult participants lay in an fMRI machine while watching a screen that showed a faint vertical grating on a similarly patterned background, or just the background alone. Participants had one second to view the screen and then one second to press a button indicating whether they had seen the vertical grating—a process repeated several hundred times for each participant.

Analysis of their brain activity showed high levels of activity in V1 both when the participants saw the grating and when they just thought they saw it. What's more, the V1 area was similarly quiet when participants did not see the grating as when they just missed it.

**This line of research could eventually help amputees who suffer from phantom limb pain. If phantom pain comes from the lowest level of the sensory system, effective drugs or therapy could target that area.**

These results, like those of the Blankenburg study, help explain why false perceptions sometimes feel quite real, says Ress.

"If you think you perceive a sensation, then the lower-level primary sensory area that is associated with that false perception actually becomes involved," he notes.

However, he cautions that fMRI data doesn't always match up with the electrical activity of the brain.

"It's a very indirect measure of neural activity, and we are still not exactly sure what it means," he notes.

That said, this line of research could eventually help amputees who suffer from phantom limb pain, Blankenburg says. If phantom pain comes from the lowest level of the sensory system, effective drugs or therapy could target that area.

In the distant future, research on the translation of sensation to perception may lead to machines that transmit visual signals directly into the brains of blind people, allowing them to see. But if higher level areas of the brain feed information to the lower areas, as is suggested by this line of research, such applications wouldn't just be able to transmit raw data straight into people's primary cortices, Ress posits.

"The design of something that emulates cortical processing becomes more complicated when the brain is a recursive network," he says.

## Critical Thinking

1. What is phantom pain?

2. What role does the brain play in experiencing this phenomenon?

# Reflections on Mirror Neurons

TEMMA EHRENFELD

In 1992, a team at the University of Parma, Italy discovered what have been termed "mirror neurons" in macaque monkeys: cells that fire both when the monkey took an action (like holding a banana) and saw it performed (when a man held a banana). Giacomo Rizzolati, the celebrated discoverer, will deliver the Keynote Address at the APS Convention in Washington DC, USA, on May 26, 2011, and report on his latest findings. To tide us over until then, here's a report on the state of mirror neuron science.

Like monkeys, humans have mirror neurons that fire when we both perceive and take an action. Locating the tiny cells means attaching electrodes deep inside the brain. As this has hardly been practical in humans, studies have had to rely on imaging, which shows which areas of the brain "light up" in different circumstances. By last year, a meta-analysis of 139 imaging studies confirmed mirroring activity in parts of the human brain where, in monkeys, mirror neurons are known to reside. Because the lit-up areas contain millions of neurons, for humans most researchers speak of a "mirror system," rather than mirror cells. Last year, single mirror neurons were recorded in humans for the first time, using in-depth electrodes, in 21 epileptic patients.

The cells showed up unexpectedly in an area known for memory, the medial temporal lobe, as well as in areas where they were expected. The discovery suggests that memory is embedded in our mirror system, says Marco Iacoboni (University of California, Los Angeles), a leading authority in the field and a co-author of the epilepsy study. Perhaps, he says, we form memory "traces" whenever we see or observe an action. "It's a lovely idea," says Rizzolati, though he adds that it's too early to say.

The mirroring system includes a mechanism that helps the brain record the difference between seeing and acting. In the epilepsy study, some neurons fired more during action and others fired more during observation. These same cells, Iacoboni proposes, help us distinguish between the self and others.

That's an important issue, to say the least. We often confuse our own actions with those of other people. In a study published recently in *Psychological Science,* Gerald Echterhoff, University of Muenster, Germany, and his co-authors reported that people who had watched a video of someone else doing a simple action—shaking a bottle or shuffling a deck of cards—often mistakenly recalled two weeks later that they had done so themselves. The mistake occurred even when participants were warned that they could mix up other people's actions with their own. Echterhoff and a co-author, Isabel Lindner, of the University of Cologne, Germany, plan to conduct imaging studies to test if the phenomenon is related to mirroring.

Mirror neurons are present in infant monkeys. Three years ago, the first abstract appeared reporting that surface electrodes had recorded mirroring in monkeys one- to seven-days old as they watched humans stick out their tongues and smack their lips. Says Pier Francesco Ferrari, of the University of Parma, and co-author of an upcoming study,

"This is the first evidence that infants have a mirror mechanism at birth that responds to facial gestures. Without any experience of stimulation, they are able to focus their attention on the most relevant stimuli and respond." Sometimes the days-old monkeys even stuck out their tongues when they saw the human tongue, Ferrari says.

In monkeys, mirror neurons are present in the insula, an emotion center. Despite all the claims linking mirror neurons to empathy, Rizzolatti says he is only now reporting the discovery of a few mirror neurons in the insula in monkeys, "a reservoir for disgust and pain. Many other factors control how we react," he says, "but mirror neurons are how we recognize an emotion in others neurally."

Mimicry, linked to mirror neurons, makes monkeys bond. The idea that mimicry helps humans bond is well-accepted, but the first controlled experiment, with a monkey, came last year, Ferrari says. In that study, reported in *Science,* his team presented monkeys with a token and rewarded them with treats if they returned it. The monkeys had a choice of returning the token to either of two investigators, only one of whom was imitating the monkey. The monkeys consistently chose to return the token to the person who imitated them and spent more time near that investigator.

Mimicry in humans reflects social cues. The idea that we're primed in one part of our brain to like those who mimic us doesn't rule out other discriminations. Unconscious mimicry is deeply social and, as such, reflects prejudice, says Rick van Baaren of Radboud University in the Netherlands. In a 2009 overview of the science of mimicry published in the *Philosophical Transactions of The Royal Society,* he points out that people are more likely to mimic a member of the same ethnic group, less likely to mimic a stigmatized person who is obese or has a scar, and less likely to mimic members of a group we view with prejudice. In fact, humans tend to react badly when mimicked by someone from an "out group."

The mirror systems of two people can move in tandem. Many researchers had proposed that the brains of two people "resonate" with each other as they interact, with one person's mirror system reflecting changes in the other. Last spring, *the Proceedings of the National Academy of Sciences* reported on the brain activity of people playing the game of charades. The observer and gesturer performing the charade did move neurologically in tandem, says co-author Christian Keysers, of the University Medical Center in Groningen, The Netherlands. Keysers says the discovery backs up the idea that mirroring plays a key role in the evolution of language. We're exquisitely responsive to gestures, he says; "Nobody had ever shown that during gestural communication the observer's mirror system tracks the moment to moment state of the gesturer's motor system."

Mirror neurons respond to sound. In monkeys, mirror neurons fire a sounds associated with an action, such as breaking a peanut or tearing paper. Mirroring has been discovered in birds hearing bird song, and in humans. Recent work, led by Emiliano Ricciardi at the University of Pisa, Italy, found that blind people, using their hearing, interpret the actions of others by recruiting the same human mirror system brain areas as sighted people.

Mirror neurons code intentions. Whether mirror neurons register the goal of an action or other higher-level systems must chip in to judge other people's intentions has been the subject of much debate. The evidence is accumulating that mirror neurons "implement a fairly sophisticated and rather abstract coding of the actions of others," says Iacoboni. One clue is that while a third of all mirror neurons fire for exactly the same action, either executed or observed, the larger number—about two thirds—fire for actions that achieve the same goal or those that are logically related—for example, first grasping and then bringing an object to the mouth. And these neurons make fine distinctions: When a monkey observed an experimenter grasping an object and pantomiming the same action, the neurons fired when the experimenter grasped the object but not during the pantomime. "In academia, there is a lot of politics and we are continuously trying to figure out the 'real intentions' of other people," Iacoboni says. "The mirror system deals with relatively simple intentions: smiling at each other, or making eye contact with the other driver at an intersection."

Mirroring increases with experience. In the first studies, monkeys mirrored when they saw a person grasping food but not if the person used a tool. That made sense because monkeys don't use tools. In later research, monkeys did mirror humans using a tool; Iacoboni suggests that their brains had "learned," adjusting to seeing researchers with tools. In humans, more mirroring activity occurs when dancers see other dancers perform routines they know well. Mirroring in blind people is more active in response to more familiar action sounds.

Stimulating the mirror system helps stroke victims. If mirroring develops as we learn, perhaps triggering mirroring can teach. Two studies with stroke victims, for example, have found that stimulating the mirror system helped them recover particular motor actions, says Ferdinand Binkofski at the University of Luebeck, Germany. When stroke victims received "action observation therapy," in which they observed an action repeatedly, they regained more ability. Compared to a control group, the stroke victims also showed more mirroring in brain scans.

Children with autistic syndromes have mirroring defects. As early as 2001, researchers hypothesized that a deficit in the mirror neuron system could explain some of the problems of autistic patients. As of September, 2010 twenty published papers using brain imaging, magnetoencephalography, electroencephalography, and transcranial magnetic stimulation support this idea, and four failed to support it, according to Iacoboni.

The hope is that basic science in the mirror system could lead to a better understanding of emotional difficulties. As Ferrari points out, some infant monkeys separated from their mothers show "symptoms like those in autistic kids. You see them rocking and avoiding your gaze." Others develop normally. Ferrari and his colleagues plan to follow the infants they studied and measure whether strong mirror neuron activity in the first week of life indicates sociability later on. "We hope to create a picture of how brain activity interacts with the social environment to put some monkeys more at risk," he says. "The obvious direction is to translate this to humans."

Mirror neuron research continues to grow fast, across disciplines. Already the number of items produced by a PubMed search, for example, increased twenty-fold between 2000 and 2010, although that number only doubled for "Stroop and brain," another popular topic. The ongoing technical challenge remains: Mirror neurons are not the majority of cells in the brain areas where they are located, so it is still difficult to pinpoint their role when those areas show spiking activity. Iacoboni suggests that mathematical modeling will help make more of this data useful. Such modeling allowed Keysers, for example, to establish the existence of resonance in the charades study. So what can we expect next? Most likely, Iacoboni, says, more work with depth electrodes in neurological patients and studies like Ferrari's to test whether mirroring is a biomarker of sociality. A promising underexplored subject is the inhibitors that keep us from mimicking (but fail recovering addicts who relapse when they see others consume). Behind all this work will be a growing consensus that mirror neurons evolved in humans so we could learn from observation and communication.

# References

Ertelt, D., Small, S., Solodkin, A., Dettmers, C., McNamara, A., Binkofski, F., & Buccino, G. (2007). Action observation has a positive impact on rehabilitation of motor deficits after stroke. *Neuroimage, 36*(Suppl 2), T164–T173.

Ferrari, P.F., Vanderwert, R., Herman, K., Paukner, A., Fox, N.A., & Suomi, S.J. (2008). Society for Neuroscience Abstract, *297*, 13.

Lindner, I., Echterhoff, G., Davidson, P.S., & Brand, M. (2010). Observation inflation: Your actions become mine. *Psychological Science, 21*, 1291–1299.

Mukamel, R., Ekstrom, A.D., Kaplan, J., Iacoboni, M., & Fried, I. (2010). Single-neuron responses in humans during execution and observation of actions. *Current Biology, 20*, 750–756.

Paukner, A., Suomi, S., Visalberghi, E., & Ferrari, P.F. (2009). Capuchin monkeys display affiliation toward humans who imitate them. *Science, 325*, 880.

Ricciardi, E., Bonino, D., Sani, L., Vecchi, T., Guazzelli, M., Haxby, J.V., Fadiga, L., Pietrini, P. (2009). Do we really need vision? How blind people "see" the actions of others. *Journal of Neuroscience, 29*, 9719-9724.

Schippers, M.B., Roebroeck, A., Renken, R., Nanetti, L., & Keysers, C. (2010). Mapping the information flow from one brain to another during gestural communication. *Proceedings of the National Academy of Sciences, USA, 107*, 9388–9393.

van Baaren, R., Janssen, L., Chartrand, T.L., & Dijksterhuis, A. (2009). Where is the love? The social aspects of mimicry. *Philosophical Transactions of the Royal Society of London, B: Biological Sciences, 364*(1528), 2381–2389.

# Critical Thinking

1. What are mirror neurons and what role do they play in learning?

2. Generally speaking, what significance does understanding neural function hold for psychology?

# UNIT 3
# Perceptual Processes

## Unit Selections

## Learning Outcomes

*After reading this Unit, you should be able to:*

- Define blindsight and describe its basic features.

- Explain how researchers study blindsight.

- Describe the power of language to influence our perception of the world.

- Summarize the factors underlying the importance of the study of sleeping and dream to the study of psychology.

- Evaluate the role of sleeping and dreaming on our waking lives.

- Explain why researchers believe that action-based video games may be useful in studying the tradeoff between reaction time and accuracy in responding.

## Student Website
www.mhhe.com/cls

## Internet References

**Five Senses Home Page**
www.sedl.org/scimath/pasopartners/senses/welcome.html
**Visual and Optical Illusions**
dragon.uml.edu/psych/illusion.html

**M**arina and her roommate Claire have been friends since their first year of college. Because they share so much in common, they decided to become roommates in their sophomore year. They both want to travel abroad one day. They both enjoy the same restaurants and share the same preference for red wine. Both date men from the same college, both are education majors, and both want to work with young children after graduation. Today they are at the local art museum. As they walk around the galleries, Marina is astonished at Claire's taste in art. Whatever Claire likes, Marina finds hideous. The paintings and sculptures that Marina admires are the very ones to which her roommate turns up her nose. "How can our tastes in art be so different when we share so much in common?" Marina wonders. What Marina and Claire experience is a difference in perception—the interpretation of the sensory stimulation provided by the artwork. Perception and its sister area of psychology, sensation, are the focus of this unit.

As you will learn in your study of psychology, the study of sensation and perception date back to psychology's earliest beginnings. Understanding how physical energy is translated to a language understood by the nervous system and interpreted by the brain have long fascinated psychologists. Although the laboratory study of sensation and perception is well over 100 years old, psychologists are still seeking to further their understanding of these phenomena.

For many years, it was popular for psychologists to consider sensation and perception as two distinct processes. Sensation was defined in passive terms as the simple event of some stimulus energy (e.g., a sound wave) impinging on a specific sensory organ (e.g., the ear) that then reflexively transmitted the appropriate information to the central nervous system and brain. Perception, on the other hand, was defined as integrative and interpretive processes that the higher centers of the brain supposedly accomplish based on sensory information and available memories of similar events.

© Ingram Publishing

The dichotomy of sensation and perception is no longer widely accepted by today's psychologists. The revolution came in the mid-1960s, when a psychologist published a then-radical treatise in which he reasoned that perceptual processes included all sensory events that he believed were directed by an actively searching central nervous system. This viewpoint provided that certain perceptual patterns, such as recognition of a piece of artwork, may be species-specific. Thus, all humans, independent of learning history, should share some of the same perceptual repertoires. This unit on perceptual processes is designed to expand your understanding of these incredibly interesting processes. It also invites you to consider the origin of your own perceptions of the world and how you acquired them.

As you will find, understanding one's perception is a complex process that made even more difficult by the fact that perception is fluid, continual, and often takes place below everyday consciousness.

# Uncanny Sight in the Blind

Some people who are blind because of brain damage have "blindsight": an extraordinary ability to react to emotions on faces and even navigate around obstacles without knowing they can see anything.

BEATRICE DE GELDER

T he video my colleagues and I shot is amazing. A blind man is making his way down a long corridor strewn with boxes, chairs and other office paraphernalia. The man, known to the medical world as TN, has no idea the obstacles are there. And yet he avoids them all, here sidling carefully between a wastepaper basket and the wall, then going around a camera tripod, all without knowing he has made any special maneuvers. TN may be blind, but he has "blindsight"—the remarkable ability to respond to what his eyes can detect without knowing he can see anything at all. [To see the film of the experiment, go to www.ScientificAmerican.com/may2010/blindsight.]

TN's blindness is of an extremely rare type, caused by two strokes he suffered in 2003. The strokes injured an area at the back of his brain called the primary visual cortex, first on his left hemisphere and five weeks later on the right. His eyes remained perfectly healthy, but with his visual cortex no longer receiving the incoming signals he became completely blind.

This study of TN navigating along the hallway is probably the most dramatic demonstration of blindsight ever reported. Other patients who have lost vision because of damage to the primary visual cortex have exhibited less spectacular but equally mysterious cases of the phenomenon—responding to things they cannot consciously see, ranging from simple geometric shapes to the complex image of a person's face expressing an emotion. Scientists have also induced a similar effect in healthy people, by temporarily "switching off" their visual cortex or by outfoxing it in other ways.

## What Is Blindsight?

Conscious vision in humans depends on a region of the brain called the primary visual cortex. Damage there causes blindness in corresponding areas of the visual field. "Blindsight" occurs when patients respond in some way to an item displayed in their blind area, where they cannot consciously see it. In a dramatic demonstration of the phenomenon, a patient called "TN" navigated an obstacle course despite his total blindness.

### Visual Pathways

Signals from the retina go to the primary visual cortex via the lateral geniculate nucleus in the midbrain and ultimately to higher areas for conscious processing. Nerves also send visual information to areas such as the pulvinar nucleus and superior colliculus in the midbrain. Those areas do not seem to produce any conscious vision, but some must underlie blindsight.

Today research into blindsight seeks to understand the range of perceptual abilities that may be retained by the cortically blind and to determine which brain regions and neuronal pathways are responsible. The knowledge being gained says something about us all, because even if we never suffer a catastrophic injury resembling TN's, the same unconscious brain functions manifest in him as the astonishing ability to see without knowing are surely a constant, invisible part of our own daily existence.

## A Controversial History

As long ago as 1917, doctors reported cases like blindsight—then called residual vision—in soldiers injured in World War I. Half a century would pass, however, before more organized and objective research into the capacity began. First, Lawrence Weiskrantz and his student Nicholas K. Humphrey, both then at the University of Cambridge, studied surgically altered monkeys in 1967. Then, in 1973, Ernst Pöppel, Richard Held and Douglas Frost of the Massachusetts Institute of Technology measured the eye movements of

## Key Concepts

- Some people who are blind because of brain damage exhibit "blindsight"—responses to objects and images they cannot consciously see.
- Blindsight can detect many visual features, including colors, motion, simple shapes, and the emotion expressed by a person's face or posture.
- Researchers are mapping the ancient brain areas responsible for blindsight and exploring the limits of this remarkable ability.

a patient and found he had a slight tendency to look toward stimuli that he could not see consciously.

These discoveries spurred further systematic investigations of animals lacking the primary visual cortex (also called V1, most of them conducted by Weiskrantz and his collaborators. A number of studies established that animals retain significant visual abilities after removal of their visual cortex (for example, detecting movement and discriminating shapes).

Weiskrantz and his co-workers also began studies in 1973 with a person known as DB who had recently lost part of his visual cortex in surgery to remove a tumor. The wider research community, however, initially greeted reports of human blindsight with great skepticism.

Disbelief about blindsight is not surprising, because the phenomenon seems counterintuitive, if not outright contradictory. After all, how could people see without knowing that they see? Just as it does not make sense to say that I do not know if I am in pain, it also does not make sense, on the face of it, to suggest that somebody can see something when he insists he is blind.

Yet we do not always know that we can see. Nor do we always know that we cannot. The relation between seeing and knowing is more complicated than we commonly assume. For instance, people with normal sight have a blind spot, although we are not usually aware of this hole in our sight or handicapped by it.

Another reason for disbelief was the paucity of human evidence: subjects with cortical blindness who can be studied are rare. The primary visual cortex is only a few centimeters across in adults, and brain damage is seldom restricted to just that area, knocking out the patient's vision yet leaving other faculties intact enough for meaningful research on what the brain continues to perceive. Even so, it is now clear that many more patients with damage to the visual cortex have blindsight than scientists realized in the past, and skepticism has abated.

> **It is now clear that many more patients with damage to the visual cortex have blindsight than scientists realized in the past.**

Most of these patients still have some functioning in the primary visual cortex. Many have damage to only a small part of V1, leading to a small island of blindness in their visual field; others lose the entire left or right half of V1, leaving them blind across the corresponding half of their visual field. Blindsight in these cases involves detecting objects or images presented in the blind area, where the patient cannot see them consciously.

Traditional methods for studying vision in humans have relied on the viewers' verbal reports of what they perceive. Tested in that way, subjects will report not seeing anything in the blind part of their visual field. More indirect methods, however, can reveal that these unseen visual stimuli actually do influence how a patient responds.

In some experiments, patients show clear physiological changes, such as constriction of the pupil, as signs of unconscious seeing. And subjects can react differently to items shown in the intact visual field depending on what is presented at the same time in the blind field. When asked to guess which of several alternative items are displayed in the blind field, a patient may answer correctly almost every time.

## What Can Be Detected?

Blindsight is strongest when visual details are about the size of a quarter viewed from five to 15 feet away. It can detect an assortment of basic visual properties, including:

- Simple shapes
- Arrays of lines
- Objects appearing or disappearing
- Movement
- Color
- Orientation of lines

BLINDSIGHT can also recognize emotions being expressed by a person, but not who the person is or what the person's gender is.

Another important experimental tool is neuroimaging, which can provide direct evidence about the brain regions involved in blindsight and the pathways that the visual information travels. Brain imaging has been instrumental in dispelling lingering suspicions that some spared pieces of cortex might explain residual vision.

Collectively, these various kinds of experiments have revealed that people can unconsciously detect a wide range of visual attributes, including color, simple shapes such as X and 0, simple motion, and the orientation of lines or gratings. Large shapes, as well as very fine detail, seem hard to detect. For instance, patients detect features of a grating most effectively if its lines are comparable to Venetian blinds viewed from about 1.5 to 4.5 meters (five to 15 feet).

We were inspired to try the navigation experiment with TN by research Weiskrantz and Humphrey did in the 1970s: a monkey with no primary visual cortex freely moved around a room cluttered with objects without bumping into any of them. Nevertheless, we were amazed when TN made his way along the hallway with no collisions at all. Personalized psychophysical tests to assess his conscious vision had not found any visual functioning, including detection of big targets.

TN's ability to move down the corridor was reminiscent of sleepwalking, another phenomenon in which people exhibit a capacity to perform in some way without having any awareness of their actions. Indeed, when we questioned him afterward, he insisted he had simply walked along the hallway: he was not only unaware of seeing anything but also oblivious to how he had maneuvered around the unseen objects. He was at a loss to explain or even to describe his actions.

## Blindsight for Emotions

Moving around is one of the most fundamental tasks an animal faces, so perhaps it should not be surprising that the brain has ways to support navigation even when the primary visual cortex and conscious vision are hobbled. As a social species, humans also depend for their survival on successful communication with others. They must recognize other people, along with their gestures and signs of what they are thinking. With such thoughts in mind, my collaborators and I began to wonder in the late 1990s if people with cortical damage could detect visual displays such as the emotion on a face or the meaning of a body posture in the usually inaccessible parts of their visual field.

In 1999 we started conducting tests using movies of faces. Vision researchers generally consider faces to be visually complex—far more difficult to process than gratings and other elementary shapes—but a face is a very natural form for the human brain to handle. Our patient, GY, had lost all of his primary visual cortex on the left side in childhood, rendering him blind on the right side of his visual field. We found he could reliably guess the expression appearing on faces he did not consciously perceive, but he seemed truly blind to a variety of non-emotional facial attributes such as personal identity and gender.

To study blindsight of emotions further, in 2009 we exploited a phenomenon called emotional contagion, a tendency to match one's own facial expressions to those of others that we see. Researchers measure emotional contagion with a procedure called facial electromyography, by which electrodes on a subject's face record nerve signals going to muscles involved in smiling or frowning. We used this technique on GY and DB while showing them still images of faces and whole bodies expressing happiness or fear.

All the stimuli triggered emotional reactions as measured by electromyography, irrespective of whether the image was on the patient's sighted side or his blind side. In fact, surprisingly, the

---

# Investigating Blindsight

Because total cortical blindness like patient TN's is rare, studies of blindsight often use patients blind on one side of their visual field. The patient stares at a fixed point while images are presented on each side. The subject may be asked to "guess" what is on the blind side or to press a button on seeing items on the sighted side. Equipment may monitor brain activity and measure involuntary responses such as tiny facial movements and pupil dilation.

## Does Blindsight See Emotions?

Patients shown images on their blind side of people expressing emotions correctly guessed the emotion most of the time. Facial muscles used in smiling and frowning reacted in ways that matched the kind of emotion in the unseen image. Thus, the emotions were recognized without involving conscious sight. The effect worked with images of faceless bodies as well as faces, implying that patients were recognizing an emotion and not merely mimicking a facial expression unconsciously.

## What Brain Areas Does Blindsight Use?

Researchers showed patients gray and purple squares, knowing the superior colliculus region in the midbrain receives no signals from the retina about purple objects. Gray squares but not purple ones triggered signs of blindsight such as greater pupil contractions. These results, along with neuroimaging of the patients in action, imply that the superior colliculus plays a critical role in blindsight.

---

# Mapping Neural Pathways

Researchers are using advanced imaging techniques to attempt to trace the neural pathways that visual information travels in the brain to produce blindsight.

One such method is a kind of magnetic resonance imaging called diffusion tensor imaging, which relies on water diffusing more rapidly along neurons than across them.

Diffusion tensor imaging has mapped bundles of neurons that may be responsible for blindsight of emotions. The pathway connects the pulvinar nucleus and superior colliculus to the amygdala, which plays a key role in processing emotions.

---

unseen images produced a faster response than those seen consciously. We also monitored pupil dilations, a measure of physiological arousal. The unseen fearful images produced the strongest effect—seemingly the more we are consciously aware of an emotional signal, the slower and weaker is our reaction.

One school of thought holds that emotional contagion arises because people unconsciously mimic the expressions they see, without necessarily recognizing the emotion itself. But because our patients reacted not only to faces but also to bodies (which had blurred faces), we concluded that they were perceiving and responding to the emotion.

# Blindsight for All

Because the number of suitable patients for blindsight studies is extremely small, inducing the phenomenon temporarily in people with completely healthy brains is a valuable tool for conducting controlled experiments. One technique uses visual "masking," more popularly known as the use of subliminal images: a visual stimulus flashes before the experimental subject very briefly, followed immediately by a pattern in the same location. The pattern interferes with conscious processing of the fleeting subliminal image, leaving the subject with no conscious awareness of seeing it, but experiments can tease out objective evidence that it was seen. Other experiments temporarily disable the visual cortex by applying magnetic fields to the back of the head, a technique called transcranial magnetic stimulation.

Numerous studies have shown that healthy subjects can reliably "guess" the nature of a stimulus even when it is presented too briefly for them to perceive it consciously or when transcranial magnetic stimulation is disabling their visual cortex. Much research has also investigated how normally sighted observers react to emotional stimuli they cannot see consciously. Even before such blindsight experiments got under way, studies in animals and humans suggested that structures in the subcortex (areas of the brain that are deeper and more evolutionarily ancient than the cortex) can initiate appropriate responses before areas such as the visual cortex have analyzed the stimulus in detail. This nonconscious system seems to operate in parallel with the normal, predominantly cortical, processing routes. These subcortical areas that are activated by subliminal emotional stimuli are the leading suspects in processing emotions detected by blindsight in permanently blind patients.

Yet scientists continue to debate whether these temporary forms of blindness induced in normally sighted people are the true functional equivalent of blindsight in patients with permanent cortical damage. In particular, visual-masking techniques, such as the use of subliminal images, permit the visual cortex to process information as usual but interfere with further conscious processing. Consequently, "blindsight" of subliminal images could be a quite distinct phenomenon from blindsight in patients, involving its own characteristic assortment of brain regions. Transcranial magnetic stimulation presumably mimics cortical damage closely, but to know whether the resulting blindsight actually involves the same neuronal pathways requires experiments that combine the technique with neuroimaging.

Conversely, after an injury, a patient's brain (even an adult's) may start rewiring itself to compensate for the loss. Such neural plasticity could well create pathways for blindsight that are not present in the normally sighted people who are studied using transcranial magnetic stimulation and visual masking. Until these issues are better understood, studies of patients with injuries will remain crucial for fathoming how noncortical regions produce residual vision.

# Neural Pathways

Research has not yet fully determined the neural structures responsible for blindsight in the cortically blind, but the most likely candidate to play a central role is a brain region called the superior colliculus (SC), which sits in a part of the subcortex called the midbrain. In nonmammals such as birds and fish, the SC is the main structure receiving input from the eyes. In mammals it is overshadowed by the visual cortex but remains involved in controlling eye movements, among other visual functions. Blindsight would exploit information that travels from the retina to the SC without first going through the primary visual cortex.

Last year my colleagues and I showed that this midbrain area is essential for translating a visual signal that cannot be consciously perceived into an action. Specifically, we had a patient press a button whenever we showed him a square on his sighted side. Sometimes we simultaneously presented a square on his blind side. Sometimes we used gray squares and sometimes purple ones. We chose a purple hue that only one type of light-detecting cone cell in the retina detects, knowing that the SC receives no inputs from that type; it is blind to this purple.

A gray square on our patient's blind side accelerated his response and made his pupils constrict more—a sign of processing the stimulus—whereas a purple square had neither effect. In other words, he exhibited blindsight of gray stimuli but not purple ones. Brain scans showed that his SC was most strongly activated only by the gray stimulus on his blind side. Some other areas in the midbrain have been suspected of being involved in blindsight instead of the SC, but in our experiment their activity seemed unrelated to the occurrence of blindsight.

These findings show that the SC acts in the human brain as an interface between sensory processing (sight) and motor processing (leading to the patient's action), thereby contributing to visually guided behavior in a way that is apparently separate from the pathways involving the cortex and entirely outside conscious visual experience. Blindsight of emotions displayed by people also involves the SC as well as other areas in the midbrain, such as the amygdala.

Blindsight has captured a lot of attention from philosophers, who are intrigued by the paradoxical idea of seeing without knowing that one sees. The idea, of course, is only a paradox if "seeing" is always taken to mean "consciously seeing." That mind-set was a stumbling block to acceptance of blindsight by scientists, delaying progress in understanding the role of unconscious seeing in human cognition.

It can also be a stumbling block for patients suffering from cortex-based loss of vision, preventing them from unlocking the potential of their residual visual skills in their everyday lives. For example, TN views himself as a blind person, and he will remain totally dependent on his white cane until he is convinced he can see without knowing it. Training may also help. After three months of daily stimulation, cortically blind patients were better at detecting targets in their blind field. Whether training in realistic conditions could lead to improved navigation skills is, like so many other features of blindsight, a question for future research.

# Critical Thinking

1. What is blindsight?
2. How do researchers study this phenomenon?
3. What are the fundamental characteristics of blindsight?

---

**BEATRICE DE GELDER** is professor of cognitive neuroscience and director of the Cognitive and Affective Neuroscience Laboratory at Tilburg University in the Netherlands. She is also on the faculty of the Athinoula A. Martinos Center for Biomedical Imaging in Charlestown, Mass. De Gelder investigates the neuroscience behind processing of faces and emotions and the ways cognition and emotion interact in both healthy and damaged brains.

# More to Explore

**Unseen Facial and Bodily Expressions Trigger Fast Emotional Reactions.** Marco Tamietto et al. in *Proceedings of the National Academy of Sciences USA,* Vol. 106, No. 42, pages 17661–17666; October 20, 2009.

**Collicular Vision Guides Nonconscious Behavior.** Marco Tamietto et al. in *Journal of Cognitive Neuroscience,* Vol. 22, No. 5, pages 888–902; May 2010.

**Affective Blindsight.** Beatrice de Gelder and Marco Tamietto in *Scholarpedia,* Vol. 2, No. 10, page 3555; 2007. Available at www.scholarpedia.org/article/Affective_blindsight

**Helen, a Blind Monkey Who Sees Everything.** Video from 1971. Available at bit.ly/blindsightmonkey

# The Color of Sin

## White and Black Are Perceptual Symbols of Moral Purity and Pollution

Gary D. Sherman and Gerald L. Clore

Abstract ideas can be clarified by comparisons with aspects of the physical world. "Love is like a rose," for example, invites people to appreciate the beauty and delicacy of love, and perhaps also the pain of its thorns. But beyond such rhetorical embellishment, some metaphors are so direct and compelling that their literal and metaphorical meanings may become conflated. For example, an admired person is often said to be "looked up to." This spatial metaphor may be so powerful that assertions about "high" or "low" status automatically evoke some of the processes involved in the perception of spatial location. Such a metaphor is "perceptually grounded," meaning that its comprehension involves an element of perceptual simulation appropriate to assertions about physical space (Barsalou, 1999; Lakoff & Johnson, 1980). For example, people have been found to attribute high status or power to individuals elevated in physical space and are able to identify powerful groups more quickly when those groups are positioned higher, rather than lower, than another group in space (Schubert, 2005). By being grounded in perceptual experience of the physical world, such analogical assertions achieve the authority of actual perceptions.

Moral cognition is embodied in this way. For example, physical purity is a metaphor for moral "purity" (Rozin, Millman, & Nemeroff, 1986). This explains why an evil person's clothing may be considered physically repulsive (Rozin, Markwith, & McCauley, 1994), and why reminders of one's moral transgressions can create desires for physical cleansing (Zhong & Liljenquist, 2006). An underappreciated, and understudied, aspect of this metaphor is that ideas of dirtiness and impurity are themselves grounded in the perceptual experience of the color black, which is seen not just as the opposite of white, but also as a potent impurity that can contaminate whiteness (Adams & Osgood, 1973; Williams & Roberson, 1967). A white object, conversely, is universally understood to be something that can be stained easily and that must remain unblemished to stay pure. This is presumably at the heart of the culturally widespread practice of dressing brides in white, which by calling to mind the experience of physical purity, provides a compelling symbol for moral purity. One can see with one's own eyes that a drop of dark paint discolors white paint more readily than the reverse. By analogy, a single immoral act can counteract an otherwise exemplary reputation, whereas a single moral act cannot compensate for a life of questionable behavior.

Little is known about associations between immorality and blackness. Most of the relevant work has focused more generally on valence. That research has revealed that children tend to assume that black boxes contain negative objects and white boxes contain positive objects (Stabler & Johnson, 1972). Also, people are quicker to evaluate a negative word when it appears in black, rather than white (Meier, Robinson, & Clore, 2004), and perceive gray patches as darker after evaluating a negative word than after evaluating a positive word (Meier, Robinson, Crawford, & Ahlvers, 2007). More relevant to morality is a study in which sports players were perceived as more aggressive, and behaved more aggressively, when wearing black uniforms than when wearing nonblack uniforms (Frank & Gilovich, 1988).

Although associations between valence and blackness operate across many domains, the aforementioned research has focused on the domain-general aspects of these associations. Black has negative connotations for many reasons; it is the color of night, uncertainty, and danger. In the case of morality, however, its association with impurity is particularly noteworthy. Because of the shared connection of blackness and immorality with impurity, associations between darkness and valence in the moral domain have a metaphorical quality. Accordingly, the concept of immorality should activate "black," not because immoral things tend to *be* black, but because immorality *acts* like the color black (e.g., it contaminates).

In addition, past research has not examined how valence-blackness associations vary with contextual factors or individual differences. Making immorality salient is enough to evoke the moral-purity metaphor: In one study, people who recalled, or hand-copied a first-person account of, unethical behavior desired physical cleansing (Zhong & Liljenquist, 2006). It is during these times—when one is currently concerned with being morally "clean"—that immorality-blackness associations should be most evident. But such associations may also relate to more chronic concerns with purity and pollution. That is, they may be especially evident among people generally concerned with cleanliness. Support for these two predictions would provide multimethod, converging evidence that immorality-blackness associations exist and are a meaningful part of the moral-purity metaphor.

The Stroop (1935) color-word task served as our measure of word-color association (MacLeod, 1991). In this task, color names or color-related words appear in different colors. Color naming is slowed when the word and color are incongruent (e.g., "lemon" in blue ink; Klein, 1964) and speeded when they are congruent. Consequently, the more one associates immorality with black, the longer it should take to identify the color of immoral words (e.g., *sin*) when they appear in white, rather than black. After first documenting such a moral Stroop effect (Study 1), we tested whether experimentally priming immorality—a procedure known to encourage physical cleansing—would amplify the effect (Study 2) and whether the effect would be strongest for people who particularly like cleaning products (Study 3).

# Study 1

Meier et al. (2004, Study 4) adapted the Stroop task to the study of valence-darkness associations and found that word color did not interact with valence (coded dichotomously) to predict naming times. We reanalyzed their data, taking into account the moral (rather than merely evaluative) connotation of the words.

# Method
## Participants

Participants were 22 undergraduates at North Dakota State University. Meier et al. (2004, Study 4) did not report the racial composition of their sample, but did note that their participant pool was 95% Caucasian.

## Word Ratings

Two independent coders rated the words on the following dimensions: immoral versus moral, wrong versus right, unpleasant versus pleasant, and undesirable versus desirable. For each dimension, 1 represented one extreme (e.g., *very immoral*), 4 represented the neutral midpoint (e.g., *neither immoral nor moral*), and 7 represented the

other extreme (e.g., *very moral*). There was substantial agreement between the raters ($\alpha$s > .91), so their ratings were averaged. The first two dimensions formed a morality composite ($\alpha$ = .98), and the latter two a pleasantness composite ($\alpha$ = .99).

## Stimuli and Procedure

Each of 100 words (50 positive, 50 negative; see Meier et al., 2004) appeared once in black or white font (randomly assigned) on a computer screen. Participants indicated the color of each word using the "1" ("black") and "9" ("white") keys.

# Results and Discussion

Before analyzing the data, we adjusted reaction times (RTs) below 300 ms to 300 ms and RTs more than 3 standard deviations above the mean to that value (we followed the same procedure for cleaning the RT data in Studies 2 and 3). Additionally, RTs on the initial trials tended to be highly irregular; in Trials 1 and 2, a substantial percentage of participants took longer than 3 standard deviations above the mean to respond (86% for Trial 1, 27% for Trial 2). By Trial 3, participants' responses stabilized (0% > 3 $SD$s above the mean). We therefore excluded data from Trials 1 and 2 from analysis. (The same pattern characterized the other two studies, so we excluded Trials 1 and 2 in those studies as well.)[1]

Because the data were nested (trials within people), we used multilevel modeling (hierarchical linear modeling, HLM; Raudenbush, Bryk, Cheong, & Congdon, 2001). We predicted RT for correct trials (98%) from the word's color (–1 = white, 1 = black), its rated morality, and their interaction. There were no main effects of either color or morality ($t$s < 1.38, $p_{rep}$s < .76), but a significant Color × Morality interaction, $\beta_3$ = 8.10, $t$(2106) = 2.99, $p_{rep}$ = .97, indicated that the effect of morality on RT depended on word color. As predicted, for words in black, greater morality predicted slower RTs, $\beta_1$ = 6.26, $t$(1054) = 1.83, $p_{rep}$ = .86. For words in white, greater morality predicted faster RTs, $\beta_1$ = –12.72, $t$(1052) = – 3.01, $p_{rep}$ = .97 (see Figure 1).[2] A separate analysis substituting pleasantness for morality found that pleasantness did not interact with color ($t$ < 1), a finding consistent with the absence of an interaction between valence (coded dichotomously) and color in predicting RT in the original analysis reported by Meier et al. (2004, Study 4).

This is the first evidence that immorality-blackness associations operate quickly and automatically. These associations influenced performance on the Stroop task, a color-identification task that requires no moral evaluation and can be performed quickly (RTs around 500 ms). Just as the word *lemon* activates "yellow," so too do immoral words activate "black" and moral words activate "white."

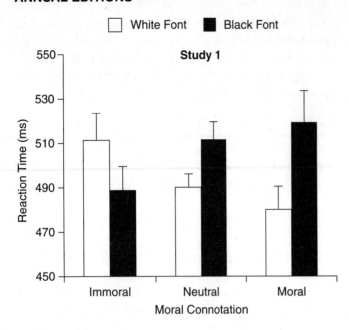

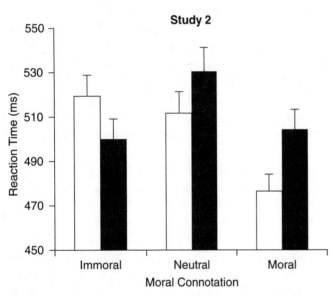

**Figure 1** Reaction time during the Stroop color-word task as a function of font color and moral connotation in Study 1 (top) and the premanipulation phase of Study 2 (bottom). Although moral connotation was a continuous variable (7-point scale) in both studies, for illustrative purposes the words are binned into three categories: immoral (1–3), neutral (3.01–5), and moral (5.01–7). Error bars represent standard errors of the mean.

# Study 2

In Study 2, we sought to (a) replicate Study 1 ourselves with a new set of words and (b) test whether the moral Stroop effect is sensitive to conditions that make immorality salient. If immorality-blackness associations are part of the moral-purity metaphor, then they should be most evident when people are feeling morally dirty. That is, the same sort of manipulations that elicit the "Macbeth effect" (Zhong & Liljenquist, 2006) should also evoke immorality-blackness associations.

## Method
### Participants

Forty University of Virginia undergraduates (19 female, 21 male) participated for partial course credit. Two participants (1 female, 1 male) experienced a computer malfunction, leaving a final sample of 38. Of these, 27 were self-identified as Caucasian (71%), 6 as Asain (16%), 3 as African American (8%), and 2 as Hispanic (5%).

### Word Ratings

At the end of the experiment, participants rated each word for morality and pleasantness (7-point scale, as in Study 1). We used each participant's ratings to predict his or her RTs.

### Stimuli and Procedure

We generated a new list of 50 words that spanned the entire range of moral connotations (Table 1). Each word was presented once (order and color assigned randomly). Participants were instructed to indicate the color of each word as quickly and as accurately as possible. After incorrect responses, "incorrect" appeared on the screen in red font for 1.5 s. Five practice trials preceded the task.

To prime immorality, we asked participants to hand-copy a story, written in the first person. The story was about a junior partner at a law firm who was competing against a colleague for a promotion and found a document of great value to the colleague. The story ended with the character either giving the document to the colleague (ethical version) or shredding it (unethical version). The materials and cover story for this task (that it measured individual differences in handwriting) were identical to those used by Zhong and Liljenquist (2006, Study 2).

The four tasks in this study were completed in the following order: baseline Stroop task, writing task, postmanipulation Stroop task, and word-rating task.

## Results and Discussion

To determine whether a moral Stroop effect was again present, we first analyzed baseline Stroop performance. In the model predicting RT for correct trials (98%), there were no main effects of either color or morality ($ts < 1.23$, $p_{rep}s < .72$), but the Color × Morality interaction was significant, $\beta_3 = 7.90$, $t(1792) = 2.30$, $p_{rep} = .93$. As in Study 1, the effect of morality depended on word color (see Figure 1). Separate models for the white and black fonts revealed that the effect was due primarily to white words, for which greater morality was associated with faster RTs, $\beta_1 = -10.72$, $t(923) = -2.33$, $p_{rep} = .92$. For words in black, the opposite pattern did not reach statistical significance, $\beta_1 = 4.73$, $t(869) = 0.92$, $p_{rep} = .60$.

We tested the effect of the writing task with a model predicting RT on the postmanipulation Stroop task from

**Table 1    Words Used in Studies 2 and 3**

Study 2

abstain, abusive, brag, cheat, compete, confess, cruel, dieting, discipline, duty, erotic, evil, exciting, forgive, freedom, gambling, gossip, gratify, greed, hate, helping, honesty, humble, indulge, justice, kind, laugh, liar, lust, money, obey, pain, partying, pleasure, polite, pray, pride, profit, respect, revenge, sacrifice, seduce, selfish, sin, smile, steal, torture, vice, virtuous, work

Study 3

Immoral: cheat, crime, devil, hell, neglect, sin, torment, vulgar

Neutral: aspect, calm, concert, east, forecast, motion, recall, sum

Moral: aid, angel, brave, charity, grace, honesty, saint, virtue

word color, word morality, and their interaction. Condition was a Level 2 (between-participants) predictor. To account for baseline Stroop performance, we computed a separate linear regression model for each participant, predicting RTs on the baseline Stroop task from word color, word morality, and their interaction. The standardized interaction coefficient—an estimate of that participant's Stroop effect—served as a Level 2 predictor, along with its interaction with condition (see Table 2).

Compared with hand-copying an ethical story, hand-copying an unethical story slowed RTs overall, $\gamma_{01} = 27.24$, $t(34) = 2.21$, $p_{rep} = .90$, and speeded the color identification of (a) immoral, relative to moral, words (Condition × Morality), $\gamma_{21} = 7.00$, $t(1781) = 2.13$, $p_{rep} = .90$, and (b) black, relative to white, words (Condition × Color), $\gamma_{11} = -5.64$, $t(1781) = -2.19$, $p_{rep} = .91$. That is, the priming manipulation primed both immorality and blackness, providing converging evidence that people automatically associate immorality with blackness.

Additionally, condition interacted with baseline Stroop effect to predict the Color × Morality interaction, $\gamma_{33} = -7.94$, $t(1781) = -3.80$, $p_{rep} > .99$. That is, the effect of the writing task on the Stroop effect depended on baseline Stroop performance. Simple-slopes analysis (Aiken & West, 1991) testing the effect of condition at two levels of baseline Stroop effect (1 $SD$ below and 1 $SD$ above the mean) revealed that for participants who did not show the Stroop effect initially, the effect of condition was as predicted, $\gamma_{31} = 8.05$, $t(1781) = 2.80$, $p_{rep} = .96$: Participants who hand-copied the unethical story subsequently exhibited a significantly larger Color × Morality interaction (i.e., Stroop effect) than those who hand-copied the ethical story (see Figure 2). For participants who did show the Stroop effect initially, hand-copying the unethical story had the opposite effect: That is, it decreased the magnitude of the Stroop effect, $\gamma_{31} = -7.87$, $t(1781) = -2.30$, $p_{rep} = .92$.

This latter effect was unexpected and is particularly interesting. Stroop effects can be diminished by several factors (see MacLeod, 1991, for a review). Manipulations that decrease the attention-drawing power of the semantic content are especially effective. For example, exposing participants to a word before the trial in which it appears (Dyer, 1971) dampens its capacity to interfere with color naming. Our priming manipulation was designed to increase the salience of moral meaning in order to create Stroop interference, but among participants for whom moral meaning was already salient, hand-copying the unethical story may have made moral content sufficiently familiar to reduce its power to draw attention away from color naming. This could account for the observed decrease in the magnitude of the Stroop effect.

Together, these findings attest to our measure's sensitivity. For people who showed no Stroop effect initially, simply exposing them to an instance of unethical behavior was sufficient to make immorality salient, which in turn allowed the morally relevant words in the Stroop task to activate their associated color. This finding suggests that whenever concerns about immorality (and perhaps also the sense of feeling morally dirty) are salient, so too are the purity-related colors of black and white. The unexpected finding for participants who had shown the Stroop effect initially suggests that moral content may lose its power with overexposure. If so, such "moral overexposure" might have troublesome behavioral consequences in that repeated thoughts or experiences of unethical behavior may cease to activate ideas of pollution and dirtiness.

Our immorality-salience manipulation is the same manipulation that in past research induced a desire for physical cleansing (Zhong & Liljenquist, 2006, Study 2). That this manipulation also primes "black" and alters the moral Stroop effect provides indirect evidence for the proposed link between immorality-blackness associations and notions of purity and contamination. In Study 3, we tested this link more directly.

# Study 3

If associating sin with blackness reflects, in part, a concern with its polluting powers, then people who tend to make such associations should be those who are generally concerned with purity and pollution. Because purity concerns can manifest themselves as desires for physical cleansing (Zhong & Liljenquist, 2006), we assessed participants' liking of various products, including several cleaning products. We predicted that participants who considered cleaning products to be especially desirable would also show the moral Stroop effect.

**Table 2** Hierarchical Linear Model Predicting Postmanipulation Stroop Performance (Reaction Time) in Study 2

| Variable | Coefficient | t | df | p |
|---|---|---|---|---|
| Intercept, $\beta_0$ | | | | |
| Intercept, $\gamma_{00}$ | 470.94 (12.09) | 38.95 | 34 | < .001 |
| Condition, $\gamma_{01}$ | 27.24 (12.31) | 2.21 | 34 | < .05 |
| Baseline Stroop effect, $\gamma_{02}$ | 4.22 (11.23) | 0.38 | 34 | .71 |
| Condition × Stroop Effect, $\gamma_{03}$ | −18.60 (11.23) | −1.66 | 34 | .11 |
| Color, $\beta_1$ | | | | |
| Intercept, $\gamma_{10}$ | −2.01 (2.58) | −0.78 | 1781 | .44 |
| Condition, $\gamma_{11}$ | −5.64 (2.58) | −2.19 | 1781 | < .05 |
| Baseline Stroop effect, $\gamma_{12}$ | −0.91 (2.17) | −0.42 | 1781 | .68 |
| Condition × Stroop Effect, $\gamma_{13}$ | −0.47 (2.17) | −0.22 | 1781 | .83 |
| Morality, $\beta_2$ | | | | |
| Intercept, $\gamma_{20}$ | −1.31 (3.33) | −0.39 | 1781 | .69 |
| Condition, $\gamma_{21}$ | 7.00 (3.28) | 2.13 | 1781 | < .05 |
| Baseline Stroop effect, $\gamma_{22}$ | 1.42 (2.45) | 0.58 | 1781 | .56 |
| Condition × Stroop Effect, $\gamma_{23}$ | −1.43 (2.45) | −0.58 | 1781 | .56 |
| Color × Morality, $\beta_2$ | | | | |
| Intercept, $\gamma_{30}$ | −2.82 (2.31) | −1.22 | 1781 | .22 |
| Condition, $\gamma_{31}$ | 0.09 (2.37) | 0.04 | 1781 | .97 |
| Baseline Stroop effect, $\gamma_{23}$ | −3.62 (2.09) | −1.73 | 1781 | .08 |
| Condition × Stroop Effect, $\gamma_{33}$ | −7.94 (2.09) | −3.80 | 1781 | < .001 |

Note. Standard errors are given in parentheses.

## Method

### Participants

Fifty-three University of Virginia undergraduates (28 female, 25 male) participated for partial course credit. Two male participants did not complete the ratings task, leaving a final sample of 51. Of these, 30 were self-identified as Caucasian (59%), 11 as Asian (22%), 5 as African American (10%), 2 as Hispanic (4%), and 3 as "other" (6%).

### Word Ratings, Stimuli, and Procedure

We created a new list of 24 words (8 immoral, 8 neutral, and 8 moral; see Table 1). To verify that the words had the intended moral connotation, at the end of the study we asked participants to rate the words themselves (as in Study 2). The ratings confirmed our categorization: All moral words had a mean rating greater than 6, all immoral words had a mean rating less than 2, and all neutral words were rated in between (minimum = 4.25, maximum = 5.66).

Each word was selected from the MRC Psycholinguistic Database (Machine-Usable Dictionary, Version 2.00; see Wilson, 1988), which supplies values for various word attributes. The different categories did not differ in concreteness, familiarity, imageability, written frequency, number of letters, or number of syllables ($F$s < 1).

The Stroop task was the same as in Study 2, except for the new words. Because we used fewer words than in Studies 1 and 2, we set the number of trials to 48. Each trial was randomly assigned 1 of the 24 words and one of the two colors. Also, participants were randomly assigned to one of two pairings of color and response key ("1" = black, "9" = white; "1" = white, "9" = black). Because the assigned pairings did not influence any result, we collapsed across them for all analyses.

After the Stroop task, participants rated the desirability of five cleaning products (Dove shower soap, Crest toothpaste, Lysol disinfectant, Windex cleaner, and Tide

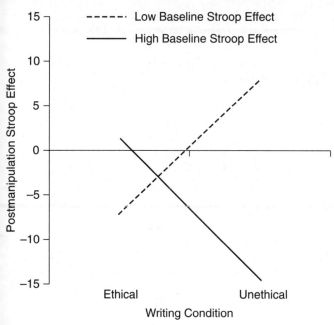

**Figure 2** Regression slopes from the hierarchical linear modeling analysis in Study 2: postmanipulation Stroop effect (Color × Morality interaction) as a function of baseline Stroop effect (1 *SD* below and 1 *SD* above the mean) and writing condition.

detergent) and five non-cleaning products (Post-it notes, Energizer batteries, Sony CD cases, Nantucket Nectars juices, and Snickers bars) on a 6-point scale (1 = *completely undesirable*, 6 = *completely desirable*). This measure was identical to the one used by Zhong and Liljenquist (2006, Study 2), who found that priming immorality increased the desirability of cleaning products.

At the end of the experiment, participants indicated their race, their political orientation (7-point scale: 1 = *very liberal*, 4 = *moderate*, 7 = *very conservative*), and the frequency with which they attended religious services (8-point scale: 0 = *never in my life*, 7 = *multiple-times per week*). The latter two measures were included to test whether any relation between the moral Stroop effect and liking of cleaning products could be explained by individual differences in religion or politics.

## Results and Discussion

In an HLM model predicting RT for correct trials (99%), Level 1 predictors were word color, word morality, and their interaction. At Level 2 (between participants), we entered participants' average rating for the cleaning products and average rating for the non-cleaning products. At Level 1, there were no significant main effects of either color, $\gamma_{10} = 7.41$, $t(628) = 1.63$, $p = .10$, or morality, $\gamma_{20} = -6.46$, $t(628) = -1.69$, $p = .09$, although both trends were notable. Unlike in Studies 1 and 2, the Color × Morality interaction was not significant, $\gamma_{30} = 5.90$, $t(628) = 1.46$, $p_{rep} = .77$, but it was in the predicted direction. Most

important, this interaction was moderated by cleaning-product desirability, $\gamma_{31} = 22.36$, $t(628) = 4.04$, $p_{rep} > .99$, such that participants who rated cleaning products as more desirable had a larger Color × Morality interaction (i.e., moral Stroop effect). No such relationship was observed for non-cleaning products, $\gamma_{32} = -5.38$, $t(628) = -1.19$, $p = .24$. When political orientation and religious attendance were added as Level 2 predictors, they were also unrelated to the moral Stroop effect ($ts < 1$).

In supplementary analyses, each participant's interaction coefficient served as an estimate of his or her moral Stroop effect (as in Study 2). A series of multiple linear regression models predicted this estimate from product-desirability ratings. A model including the cleaning and noncleaning composite ratings replicated the HLM results: The cleaning composite was again a significant, positive predictor, $\beta = -.39$, $p_{rep} = .90$, whereas the noncleaning composite was unrelated to the moral Stroop effect, $\beta = -.07$, $p = .72$. To see which cleaning products were responsible for this relationship, we tested another model, with all 10 products as separate, simultaneous predictors. The only significant predictors were Crest toothpaste, $\beta = .46$, $p_{rep} = .94$, and Dove shower soap, $\beta = .35$, $p_{rep} = .90$. All other products were unrelated to the moral Stroop effect ($ts < 1$). Notably, the two items that were significant predictors are the only products that deal specifically with cleaning oneself. This result fits nicely with Zhong and Liljenquist's (2006) finding that people who had recalled a past unethical behavior preferred a hand-sanitizing antiseptic wipe to a pencil as a gift and that those who had actually cleansed their hands felt absolved of their moral guilt. Together, these findings suggest that the moral-purity metaphor may be particularly important for regulating one's own moral behavior. If the thought of acting immorally evokes images of dark, dirty impurities, it may facilitate avoidance of such behavior, thus protecting against moral contamination and ensuring that one's moral self stays clean and pure (i.e., "white").

## General Discussion

There exists a moral-purity metaphor that likens moral goodness to physical cleanliness (Rozin et al., 1986; Zhong & Liljenquist, 2006). In three studies, we explored an unstudied, and underappreciated, aspect of this metaphor—its grounding in the colors black and white. We documented a moral Stroop effect indicating that people make immorality-blackness associations quickly and relatively automatically (Studies 1 and 2). Moreover, a manipulation known to induce a desire for physical cleansing primed both immorality and the color black

(Study 2). The increased salience of immorality, in turn, altered the magnitude of the Stroop effect. Finally, individuals who showed the moral Stroop effect considered cleaning (especially self-cleaning) products to be highly desirable (Study 3), a finding indicating a direct link between immorality-blackness associations and purity concerns.

Although the metaphor of moral purity is well documented, this is the first demonstration that black and white, as representative of negative contagion (black contaminates white), are central parts of this metaphor. Sin is not just dirty, it is black. And moral virtue is not just clean, but also white. Our most unexpected finding—that the effect of priming immorality depended on an individual's baseline Stroop effect—contributes to understanding of embodied moral cognition by suggesting that seeing moral purity in black and white is not always a given. Just as easily as the metaphor can be evoked in people who do not generally show it, it can be diminished in those who do.

These findings may have implications for understanding racial prejudice. The history of race-related practices in the United States (e.g., the "one drop of blood" rule for racial categorization and segregation) has demonstrated that the tendency to see the black-white spectrum in terms of purity and contamination extends to skin color (for a discussion, see Rozin & Royzman, 2001). Given that both blackness and immorality are considered powerful contaminants to be avoided, and that the category labels "black" and "white" are often applied to race, dark skin might also be easily associated with immorality and impurity. This may explain, in part, why stereotypes of darker-skinned people often allude to immorality and poor hygiene, and why the typical criminal is seen as both dark skinned and physically dirty (MacLin & Herrera, 2006).

A morally virtuous person is said to be as "pure as the driven snow." In contrast to the pure whiteness of newly fallen snow, impurities are dirty, are dark, and visibly stain otherwise pristine surfaces. Equating immorality with these contaminants animates the abstract notions of sin and evil by grounding them in visceral, evocative qualities of one's experience of the physical world (Lakoff & Johnson, 1980). More than merely a rhetorical device for moral discourse, the moral-purity metaphor is a deep, embodied phenomenon covertly shaping moral cognition.

## Notes

1. Because RT data are often positively skewed, we also analyzed the data using log-transformed RTs. The results were nearly identical to those reported here.

2. This interaction remained significant when we controlled for word extremity (provided by Meier et al., 2004) and written frequency (Kucera & Francis, 1967).

# References

Adams, F.M., & Osgood, C.E. (1973). A cross-cultural study of the affective meanings of color. *Journal of Cross-Cultural Psychology, 4,* 135–156.

Aiken, L.S., & West, S.G. (1991). *Multiple regression: Testing and interpreting interactions.* Thousand Oaks, CA: Sage.

Barsalou, L.W. (1999). Perceptual symbol systems. *Behavioral and Brain Sciences, 22,* 577–609.

Dyer, F.N. (1971). The duration of word meaning responses: Stroop interference for different preexposures of the word. *Psychonomic Science, 25,* 229–231.

Frank, M.G., & Gilovich, T. (1988). The dark side of self- and social perception: Black uniforms and aggression in professional sports. *Journal of Personality and Social Psychology, 54,* 74–85.

Klein, G.S. (1964). Semantic power measured through the interference of words with color-naming. *American Journal of Psychology, 77,* 576–588.

Kucera, H., & Francis, W. (1967). *Computational analysis of present-day American English.* Providence, RI: Brown University Press.

Lakoff, G., & Johnson, M. (1980). *Metaphors we live by.* Chicago: University of Chicago Press.

MacLeod, C.M. (1991). Half a century of research on the Stroop effect: An integrative review. *Psychological Bulletin, 109,* 163–203.

MacLin, M.K., & Herrera, V. (2006). The criminal stereotype. *North American Journal of Psychology, 8,* 197–207.

Meier, B.P., Robinson, M.D., & Clore, G.L. (2004). Why good guys wear white: Automatic inferences about stimulus valence based on brightness. *Psychological Science, 15,* 82–87.

Meier, B.P., Robinson, M.D., Crawford, L.E., & Ahlvers, W.J. (2007). When 'light' and 'dark' thoughts become light and dark responses: Affect biases brightness judgments. *Emotion, 7,* 366–376.

Raudenbush, S., Bryk, A., Cheong, Y.F., & Congdon, R. (2001). *HLM5: Hierarchical linear and nonlinear modeling.* Chicago: Scientific Software International.

Rozin, P., Markwith, M., & McCauley, C. (1994). Sensitivity to indirect contacts with other persons: AIDS aversion as a composite of aversion to strangers, infection, moral taint, and misfortune. *Journal of Abnormal Psychology, 103,* 495–504.

Rozin, P., Millman, L., & Nemeroff, C. (1986). Operation of the laws of sympathetic magic in disgust and other domains. *Journal of Personality and Social Psychology, 50,* 703–712.

Rozin, P., & Royzman, E.B. (2001). Negativity bias, negativity dominance, and contagion. *Personality and Social Psychology Review, 5,* 296–320.

Schubert, T.W. (2005). Your highness: Vertical positions as perceptual symbols of power. *Journal of Personality and Social Psychology, 89,* 1–21.

Stabler, J.R., & Johnson, E.E. (1972). The meaning of black and white to children. *International Journal of Symbology, 3,* 11–21.

Stroop, J.R. (1935). Studies of interference in serial verbal reactions. *Journal of Experimental Psychology, 18,* 643–662.

Williams, J.E., & Roberson, J.K. (1967). A method for assessing racial attitudes in preschool children. *Educational and Psychological Measurement, 27,* 671–689.

Wilson, M. (1988). MRC Psycholinguistic Database: Machine-usable dictionary, version 2.00. *Behavior Research Methods, Instruments, & Computers, 20,* 6–10.

Zhong, C., & Liljenquist, K.A. (2006). Washing away your sins: Threatened morality and physical cleansing. *Science, 313,* 1451–1452.

# Critical Thinking

1. In what interesting ways does language influence or shape our perception of life's experiences?

Address correspondence to **GARY D. SHERMAN,** Department of Psychology, University of Virginia, P.O. Box 400400, Charlottesville, VA 22904-4400, e-mail: gds6d@virginia.edu.

**Acknowledgments**—This research was supported in part by a National Science Foundation Graduate Research Fellowship to Gary Sherman and by National Institute of Mental Health Research Grant MH 50074 to Gerald Clore. We thank Brian Meier and Michael Robinson for providing the data for the reanalysis reported in Study 1.

# What Dreams Are Made Of

**Technologies that reveal the inner workings of the brain are beginning to tell the sleeping mind's secrets.**

MARIANNE SZEGEDY-MASZAK

Strange images appear from long-forgotten memories. Or out of nowhere: You're roller-skating on water; your mother flashes by on a trapeze; your father is in labor; a friend dead for years sits down at the dinner table. Here are moments of unspeakable terror; there, moments of euphoria or serenity. Shakespeare wrote, "We are such stuff as dreams are made on," and 300 years later, Sigmund Freud gave the poetry a neat psychoanalytic spin when he called dreams "the royal road to the unconscious." The movies that unfold in our heads some nights are so powerfully resonant they haunt us for days—or inspire us. Mary Shelley dreamed of Frankenstein before she created him on paper; the melody to "Yesterday" came to Paul McCartney as he slept.

Everybody dreams—yet no one, throughout history, has fully grasped what the dreaming mind is doing. Are the nightly narratives a message from the unconscious to the conscious mind, as Freud believed? Or are they simply the product of random electrical flashes in the brain? Today, researchers aided by powerful technologies that reveal the brain in action are concluding that both schools of thought hold truth. "This is the greatest adventure of all time," says Harvard psychiatrist and dream researcher J. Allan Hobson. "The development of brain imaging is the equivalent of Galileo's invention of the telescope, only we are now exploring inner space instead of outer space."

## Freud saw dreams as buried wishes disguised by symbols.

**Mind-brain dance.** The dream researchers' new tools, functional magnetic resonance imaging and positron emission tomography (PET) scanning, have been used for some time to capture the waking brain at work—making

decisions, feeling frightened or joyous, coping with uncertainty. And those efforts have shown clearly that psychology and physiology are intimately related: In someone suffering from an anxiety disorder, for example, the fear center of the brain—the amygdala—"lights up" as neurons fire in response to images that trigger anxiety; it flickers in a minuet with the center of memory, the hippocampus. Scanning people who are sleeping, too, suggests that the same sort of mind-brain dance continues 24 hours a day.

"Psychology has built its model of the mind strictly out of waking behavior," says Rosalind Cartwright, chair of the department of behavioral science at Rush University Medical Center in Chicago, who has studied dreams for most of her 83 years. "We know that the mind does not turn off during sleep; it goes into a different stage." Brain cells fire, and the mind spins. Problems find solutions; emotional angst seems to be soothed; out-of-the-box ideas germinate and take root.

> The door between the kitchen and the garage was split, so you could open the top half without opening the bottom half. It was the only safe way of doing it, because we had a rhinoceros in the garage. The garage was a lot bigger, though; it was also sort of a basement, and led underneath the rest of the house. My mother was cooking dinner, and I went into the bathroom where my brother Stuart was. The rhinoceros punched a hole in the floor with his horn.
>
> **Madeline,** third grade

What to make of young Madeline's dream? To Freud, had he met her, Madeline's rhinoceros horn would almost certainly have symbolized a penis, and the animal's violence would have been an expression of normal but threatening sexual feelings toward her brother—or perhaps of a fear of men in general. Freud saw dreams as deeply

## Frankenstein and Mary Shelley

### A Dream Come True

Can man create life? A talk on evolution that considered the possibility so disturbed Mary Godwin that she went to bed and dreamed up Frankenstein. She and three other writers, including her soon-to-be-husband, Percy Shelley, were staying at Lake Geneva in Switzerland during that summer of 1816, entertaining one another by telling and competing to write the best ghost stories. Shelley's vivid dream, in which she saw a "hideous phantasm of a man stretched out" and a scientist using a machine to try to bring him to life, inspired hers. She began to write the next day.

—Betsy Querna

## Joseph and a Word from God

### A Dream Come True

When Joseph discovered that Mary was pregnant during their engagement, he was "just crushed," says Father Gerald Kleba, a Roman Catholic priest in St. Louis who wrote the historical novel *Joseph Remembered*. Assuming that she had committed adultery, Joseph figured he would have to leave her. But an angel visited him in a dream, according to the Bible, and told him not be afraid. Mary had conceived through the Holy Spirit and would bear a special child. That "huge aha moment" shaped the rest of Joseph's life, says Kleba, and still speaks to many Christians of the power of faith.

—B.Q.

buried wishes disguised by symbols, a way to gratify desires unacceptable to the conscious mind. His ideas endured for years, until scientists started systematically studying dream content and decided that actually, something less exotic is going on.

"Dreams do enact—they dramatize. They are like plays of how we view the world and oneself in it," says William Domhoff, who teaches psychology and sociology at the University of California-Santa Cruz. "But they do not provide grandiose meanings." Domhoff bases his view on a study of themes and images that recur in a databank of some 16,000 dreams—including Madeline's—that have been collected as oral narratives and are held at Santa Cruz. (The narratives can be read at www.dreambank.net.)

Post-Freudians might argue that the monsters lurking in children's dreams signal a growing awareness of the world around them and its dangers. Young children describe very simple and concrete images, while the dreams of 9- and 10-year-olds get decidedly more complex. A monster that goes so far as to chase or attack might represent a person who is frightening to the child during waking hours. "Dreaming serves a vital function in the maturation of the brain and in processing the experiences of the day," says Alan Siegel, professor of psychology at UC-Berkeley and author of *Dream Wisdom*.

### The experience of dreaming is as universal as a heartbeat.

**Nonsense.** Physiology purists, who would say that Madeline's brain is simply flashing random images, got their start in 1953 with the discovery of rapid eye movement sleep. Using primitive electroencephalograms,

researchers watched as every 90 minutes, sleepers' eyes darted back and forth and brain waves surged. Then, in 1977, Harvard psychiatrists Hobson and Robert McCarley reported that during sleep, electrical activity picked up dramatically in the most primitive area of the brain—the pons—which, by simply stimulating other parts of the brain, produced weird and disconnected narratives. Much like people looking for meaning in an inkblot, they concluded, dreams are the brain's vain attempt to impose coherence where there is none.

Or maybe that's not the whole story, either, said a young neuropsychologist at the Royal London School of Medicine 20 years later, when his findings hinted that dreaming is both a mental and a physical process. Mark Solms showed that dreams can't be explained as simple physical reactions to flashes from the primitive pons, since some of the most active dreamers in his study had suffered brain damage in that area. On the other hand, in those with damage to regions of the brain associated with higher-order motivation, passionate emotions, and abstract thinking, the nightly movies had stopped. That seemed a sign that dreams might indeed express the mind's ideas and motivations. "It is a mistake to think that we can study the brain using the same concepts we use for the liver," says Solms.

"From my perspective, dreaming is just thinking in a very different biochemical state," says Deirdre Barrett, who teaches psychology at Harvard and is editor of the journal *Dreaming*. The threads can be "just as complex as waking thought and just as dull. They are overwhelmingly visual, and language is less important, and logic is less important."

I am a traveler carrying one light bag and looking for a place to spend the night. I . . . discover a hostel of a sort in a large indoor space big enough to house a gymnasium. I find a spot near a corner and

## Paul McCartney and "Yesterday"

### A Dream Come True

"I woke up with a lovely tune in my head," Paul McCartney recalled to his biographer, Barry Miles. "I thought, 'That's great. I wonder what that is?'" He got up that morning in May 1965, went to the piano, and began playing the melody what would become "Yesterday." At first, lacking lyrics, he improvised with "Scrambled eggs, oh my baby, how I love your legs." While he really liked the tune, he had some reservations: "Because I'd, dreamed it, I couldn't believe I'd written it." Today, with more than 1,600 covers, that song holds the Guinness world record for most recorded versions.

—B.Q.

prepare for bed. I think to myself, "Luckily, I have my high-tech pillow." I take out of my bag a light, flat panel about 8 by 10 inches and the thickness of a thick piece of cardboard. "It works by applying a voltage," I say. "There's a new kind of material which fluffs up when you apply a voltage." On the face of the panel is a liquid-crystal display with two buttons, one labeled "on" and one labeled "off." I touch the "on" button with my index finger, and the flat panel magically inflates to the dimensions of a fluffy pillow. I lay it down on the ground and comfortably go to sleep.

**Chuck,** scientist (from Dreambank.net)

If Chuck's experience is an example of logic gone to sleep, no wonder dreamers so often wake up shouting, "Eureka!" Indeed, history is filled with examples of inspiration that blossomed during sleep and eventually led to inventions or works of art or military moves. Exactly what happens to inspire creativity is unclear, but the new technology is providing clues.

**Crazy smart.** Brain scans performed on people in REM sleep, for example, have shown that even as certain brain centers turn on—the emotional seat of the brain and the part that processes all visual inputs are wide awake— one vital area goes absolutely dormant: the systematic and clear-thinking prefrontal cortex, where caution and organization reside. "This can explain the bizarreness you see in dreams, the crazy kind of sense that your brain is ignoring the usual ways that you put things together," says Robert Stickgold, associate professor of psychiatry at Harvard and director of the Center for Sleep and Cognition at Beth Israel Deaconess Medical Center. "This is what you want in a state in which creativity is enhanced. Creativity is nothing more and nothing less than putting

memories together in a way that they never have been before."

## No wonder dreamers so often wake up shouting, "Eureka!"

Putting memories together is also an essential part of learning; people integrate the memory of new information, be it how to tie shoelaces or conjugate French verbs, with existing knowledge. Does dreaming help people learn? No one knows—but some sort of boost seems to happen during sleep. Many studies by sleep researchers have shown that people taught a new task performed it better after a night of sleep.

A study of how quickly dreamers solve problems supports Stickgold's theory that the sleeping mind can be quite nimble and inventive. Participants were asked to solve scrambled word puzzles after being awakened during both the REM phase of sleep and the less active non-REM phase. Their performance improved by 32 percent when they worked on the puzzles coming out of REM sleep, which told researchers that that phase is more conducive to fluid reasoning. During non-REM sleep, it appears, our more cautious selves kick into gear.

Indeed, PET scans of people in a non-REM state show a decline in brain energy compared with REM sleep and increased activity in those dormant schoolmarmish lobes. Does this affect the content of dreams? Yes, say researchers from Harvard and the Boston University School of Medicine.

Since people should theoretically be more uninhibited when the controlling prefrontal cortex is quiet, the team tracked participants for two weeks to see if their REM dreams were more socially aggressive than the ones they reported during non-REM sleep. The REM dreams, in fact, were much more likely to involve social interactions and tended to be more aggressive.

I had a horrible dream. Howard was in a coffin. I yelled and screamed at his mom that it was all her fault. I kicked myself that I hadn't waited to become a widow rather than a divorcée in order to get the insurance. I woke up feeling miserable, the dream was so icky.

**Barb** (from Dreambank.net)

To many experts, Barb's bad dream would be a good sign, an indication that she would recover from the sorrow of her divorce. A vivid dream life, in which troubled or anxious people experience tough emotions while asleep, is thought to act, in the words of Cartwright, as "a kind of internal therapist."

## Saddam and His Winning Strategy

### A Dream Come True

Saddam Hussein used his dreams to guide policy, sometimes to the befuddlement of his closest advisers. The dictator's personal secretary told U.S. military investigators in an interview in 2003 that Hussein would sleep on difficult problems and report the solutions the next morning. One time that his dream got it right: During the Iran-Iraq War of the 1980s, Hussein dreamed that the Iranians would launch an offensive through a large marshland, so he ordered more troops there. His generals thought the move illogical but acquiesced. The Iranians attacked there, and the Iraqis prevailed.

—B.Q.

## Jack Nicklaus and His Grip

### A Dream Come True

In the summer of 1964, Jack Nicklaus was in a slump: "It got to the point where a 76 looked like a great score to me," the golfer told the Cleveland *Plain Dealer.* One night, during the Cleveland Open, he dreamed he was hitting the ball with a different grip—and it worked better. So he tried it the next day, shot a 68, then a 65, and ended the tournament tied for third place. For the year, he shot about a 70 average, the lowest in professional golf. "I'm almost embarrassed to admit how I changed my grip this week," he told the reporter at the time. "But that's how it happened. It's kinda crazy, isn't it?"

—B.Q.

The enduring and vexing question is: How much of value do dreams say? Despite all the efforts to quantify, to measure, no one has an answer yet. But dreams have played a role in psychotherapy for over a century, since Freud theorized that they signal deep and hidden motivations. "A dream is the one domain in which many of a patient's defenses are sufficiently relaxed that themes emerge that ordinarily would not appear in waking life," says Glen Gabbard, professor of psychiatry and psychoanalysis at Baylor College of Medicine.

## A vivid dream life is thought to act as an "internal therapist."

Sometimes, dreams can be a helpful diagnostic tool, a way of taking the emotional temperature of a patient. The dreams of clinically depressed people are notable for their utter lack of activity, for example.

Might there be a physiological reason? Eric Nofzinger, director of the Sleep Neuroimaging Research Program at the University of Pittsburgh medical school, has studied PET scans of depressed patients and has found that the difference between their waking and sleeping states is far less dramatic than normal. On the one hand, he says, "we were shocked, surprised, and amazed at how much activity" there was in the emotional brain of healthy people during sleep. In depressed patients, by contrast, the vigilant prefrontal cortex, which normally is not active during sleep, worked overtime. Never surrendering to the soothing power of dreams, the brain is physically constrained, and its dream life shows it.

**Healing power.** Is it possible that dreaming can actually heal? "We know that 60 to 70 percent of people who go through a depression will recover without treatment,"

says Cartwright, who recently tested her theory that maybe they are working through their troubles while asleep. In a study whose results were published this spring in the journal *Psychiatry Research,* she recruited 30 people going through a divorce and asked them to record their dreams over five months. Depressed patients whose dreams were rich with emotion—one woman reported seething while her ex-husband danced with his new girlfriend—eventually recovered without the need for drugs or extensive psychotherapy. But those whose dreams were bland and empty of feeling were not able to recover on their own.

I've sat straight up in bed many times, reliving it, reseeing it, rehearing it. And it's in the most absurd ways that only a dream could depict . . . the one that comes to mind most, dreaming of a green pool in front of me. That was part of the radarscope. It was a pool of gel, and I reached into the radarscope to stop that flight. But in the dream, I didn't harm the plane. I just held it in my hand, and somehow that stopped everything.

**Danielle O'Brien,** air traffic controller
for American Airlines Flight 77, which
crashed into the Pentagon on Sept. 11, 2001
(in an interview with ABC News)

Many clinicians working with traumatized patients have found that their nightmares follow a common trajectory. First, the dreams re-create the horrors; later, as the person begins to recover, the stories involve better outcomes. One way to help victims of trauma move on is to encourage them to wake themselves up in the midst of a horrifying dream and consciously take control of the narrative, to take action, much as O'Brien appears to have done in her dream. This can break the cycle of nightmares by offering a sense of mastery. "If you can change the dream content," says Harvard's Barrett, author of *Trauma and Dreams,* "you see a reduction in all the other post-traumatic symptoms."

Cartwright recalls helping a rape victim who came in suffering from nightmares in which she felt an utter lack of control; together, they worked to edit the young woman's dreams of being in situations where she was powerless—of lying on the floor of an elevator without walls as it rose higher and higher over Lake Michigan, for example. "I told her, 'Remember, this is your construction. You made it up, and you can stop it,'" says Cartwright, who coached the woman to recognize the point at which the dream was becoming frightening and try to seize control. At the next session, the woman reported that, as the elevator rose, she decided to stand in her dream and figure out what was happening. The walls rose around her until she felt safe.

A window? A royal road? A way for the brain to integrate today with yesterday? While definitive answers remain elusive, the experience of dreaming is clearly as universal as a heartbeat and as individual as a fingerprint—and rich with possibilities for both scientist and poet.

## Critical Thinking

1. Why do psychologists study sleep and dreaming?
2. What impact does sleeping and dreaming appear to have on what we do while we are awake?

From *U.S. News & World Report,* May 15, 2006, pp. 55–64. Copyright © 2006 by U.S. News & World Report, L.P. Reprinted by permission via Wright's Media.

# Increasing Speed of Processing with Action Video Games

MATTHEW W. G. DYE, C. SHAWN GREEN, AND DAPHNE BAVELIER

Playing action video games—contemporary examples include *God of War, Halo, Unreal Tournament, Grand Theft Auto,* and *Call of Duty*—requires rapid processing of sensory information and prompt action, forcing players to make decisions and execute responses at a far greater pace than is typical in everyday life. During game play, delays in processing often have severe consequences, providing large incentive for players to increase speed. Accordingly, there is anecdotal evidence that avid game players react more readily to their environment. However, it remains unknown whether any reduction in reaction time (RT) really generalizes to tasks beyond video-game playing and, if it does, whether it makes gamers more impulsive and prone to making errors. In short, are expert video-game players (VGPs) just "trigger happy," or does video-game playing really improve RTs on a variety of tasks without a concomitant decrease in accuracy? The possibility of identifying a single training task that can lead to RT improvements across a variety of unrelated tasks is of great interest but remains controversial in the field of speeded-response-choice tasks (in which observers must choose among alternative responses or actions as rapidly as possible). On such tasks, decreases in RT are typically accompanied by decreases in accuracy. This is termed a speed–accuracy trade-off, with speeding up resulting in more mistakes. One exception is when individuals are trained on such speeded tasks. Performance on the trained task is then improved (faster RTs, but no speed–accuracy trade-off); however, little or at best limited transfer to new tasks is observed, limiting the benefits of training (Pashler & Baylis, 1991). Interestingly, flexible or integrated training regimens—requiring constant switching of processing priorities and continual adjustments to new task demands—have been argued to lead to greater transfer (Bherer et al., 2005). Action-video-game playing may be an extreme case of such flexible training.

Here we consider the possibility that action-video-game training leads to faster RTs on tasks unrelated to the training and, thus, for the first time may offer a regimen leading to generalized speeding across tasks in young adults.

## Action Video Games and Speeded-Choice RT Tasks

The possibility that playing video games affects perceptual and cognitive skills has received much interest lately. Most past studies have compared VGPs to novice video-game players (NVGPs) using tasks that measure RTs in order to draw conclusions about performance. Although usually not the primary focus of these studies, they invariably show that the VGPs are faster overall than those who do not play such games (Bialystok, 2006; Castel, Pratt, & Drummond, 2005; Clark, Lanphear, & Riddick, 1987; Greenfield, deWinstanley, Kilpatrick, & Kaye, 1994). This is perhaps unsurprising given the fast pace of games considered in these studies. There are, however, two surprising characteristics of these RT decreases: (a) the consistency in speed-of-processing advantages for VGPs across a range of tasks, and (b) the fact that there is no speed–accuracy trade-off. These points are illustrated by the following meta-analysis, which examines the reported RTs of avid action gamers versus those of novices across a number of studies. . . .

It is important to note that a few studies (Clark et al., 1987; Green, 2008) have indicated that these faster RTs can be trained by action-video-game play, therefore establishing causality (as opposed to strictly correlative studies where population bias is a significant concern). RTs in NVGP individuals were assessed before and after action-video-game training, and these results were then compared to NVGP individuals trained on control non-action video games. The control video games were chosen to be as engrossing as the experimental game,

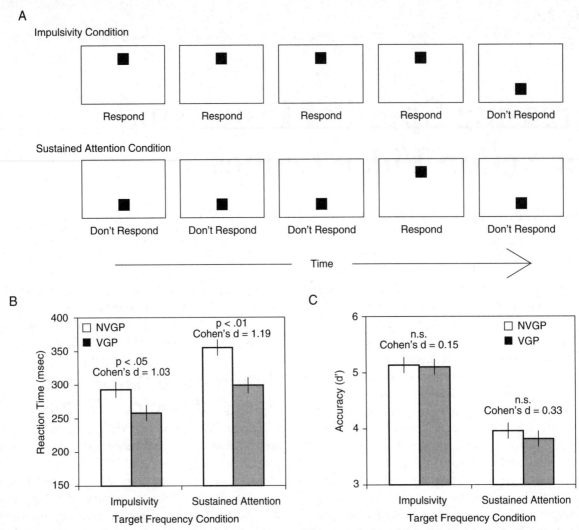

**Figure 1** The Test of Variables of Attention (A), used to assess differences in impulsivity and sustained attention between non-video-game players (NVGPs) and expert video-game players (VGPs), and results for both reaction time (B) and accuracy (C) measures. VGPs were faster at responding than NVGPs on both the impulsivity and sustained attention measures, but the groups did not differ on the accuracy measure, suggesting that the faster responses of VGPs were not due to impulsive responses to the stimuli and that they did not have greater problems sustaining their attention (n.s. stands for nonsignificant; $p$ values are given for statistical significance and Cohen's $d$ for the strength of the effect).

minimizing differences in motivation across groups and thus controlling for both test–retest effects (i.e., improvement expected simply from taking the test a second time) and Hawthorne-like effects (wherein individuals who have an active interest taken in their behavior tend to, all other things being equal, outperform individuals in which no such interest is taken). Furthermore, by evaluating subject behavior a few days before and a few days after the end of training (rather than immediately prior to and after training), these training studies attempt to exclude possible short-term effects of gaming on behavior, such as changes in arousal state or frame of mind. . . .

Thus, unlike what has been reported in the majority of the literature on the training of speeded responses, the learning that occurs during action-video-game experience generalizes well beyond the act of playing games itself.

# Action Video Games and Impulsivity

The increased speed of processing noted in VGPs is often viewed as a "trigger-happy" behavior, in which VGPs respond faster but make more anticipatory errors (responding incorrectly because they do not wait for enough information to become available). Available research suggests this is not the case. First, the meta-analysis above reveals that VGPs have equivalent accuracy to NVGPs in the face of an 11% decrease in RTs. Second, a more direct evaluation of impulsivity using the Test of Variables of Attention (T.O.V.A.®) indicates equivalent performance in VGPs and NVGPs. Briefly, this test requires subjects to look at a computer monitor and make a timed response to shapes appearing at one location (targets), while ignoring the same shapes if they appear at another location (nontargets). In different parts of the experiment, the target can appear either often or very rarely (Figure 1A). The T.O.V.A. therefore offers a measure of both impulsivity (is the observer able to withhold a response to a nontarget when most of the stimuli are targets?) and a measure of sustained attention (is the observer able to stay on task and respond quickly to a target when most of the stimuli are nontargets?).

VGPs were selected based on self-reports of playing 5 hours per week (or more) of action video games in the previous year, and compared to NVGPs who reported little or no video gaming (and no action gaming for several years). VGPs responded more quickly than did NVGPs on both task components (Figure 1B), confirming increased processing speed in this group. Crucially, accuracy did not differ for the two groups, this being the case for both the impulsivity and the sustained-attention measures (Figure 1C). VGPs were therefore faster but not more impulsive than NVGPs and were equally capable of sustaining their attention. Thus, in contrast to the "trigger-happy" hypothesis, VGPs did not compensate for their faster RTs by making more anticipatory errors than NVGPs.

## Action Video Games and Accuracy Measures

Although earlier studies typically used speeded RT tasks, more recent studies of action-video-game players have focused on accuracy measures. This choice was motivated by the difficulty of making fair comparisons regarding cognitive processes across populations that have large differences in how quickly they make their responses. This problem is well acknowledged in the aging literature, and we refer the reader to Madden, Pierce, and Allen (1996) for a comprehensive discussion of the issue.

One area that has received considerable attention is the effect of action video games on visual cognition. Video-game players have been reported to show improved hand–eye coordination, increased visual processing in the periphery, enhanced mental-rotation skills, greater divided attention, and enhanced visuospatial memory. A series of published accuracy studies have established that playing action video games enhances performance on tasks thought to measure different aspects of visual attention, including the ability to (a) distribute attention across space, (b) efficiently perform dual tasks, (c) track several moving objects at once, and (d) process streams of briefly presented visual stimuli (Green & Bavelier, 2003, 2007). One such study focusing on visuospatial skills

has suggested that action-game playing may provide a reliable training regimen to reduce gender differences in visuospatial cognition (Feng, Spence, & Pratt, 2007). In each of these instances, a causative role for action video games was demonstrated by conducting training studies with college students who did not play video games.

While these results in accuracy-based tasks have been previously interpreted as an increase in attentional resources in action-video-game players and/or an enhancement in the ability to allocate those resources across space and time, the Brinley plot in Figure 1 suggests an alternative hypothesis that parsimoniously explains the entire pattern of previous data, both RT-and accuracy-based. The consistent multiplicative VGP advantage in reaction time observed in the Brinley plot suggests a clear difference in the speed with which visual information is processed between the groups. In tasks in which RT is the primary dependent measure, this difference will be manifested as predictably faster RTs in VGPs than in NVGPs. However, such a difference in the speed of processing also predicts higher accuracy in VGPs in accuracy-based tasks in which the stimulus is typically quickly flashed or moving. This prediction was confirmed by Li, Polat, Makous, and Bavelier (2009), who show that VGPs acquire visual information more rapidly than NVGPs do. In fact, such a hypothesis predicts VGP advantages on virtually any task for which speeded visual processing is at the root of performance. To some extent, this hypothesis can be thought of as the converse of the generalized-slowing hypothesis for cognitive aging—that is, the suggestion that the observed decrements on a wide range of tasks in the elderly can be explained by a single underlying mechanism, decreases in the speed of information processing.

## Implications and Future Directions

A training regimen that efficiently increases processing speed is potentially greatly interesting, as faster RTs are reported to correlate with higher performance on tests of high-level cognition (Conway, Cowen, Bunting, Therriault, & Minkoff, 2002) and to be responsible for many of the observed changes in cognitive performance across the lifespan (Kail & Salthouse, 1994). For example, age-related declines in visual search, memory, and spatial-reasoning tasks appear to be largely due to task-independent slowing of processing speed in elderly subjects. Action-video-game training may therefore prove to be a helpful training regimen for providing a marked increase in speed of information processing to individuals with slower-than-normal speed of processing, such as the elderly or victims of brain trauma (Clark et al., 1987; Drew & Waters, 1986).

While the evidence reviewed here shows that these improvements generalize to a wide range of perceptual and attentional tasks, the extent of this generalization remains unknown. Because available work has focused on visual tasks, there is no information about generalization to other modalities, such as audition or touch. Similarly, because the focus has so far been on relatively fast tasks requiring decisions between just two alternatives (with RTs less than 2,000 milliseconds), it remains unknown whether more cognitively demanding tasks would benefit in any way.

While the mechanism of this generalization remains unknown, the need to maximize the number of actions per unit of time to achieve the greatest reward when playing action video games may well be a key factor. This will certainly be a promising avenue of research for future studies. A second important goal for future work is to gain a clearer understanding of the characteristics of the action-video-game play experience that favor performance enhancement. Much of what is currently known is descriptive (for instance, that fast-paced and visually complex games promote greater levels of learning than do slower games; see Cohen, Green, & Bavelier, 2007); there is a clear need to move toward more explanatory accounts. Hand-in-hand with such accounts, it will be important to isolate the characteristics of action video games that cause the observed changes and relate those characteristics to the mechanisms by which performance is altered. Finally, most of the games found to enhance performance are unsuitable for children in terms of their content and difficult for elderly gamers in terms of the dexterity of response and visual acuity required. Identifying which aspects of the games are relevant will allow the development of games that have a wide range of suitability and accessibility that can be used in clinical as well as educational applications. As with any research endeavor, a combination of basic theoretical research combined with evidence-led practical applications is the most likely to produce tangible results.

## Recommended Reading

Green, C.S., & Bavelier, D. (2003). (See References). The first study reporting changes in several different aspects of visual attention as a result of action-video-game playing incorporating a training study designed to establish causality.

Green, C.S., & Bavelier, D. (2006). The cognitive neuroscience of video games. In P. Messaris & L. Humphreys (Eds.), *Digital Media: Transformations in Human Communication.* New York: Peter Lang. A review of existing studies on the effects of action video games on perception and cognition as well as brain organization.

Kail, R., & Salthouse, T.A. (1994). (See References). A discussion of the role of processing speed in cognition.

## Reference

Bavelier, D., & Bailey, S. (2007). [N-back and pro-active interference memory tasks in action gamers]. Unpublished raw data.

Bherer, L., Kramer, A.F., Peterson, M.S., Colcombe, S., Erickson, K., & Becic, E. (2005). Training effects on dual-task performance: Are there age-related differences in plasticity of attentional control? *Psychology and Aging, 20,* 695–709.

Bialystok, E. (2006). Effect of bilingualism and computer video game experience on the Simon task. *Canadian Journal of Experimental Psychology, 60,* 68–79.

Cameron, E.L., Tai, J.C., Eckstein, M.P., & Carrasco, M. (2004). Signal detection theory applied to three visual search tasks— identification, yes/no detection and localization. *Spatial Vision, 17,* 295–325.

Castel, A.D., Pratt, J., & Drummond, E. (2005). The effects of action video game experience on the time course of inhibition of return and the efficiency of visual search. *Acta Psychologica, 119,* 217–230.

Clark, J.E., Lanphear, A.K., & Riddick, C.C. (1987). The effects of videogame playing on the response selection processing of elderly adults. *Journal of Gerontology, 42,* 82–85.

Cohen, J.E., Green, C.S., & Bavelier, D. (2007). Training visual attention with video games: Not all games are created equal. In H. O'Neil & R. Perez (Eds.), *Computer games and adult learning* (pp. 205–227). Oxford, England: Elsevier.

Conway, A.R.A., Cowan, N., Bunting, M.F., Therriault, D.J., & Minkoff, S.R.B. (2002). A latent variable analysis of working memory capacity, short-term memory capacity, processing speed, and general fluid intelligence. *Intelligence, 30,* 163–183.

Drew, D., & Waters, J. (1986). Video games: Utilization of a novel strategy to improve perceptual motor skills and cognitive functioning in the non-institutionalized elderly. *Cognitive Rehabilitation, 4,* 26–31.

Dye, M.W.G., Green, C.S., & Bavelier, D. (2009). The development of attention skills in action video game players. *Neuropsychologia, 47,* 1780–1789.

Feng, J., Spence, I., & Pratt, J. (2007). Playing action video games reduces or eliminates gender differences in spatial cognition. *Psychological Science, 18,* 850–855.

Green, C.S. (2008). *The effects of action video game experience on perceptual decision making.* Unpublished doctoral dissertation, University of Rochester, Rochester, NY.

Green, C.S., & Bavelier, D. (2003). Action video game modifies visual selective attention. *Nature, 423,* 534–537.

Green, C.S., & Bavelier, D. (2007). Action video game experience alters the spatial resolution of attention. *Psychological Science, 18,* 88–94.

Greenfield, P.M., deWinstanley, P., Kilpatrick, H., & Kaye, D. (1994). Action video games and informal education: Effects on strategies for dividing visual attention. *Journal of Applied Developmental Psychology, 15,* 105–123.

Kail, R., & Salthouse, T.A. (1994). Processing speed as a mental capacity. *Acta Psychologica, 86,* 199–225.

Li, R., Polat, U., Makous, W., & Bavelier, D. (2009). Enhancing the contrast sensitivity function through action video game training. *Nature Neuroscience, 12,* 549–551.

Madden, D.J., Pierce, T.W., & Allen, P.A. (1996). Adult age differences in the use of distractor homogeneity during visual search. *Psychology and Aging, 11,* 454–474.

Monsell, S., Sumner, P., & Waters, H. (2003). Task-set reconfiguration with predictable and unpredictable task switches. *Memory and Cognition, 31,* 327–342.

Palmer, J., Huk, A., & Shadlen, M. (2005). The effect of stimulus strength on the speed and accuracy of a perceptual decision. *Journal of Vision, 55,* 376–404.

Pashler, H., & Baylis, G. (1991). Procedural learning: I. Locus of practice effects in speeded choice tasks. *Journal of Experimental Psychology: Learning, Memory and Cognition, 17,* 20–32.

## Critical Thinking

1. How can psychologists use video gaming to study human thought and action?

2. Why is the study of reaction time and response accuracy important topics in the study of psychology?

# UNIT 4
# Learning

## Unit Selections

13. **Finding Little Albert : A Journey to John B. Watson's Infant Laboratory,** Hall P. Beck, Sharman Levinson, and Gary Irons
14. **Psychological Science and Safety: Large-Scale Success at Preventing Occupational Injuries and Fatalities,** E. Scott Geller
15. **The Perils and Promises of Praise,** Carol S. Dweck

## Learning Outcomes

*After reading this Unit, you should be able to:*

- Describe who "Little Albert" was and how identifying him solved an intriguing mystery in the annals of the history of psychology.

- Summarize the research involved in tracing the history and conditions surrounding Watson and Raynor's famous study with Little Albert.

- Discuss the origins of behavior-based safety initiatives.

- Explain the key elements of behavior-based safety programs and their effectiveness in reducing injuries and fatalities in the workplace.

- Describe the various ways that praise may motivate students to learn and the ways in which praise may impair learning.

- Distinguish between a "fixed mind-set" and a "growth mind-set."

## Student Website
www.mhhe.com/cls

## Internet References

**Classical Conditioning**
http://psychology.about.com/od/behavioralpsychology/a/classcond.htm

**Operant Conditioning**
psychology.about.com/od/behavioralpsychology/a/introopcond.htm

**Social Learning Theory**
teachnet.edb.utexas.edu/~lynda_abbott/Social.html

Do you remember your first week of college classes? There were so many new buildings and so many people's names to remember. You had to recall accurately where all your classes were as well as your professors' names. Just remembering your class schedule was problematic enough. For those of you who lived in residence halls, the difficulties multiplied. You had to remember where your residence was, recall the names of individuals living on your floor, and learn how to navigate from your room to other places on campus, such as the dining halls and library. Did you ever think you would survive college exams? The material, in terms of difficulty level and amount, was perhaps more than you thought you could manage.

What a stressful time you experienced when you first came to campus! Much of what created the stress was the strain on your learning and memory systems, two complicated processes unto themselves. Indeed, most of you survived just fine—and with your memories, learning strategies, and mental health intact.

Today, with their sophisticated experimental techniques, psychologists have distinguished several types of memory processes and have discovered what makes learning more efficient, so that subsequent memory is more accurate. We also have discovered that humans aren't the only organisms capable of these processes. Nearly all types of animals can learn, even if the organism is as simple as an earthworm or amoeba.

You may be surprised to learn, though, that in addition to researching memory processes and the types of learning you most often experience in school, psychologists have spent a considerable amount of time and effort studying other types of learning, particularly classical conditioning, operant conditioning, and social learning. Classical conditioning is a form of learning that governs much of our involuntary responses to stimuli, such as our emotions. Operant conditioning centers on how the consequences of our behavior shape and otherwise influence the frequency with which those behaviors subsequently occur and the circumstances under which they take place. Social

© Mike Kemp/Rubberball Images/Getty Images

learning happens when we learn from watching what other people do and how others' actions change the environment.

Historically, psychologists used nonhuman laboratory animals to study learning processes. Such research has led to many widely accepted principles of learning that appear to be universal across many species, including humans. Although nonhuman laboratory research is still a popular area of psychological inquiry, many psychologists today test and extend the application of these principles to humans under a wide array of laboratory and nonlaboratory settings. We explore these principles and their applications in this unit.

# Finding Little Albert
## *A Journey to John B. Watson's Infant Laboratory*

In 1920, John Watson and Rosalie Rayner claimed to have conditioned a baby boy, Albert, to fear a laboratory rat. In subsequent tests, they reported that the child's fear generalized to other furry objects. After the last testing session, Albert disappeared, creating one of the greatest mysteries in the history of psychology. This article summarizes the authors' efforts to determine Albert's identity and fate. Examinations of Watson's personal correspondence, scientific production (books, journal articles, film), and public documents (national census data, state birth and death records) suggested that an employee at the Harriet Lane Home was Albert's mother. Contact with the woman's descendents led the authors to the individual they believe to be "Little Albert."

HALL P. BECK, SHARMAN LEVINSON, AND GARY IRONS

In 1920, John Broadus Watson and Rosalie Alberta Rayner attempted to condition an 11-month-old boy, Albert B., to fear a laboratory rat. They subsequently reported generalization of the fear response to other furry objects (Watson & Rayner, 1920). Despite the investigation's lack of methodological rigor (Harris, 1979; Paul & Blumenthal, 1989; Samelson, 1980) and questionable ethics (Cornwell & Hobbs, 1976), the "Little Albert" study remains one of the most frequently cited articles in textbook psychology.

The interest created by Watson and Rayner's (1920) investigation is not due solely to the significance of the researchers' findings. Much of the attention the study has received has centered upon Albert. Without having been deconditioned, Albert moved from his home on the Johns Hopkins University campus, creating one of the greatest mysteries in the history of psychology. "Whatever happened to Little Albert?" is a question that has intrigued generations of students and professional psychologists (e.g., Blair-Broeker, Ernst, & Myers, 2003; Griggs, 2009; Harris, 1979; LeUnes, 1983; Murray, 1973; Resnick, 1974).

This article is a detective story, a narrative summarizing our efforts to resolve an almost 90-year-old cold case. It chronicles how seven years of searching, logic, and luck led my co-authors, my students, and me (Hall P. Beck) to the individual we believe to be Little Albert.

The investigation proceeded in two stages. First, we tried to learn as much as possible about Albert. Then we looked for an individual who matched these attributes. In this article, we introduce the lost boy's mother and surviving members of his family. We conclude by addressing the often-asked question: Whatever happened to Little Albert?

## The Setting of the Watson and Rayner Study

The Albert study emerged during two of the most productive and turbulent years of John Watson's life. Between his return to Johns Hopkins University following World War I and his resignation from the faculty in October 1920 (Buckley, 1989), Watson conducted pioneering research on infant development, the psychology of emotion (Watson, 1919f), and sex education (Watson & Lashley, 1920). In addition, he planned tests of the effects of alcohol on manual and mental performance (Watson, 1920a), edited a major journal, promoted scientific psychology to the general public, and corresponded with such prominent scholars as Robert Yerkes, James McKeen Cattell, Edward B. Titchener, Edward Lee Thorndike, and Bertrand Russell.

Watson also became romantically involved with his graduate student, Rosalie Rayner. Their relationship resulted in a highly publicized divorce trial and Watson's dismissal. The Little Albert investigation was the last published research of Watson's academic career.

## What Was Known About Albert

When we began our investigation, not a single fact had been verified about Albert after he left Johns Hopkins. Fortunately, more was known about Albert before he left the hospital. Watson's many descriptions of the study (e.g., Watson, 1924a, 1924b, 1925, 1928a, 1928b; Watson & Rayner, 1920; Watson & Watson, 1921) contain detailed reports of the conditioning procedures as well as personal information about Albert. Although there are troubling inconsistencies in Watson's various accounts (see Harris, 1979), his information offered the most reliable foundation from which we could begin to search for Albert.

According to Watson and Rayner (1920), Albert was assessed at 8 months 26 days, 11 months 3 days, 11 months 10 days, 11 months 15 days, 11 months 20 days, and 12 months 21 days of age. He "was reared almost from birth in a hospital environment" (p. 1). His mother was a wet nurse in the Harriet Lane Home for Invalid Children, a pediatric facility on the Johns Hopkins campus.

Albert was a healthy, unemotional child who rarely cried. The investigators chose him for conditioning because they reasoned that such a stolid child would experience "relatively little harm" (Watson & Rayner, 1920, p. 2). Convenience may also have influenced his selection. The Harriet Lane Home was adjacent to the Phipps Clinic, where Watson's Infant Laboratory was housed. A corridor connected the two buildings, which allowed the baby to be brought to the laboratory without exposing him to the winter air.

Although we cannot be sure why Albert's mother permitted him to be tested, financial incentives may have been offered. On January 12, 1920, Watson (1920b) wrote to Frank Goodnow, president of Johns Hopkins, that paying mothers $1.00 (2009 currency = $12.36, Bureau of Labor Statistics, 2009) per visit strained the departmental budget. One dollar may have been a significant sum to a young woman who supported herself and her child by selling breast milk.

A motion picture of the baby studies, made by Watson in 1919 and 1920 and distributed by the Stoelting Company in 1923 (Watson, 1923), provided a second valuable source of information. In 2004, Ben Harris kindly lent me a 16-mm version of Watson's movie that I converted to DVD format. The digitized images used in this investigation were made from Harris's copy.

The *Experimental Investigation of Babies* is the first (or one of the first) films made by a psychologist to disseminate research. In the initial scene, Watson and Rayner are shown preparing a baby for testing. Assessments were made of the baby's grasping, Babinski, nursing, and defensive reflexes as well as its infolded thumb, handedness, swimming movements, blinking, head steadiness, and reaching.

The film culminated in the sequences with Albert. A comparison of the movie and the Watson and Rayner (1920) article indicates that Albert was filmed at 8 months 26 days of age. During what today would be called baseline, he responded inquisitively but not fearfully to blocks, a marble, a crayon, a fire, a monkey, a dog, a rabbit, and a white laboratory rat. Overall, he fit Watson and Rayner's description of a robust and somewhat phlegmatic baby. In the film, Albert appears to be Caucasian.

Watson made no effort to condition Albert until he was more than 11 months old. The film shows Albert's response after seven pairings of the rat and a loud noise. The previously innocuous rat now evoked what Watson interpreted as fear. Similar but less intense reactions were then observed to a rabbit, a dog, a fur coat, and a Santa Claus mask.

We do not know why Watson waited almost two months to begin the conditioning phase of the study. The university closed for Christmas vacation from December 24 through January 4 ("University Register 1919–20," 1919), but that accounts for only part of the interval. Perhaps other professional and personal affairs intervened.

Information from *The Experimental Investigation of Babies* and Watson's write-ups were the starting points for our inquiry. The facts they provided were critical, but they were known to many investigators. Why, then, had no one located Albert? The obvious answer was that crucial information was missing. Therefore, my students and I set out to learn more about Albert and Watson's baby studies.

## When Did Watson and Rayner Test Albert?

Watson and Rayner (1920) reported Albert's age at each assessment, but they did not indicate the dates on which the study was performed. For their purposes, the testing dates were inconsequential. For our purposes, the testing dates were of great importance. If we could determine the assessment dates, then we could easily calculate Albert's birthday.

Most investigators (Beck, 1938; Buckley, 1989; Samelson, 1980) agree that the study was performed during the winter of 1919–1920. We hoped to narrow that time frame by concurrently examining Watson's descriptions of the study, his correspondence, and the film.

Mary Cover Jones (1974, 1975, 1976) recalled listening to Watson lecture on his work with Albert in the spring of 1919. However, the presence of Rosalie Rayner in many of the movie scenes, including those with Albert, is at odds with Jones's recollections. Rayner was taking classes at Poughkeepsie during the spring semester of 1919 ("Vassar College Transcript," 1919) and did not graduate until June 10, 1919 (D. M. Rogers, personal communication, September 30, 2008).

It is also unlikely that Albert was filmed in the summer or early fall. Watson left Baltimore to vacation in Ontario on June 6 and did not return until mid- or late September (Watson, 1919a). Classes started on September 30 ("University Register," 1919), at which time Rayner began working as Watson's graduate assistant. Watson may have been ready to film by early October, but an exchange of letters with President Goodnow reveals that he lacked the resources to do so.

During October and November, Watson made his case for the purchase of 1,000 ft (304.8 m) of film. The cost was $450.00 (2009 currency = $5,562.73), a considerable expenditure for the small, financially stressed university (Watson, 1919d). Although Goodnow (1919) doubted that the Budget Committee would approve the appropriation, he agreed to present a letter from Watson (1919c) detailing the benefits of making the movie. Watson's letter and the president's probable endorsement proved effective. Funds to purchase the film were authorized on November 19.

In a letter dated December 5, Watson (1919b) thanked Goodnow for procuring money for the motion picture. He wrote that he was only "waiting for a warm spell to start in on the work." The Watson–Goodnow correspondence suggests that filming commenced around December 5, 1919.

Efforts to determine the exact date that shooting began were inconclusive. As his letter implies, Watson may have begun filming on or shortly after December 5. Other documents in the Alan Mason Chesney Medical Archives of the Johns Hopkins Medical Institutions, however, leave open the possibility that shooting started before the 5th. Watson frequently complained to Johns Hopkins officials of a lack of staff support. Among other duties, the departmental stenographer sometimes served as a research and editorial assistant (Watson, 1918).

If the stenographer was otherwise occupied, the December 5 letter may have been dictated or handwritten some days before. In 1920, Johns Hopkins was a small university, so Watson probably knew that funding had been approved on November 19, 1919. He may then have bought the film and started shooting before his "thank you" note to Goodnow was typed. Although a precise date cannot be established, a reasonable estimate is that the first filming session occurred within a two-week period between November 28 and December 12, 1919.

Subtracting 8 months 26 days (baseline) from these dates allows one to approximate Albert's birth date. Albert was born between March 2 and March 16, 1919. Given that he was last tested at 12 months 21 days of age, we estimate that the final assessment occurred between March 23 and April 6, 1920.

One important document is inconsistent with these calculations. The Watson and Rayner (1920) article was published in the February 1920 issue of the *Journal of Experimental Psychology (JEP)*. If *JEP* was printed on schedule, then the investigation must have begun much earlier than we anticipated. Conversely, if the publication was delayed, Watson could have completed data collection in late March or early April and still included the study in the February issue.

# When Was the Watson and Rayner Study Published?

Watson was the founding editor of *JEP*, inaugurating the journal in 1915. By the time the United States entered World War I on April 6, 1917, two volumes had been printed and the journal was enjoying scholarly success. Publication was suspended as Watson and other psychologists joined the war effort. The Armistice was signed on November 11, 1918, and by early December, Watson was once more working at Johns Hopkins.

Before Watson could publish the third volume, he needed to solicit articles and reestablish subscriptions that had lapsed during the war. We wrote to the current editor of *JEP: General* hoping to discover when the first postwar issue was printed. Not unexpectedly, journal records do not go back to 1920 (F. Ferreira, personal communication, August 30, 2008). Searches of the Alan Mason Chesney Medical Archives and the Ferdinand Hamburger, Jr., Archives at Johns Hopkins as well as inquiries submitted to the Archives of the American Psychological Association and the Archives of the History of American Psychology at the University of Akron also failed to turn up any information on the publication date of the February issue.

An electronic mailing was sent to serialists throughout the United States asking if their libraries recorded when they received the first issue of Volume 3. A serialist at Johns Hopkins responded to a special request but was unable to find a receipt date. Fortunately, librarians at Kansas State University, Harvard University, and Cornell University located receipt stamps on their issues of the third volume (E. Cook, personal communication, July 14, 2008). The earliest of these was August 23, 1920, at Cornell. The stamp on that issue, however, is difficult to read; the year could be 1921. Two stamps were on the volume at Harvard, the first documenting receipt of Issues 1 through 5 and the second receipt of Issue 6. This might indicate that the first five issues were mailed as a package.

Our attempts to determine when the Watson and Rayner (1920) article was published included an examination of each page of the third volume for a telltale date. This effort furnished no pertinent information. We did uncover a letter to Adolf Meyer dated December 14, 1922, in which Watson (1922) commented that "the issues now come out on time." Presumably, Watson would not have made this statement unless previous issues of *JEP* were delayed.

Correspondence between Goodnow and Watson regarding the purchase of the film is also inconsistent with a February publication date. To illustrate, assume that the testing of Albert at 12 months 21 days occurred near the end of January 1920. That would place the filming of the baseline, when Albert was 8 months 26 days of age, in late September or early October of 1919.

Throughout October and November, Watson was seeking funds to buy film. Although investigators sometimes expend monies for which they are later reimbursed, Watson's letters to Goodnow imply that he had not yet purchased the film. In fact, Watson (1919c) claimed that "such a work has never hitherto been undertaken." Furthermore, he included four still photographs with his November 13, 1919, letter showing some of the tests he wanted to record.

It is hard to believe that Watson would have been so foolish as to try to mislead President Goodnow. If Watson were dishonest, his deception would have been revealed. The Phipps Clinic is a modest-sized building. Extensive filming could not have been conducted without the knowledge of Meyer, the clinic director, and other administrators.

Our estimation of the publication date also needed to account for the review process. Usually, several months or more pass between the submission and acceptance of a manuscript. As editor of *JEP*, however, Watson could have expedited publication by not sending the Albert article for review. Our searches found no document indicating that the Watson and Rayner (1920) study was ever reviewed.

The dates that universities received the journal, Watson's (1922) letter to Meyer, and his correspondence with Goodnow (1919; Watson, 1919b) all suggest that the first issue of the third volume was substantially delayed. The initial issue was probably dated as February because *JEP* was a bimonthly publication and not because it was printed at that time. As Boring (1937) noted, it was not uncommon to print early psychological journals after the dates on the covers of the issue. Although we were unable to establish the month of publication, we found no evidence indicating that Watson did not complete data collection in late March or early April of 1920. He could then have included the Albert study in the February 1920 issue of *JEP*.

# Traces of Albert

We had learned a great deal about Albert, but the most difficult part of our investigation, matching an individual to known Albert attributes, now awaited us. The early records from Johns Hopkins and the Harriet Lane Home (Park, 1957; Park, Littlefield, Seidel, & Wissow, 2006) mostly describe decisions and actions by administrators and physicians. They provide little information about the often nameless nurses, students, maids, cooks, and laundresses who labored in the university and its hospitals. We were especially interested in hearing the quiet voices of the wet nurses.

What evidence would Albert or those who knew him have left behind? Watson burned his papers late in life (Buckley, 1989), declaring, "When you're dead, you're all dead" (p. 182). No one knows whether those lost manuscripts included write-ups or notes on the baby studies.

If the child's actual name was Albert and if he had been treated at the hospital, then an examination of patient records might establish the boy's identity. Unfortunately, no patient records from the Harriet Lane Home remain from 1919–1920 (A. Harrison, personal communication, August 6, 2008). An attempt to examine the employee records for the names of wet nurses proved equally futile. All employee files from that time were either lost or destroyed (A. Harrison, personal communication, August 6, 2008).

There were no notes left by Watson and Rayner, no patient records, and no employee files. Although I could offer my students no direction at this point, Albert and his mother remained in the forefront of my thinking. I then remembered that 1920 was a census year. If a census taker came to Johns Hopkins, Albert's and his mother's names may have been recorded. A quick check revealed that a census had been taken of people living on campus (U.S. Bureau of the Census, 1920).

# Albert and the Missing Pearl

My co-author Sharman Levinson and I met in the refreshment line at the 2005 conference of the European Congress of Psychology in Granada, Spain. We discovered a mutual interest in Watson's career. Soon we were discussing Watson's views of psychoanalysis (Rilling, 2000), Adolf Meyer's role in Watson's dismissal, rumors that Watson made physiological recordings during intercourse (Benjamin, Whitaker, & Ramsey, 2007; Magoun, 1981) and, of course, the fate of Albert. Levinson expressed interest in the materials my students and I had collected, so after the conference I sent her digitized files of these documents. Among them was a copy of the Johns Hopkins census of 1920.

The Hopkins census was taken on January 2, 1920, between the baseline and conditioning phases of the study. Of 379 persons listed as living in Enumeration District 82 (U.S. Bureau of the Census, 1920), only one, the superintendent of the hospital, was designated as the head of a household. Everyone else, save the superintendent's wife, was listed as an "inmate." These inmates were not patients; they were employees or students.

According to Watson's writings and the film's subtitles, Albert lived almost his entire first year at Johns Hopkins. Hopes that his name would be recorded on the census were unfounded; no one younger than 14 years of age was listed. Evidence would later show that some employees living on the Johns Hopkins campus were parents of young children. Why then were no family members included in the census?

A likely explanation is that the census taker did not go to the residences, where she may have encountered children. Instead, she may have set up a desk in a central location and waited for the employees to come to her. Almost everyone she recorded was unmarried or widowed. Quite likely, the census taker never asked about children or spouses because she assumed that no families lived on campus.

A close examination of the census itself furnishes some support for this analysis. Most census records include an exact address, such as a street and house number. The Johns Hopkins census is unusual in that all the respondents are simply listed as living at "Johns Hopkins Hospital"; no attempt was made to specify the particular building or room where they resided.

The occupation of the employees provided the key to locating the woman that we believe to be Albert's mother. "Wet nurse" was not one of the occupations included in the census. Levinson, however, noticed that three women, Pearl Barger, Ethel Carter, and Arvilla Merritte, were listed as "foster mothers." Of all occupations reported for Enumeration District 82, this was the only one that could include wet nurses. *Foster mother* is a term encompassing a variety of activities involving maternal care for someone else's child. To advance our investigation, we needed to determine if these foster mothers were lactating during the winter of 1919–1920.

We were particularly interested in Pearl because she was Caucasian and her last name began with "B." Could Albert B. be Albert Barger? Several hundred hours of examining birth, death, census, marriage, and other records yielded no evidence of Pearl's motherhood. We remained open to the possibility that Pearl was a wet nurse. Still, all we had determined was that she lived on campus at the time of the Watson and Rayner (1920) study and probably worked with children.

After failing to find an association between Pearl Barger and Albert, we shifted our attention to the remaining foster mothers. Ethel Carter could have been a wet nurse; she had a baby on August 26, 1919 ("Johns Hopkins Hospital Records of Births," 1919). Ethel probably knew Albert, but she was not his mother. Ethel Carter was a Black woman, the only Black residing in Enumeration District 82.

The third foster mother, Arvilla Merritte, was White, 22 years old, and literate. Hospital records and documents from the Maryland State Archives revealed that Arvilla gave birth to an unnamed male Caucasian on March 9, 1919, at Johns Hopkins (Department of Health and Mental Hygiene, 1919; "Johns Hopkins Hospital Records of Births," 1919). These documents identify the father as William Merritte, age 25, born in Maryland. Mother and child were released from the hospital on March 21. Today, a hospitalization of 12 days would be indicative of a medical problem. Such lengthy stays, however, were commonplace at Johns Hopkins in 1919.

Further searching revealed no traces of Arvilla Merritte. Like Pearl Barger and Albert, she disappeared. Once more we were without direction. Despite these setbacks, we remained optimistic that somewhere there was a thread that would lead us to Albert. That thread turned up on Baby Merritte's birth record.

Arvilla resided on the Johns Hopkins campus, presumably with her son. If mother and son were living together, where was William Merritte? Father, mother, and son shared the same last name, but the relationship between the husband and wife seemed distal. Or, perhaps the marriage was fictitious.

The motivation for feigning marriage was obvious. In 1919, unwed mothers faced severe censure. A marriage, even an imaginary one, might protect the dignity of mother and child. The birth certificate listed Irons as Arvilla's maiden name. I asked one of my most trusted research assistants to begin looking for Arvilla Irons.

## A Johns Hopkins Foster Mother Introduces Her Family

A genealogical search revealed that Arvilla was the mother of Maurice Irons, who was the father of Larry and Gary Irons. Arvilla was an unusual name, and Larry and Gary Irons were currently living in Maryland. Most likely, we had found the family of the foster mother listed in the 1920 Johns Hopkins census.

Larry left an e-mail address on the genealogical website so that relatives might contact him. His invitation presented an opportunity laced with a problem. How does one explain to strangers one's interest in their grandmother's personal life? I composed a message describing the significance of Albert to psychology and requesting permission for further contact.

It was an exhilarating moment when I received a phone call from Gary Irons. Gary was more interested in family history than was his brother Larry, so it fell to him to call me. He confirmed that his grandmother worked at the Harriet Lane Home and gave birth to a son on March 9, 1919. She named the baby Douglas Merritte.

After speaking with Gary, I pondered the possibility that Douglas might be Albert. Arvilla was working at Johns Hopkins on January 2, 1920. The census placed her on campus when Watson and Rayner were conducting their investigation. If Douglas was born on March 9, Arvilla was probably lactating at the time of the Watson and Rayner study. Douglas shared three other Albert attributes; he was male, Caucasian, and born between March 2 and March 16.

How likely was it that a child born to a Johns Hopkins wet nurse would meet these three criteria? Rather than informally perform the computations, I made the necessary assumptions explicit. It seemed reasonable to estimate that half the wet nurses' children would be male, that half would be Caucasian, and that their births would be randomly distributed throughout the year. If these assumptions were correct, then the odds were 1 in 104 ($1/2 \times 1/2 \times 1/26$) that a child of a 1920 Johns Hopkins wet nurse would be male, Caucasian, and born between March 2 and March 16. Even if my assumptions lacked precision, the calculations demonstrated that it would be unusual for two individuals to have as much in common as Douglas and Albert.

The likelihood that Douglas was Albert also depended on the number of wet nurses living in the Harriet Lane Home. We identified two potential in-residence wet nurses from the 1920 census, but could there have been more? Initial plans called for as many as 10 wet nurses to be housed in the Harriet Lane Home (Park, 1957). However, blueprints (Wyatt and Nolting Architects, 1909), an early description of the facilities (Howland, 1912–1913), and the recollections of one of the original staff physicians (Park, n.d.) suggest that there were never 10, and probably no more than four, wet nurses concurrently living in the Harriet Lane Home.

If, as we suspect, Arvilla was a wet nurse, then Douglas is one of a very few children who could be Albert. But were Douglas and Albert the same person or nursery mates? The strongest argument against Douglas's being Albert was his name. In the following section we first make the case for Albert B. being the actual name of the baby in the Watson and Rayner (1920) study. Then we consider why, if the baby in the study was Douglas, Watson and Rayner may not have called him Douglas when writing their article.

## What's in a Name?

The main reason to believe that Albert was the baby's name is that in 1920 psychologists were not obligated to conceal the identity of their participants. The American Psychological Association did not adopt a formal ethics code until 1953 (American Psychological Association, 1953). Although Watson and Rayner (1920) have been castigated for not removing Albert's conditioned fear (Cornwell & Hobbs, 1976; Harris, 1979), we are not aware that they have been criticized for breeching confidentiality.

The lack of a formal ethics code does not mean that Watson or other psychologists were insensitive to confidentiality issues. Watson's other writings do little to clarify his views on confidentiality. In *Psychology From the Standpoint of a Behaviorist*, Watson (1919e) described assessments of babies Thorne, Nixon, and Lee. These names could be pseudonyms, but they could also be actual last names. In the same text, at least 18 babies are identified only by their initials. These initials may reflect a desire to maintain confidentiality, but they may simply be abbreviations.

To our knowledge, Albert is the only baby that Watson refers to by first name. Whether intentional or not, using the first name was a publicity-generating masterstroke. Giving the baby a name made him easier to relate to. Calling him "Baby A" or assigning him a number would have stolen his warmth, psychologically distancing him from readers. Watson may have realized early on a negative side effect of psychologists' later ethical practices. Confidentiality transforms people into faceless data points, often making it difficult for the general public to identify with participants and to fully appreciate the importance of psychologists' work.

The impetus for confidentiality may have come from Arvilla herself. As her grandchildren reported, she sometimes refused to share important parts of her life with her immediate family. It would have been within character for Arvilla to ask Watson to conceal her son's name.

Apart from confidentiality, there may be another reason why Watson did not write about Baby Douglas. He may never have known or cared what Arvilla named her child. Johns Hopkin had a rigid social system, and wet nurses were near the bottom of that hierarchy (Park, n.d.). Professors did not socialize with wet nurses. The information Watson and Rayner (1920) furnished about Albert is the type of data that would be expected in a case study and does not necessarily demonstrate a personal interest in the baby or his mother.

If Watson used a pseudonym, why did he choose Albert B.? Charles Brewer may have the answer to that question. At the 2008 meeting of the Southeastern Psychological Association, Brewer entertained my students and me with fascinating Watson stories. Between tales, I asked if Watson might have coined the name Albert B. Brewer reminded me that Watson's mother and maternal grandmother were very religious. Watson was named John Broadus in honor of a prominent Baptist minister, John Albert Broadus (Robertson, 1901; Watson, 1936).

If Brewer's inference is correct, then Albert B. may not have been the only instance of Watson's playful use of names. Shortly after his divorce was finalized, John and Rosalie married. They had two sons, William, born in 1921, and James, born in 1924. Brewer (1991) questioned whether "the combination of their sons' first names into 'William James' was fortuitous" (p. 180). Although Watson and William James advocated very different systems of psychology, Watson was a great admirer of his predecessor. There is no way to determine if these combinations are due to chance or were the product of a clever and verbally facile mind. My guess is that Albert B. derives from John Albert Broadus.

Our investigation would have ended at this point if not for the discovery of an old trunk. Inside were contents private and precious, the milestones of Arvilla Irons Merritte's life. Unless otherwise referenced, the following account was supplied by co-author Gary Irons, Arvilla's grandson.

## Arvilla's Story

Arvilla was born in 1898 in New Jersey, the youngest of John and Lizzie Irons's eight children. The family moved to rural Amelia, Virginia, around 1910. Arvilla's father was a carpenter and painter. Her mother was well educated and served as her church's pianist. Arvilla was an attractive teenager but possessed a volatile temper. Her family's nickname for her, "Cyclone Bill," suggests a less than tranquil disposition.

On December 18, 1915, Arvilla gave birth to Maurice Albert Irons, father unknown. All accounts agree that she was a devoted mother. Nevertheless, in 1918 or early 1919, Arvilla left Maurice to be raised by his grandparents and moved to Baltimore. Her departure was precipitated by another pregnancy. According to an 89-year-old niece, two friends told Arvilla that she could give birth at Johns Hopkins and then get a job at the hospital. Our first record of Arvilla in Maryland is the birth of her son Douglas on March 9, 1919.

No specific details of Arvilla's life at Johns Hopkins are known. Early in the early 1920s, Arvilla and Douglas left Johns Hopkins and moved near Mt. Airy, Maryland. There, Arvilla obtained employment with a farmer, Raymond Brashears. Raymond's wife, Flora Hood Brashears, was sickly and needed help caring for her home and young daughter.

Mrs. Brashears ("Deaths: Mrs. Flora Belle Brashears," 1924) succumbed to meningitis on May 15, 1924. In 1926, Arvilla married Wilbur Hood, known to the Irons family as Hoody. After 13 years of marriage, a daughter, Gwendolyn, was born to Arvilla and Hoody. Following Gwendolyn's birth, Arvilla's attention centered on home and daughter, but Hoody was more interested in socializing with his friends. The two grew apart and divorced about 1945. Arvilla remained healthy and vigorous throughout most of her senior years, dying in 1988 at the age of 89.

Gwendolyn came across her mother's trunk as she was preparing for the funeral. Inside were two colorized photographic portraits; one of Maurice when he was 4 or 5 years old and the second of an infant she did not recognize. The baby may have remained unidentified if not for a fortuitous event many years before. As a child, Gary inadvertently came across the open trunk. He questioned his mother about the pictures. She told him that the photographs were of Maurice and Douglas. The discovery of Douglas was understandably upsetting to Gwendolyn. Her mother had never told her that she had a second brother.

Gwendolyn gave the two portraits to Gary and his wife Helen. A short time later, their oldest daughter, Dana, found Gwendolyn still examining the contents of the trunk. Dana was given a small mitten, a baby's shoe similar to the one Douglas was wearing in his picture, and a black and white photograph from which Douglas's colorized portrait was produced. On the back of the photograph was written "Vincent Mitchell Studios, 111 W. Lexington Street, Baltimore." The studio was less than two miles from the Harriet Lane Home.

## Comparisons of the Portrait and Film

Gary agreed to mail me a photograph of Douglas's portrait. As I awaited the picture of Douglas, I made stills from Watson's (1923) movie. Regrettably, there were no close-ups of Albert, so enlargements were made to better observe the baby's features. Multiple stills were developed, because there was no single "best" shot. One frame revealed a distinctive eyebrow, another yielded a good look at the nose, and so on.

After the photograph of Douglas arrived, several colleagues and I scrutinized the images. We agreed that both boys had long arching eyebrows, an upturned nose, and a "Cupid's bow mouth." Several stills showed a dark vertical area near the center of Albert's chin. This could be the distinct dimple seen in Douglas's portrait. Alternatively, the low resolution of the old film leaves open the possibility that this area is a shadow.

Examinations of the eyes, eye sockets, and ears were less informative. In the stills, Albert's eyes look like black dots. The eye sockets lacked definition; we could not determine their lengths or the space between them. Also, in his portrait, Douglas was wearing a bonnet that obscured his ears. Although the photographic data were not ideal, neither I nor my colleagues saw any evidence to indicate that Douglas was not Albert. Thus, I deemed that a more thorough and expert biometric analysis was warranted.

An argument can be made that the shortcomings of the photographic evidence precluded meaningful biometric comparisons. The quality of Watson's (1923) movie limited the precision with which Albert's facial features could be measured. The enlargements of Albert's face were of such low resolution that they would not reproduce well in a journal.

An even greater problem was that we did not know Douglas's age when his portrait was taken. Infant facial features change rapidly, making it difficult or impossible to determine if photographs of babies of different ages show the same person (Wilkinson, 2004). I recognized that we could not conduct a confirmatory test, but a disconfirmatory evaluation might be possible. That is, the difference between Albert and Douglas might be so great that a biometric assessment could establish that the two boys could not be the same individual.

When in need, I have always relied on the kindness of scientists. Alan Brantley, formerly of the Federal Bureau of Investigation, and Randy Palmer, retired from the North Carolina Department of Corrections, began calling their contacts for me. Eventually they put me in touch with William Rodriguez of the Armed Forces Institute of Pathology. He graciously consented to compare the photograph of Douglas with stills of Albert taken from the Watson film.

As expected, Rodriguez (personal communication, June 13, 2008) pointed out that the fast rate of tissue growth during infancy ruled out a definitive identification of Albert. He then addressed the question: Did the photographic evidence reveal that Douglas and Albert were different people?

> My examination using a simplified cross-sectional ratio comparison appears to suggest that one cannot exclude the subject in question as possibly being baby Albert. There are certainly facial similarities based upon my observations, even taking into account the differential chronological age of the subjects depicted. In conclusion, the two photographs could be the same individual. (W. Rodriguez, personal communication, June 13, 2008)

The visual and biometric comparisons revealed a resemblance between the two boys. Nevertheless, if we possessed only the photographic data, we could not say with confidence that Douglas was Albert. Thankfully, the photographic evidence does not need to be considered in isolation. The photographic data can be examined in conjunction with our other findings to determine the likelihood that Douglas and Albert are the same person.

## Conclusion

This article describes our search for Little Albert. First, we sought to learn as much as possible about Albert. Then we tried to find a child who matched these attributes. After seven years, we discovered an individual, Douglas Merritte, who shared many characteristics with Albert. The findings are summarized below.

1. Watson and Rayner (1920) tested Albert during the winter of 1919–1920. At the time of the study, Albert and his mother were living on the Johns Hopkins campus. Census data show that Douglas's mother, Arvilla, resided on the Johns Hopkins campus on January 2, 1920.

2. Watson and Rayner (1920) stated that Albert's mother was a wet nurse in the Harriet Lane Home. According to family history, Arvilla worked in the Harriet Lane Home.

3. Douglas was born on March 9, 1919, so Arvilla was probably lactating at the time of the investigation. She could then have served as a wet nurse.

4. Documents suggest that there were never many, probably no more than four, wet nurses concurrently residing in the Harriet Lane Home.

5. Douglas was born at Johns Hopkins and was cared for by his mother after she left the hospital. Thus, it is highly probable that Douglas lived on campus with his mother during the winter of 1919–1920.

6. Assuming that Douglas lived with Arvilla, he, like Albert, spent almost his entire first year at Johns Hopkins.

7. Like Albert, Douglas left the institution during the early 1920s.

8. Albert's baseline was assessed when he was 8 months 26 days of age. By jointly considering Watson and Rayner's (1920) article, the film (Watson, 1923), and Watson's correspondence with Goodnow (1919; Watson, 1919b), we determined that baseline was recorded on or around December 5, 1919. Douglas was 8 months 26 days old on December 5, 1919.

9. Albert and Douglas were Caucasian males.

10. There are physical resemblances between the two boys. Visual inspection and biometric analyses of the Douglas portrait and the Little Albert film stills revealed "facial similarities." No features were so different as to indicate that Douglas and Albert could not be the same individual.

It is possible, but improbable, that these commonalities are happenstance. Although some of these attributes apply to more than one person, the likelihood that the entire set applies to anyone other than Albert is very small. The available evidence strongly supports the hypothesis that Douglas Merritte is Little Albert. After 89 years, psychology's lost boy has come home.

## Epilogue to a Quest

Gary Irons, his wife Helen, and I drove to the Prospect Cemetery where Arvilla is buried. Then we traveled several miles to the Locust Grove Church. Beside the church is a small well-kept cemetery. The heading on Douglas's gravestone reads, "Douglas, Son of Arvilla Merritte, March 9, 1919 to May 10, 1925." Below is an inscription, taken from Felicia Hemans's (189-?, p. 331) *Dirge of a Child:*

> *The sunbeam's smile, the zephyr's breath,*
> *All that it knew from birth to death.*

As I watched Gary and Helen put flowers on the grave, I recalled a daydream in which I had envisioned showing a puzzled old man Watson's film of him as a baby. My small fantasy was among the dozens of misconceptions and myths inspired by Douglas.

None of the folktales we encountered during our inquiry had a factual basis. There is no evidence that the baby's mother was "outraged" at her son's treatment (Rathus, 1987) or that Douglas's phobia proved resistant to extinction (Blum, 2002; Kleinmuntz, 1974). Douglas was never deconditioned (Prytula, Oster, & Davis, 1977), and he was not adopted by a family north of Baltimore (Cohen, 1979).

Nor was he ever an old man. Our search of seven years was longer than the little boy's life. I laid flowers on the grave of my longtime "companion," turned, and simultaneously felt a great peace and profound loneliness.

We will probably never know if Douglas experienced any long-term effects from Watson and Rayner's (1920) attempts to condition him. No family stories suggest that Douglas was afraid of furry objects or loud noises. Of course, a lack of evidence does not necessarily mean that the conditioning procedure had no ill effects or that Douglas's treatment was ethical.

Whatever happened to Douglas, better known as Little Albert? After leaving the Harriet Lane Home, the robust child shown in Watson's (1923) film became sickly. According to his death certificate (Department of Health, Bureau of Vital Statistics, 1925), Douglas developed hydrocephalus in 1922. Acquired hydrocephalus is often caused by a disease or condition such as encephalitis, meningitis, or a brain tumor (Turkington, 2002). We were unable to determine the source of Douglas's illness, but a reasonable conjecture is that he contracted meningitis from Flora Brashears.

The Albert saga did not end in a rural Maryland graveyard. It is still being written in his legacy to psychology. Although his conditioning apparently did not produce an outcry at the time the study was published (Buckley, 1989; Simpson, 2000), his treatment has come to exemplify the need for an ethical code to protect the rights of participants.

For all its methodological limitations, the Little Albert study (Watson & Rayner, 1920) became a landmark in behavioral psychology. Albert's conditioning helped stimulate a movement that reshaped the conduct and practice of our discipline (Benjamin, 2007). All behavior therapies trace their lineage to Mary Cover Jones's (1924) counterconditioning of Peter, a follow-up to the Albert investigation. Watson and Rayner's simple study of fear acquisition and generalization initiated the development of effective treatments for phobias (Field & Nightingale, 2009; Wolpe, 1958) and an array of other behavioral problems (Masters & Rimm, 1987; Rachman, 1997).

Albert's fame now transcends the Watson and Rayner (1920) study. As much as Pavlov's dogs, Skinner's pigeons, and Milgram's obedience experiments, the conditioning of Albert is the face of psychology. To many, Little Albert embodies the promise and, to some, the dangers inherent in the scientific study of behavior.

# References

American Psychological Association. (1953). *Ethical standards of psychologists.* Washington, DC: Author.

Beck, L. F. (1938). A review of sixteen-millimeter films in psychology and allied sciences. *Psychological Bulletin, 35,* 127–169.

Benjamin, L. T., Jr. (2007). *A brief history of modern psychology.* Malden, MA: Blackwell.

Benjamin, L. T., Jr., Whitaker, J. L., & Ramsey, R. M. (2007). John B. Watson's alleged sex research: An appraisal of the evidence. *American Psychologist, 62,* 131–139.

Blair-Broeker, C. T., Ernst, R. M., & Myers, D. G. (2003). *Thinking about psychology. The science of mind and behavior.* New York: Worth.

Blum, D. (2002). *Love at Goon Park: Harry Harlow and the science of affection.* Cambridge, MA: Perseus.

Boring, E. G. (1937). The lag of publication in journals of psychology. *The American Journal of Psychology, 49,* 137–139.

Brewer, C. L. (1991). Perspectives on John B. Watson. In G. A. Kimble, M. Wertheimer, & C. L. White (Eds.), *Portraits of pioneers in psychology* (pp. 171–186). Washington, DC: American Psychological Association.

Buckley, K. W. (1989). *Mechanical man: John Broadus Watson and the beginnings of behaviorism.* New York: Guilford Press.

Bureau of Labor Statistics, U.S. Department of Labor. (2009). *CPI inflation calculator.* Retrieved June 29, 2009, from www.bls.gov/data/inflation_calculator.htm

Cohen, D. (1979). *J. B. Watson—The founder of behaviourism: A biography.* London: Routledge & Kegan Paul.

Cornwell, D., & Hobbs, S. (1976, March 18). The strange saga of little Albert. *New Society,* pp. 602–604.

Deaths: Mrs. Flora Belle Brashears. (1924, May 24). *The Frederick Post,* p. 5.

Department of Health and Mental Hygiene, Division of Vital Records (Birth Record, BC). (1919). *Baby Merritte, 70288, 02/25/04/006.* In the Maryland State Archives (MSA T310–230), Annapolis, MD.

Department of Health, Bureau of Vital Statistics (Death Record Counties). (1925). *Douglas Merritte, Carroll County, 10 May 1925.* In the Maryland State Archives (MSA S1179, MdHR 50, 259–375, 2/56/62)(1), Annapolis, MD.

Field, A. P., & Nightingale, Z. C. (2009). Test of time: What if Little Albert had escaped? *Clinical Child Psychology and Psychiatry, 14,* 311–319.

Goodnow, F. J. (1919). Letter to John B. Watson, October 28, 1919. In the Ferdinand Hamburger, Jr., Archives of The Johns Hopkins University (Record Group 02.001/Office of the President/Series 1/File 115, Department of Psychology, 1913–1919), Baltimore, MD.

Griggs, R. A. (2009). *Psychology: A concise introduction.* New York: Worth.

Harris, B. (1979). Whatever happened to little Albert? *American Psychologist, 34,* 151–160.

Hemans, F. (189-?). *The poetical works of Mrs. Hemans.* New York: Thomas Y. Crowell.

Howland, J. (1912–1913). The Harriet Lane Home for Invalid Children. *Johns Hopkins Alumni Magazine, 1,* 115–121.

*Johns Hopkins Hospital Records of Births March 11, 1916 to October 28, 1919.* (1919). In the Alan Mason Chesney Medical Archives of The Johns Hopkins Medical Institutions (Box 504923), Baltimore, MD.

Jones, M. C. (1924). A laboratory study of fear: The case of Peter. *Pedagogical Seminary, 31,* 308–315.

Jones, M. C. (1974). Albert, Peter, and John B. Watson. *American Psychologist, 29,* 581–583.

Jones, M. C. (1975). A 1924 pioneer looks at behavior therapy. *Journal of Behavior Therapy and Experimental Psychiatry, 6,* 181–187.

Jones, M. C. (1976). Letter to Cedric A. Larson, July 28, 1976. In the Cedric Larson Papers, Archives of the History of American Psychology, University of Akron, Akron, OH.

Kleinmuntz, B. (1974). *Essentials of abnormal psychology.* New York: Harper & Row.

LeUnes, A. (1983). Little Albert from the viewpoint of abnormal psychology textbook authors. *Teaching of Psychology, 10,* 230–231.

Magoun, H. W. (1981). John B. Watson and the study of human sexual behavior. *Journal of Sex Research, 17,* 368–378.

Masters, J. C. & Rimm, D. C. (1987). *Behavior therapy: Techniques and empirical findings.* San Diego, CA: Harcourt Brace Jovanovich.

Murray, F. S. (1973). In search of Albert. *Professional Psychology, 4,* 5–6.

Park, E. A. (1957). [Description of the Harriet Lane Home]. In the Alan Mason Chesney Medical Archives of The Johns Hopkins Medical Institutions (Records of the Harriet Lane Home, Collection Harriet Lane Home, Series 4b), Baltimore, MD.

Park, E. A. (n.d.). *The Howland period from 1912 to 1926.* In the Alan Mason Chesney Medical Archives of The Johns Hopkins Medical Institutions (Records of the Harriet Lane Home, Collection Harriet Lane Home, Series 4b), Baltimore, MD.

Park, E. A., Littlefield, J. W., Seidel, H. M., & Wissow, L. S. (2006). *The Harriet Lane Home: A model and a gem.* Baltimore: Johns Hopkins University, Department of Pediatrics.

Paul, D. B., & Blumenthal, A. L. (1989). On the trail of Little Albert. *Psychological Record, 39,* 547–553.

Prytula, R. E., Oster, G. D., & Davis, S. F. (1977). The "rat-rabbit" problem: What did John B. Watson really do? *Teaching of Psychology, 4,* 44–46.

Rachman, S. (1997). The evolution of cognitive behaviour therapy. In D. M. Clark & C. G. Fairburn (Eds.), *Science and practice of cognitive behavior therapy* (pp. 1–26). New York: Oxford University Press.

Rathus, S. A. (1987). *Psychology.* New York: Holt, Rinehart & Winston.

Resnick, J. H. (1974). In pursuit of Albert. *Professional Psychology, 5,* 112–113.

Rilling, M. (2000). John Watson's paradoxical struggle to explain Freud. *American Psychologist, 55,* 301–312.

Robertson, A. T. (1901). *Life and letters of John Albert Broadus.* Philadelphia: American Baptist Publication Society.

Samelson, F. (1980). J. B. Watson's Little Albert, Cyril Burt's twins, and the need for a critical science. *American Psychologist, 35,* 619–625.

Simpson, J. C. (2000, April). It's all in the upbringing. *Johns Hopkins Magazine, 52,* 62–65.

Turkington, C. (2002). Hydrocephalus. In *The encyclopedia of the brain and brain disorders* (2nd ed., pp. 134–135). New York: Facts on File.

University Register 1919–20. (1919, November). *Johns Hopkins University Circular, 38*(9, Whole No. 319, New Series).

U.S. Bureau of the Census. (1920). Johns Hopkins Hospital, Baltimore City, Maryland. In *Fourteenth Census of the United States, 1920* (Enumeration District 82, Sheet 4A; Roll: T625_661). Retrieved June 29, 2009 from Ancestry Library database.

[Vassar College transcript of Rosalie Alberta Rayner]. (1919). In the Cedric Larson Papers, Archives of the History of American Psychology, University of Akron, Akron, OH.

Watson, J. B. (1918). Letter to Frank J. Goodnow, December 31, 1918. In the Ferdinand Hamburger, Jr., Archives of The Johns Hopkins University (Record Group 02.001/Office of the President/Series 1/ File 115, Department of Psychology, 1913–1919), Baltimore, MD.

Watson, J. B. (1919a). Letter to Bertrand Russell, October 4, 1919. In the Cedric Larson Papers, Archives of the History of American Psychology, University of Akron, Akron, OH.

Watson, J. B. (1919b). Letter to Frank J. Goodnow, December 5, 1919. In the Ferdinand Hamburger, Jr., Archives of The Johns Hopkins University (Record Group 02.001/Office of the President/Series 1/File 115, Department of Psychology, 1913–1919), Baltimore, MD.

Watson, J. B. (1919c). Letter to Frank J. Goodnow, November 13, 1919. In the Ferdinand Hamburger, Jr., Archives of The Johns Hopkins University (Record Group 02.001/Office of the President/Series 1/File 115, Department of Psychology, 1913–1919), Baltimore, MD.

Watson, J. B. (1919d). Letter to Frank J. Goodnow, October 27, 1919. In the Ferdinand Hamburger, Jr., Archives of The Johns Hopkins University (Record Group 02.001/Office of the President/Series 1/ File 115, Department of Psychology, 1913–1919), Baltimore, MD.

Watson, J. B. (1919e). *Psychology from the standpoint of a behaviorist* (1st ed.). Philadelphia: J. B. Lippincott.

Watson, J. B. (1919f). A schematic outline of the emotions. *Psychological Review, 26,* 165–196.

Watson, J. B. (1920a). Letter to E. L. Thorndike, May 13, 1920. In the Ferdinand Hamburger, Jr., Archives of The Johns Hopkins University (Record Group 02.001/Office of the President/ Series 1/File 115, Department of Psychology, 1920–1921), Baltimore, MD.

Watson, J. B. (1920b). Letter to Frank J. Goodnow, January 12, 1920. In the Ferdinand Hamburger, Jr., Archives of The Johns Hopkins University (Record Group 02.001/Office of the President/Series 1/ File 115, Department of Psychology, 1920–1921), Baltimore, MD.

Watson, J. B. (1922). Letter to Adolf Meyer, December 14, 1922. In the Adolf Meyer Papers (Unit I/3974/21), Alan Mason Chesney Medical Archives of The Johns Hopkins Medical Institutions, Baltimore, MD.

Watson, J. B. (Writer/Director). (1923). *Experimental investigation of babies* [motion picture]. (Distributed by C. H. Stoelting Co., 424 N. Homan Ave, Chicago, IL).

Watson, J. B. (1924a). *Behaviorism.* New York: Norton.

Watson, J. B. (1924b). *Psychology from the standpoint of a behaviorist* (2nd ed.). Philadelphia: J. B. Lippincott.

Watson, J. B. (1925). Experimental studies on the growth of the emotions. *Pedagogical Seminary, 32,* 328–348.

Watson, J. B. (1928a, February). The heart or the intellect? *Harper's Magazine,* pp. 345–352.

Watson, J. B. (1928b). *Psychological care of infant and child.* New York: Norton.

Watson, J. B. (1936). Letter to Thomas W. Harrell and Ross Harrison, June 16, 1936. In the Cedric Larson Papers, Archives of the History of American Psychology, University of Akron, Akron, OH.

Watson, J. B., & Lashley, K. S. (1920). A consensus of medical opinion upon questions relating to sex education and venereal disease campaigns. *Mental Hygiene, 4,* 769–847.

Watson, J. B., & Rayner, R. (1920). Conditioned emotional reactions. *Journal of Experimental Psychology, 3,* 1–14.

Watson, J. B., & Watson, R. R. (1921). Studies in infant psychology. *Scientific Monthly, 13,* 493–515.

Wilkinson, C. (2004). *Forensic facial recognition.* Cambridge, England: Cambridge University Press.

Wolpe, J. (1958). *Psychotherapy by reciprocal inhibition.* Stanford, CA: Stanford University.

Wyatt and Nolting Architects. (1909). [Fourth floor plan, Harriet Lane Home]. In the Architectural Drawing Collection Harriet Lane Home (HLH 004A), Alan Mason Chesney Medical Archives of The Johns Hopkins Medical Institutions, Baltimore, MD.

## Critical Thinking

1. Who was "Little Albert"?
2. What were the research steps involved in discovering his true identity?
3. Was the "Little Albert" study ethical?

**HALL P. BECK,** Department of Psychology, Appalachian State University; **SHARMAN LEVINSON,** Department of Psychology, The American University of Paris, Paris France; **GARY IRONS,** Finksburg, Maryland.

We are indebted to Charles Brewer for sharing his wonderful collection of Watson materials and for his editorial comments on an earlier version of this article. We also thank Ben Harris for imparting his extensive knowledge of the Watson and Rayner investigation. This research would have been impossible without the efforts of David B. Baker, director of the Archives of the History of American Psychology at the University of Akron; James Stimpert, archivist of the Ferdinand Hamburger, Jr., Archives of The Johns Hopkins University; Andrew Harrison, archivist of the Alan Mason Chesney Medical Archives of the Johns Hopkins Medical Institutions; and their staffs. Our greatest debt is to the many students who collectively volunteered thousands of hours on what was probably the most time-intensive baby hunt in the history of psychology.

Correspondence concerning this article should be addressed to Hall P. Beck, Psychology Department, 222 Joyce Lawrence Lane, Appalachian State University, Boone, NC 28608. E-mail: beckhp@appstate.edu

# Psychological Science and Safety: Large-Scale Success at Preventing Occupational Injuries and Fatalities

E. Scott Geller

At the time of this writing, the eyes of the world are on the oil crisis in the Gulf of Mexico—an ongoing, massive environmental catastrophe resulting from an April 20, 2010, oil-well blowout and explosion that killed 11 platform workers and injured 17 others. Most of these eyes are sympathetic, realizing the severe devastation to marine and wildlife habitats and the fishing and tourism industries. Many are also empathic, because they themselves have experienced similar disastrous consequences to humanity and its milieu as the result of a sudden unforeseen calamity.

However, many are also accusatory, attempting to find a "root cause" of this tragedy by assigning blame to the leader or CEO of one of the organizations involved. For example, the chief executive of British Petroleum, who had leased the oil rig from Transocean Ltd., condemned Transocean because it was their equipment and operating system that failed. But British Petroleum shareholders and the U.S. government criticize British Petroleum for insufficient oversight of its contractors. Other fault-finding parties hold Halliburton responsible because the rig explosion occurred about 20 hours after Halliburton workers cemented the production lines in the well casing to seal off the oil reservoir from the well bore. Plus, some accuse the U.S. government for allowing deep-well drilling in the first place and not imposing sufficient safety standards, supervision, and enforcement.

Many of these condemning eyes are looking for ways to punish the individuals who caused this horrific event. With substantial media attention, they seemingly believe large fines and incarceration will prevent such disasters in the future. Others appear convinced the only answer is to stop all off-shore oil drilling completely.

With 40 years of research and scholarship related to industrial and community safety, I see a missing link in all of these viewpoints. Here I explain how psychological science has been applied in organizations worldwide to turn human dynamics into an asset rather than a liability for preventing occupational injuries, fatalities, and calamities like the Deepwater Horizon oil spill.

## The Vision of a Total Safety Culture

Imagine a workplace in which everyone feels responsible for safety and does something about it on a daily basis. Top managers, supervisors, and line workers frequently go beyond the call of duty to identify hazards and at-risk behaviors, and they intervene to correct them as soon as possible. Safety is not considered a priority that can be conveniently shifted depending on the demands of the situation; rather, safety is a value linked to every priority of a given situation (Geller, 2001a).

In this Total Safety Culture, "accident investigations" are not conducted to find the "root cause" of an injury. In fact, the popular term *accident* is not used at all to refer to unintentional property damage or an injury that could have been prevented with the proper execution of a safety-related process or procedure. The terms *investigation* and *root cause* are also eliminated because these reflect a blame game and the unwarranted assumption the "accident" was caused by one independent variable.

Advocates for the Total Safety Culture realize severe punitive consequences following an undesirable behavior can cause more harm than good, by activating negative attitudes and instilling fear into the organizational culture, thereby stifling the reporting of close calls and minor injuries and discouraging the kinds of safety-related conversations needed to learn from mistakes and prevent more serious casualties.

An injury or close-call analysis replaces the accident investigation, and contributing factors are identified, rather than a root cause, in a fact-finding process that involves every relevant employee. The Total Safety Culture participants realize many behavioral, environmental, and person (e.g., attitudinal and cognitive) factors potentially contribute to a close call, injury, or fatality. This vision of a Total Safety Culture is actually a reality at numerous companies worldwide. How was this cultural shift attained? These corporations implemented an employee-driven behavior-based safety process (e.g., Grindle, Dickinson, & Boettcher, 2000; Sulzer-Azaroff & Austin, 2000).

# The Beginning of Behavior-Based Safety

In 1983, the Corporate Safety Director of Ford Motor Company asked me to help his safety management team increase safety-belt use among Ford employees at approximately 110 facilities. In brief, I developed training materials that explicated the basics of applying principles of behavior analysis to *define* the target behavior (in this case, vehicle safety-belt use), *observe* its frequency of occurrence, *intervene* to increase the frequency of the target behavior, and subsequently *test* the impact of the intervention by comparing frequencies of the target behavior during baseline, intervention, and follow-up phases. The process was labeled "DO IT," and the overall approach was termed *behavior-based safety*—a label I had been using since 1979 to refer to field research evaluating the impact of interventions designed to decrease risky behavior and/or increase safe behavior.

Besides teaching and implementing the evidence-based principles of applied behavior analysis (Baer, Wolf, & Risley, 1968), this large-scale program included the following components, which facilitate the sustained success of current behavior-based safety programs: (a) Safety leaders selected from each site attended a 2-day education/training session to learn behavior-based safety principles and customize practical applications for their work culture; (b) with a teaching manual, discussion, and practice workbooks,[1] the leaders were held accountable to select and train a behavior-based safety-steering committee at their site with the mission to develop and coordinate a DO IT process for increasing employee safety-belt use; (c) directed to follow the basic principles of behavior-based safety and report pre- and postintervention data (i.e., the weekly use of vehicle safety belts at their site), each behavior-based safety team designed an observation schedule and intervention plan to fit their situation; (d) behavior-based safety facilitators attended follow-up information-sharing sessions off site to learn from the successes and failures of other behavior-based safety teams and receive refresher instruction from me; and (e) the corporate safety office periodically distributed a newsletter that reported site-specific and overall results of the corporate-wide behavior-based safety program designed to increase safety-belt use, and it also described various innovative interventions developed by certain behavior-based-safety steering teams.

Following the success of this corporate-wide behavior-based safety program, which increased vehicle safety-belt use among all Ford employees from 9% to 54% in 1984,[2] the Corporate Safety Director asked me to help him expand the behavior-based safety process to address the human side of safety within Ford plants. This led to me teaching the principles of behavior-based safety at the facilities of several automobile-manufacturing companies, including Ford, General Motors, and Chrysler.

1. Focus intervention on observable behavior.
2. Look for external factors to understand and improve behavior.
3. Direct with activators and motivate with consequences.
4. Focus on positive consequences to motivate behavior.
5. Apply a DO IT process to improve intervention.
6. Use theory to integrate information, not to bias observation or limit exploration.
7. Design interventions with consideration of internal feelings and attitudes.

**Figure 1   The seven principles of behavior-based safety.**

After learning the seven basic principles of behavior-based safety (see Figure 1), representatives of work teams at an industrial site learned how to expand the DO IT process beyond one behavior. More specifically, they were shown how to develop and apply a critical behavior checklist to help achieve an injury-free workplace.

# Interpersonal Coaching

Employee teams used the worksheet shown in Figure 2 to develop a critical behavior checklist to fit their work process. Through interactive discussions, each work team defined safe and risky behaviors in their work areas relevant to each operating procedure shown in Figure 2. Some categories were irrelevant for a particular work group, and many behavior-based safety teams added another operating process to cover a distinct set of relevant work behaviors.

Workers used the specific critical behavior checklist designed for their work area to observe a coworker (always with the employee's permission) and then to offer behavior-based feedback by revealing the critical behavior checklist results. Percent-safe scores were calculated per one-on-one coaching sessions (with only the observer's name reported on the critical behavior checklist). These achievement percentages were then averaged across individual critical behavior checklists to obtain percent-safe averages per behavior, per work team, per department, and per plant. Work teams changed their critical behavior checklists regularly to target behaviors with the lowest percent-safe scores. This behavior-based safety coaching process was also used to assess barriers to safe behavior and facilitators of risky behavior, as well as environmental hazards.

# Worldwide Dissemination of Behavior-Based Safety

Starting in the mid-1980s, behavior-based safety became increasingly popular in industrial settings nationwide and subsequently, throughout the world. Several books detail the principles and procedures of behavior-based safety (e.g., Cooper, 2009; Geller, 1998, 2001a, 2001b; Krause, Hidley, & Hodson, 1996; McSween, 1995), and a number of systematic reviews of the literature provide solid evidence for the success of this approach to injury prevention (e.g., Grindle et al., 2000; McAfee & Winn, 1989; Sulzer-Azaroff & Austin, 2000).

| Operating Procedures | Safe Observation | Risky Observation |
|---|---|---|
| BODY POSITIONING/PROTECTING | | |
| Positioning/protecting body parts (e.g., avoiding line of fire by using personal protective equipment, equipment guards, barricades) | | |
| VISUAL FOCUSING | | |
| Eyes and attention devoted to ongoing task(s) | | |
| COMMUNICATING | | |
| Verbal or nonverbal interaction that affects safety | | |
| PACING OF WORK | | |
| Rate of ongoing work (e.g., spacing breaks appropriately, rushing) | | |
| MOVING OBJECTS | | |
| Body mechanics while lifting, pushing/pulling | | |
| COMPLYING WITH LOCKOUT/TAGOUT | | |
| Following procedures for lockout/tagout | | |
| COMPLYING WITH PERMITS | | |
| Obtaining, then complying with permit(s) (e.g., confined space entry, hot work, excavation, open line, hot tap) | | |

**Figure 2  A worksheet for developing a critical behavior checklist.**

Since the early 1990s, an annual "Behavioral Safety Now" convention, sponsored in part by the Cambridge Center for Behavioral Studies, has enabled several hundred employees from organizations around the world to share their behavior-based safety innovations and learn more about the human dynamics of injury prevention from leading consultants and researchers. In addition, several behavior-based safety consulting firms host their own annual "Behavior-Based Safety Users" conference to provide continuous learning and momentum for their clients.

# The Behavior-Based Safety Principles

Some labor unions have rejected behavior-based safety because they believe the process puts improper blame on the injured worker (Hoyle, 1998), perhaps because of the fault-finding bias referred to at the start of this article. In fact, when presented correctly, behavior-based safety targets employee behavior as only one dimension of an injury-prevention system while also engaging the wage worker in the discovery and improvement of environmental, engineering, and cultural factors related to hazard removal and injury prevention.

How does behavior-based safety facilitate open conversation about safety-related issues and ways to address them? When the principles and procedure of behavior-based safety are understood and followed by both managers and wage workers (as explained and explicated elsewhere; Geller, 1998, 2001a, 2001b), employees perceive increased choice and personal control over the safety and health of themselves and others. Their

paradigm for attaining and sustaining an injury-free workplace is transformed from reactive, failure-oriented, and individualistic to proactive, achievement-focused, and collectivistic.

The behavior-based safety principles listed in Figure 1 are founded on behavioral science as conceptualized and researched by B.F. Skinner (1953). The focus is on examining external factors (Principle 2) to explain and improve behavior and then applying the ABC model—A for activator, B for behavior, and C for consequence (Principle 3)—to design interventions for improving behavior at individual, group, and organizational levels (Cooper, 2009; Geller, 1998, 2001a, 2001b). Continuous learning and improvement occurs with a DO IT process (Principle 5) that monitors the impact of a behavior-change intervention and then uses process and outcome data to refine the intervention. The systematic evaluation of a number of DO IT processes can lead to a body of knowledge worthy of integrating into a theory (Principle 6).

Principles 4 and 7 reflect Skinner's concern for people's feelings and attitudes, even though he rejected unobservable constructs from scientific study as causes or outcomes of behavior. In Skinner's words, "the problem is to free men, not from control, but from certain kinds of control" (Skinner, 1971, p. 41). He goes on to explain why control by negative consequences must be reduced in order to increase perceptions of personal freedom. Similarly, subsequent researchers have demonstrated the detrimental motivational effects of contingencies that restrict an individual's perception of autonomy (e.g., Deci & Ryan, 1995).

Organizations that have implemented a behavior-based safety observation and feedback process have made great strides in achieving an injury-free workplace. However, the typical behavior-based safety approach does not address the person domain of safety reflected in Principle 7, including perceptions, attitudes, beliefs, expectancies, and cognitions of employees. Indeed, since the mid-1990s, several consultant groups have been marketing their services for industrial safety as more comprehensive or holistic than those providing behavior-based safety training and consultation.

Actually, many of the behavior-based safety trainers present a rather narrow view of the human element in injury prevention, with some of their teaching being potentially detrimental to safety. For example, it is common for a consultant to teach the ABC model as if antecedent stimuli "trigger" or cause behavior to occur, as when a conditioned stimulus elicits a conditioned response in classical conditioning. In other words, the critical role of choice is left out of the explanation of the three-term contingency, thus missing an opportunity to explain the impact of perceived autonomy on self-determinism (Deci & Ryan, 1995).

Furthermore, behavior-based safety consultants often state the ultimate goal is to make safe behavior habitual whereby individuals perform safely without thinking. While there are certainly circumstances when it is beneficial to respond automatically (as in emergencies and some sports activities), in most safety-related situations it is better to accompany the behavior with cognition. Self-talk before, during, and after a safe behavior enables the participant to anticipate and perform slight variations in a certain response as a function of situational changes while also providing personal affirmation and self-persuasion for the behavior, which in turn enhances self-accountability (Aronson, 1999) and self-motivation (Geller, 2005).

Moreover, almost every consulting firm targeting the human dynamics of industrial safety (and there are many such firms) includes a perception survey as an initial diagnostic tool. Subsequently, they purport to use the results of this survey to customize an intervention program for the organization. This approach clearly reflects a consideration of factors beyond overt behavior as contributors to hazard recognition and injury prevention.

These perspectives, especially the narrow and incomplete presentations by the army of behavior-based safety consultants worldwide, led me to develop an expanded version of behavior-based safety. The approach is called people-based safety and is described in books (Geller, 2005, 2008; Geller & Veazie, 2009), as well as in DVDs and accompanying workbooks I have developed and that have been disseminated by a leading training and consulting corporation.[3] This approach was also customized for application among health care professionals to reduce medical error and keep patients safe (Geller & Johnson, 2007) and is called people-based patient safety.[3]

The people-based safety and people-based patient safety approaches are not marketed as an alternative to behavior-based safety but rather as an evolution that integrates the best of behavior-based and person-based safety, as signified by the acronym ACTS: acting, coaching, thinking, and seeing.[3] The Acting and Coaching components are essentially behavior-based safety, except

self-coaching and self-management techniques are incorporated. These added processes are supported through self-talk, which involves the Thinking component of people-based safety and people-based patient safety.

The Seeing dimension of people-based safety and people-based patient safety takes into consideration the divergent views of safety-related issues, which should be assessed with a perception survey and considered when designing and evaluating interventions to improve safety performance. Person factors are addressed in this domain of people-based safety, including five person states shown to increase one's propensity to go beyond the call of duty to help another person (i.e., self-esteem, self-efficacy, personal control, optimism, and belongingness; Geller, 2001a, 2001b; Geller, Roberts, & Gilmore, 1996). After workshop participants learn the psychological definitions of these five states and take a survey to assess their current score per each state, they entertain practical ways to enhance these states in themselves and others, thereby increasing the likelihood workers will actively care for each other's safety.

## Conclusion

The example of the British Petroleum Deepwater Horizon tragedy illustrates a potential outcome of a worksite that does not report hazards, close calls, and minor injuries on a regular basis, thereby missing opportunities to correct environmental and behavioral factors that could contribute to a serious injury or even a fatality. These worksites, common in industries worldwide, measure their safety success exclusively by counting injuries per work hours (e.g., total recordable injury rate). By prioritizing such after-the-fact numbers over leading indicators of possible injuries, these industries cultivate a loss-control or failure-avoiding culture wherein workers are reluctant to report and discuss their safety-related mistakes.

News reports have suggested the oil-rig employees on the Deepwater Horizon worked in a culture that discouraged the reporting of hazards, close calls, minor injuries, and other factors that could have led to a serious injury if not corrected. While such a work culture is not unusual, it is inappropriate to claim such a culture existed on that Transocean oil rig without a systematic and objective analysis. Furthermore, it is unfair to assume a direct cause-and-effect connection between such a culture (if it existed) and the oil-well blowout and explosion.

However, it is intuitive that a work culture that attends to leading indicators of occupational injuries by encouraging the report and correction of factors that contributed to a close call or minor injury would prevent major injuries and fatalities. Here I have reviewed an ongoing approach in industries worldwide that successfully cultivates such a work culture by engaging workers in creating, applying, and evaluating a peer-to-peer behavior-based coaching process. Evidence-based reviews in books and journal articles support this kind of beneficial culture change accompanying behavior-based and people-based safety.

Nevertheless, the behavior-based and people-based safety procedures reviewed here may not be the only or most cost-effective way to develop a work culture that activates and reinforces proactive reporting and follow-up correcting of behavioral and environmental factors that might predict a serious injury or fatality. While the existing evidence gives a deciding edge to behavior-based and people-based safety in this regard, follow-up research is needed to explore alternative intervention paradigms and reveal procedures for enhancing the impact and durability of behavior-based and people-based safety programs, as well as to demonstrate the advantages (if any) of people-based safety over behavior-based safety.

## Notes

1. These original materials (including a manual, discussion guide, and practice workbook), expanded to address all safety-related behavior, are available from the author upon request at esgeller@vt.edu.

2. In personal communication, the corporate safety director (Dale A. Gray) estimated this program enabled Ford Motor Company to realize "a savings of over $22 million" and it "saved at least 20 lives and reduced injuries to more than 800 others."

3. In addition to the referenced books on people-based safety and people-based patient safety, more details about this approach to industrial and health care safety are available from Safety Performance Solutions, Inc., Suite 228, 610 N. Main St., Blacksburg, VA 24060; Tel: 540 951 7233; e-mail: safety@ safetyperformance.com. Log on to www.safetyperfonnance .com for more information and links to obtain numerous behavior-based safety, people-based safety, and people-based patient safety articles at no cost.

## Recommended Reading

Deci, E.L., & Flaste, R. (1995). *Why we do what we do: Understanding self-motivation.* New York, NY: Penguin Books. An easy-to-read review of the evidence-based determinants of self-motivation: competence, choice, and connections with others.

Geller, E.S. (2001). *Working safe: How to help people actively care for health and safety* (2nd ed.). New York, NY: Lewis Publishers. A step-by-step practical look at how to use behavioral science to improve health and safety in organizations and throughout communities.

Geller, E.S., & Johnson, D. (2007). (See References). Addresses the human dynamics of error prevention in health care by improving communication, teamwork, and the proactive examination of leading indicators of potential harm to patients.

Geller, E.S., & Veazie, B. (2010). *When no one's watching: Living and leading self-motivation.* Newport, VA: Make A Difference, LLC. An engaging, fast-paced, and true-to-life narrative, laced with leadership lessons, that teaches evidence-based ways to increase self-motivation in yourself and others.

Williams, J. (2010). *Keeping people safe: The human dynamics of injury prevention.* Lanham, MD: The Rowman & Littlefield Publishing Group, Inc. An easy-to-read procedural text providing the tools for developing an effective organizational safety culture, based on the principles of psychological science.

## Declaration of Conflicting Interests

The author declared he had no conflicts of interest with respect to his authorship or the publication of this article.

## References

Aronson, E. (1999). The power of self-persuasion. *American Psychologist, 54,* 875–884.

Baer, D.M., Wolf, M.M., & Risley, T.R. (1968). Some current dimensions of applied behavior analysis. *Journal of Applied Behavior Analysis, 1,* 91–97.

Cooper, D. (2009). *Behavioral safety: A framework for success.* Franklin, IN: B-Safe Management Solutions.

Deci, E.L., & Ryan, R.M. (1995). *Intrinsic motivation and self-determinism in human behavior.* New York, NY: Plenum.

Geller, E.S. (1998). *Understanding behavior-based safety: Step-by-step methods to improve your workplace.* (2nd ed.). Neenah, WI: J.J. Keller & Associates.

Geller, E.S. (2001a). Behavior-based safety in industry: Realizing the large-scale potential of psychology to promote human welfare. *Applied & Preventive Psychology, 10,* 87–105.

Geller, E.S. (2001b). *The psychology of safety handbook.* Boca Raton, FL: CRC Press.

Geller, E.S. (2005). *People-based safety: The source.* Virginia Beach, VA: Coastal Training Technologies Corporation.

Geller, E.S. (2008). *Leading people-based safety: Enriching our culture.* Virginia Beach, VA: Coastal Training Technologies Corporation.

Geller, E.S., & Johnson, D. (2007). *People-based patient safety: Enriching your culture to prevent medical error.* Virginia Beach, VA: Coastal Training Technologies Corporation.

Geller, E.S., Roberts, D.S., & Gilmore, M.R. (1996). Predicting propensity to actively care for occupational safety. *Journal of Safety Research, 27,* 1–8.

Geller, E.S., & Veazie, B. (2009). *The courage factor: Leading people-based culture change.* Virginia Beach, VA: Coastal Training Technologies Corporation.

Grindle, A.C., Dickinson, A.M., & Boettcher, W. (2000). Behavioral safety research in manufacturing settings: A review of the literature. *Journal of Organizational Behavior Management, 20,* 29–68.

Hoyle, B. (1998). *Fixing the workplace, not the worker: A workers' guide to accident prevention.* Lakewood, CO: Oil, Chemical and Atomic Workers International Union.

Krause, T.R., Hidley, J.H., & Hodson, S.J. (1996). *The behavior-based safety process: Managing improvement for an injury-free culture.* (2nd ed.). New York, NY: Van Nostrand Reinhold.

McAfee, R.B., & Winn, A.R. (1989). The use of incentives/feedback to enhance workplace safety: A critique of the literature. *Journal of Safety Research, 20,* 7–19.

McSween, T.E. (1995). *The values-based safety process: Improving your safety culture with a behavioral approach.* New York, NY: Van Nostrand Reinhold.

Skinner, B.F. (1953). *Science and human behavior.* New York, NY: Macmillan.

Skinner, B.F. (1971). *Beyond freedom and dignity.* New York, NY: Alfred A. Knopf.

Sulzer-Azaroff, B., & Austin, J. (2000). Does BBS work? Behavior-based safety and injury reduction: A survey of the evidence. *Professional Safety, 45*(7): 19–24.

# Critical Thinking

1. Describe how psychological scientists are applying behavior-analytic methods to reduce injury and death in the workplace.

2. Describe in detail the specific aspects of safety training in the workplace that seem to be particularly effective in reducing injury and death.

From *Current Directions in Psychological Science,* vol. 20, no. 2, April 2011, pp. 109–114. Copyright © 2011 by the Association for Psychological Science. Reprinted by permission of Sage Publications via Rightslink.

# The Perils and Promises of Praise

**The wrong kind of praise creates self-defeating behavior.
The right kind motivates students to learn.**

CAROL S. DWECK

We often hear these days that we've produced a generation of young people who can't get through the day without an award. They expect success because they're special, not because they've worked hard.

Is this true? Have we inadvertently done something to hold back our students?

I think educators commonly hold two beliefs that do just that. Many believe that (1) praising students' intelligence builds their confidence and motivation to learn, and (2) students' inherent intelligence is the major cause of their achievement in school. Our research has shown that the first belief is false and that the second can be harmful—even for the most competent students.

As a psychologist, I have studied student motivation for more than 35 years. My graduate students and I have looked at thousands of children, asking why some enjoy learning, even when it's hard, and why they are resilient in the face of obstacles. We have learned a great deal. Research shows us how to praise students in ways that yield motivation and resilience. In addition, specific interventions can reverse a student's slide into failure during the vulnerable period of adolescence.

## Fixed or Malleable?

Praise is intricately connected to how students view their intelligence. Some students believe that their intellectual ability is a fixed trait. They have a certain amount of intelligence, and that's that. Students with this fixed mind-set become excessively concerned with how smart they are, seeking tasks that will prove their intelligence and avoiding ones that might not (Dweck, 1999, 2006). The desire to learn takes a backseat.

Other students believe that their intellectual ability is something they can develop through effort and education. They don't necessarily believe that anyone can become an Einstein or a Mozart, but they do understand that even Einstein and Mozart had to put in years of effort to become who they were. When students believe that they can develop their intelligence, they focus on doing just that. Not worrying about how smart they will appear, they take on challenges and stick to them (Dweck, 1999, 2006).

> **When students believe that they can develop their intelligence, they focus on doing just that.**

More and more research in psychology and neuroscience supports the growth mind-set. We are discovering that the brain has more plasticity over time than we ever imagined (Doidge, 2007); that fundamental aspects of intelligence can be enhanced through learning (Sternberg, 2005); and that dedication and persistence in the face of obstacles are key ingredients in outstanding achievement (Ericsson, Charness, Feltovich, & Hoffman, 2006).

Alfred Binet (1909/1973), the inventor of the IQ test, had a strong growth mind-set. He believed that education could transform the basic capacity to learn. Far from intending to measure fixed intelligence, he meant his test to be a tool for identifying students who were not profiting from the public school curriculum so that other courses of study could be devised to foster their intellectual growth.

## The Two Faces of Effort

The fixed and growth mind-sets create two different psychological worlds. In the fixed mind-set, students care first and foremost about how they'll be judged: smart or not smart. Repeatedly, students with this mind-set reject opportunities to learn if they might make mistakes (Hong, Chiu, Dweck, Lin, & Wan, 1999; Mueller & Dweck, 1998). When they do make mistakes or reveal deficiencies, rather than correct them, they try to hide them (Nussbaum & Dweck, 2007).

They are also afraid of effort because effort makes them feel dumb. They believe that if you have the ability, you shouldn't need effort (Blackwell, Trzesniewski, & Dweck, 2007), that ability should bring success all by itself. This is one of the worst beliefs that students can hold. It can cause many bright students to stop working in school when the curriculum becomes challenging.

Finally, students in the fixed mind-set don't recover well from setbacks. When they hit a setback in school, they *decrease* their efforts and consider cheating (Blackwell et al., 2007). The idea of fixed intelligence does not offer them viable ways to improve.

Let's get inside the head of a student with a fixed mind-set as he sits in his classroom, confronted with algebra for the first time. Up until then, he has breezed through math. Even when he barely paid attention in class and skimped on his homework, he always got As. But this is different. It's hard. The student feels anxious and thinks, "What if I'm not as good at math as I thought? What if other kids understand it and I don't?" At some level, he realizes that he has two choices: try hard, or turn off. His interest in math begins to wane, and his attention wanders. He tells himself, "Who cares about this stuff? It's for nerds. I could do it if I wanted to, but it's so boring. You don't see CEOs and sports stars solving for *x* and *y*."

By contrast, in the growth mind-set, students care about learning. When they make a mistake or exhibit a deficiency, they correct it (Blackwell et al., 2007; Nussbaum & Dweck, 2007). For them, effort is a *positive* thing: It ignites their intelligence and causes it to grow. In the face of failure, these students escalate their efforts and look for new learning strategies.

Let's look at another student—one who has a growth mind-set—having her first encounter with algebra. She finds it new, hard, and confusing, unlike anything else she has ever learned. But she's determined to understand it. She listens to everything the teacher says, asks the teacher questions after class, and takes her textbook home and reads the chapter over twice. As she begins to get it, she feels exhilarated. A new world of math opens up for her.

It is not surprising, then, that when we have followed students over challenging school transitions or courses, we find that those with growth mind-sets outperform their classmates with fixed mind-sets—even when they entered with equal skills and knowledge. A growth mind-set fosters the growth of ability over time (Blackwell et al., 2007; Mangels, Butterfield, Lamb, Good, & Dweck, 2006; see also Grant & Dweck, 2003).

# The Effects of Praise

Many educators have hoped to maximize students' confidence in their abilities, their enjoyment of learning, and their ability to thrive in school by praising their intelligence. We've studied the effects of this kind of praise in children as young as 4 years old and as old as adolescence, in students in inner-city and rural settings, and in students of different ethnicities—and we've consistently found the same thing (Cimpian, Arce, Markman, & Dweck, 2007; Kamins & Dweck, 1999; Mueller & Dweck, 1998): Praising students' intelligence gives them a short burst of pride, followed by a long string of negative consequences.

In many of our studies (see Mueller & Dweck, 1998), 5th grade students worked on a task, and after the first set of problems, the teacher praised some of them for their intelligence ("You must be smart at these problems") and others for their effort ("You must have worked hard at these problems"). We then assessed the students' mind-sets. In one study, we asked students to agree or disagree with mind-set statements, such as, "Your intelligence is something basic about you that you

can't really change." Students praised for intelligence agreed with statements like these more than students praised for effort did. In another study, we asked students to define intelligence. Students praised for intelligence made significantly more references to innate, fixed capacity, whereas the students praised for effort made more references to skills, knowledge, and areas they could change through effort and learning. Thus, we found that praise for intelligence tended to put students in a fixed mind-set (intelligence is fixed, and you have it), whereas praise for effort tended to put them in a growth mind-set (you're developing these skills because you're working hard).

We then offered students a chance to work on either a challenging task that they could learn from or an easy one that ensured error-free performance. Most of those praised for intelligence wanted the easy task, whereas most of those praised for effort wanted the challenging task and the opportunity to learn.

Next, the students worked on some challenging problems. As a group, students who had been praised for their intelligence *lost* their confidence in their ability and their enjoyment of the task as soon as they began to struggle with the problem. If success meant they were smart, then struggling meant they were not. The whole point of intelligence praise is to boost confidence and motivation, but both were gone in a flash. Only the effort-praised kids remained, on the whole, confident and eager.

When the problems were made somewhat easier again, students praised for intelligence did poorly, having lost their confidence and motivation. As a group, they did worse than they had done initially on these same types of problems. The students praised for effort showed excellent performance and continued to improve.

Finally, when asked to report their scores (anonymously), almost 40 percent of the intelligence-praised students lied. Apparently, their egos were so wrapped up in their performance that they couldn't admit mistakes. Only about 10 percent of the effort-praised students saw fit to falsify their results.

Praising students for their intelligence, then, hands them not motivation and resilience but a fixed mind-set with all its vulnerability. In contrast, effort or "process" praise (praise for engagement, perseverance, strategies, improvement, and the like) fosters hardy motivation. It tells students what they've done to be successful and what they need to do to be successful again in the future. Process praise sounds like this:

- You really studied for your English test, and your improvement shows it. You read the material over several times, outlined it, and tested yourself on it. That really worked!
- I like the way you tried all kinds of strategies on that math problem until you finally got it.
- It was a long, hard assignment, but you stuck to it and got it done. You stayed at your desk, kept up your concentration, and kept working. That's great!
- I like that you took on that challenging project for your science class. It will take a lot of work—doing the research, designing the machine, buying the parts, and building it. You're going to learn a lot of great things.

What about a student who gets an *A* without trying? I would say, "All right, that was too easy for you. Let's do something more challenging that you can learn from." We don't want to make something done quickly and easily the basis for our admiration.

What about a student who works hard and *doesn't* do well? I would say, "I liked the effort you put in. Let's work together some more and figure out what you don't understand." Process praise keeps students focused, not on something called ability that they may or may not have and that magically creates success or failure, but on processes they can all engage in to learn.

## Motivated to Learn

Finding that a growth mind-set creates motivation and resilience—and leads to higher achievement—we sought to develop an intervention that would teach this mind-set to students. We decided to aim our intervention at students who were making the transition to 7th grade because this is a time of great vulnerability. School often gets more difficult in 7th grade, grading becomes more stringent, and the environment becomes more impersonal. Many students take stock of themselves and their intellectual abilities at this time and decide whether they want to be involved with school. Not surprisingly, it is often a time of disengagement and plunging achievement.

We performed our intervention in a New York City junior high school in which many students were struggling with the transition and were showing plummeting grades. If students learned a growth mind-set, we reasoned, they might be able to meet this challenge with increased, rather than decreased, effort. We therefore developed an eight-session workshop in which both the control group and the growth-mind-set group learned study skills, time management techniques, and memory strategies (Blackwell et al., 2007). However, in the growth-mind-set intervention, students also learned about their brains and what they could do to make their intelligence grow.

They learned that the brain is like a muscle—the more they exercise it, the stronger it becomes. They learned that every time they try hard and learn something new, their brain forms new connections that, over time, make them smarter. They learned that intellectual development is not the natural unfolding of intelligence, but rather the formation of new connections brought about through effort and learning.

Students were riveted by this information. The idea that their intellectual growth was largely in their hands fascinated them. In fact, even the most disruptive students suddenly sat still and took notice, with the most unruly boy of the lot looking up at us and saying, "You mean I don't have to be dumb?"

Indeed, the growth-mind-set message appeared to unleash students' motivation. Although both groups had experienced a steep decline in their math grades during their first months of junior high, those receiving the growth-mind-set intervention showed a significant rebound. Their math grades improved. Those in the control group, despite their excellent study skills intervention, continued their decline.

What's more, the teachers—who were unaware that the intervention workshops differed—singled out three times as many students in the growth-mindset intervention as showing marked changes in motivation. These students had a heightened desire to work hard and learn. One striking example was the boy who thought he was dumb. Before this experience, he had never put in any extra effort and often didn't turn his homework in on time. As a result of the training, he worked for hours one evening to finish an assignment early so that his teacher could review it and give him a chance to revise it. He earned a *B+* on the assignment (he had been getting *C*s and lower previously).

Other researchers have obtained similar findings with a growth-mind-set intervention. Working with junior high school students, Good, Aronson, and Inzlicht (2003) found an increase in math and English achievement test scores; working with college students, Aronson, Fried, and Good (2002) found an increase in students' valuing of academics, their enjoyment of schoolwork, and their grade point averages.

To facilitate delivery of the growth-mind-set workshop to students, we developed an interactive computer-based version of the intervention called *Brainology*. Students work through six modules, learning about the brain, visiting virtual brain labs, doing virtual brain experiments, seeing how the brain changes with learning, and learning how they can make their brains work better and grow smarter.

We tested our initial version in 20 New York City schools, with encouraging results. Almost all students (anonymously polled) reported changes in their study habits and motivation to learn resulting directly from their learning of the growth mind-set. One student noted that as a result of the animation she had seen about the brain, she could actually "picture the neurons growing bigger as they make more connections." One student referred to the value of effort: "If you do not give up and you keep studying, you can find your way through."

Adolescents often see school as a place where they perform for teachers who then judge them. The growth mind-set changes that perspective and makes school a place where students vigorously engage in learning for their own benefit.

## Going Forward

Our research shows that educators cannot hand students confidence on a silver platter by praising their intelligence. Instead, we can help them gain the tools they need to maintain their confidence in learning by keeping them focused on the *process* of achievement.

Maybe we have produced a generation of students who are more dependent, fragile, and entitled than previous generations. If so, it's time for us to adopt a growth mind-set and learn from our mistakes. It's time to deliver interventions that will truly boost students' motivation, resilience, and learning.

## References

Aronson, J., Fried, C., & Good, C. (2002). Reducing the effects of stereotype threat on African American college students by shaping theories of intelligence. *Journal of Experimental Social Psychology, 38,* 113–125.

Binet, A. (1909/1973). *Les idées modernes sur les enfants* [Modern ideas on children]. Paris: Flamarion. (Original work published 1909)

Blackwell, L., Trzesniewski, K., & Dweck, C. S. (2007). Implicit theories of intelligence predict achievement across an adolescent transition: A longitudinal study and an intervention. *Child Development, 78,* 246–263.

Cimpian, A., Arce, H., Markman, E. M., & Dweck, C. S. (2007). Subtle linguistic cues impact children's motivation. *Psychological Science, 18,* 314–316.

Doidge, N. (2007). *The brain that changes itself: Stories of personal triumph from the frontiers of brain science.* New York: Viking.

Dweck, C. S. (1999). *Self-theories: Their role in motivation, personality and development.* Philadelphia: Taylor and Francis/ Psychology Press.

Dweck, C. S. (2006). *Mindset: The new psychology of success.* New York: Random House.

Ericsson, K. A., Charness, N., Feltovich, P. J., & Hoffman, R. R. (Eds.). (2006). *The Cambridge handbook of expertise and expert performance.* New York: Cambridge University Press.

Good, C., Aronson, J., & Inzlicht, M. (2003). Improving adolescents' standardized test performance: An intervention to reduce the effects of stereotype threat. *Journal of Applied Developmental Psychology, 24,* 645–662.

Grant, H., & Dweck, C. S. (2003). Clarifying achievement goals and their impact. *Journal of Personality and Social Psychology, 85,* 541–553.

Hong, Y. Y., Chiu, C., Dweck, C. S., Lin, D., & Wan, W. (1999). Implicit theories, attributions, and coping: A meaning system approach. *Journal of Personality and Social Psychology, 77,* 588–599.

Kamins, M., & Dweck, C. S. (1999). Person vs. process praise and criticism: Implications for contingent self-worth and coping. *Developmental Psychology, 35,* 835–847.

Mangels, J. A., Butterfield, B., Lamb, J., Good, C. D., & Dweck, C. S. (2006). Why do beliefs about intelligence influence learning success? A social-cognitive-neuroscience model. *Social, Cognitive, and Affective Neuroscience, 1,* 75–86.

Mueller, C. M., & Dweck, C. S. (1998). Intelligence praise can undermine motivation and performance. *Journal of Personality and Social Psychology, 75,* 33–52.

Nussbaum, A. D., & Dweck, C. S. (2007). Defensiveness vs. remediation: Self-theories and modes of self-esteem maintenance. *Personality and Social Psychology Bulletin.*

Sternberg, R. (2005). Intelligence, competence, and expertise. In A. Elliot & C. S. Dweck (Eds.), *The handbook of competence and motivation* (pp. 15–30). New York: Guilford Press.

# Critical Thinking

1. How does praise motivate students to learn?

2. In what ways might praise impair learning?

3. What is the difference between a "fixed mind-set" and a "growth mind-set"?

---

CAROL S. DWECK is the Lewis and Virginia Eaton Professor of Psychology at Stanford University and the author of *Mindset: The New Psychology of Success* (Random House, 2006).

# UNIT 5
# Cognitive Processes

## Unit Selections

## Learning Outcomes

*After reading this Unit, you should be able to:*

- Describe the interesting roles that superstition plays in many of our lives.

- Summarize the causes superstitious.

- Explain working memory and its importance in everyday life.

- Discuss the central capacity limits of working memory.

- Debate both sides of the issues regarding which developed first, language or hand gestures.

- Summarize the current state of theory and research regarding the evolution of language.

- Describe the ways that our use of advanced technology is sometimes dangerous.

- Summarize the suggestions that psychologists offer for using advanced technology more safely.

## Student Website
www.mhhe.com/cls

## Internet References

**American Association for Artificial Intelligence (AAAI)**
www.aaai.org/AITopics/index.html
**Cognition and Thinking**
www.simplypsychology.pwp.blueyonder.co.uk/cognitive.html
**Cognitive Science Society**
http://cognitivesciencesociety.org/index.html

As Rashad watches his 4-month-old child, he is convinced that the baby possesses some degree of understanding of the world around her. In fact, Rashad is sure he has one of the smartest babies in the neighborhood, if not the world. Although he is a proud father, he keeps his thoughts to himself so as not to alienate the parents of less capable babies.

Gustav lives in the same neighborhood as Rashad. Gustav doesn't have any children, but he does own two dachshunds. Despite Gustav's most concerted efforts, the dogs never come to him when he calls them. In fact, the dogs have been known to run in the opposite direction on occasion. Instead of being furious, Gustav accepts his dogs' disobedience because he is sure the dogs are just not all that bright. Indeed, he is quite tolerant of his dogs' ignoring his pleas to come to him.

Both of these vignettes illustrate important and interesting ideas about cognition or thought processes. In the first vignette, Rashad ascribes cognitive abilities and high intelligence to his child; in fact, Rashad perhaps ascribes too much cognitive ability to his 4-month-old. On the other hand, Gustav assumes that his dogs are not intelligent—more specifically, incapable of premeditated disobedience—and therefore forgives the dogs.

As you read about Rashad and his child and Gustav and his dogs, you are using many well-researched cognitive resources. You must decipher lots of little marks on the page that we call words and make sense of them. As you go through this process of comprehension, you are forming thoughts—effortlessly and automatically—about the meaning of what you are reading. You may think to yourself, "Rashad is really biased about his baby's intellectual abilities" or that "It's not Gustav's dogs who lack intelligence, it is Gustav," after all, you've probably heard the old saying that "dogs are only as smart as their owners." As you are processing this information, you are also drawing on your memories of any experiences you may have had with babies or with dachshunds or both—although before you

© The McGraw-Hill Companies, Inc./Christopher Kerrigan, photographer

started reading this vignette, you probably were not thinking about babies or dachshunds. The story tapped your long-term memory story, and your previous experiences were brought to mind.

What you are experiencing firsthand is cognition, which psychologists like to define as the mental abilities involved in the acquisition, maintenance, and use of knowledge. Cognition is critical to our survival as adults. Of course, people think differently. Thus, psychologists have found interesting differences in cognitive development and in adult cognition. Psychologists have also studied, and continue to study, nonhuman animal cognition and how it helps these creatures adapt to their unique ecological niches in the world. These and other related phenomena form the heart and soul of cognitive science, which we showcase in this unit.

# The Many Lives of Superstition

Eric Wargo

We're nearing the end of a long campaign season in which every factor under the sun has come into play: Issues of age, race, gender, experience/inexperience. Round and round it goes, how it ends, nobody knows. At least one of the candidates on the ticket is not leaving anything up to chance. Famously superstitious, John McCain avoids taking salt shakers handed to him, tossing his hat on a bed, or commenting on his prospects without touching wood. An aide always has his lucky pen at the ready. And, a confirmed triskaidekophobe, he always carries 31 cents in his pocket (that's 13 backwards)—in lucky coins. Also, since his campaign headquarters happened to be on the 13th floor of an Arlington, VA office building, he renamed the floor. He's a powerful guy. It's the "M" floor now.

McCain's isn't the first campaign to make room for superstitious thinking. For example, when running Bill Clinton's 1992 campaign, James Carville was rumored to not change his underwear when his candidate was on a hot streak. McCain is reported to have developed his habits in his past life as a Navy pilot; aviation is another occupation that, like gambling and sports (see sidebar), seems to invite more than its share of rituals aimed at appeasing fickle fate. When there's a lot at stake, it can't hurt, right?

It appears to be human nature to believe our thoughts, our words, or our rituals can influence remote outcomes. Yet in his classic 1948 paper on the subject, "'Superstition' in the Pigeon," B.F. Skinner revealed that superstition isn't particularly human at all (Skinner, 1948). If you put a hungry pigeon inside a box that automatically dispenses food at regular intervals, a funny thing happens: After a while, the pigeon will acquire some sort of idiosyncratic behavior or tic—perhaps spinning in circles, or bobbing its head rhythmically, or some other strange, random, senseless behavior. In effect, the pigeon has developed a superstition about the source of the food and behaves just like a baseball player before a big game or a candidate before an election: just doing whatever it thinks it takes to guarantee a good outcome.

What made a fool of Skinner's pigeons is what makes fools of us all: conditioning. Specifically, what APS Charter Member Stuart A. Vyse (Connecticut College) calls "conditioning by coincidence" (Vyse, 1997, p. 71). Essentially, the food was dispensed, and the pigeon thought that whatever it happened to be doing at the time was the cause, so it kept on doing it. Subsequent feedings serve only to reinforce the behavior: The pigeon repeats its action, the food keeps coming, so why mess with a good thing?

If Skinner's pigeons had spoke Latin they may not have been so easily tripped up. Their error is a classic case of the common logical fallacy *post hoc ergo propter hoc*—"after this, therefore because of this." Temporal contiguity does not imply causality, as every good scientist knows, but the brain is a voracious and often indiscriminate pattern detector, always on the lookout for connections among phenomena and between the individual's own actions and favorable or unfavorable outcomes. Superstition arises from the natural tendency to seek connections that could, even remotely, be useful in controlling the world.

## An Acausal Connecting Organ

I'm writing about coincidence and superstitious connections, my thoughts wander, I'm thinking about my father, when unexpectedly the phone rings and—lo and behold—it's him on the other end. The famous psychiatrist and mystic Carl Jung coined the term "synchronicity" to describe meaningful coincidences that appear to defy the laws of probability (Jung, 1960/1973). In Jung's theory, unconscious archetypes appear to exert an influence on events in the world. His idea made sense not only to the magically minded (and to Sting, who wrote a hit song about it), but even to some hard-headed scientists at a time when people were first grappling with the implications of indeterminacy in physics. The rigorous theoretical physicist Wolfgang Pauli (one of Jung's patients) was persuaded that uncertainty on a quantum scale could allow the unconscious mind to have a hand in events.

As a theory of how things actually occur in the material world, synchronicity is easily debunked by the statistician. People are notoriously bad at understanding probabilities and statistics, and they generally underestimate the likelihood of "impossible" coincidences (see Vyse, 1997, for a discussion). The law of large numbers ensures that improbable events happen all the time. What's more, the *egocentric bias* causes us to disproportionly notice chance occurrences that have some bearing on our own interests and priorities. Ruma Falk, a specialist in the psychology of coincidence at Hebrew University, found that participants were more surprised by coincidences that happened in their own lives (either in the past or in the course of an experiment) than they were by identical coincidences that happened to another person. A coincidence that happens to another person, she says, seems unremarkable, just "one of many events that could have happened" (Falk, 1989, p. 477).

So the odds of my father calling on the phone at exactly the moment I am thinking of him are probably a lot larger than I imagine and are probably not too different from the odds against any number of other chance occurrences that I fail to notice because they don't matter to me personally. If they happen to someone else, I'll be much more sober in my interpretation.

Whether or not the coincidence of a phone call from someone one happens to be thinking of is random from the point of view of the indifferent universe, it is meaningful in terms of the associative links in one's head, and those links bias how we perceive and interpret the world. To be fair, this was part of Jung's point: Coincidences, in the end, tell us about ourselves. If we take it simply as a description of the brain's appetite for "meaningful" association and not as a statement of how the external world works, his oft-quoted definition of synchronicity, "an acausal connecting principle," fits quite well. The brain could be described as an "acausal connecting organ"—an insatiable meaning maker.

## The Power of Connection

The acausal connections that give rise to superstition may be temporal, as in the case of conditioning by coincidence, and they may also involve physical contact or similarities in form between objects. Perhaps the most familiar example of superstitious or magical thinking involves objects that are imbued with special significance because of what they resemble—for example, a picture of one's spouse or a religious icon. The *law of similarity* holds that a representation is linked to what it represents. People have difficulty throwing darts at a picture of a baby, for example (King, Burton, Hicks, & Drigotas, 2007). Objects also become special by virtue of what or whom they been in contact with—the *law of contagion.*

The laws of similarity and contagion are part of what is known as *sympathetic magic* (Rozin & Nemeroff, 1990).

Early anthropologists readily identified such forms of reasoning in non-Western cultures, but argued that they were really universal. What makes such beliefs superstitions is when they run counter to the causal theories held in one's culture. Vyse (1999) defines superstition as "beliefs or practices groundless in themselves and inconsistent with the degree of enlightenment reached by the community to which one belongs" (p. 19). One person's enlightenment might be another person's superstition, of course, and a devout Catholic might justifiably balk at being called superstitious when kissing a crucifix, as it reflects his consciously held belief system and that of his community. Yet like most people in our culture, he might readily cop to the charge of superstition if he wears his lucky sweater to a poker game.

In research on superstitions and contagion, sweaters are favorite props. APS Fellow Paul Rozin (University of Pennsylvania) and APS Charter Member Carol J. Nemeroff (University of Southern Maine) found that people are reluctant to wear sweaters that have previously been worn by those who have suffered a misfortune, such as an amputation, or by those with a strong moral taint, such as a convicted killer (Rozin & Nemeroff, 1990, 2002). And despite knowing that hepatitis or HIV can't be transmitted merely through bodily contact, people still feel averse to wearing clothes or touching objects that have belonged to people with those diseases (Rozin, Markwith, & Nemeroff, 1992). The law of contagion holds that "once in contact, always in contact"—thus some essence of the previous sweater wearer stays with the garment.

Rozin and Nemeroff point out that such beliefs have an evolutionary psychological rationale. Even if you can't catch a car accident or AIDS by wearing a victim's sweater, invisible germs are the means of contracting many of the diseases that would have afflicted our ancestors. Contagion thus would have been an adaptive heuristic for dealing with sickness before the advent of the germ theory of disease (Rozin & Nemeroff, 2002).

The notion that an object's history magically adheres to it also accounts for the positive value we place on original works of art, objects that have belonged to famous people, and objects of sentimental value. Bruce Hood (University of Bristol) and Paul Bloom (Yale) found that small children already sense that "authentic" objects have a special essence that remains with them and can't be copied. In their study, kids between the ages of three and six were shown a "copying machine" that could make duplicates of objects. Although the participants felt that a "copied" random toy or silver goblet was just as good as its original, they were uninterested in a duplicate of a spoon that had belonged to Queen Elizabeth II, because it wasn't the original. They also would not accept a duplicate of their favorite toy; they would only accept the original, "because it's mine" (Hood & Bloom, 2008, p. 459).

# Because It's Mine

Superstitious beliefs have historically been attributed to the lingering influence of childhood understandings about the world (see Rozin & Nemeroff, 1990) and were once considered mainly a problem for neurotics like baseball players and politicians. But using the framework of biases and heuristics pioneered by APS Fellow and Nobel laureate Dan Kahneman (Princeton) and his collaborator, the late Amos Tversky, psychology researchers have shown that superstitious behaviors and thought processes arise from the rapid, automatic judgments ordinary people routinely use to help navigate a highly uncertain world. Some are even at the heart of some of our most cherished beliefs about the self.

The already-mentioned tendency to be disproportionately fascinated with our own life and priorities is one of these biases. So is the tendency to over-attribute causal efficacy to one's own thoughts. According to Emily Pronin (Princeton) and colleagues at Princeton and Harvard, this tendency helps account for people's superstitious beliefs in their ability to supernaturally influence or cause real-world outcomes (Pronin, Wegner, McCarthy, Rodriguez, 2006).

In an experiment ostensibly having to do with the effects of voodoo curses on physical health, participants stuck pins into a doll representing a research confederate, who thereafter reported a mild headache. In one condition, the confederate arrived late, wore an offensive tee-shirt, and behaved in various irritating ways in order to provoke malevolent thoughts on the part of the participant. Participants in this "evil thoughts" condition subsequently confirmed having negative feelings toward the confederate and, more to the point, were more likely to think that their "voodoo hex" had caused his headache than were those in the control condition (in which the confederate had done nothing to make the participant dislike him). A second study showed something similar in the domain of sports spectatorship. Participants watching a blindfolded confederate attempt to shoot baskets with a toy basketball believed that their own visualizations (either of the shooter making the shot or of the shooter performing an unrelated action) helped the shooter when their visualizations were consistent with the shooters' successes.

These studies demonstrate that sympathetic magic has much to do with *apparent mental causation,* a principle that has been studied extensively by Pronin's coauthor, APS Fellow Daniel M. Wegner (Harvard). Wegner has shown that people infer themselves to be the cause of actions when they have had thoughts consistent with those actions immediately beforehand (and in the absence of other possible causes). In an experiment demonstrating this effect, participants mistakenly thought they had caused a cursor to stop moving on a computer screen if immediately beforehand they had been induced to think about stopping it, even though they did not in fact actually do so (Wegner & Wheatley, 1999).

> Very superstitious, writing's on the wall.
> Very superstitious, ladders bout' to fall.
> Thirteen month old baby, broke. The lookin' glass.
> Seven years of bad luck, the good things in your past.
> When you believe in things that you don't understand
> Then you suffer. Superstition ain't the way.
>
> —Stevie Wonder

Apparent mental causation explains more than just voodoo spells or our emotional investment in watching sports. According to Wegner, it is no less than the basis of the human experience of conscious will in a deterministic universe (Wegner, 2002, 2003). He argues that conscious will may be an illusion not unlike a magician's stage trick: We attribute to ourselves authorship of our own actions due to the fact that our self-monitoring thoughts coincide with them, yet the actions themselves actually have other, nonconscious causes. Neuroscientists have provided compelling evidence to support this view. In a famous (and to many, still mind-bending) finding by neurophysiologist Benjamin Libet, motor movements that were experienced by participants as consciously willed were actually shown to be initiated in the brain prior to conscious intention (Libet, 1985).

As we learn more about the brain's inner workings, it may turn out that belief in free will is just a somewhat less foolish-looking version of one of Skinner's gyrating pigeons: a superstitious belief arising from an understandable inference error about how events connect and unfold—a belief that, gratifyingly, puts our own thoughts center stage.

# Tempting Fate

The persistence of secret beliefs in the mind's influence over reality is particularly apparent when it comes to questions of luck. Going around casting spells or sticking pins into dolls will make people look at you funny, but no one bats an eye when someone knocks on wood after commenting on their own good fortune. McCain's campaign reportedly resounds with the rapping of knuckles on all available wooden surfaces. And McCain himself, like many people, avoids commenting on his fortunes at all. (At a New Jersey campaign event last winter, he refused to comment on what he would do after winning his party's nomination: "For me to start talking about what would happen after I win the nomination, when I have not won it yet, is in direct violation of my superstitious tenets" [Simon, 2008]). The ancient dramatic principle, "When hubris rises, nemesis falls," remains a widespread, deeply held intuition about fate; it's one that may also be explained in terms of heuristics and biases.

Jane L. Risen (University of Chicago) and APS Fellow Thomas Gilovich (Cornell) recently reported a series of experiments about tempting fate and why it is felt to be bad luck (Risen & Gilovich, 2008). In their first study, participants read a story about a student, "Jon," who had applied to grad school at Stanford. Jon's mother, being constitutionally optimistic, sent him a Stanford tee shirt as a gift even before Jon had heard whether he was accepted. One group of participants read a version of the story in which Jon, also optimistic, wore the tee-shirt after receiving it; the other group read a version in which Jon stuffed the shirt in the bottom of a drawer while awaiting Stanford's decision. As the researchers expected, Jon's acceptance prospects were rated higher if he avoided tempting fate by refusing to wear the tee shirt. In a second study, participants rated the likelihood of a student being randomly called upon in a large lecture class to discuss assigned reading that they either had or had not completed; results showed the same trend: Not doing the reading—again, tempting fate—seemed to make the prospect of being "randomly" called upon more likely.

Risen and Gilovich suggest that a negative outcome following a fate-tempting action will be anticipated by people as especially negative, due to the added embarrassment or regret of having knowingly harmed their prospects, as well as from having gone out on a limb by flaunting a well-known societal norm. They hypothesize that such an outcome becomes more cognitively accessible than its more positive alternative due to the tendency for people's attention to be drawn disproportionally to negative stimuli (a tendency especially found in younger people, such as the college students used in these studies; for a discussion of changes in this tendency with age, see Carstensen & Mikels, 2005). And since ease of thinking about something biases us toward seeing that thing as likely—what Tversky and Kahneman (1973) called the *availability heuristic*—the negative outcome seems disproportionally probable.

In short, people's beliefs about tempting fate are due to their tendency to accentuate the negative coupled with their tendency to believe in the likelihood of what they can readily imagine.

## Being of Two Minds

Risen and Gilovich tested their ideas about tempting fate in subsequent studies by measuring participants' response times when rating the appropriateness/inappropriateness of different one-sentence endings to variants of the stories used in the earlier studies. They discovered that Jon's wearing of the tee-shirt, for example, caused negative outcomes to spring to mind more rapidly than other possibilities. They also found that the tendency to interpret events in a

story superstitiously was increased when participants were put under the added mental burden of having to count backwards from 564, by threes, while reading.

The researchers interpret these findings in terms of *dual-process* accounts of cognition. The heuristics and biases giving rise to magical beliefs belong to associative, intuitive thought processes sometimes called "System 1" (Stanovich & West, 2002). System 1 thinking is fast and effortless, rapidly making judgments and associations. It is this system that enables us to react quickly to the ever-changing situations life throws at us. The downside is that its errors can be hard to detect or correct on the fly.

When we are not under time pressure or mental burden, though, System 1 thinking may be tempered or even countered by the slower, deliberative reasoning of "System 2." This system gives us the capacity to reflect critically on whether leaving one's umbrella at home really makes it more likely that it will rain, or on whether not doing the reading makes it more likely that we will be called on in class. In the Skinner Box called life, humans, unlike pigeons, can sit back and turn on the System 2 brain: "Well, what if I try *not* bobbing my head once, just to verify that my head-bobbing is what is causing the food to come out that hole?" We can even experiment, altering our head-bobs or speeding them up, or maybe adding in a little twist of the hips and a tap on desk, to see if that modifies the outcome in a favorable way. This ability to reason and reflect critically on apparent associations helps us not veer too far in the direction of mystical folly.

## What Do You Have to Lose?

The persistence of superstition in a society that values reason may be explained by how little it seems to matter. It is part of the very definition of a superstition that people will admit they don't rationally believe that rituals and thoughts have a causal influence; it just makes them feel better to pay their superstitions a certain heed, because what can it hurt? In the mental balance sheet, the trivial cost of seeming slightly irrational is generally outweighed by the size of the possible benefits.

Vyse (1997) notes that, perhaps even for Skinner's pigeons, there is a certain bet-hedging quality in superstitious behavior, making it reminiscent of Pascal's famous wager: Even if you doubt the existence of God or heaven and hell, you are better off behaving as if they exist, because you stand to lose in the one case more than you stand to benefit in the other. As Kahneman and Tversky (1979) show in their Nobel Prize-winning work, *loss aversion* is a stronger motivator than the promise of gain.

Pascal's Wager helps explain why superstitions are such a familiar feature in high-stakes domains like politics, aviation, and sports. In all these realms, there's a lot to lose. The statistics-obsessed sport of baseball, for example, is

# A Sporting Chance

Professional sporting competitions are not only notoriously high-stakes events, but are notoriously unpredictable. No matter how well an athlete performs, the outcome of a game or match is never entirely under his or her control. In the face of this uncertainty, it is not surprising that professional athletes and spectators alike take part in often elaborate superstitious rituals to ward off bad luck and ensure victory. Here are a few of those quirky rituals we've all come to know and love.

### Wade Boggs' Ritual Eccentricities

We all know about the pre-game chicken, but Boggs' rituals also included tracing the Hebrew letter *chai* in the dirt before batting, running wind-sprints at precisely 7:17 P.M., and touching the foul line only on his way back to the dugout.

### Michael Jordan's Shorts

Throughout his career, Jordan wore his NC State shorts beneath his Bulls uniform for good luck.

### Tiger Woods' Red Shirts

Tiger wears only red shirts on Sundays, as his mother believes it is a lucky color for him.

### Detroit Octopus Tossing

In 1952, a Red Wings fan tossed an octopus onto the ice to symbolize the eight wins needed to win the Stanley Cup. The Red Wings won eight in a row that year, and flying octopi have been a part of the playoffs in Detroit since 1979. Al Sobotka, the head ice manager, is responsible for cleaning up the creatures. He relished the opportunity to be part of the tradition, often twirling them over his head to excite the crowd. Although the big bad NHL won't let him twirl cephalopods on the ice any longer, the practice continues in the Zamboni entrance, so the Detroit fans can breathe easy.

### The World Cup Kiss

During the 1998 World Cup, French footballer Laurent Blanc would kiss goalie Fabian Barthez on his bald head before every game. France won that year.

### The Silent No-Hitter

Don't ever talk about a no-hitter during the game. Ever.

And where would sports be without curses?

### The Madden Curse

In 2000, the cover of Madden NFL began featuring images of NFL Players. All nine of the players featured since then have been plagued by some injury and six of them missed multiple games as a result, causing their team's record to suffer significantly.

### The Curse of the Bambino

After winning 5 World Series Championships in 15 years, the Boston Red Sox sold Babe Ruth to the New York Yankees, supposedly prompting the Bombers to win the most championship titles of any sports franchise in history and causing Boston's 86-year World Series drought. This is possibly the most famous curse in sports, both for how long it stood and for its dramatic breaking in 2004.

### The Curse of the Billy Goat

In 1945, Greek immigrant Billy Sianis brought his pet goat with him to Game 4 of the World Series, the last Series the Chicago Cubs have ever played in. After eventually being ejected from the stadium, Sianis allegedly placed a curse on the team, claiming that the Cubs would never play in another World Series at Wrigley Field. So far he's been right, and according to Sianis' nephew Sam Sianis, the Cubs may only dispel the curse by demonstrating a genuine affection for goats.

also famously superstition-obsessed. Wade Boggs, former NY Yankees third baseman, is a well-known example: He consumed chicken before every game, along with a host of other rituals, to help ensure success (See Vyse, 1997, and the sidebar).

High stakes are often compounded by unpredictability of outcome; in sports, outcomes are (almost by definition) unpredictable and subject to many variables outside an individual athlete's control. Dutch psychologists Michaela Schippers (Erasmus University, Rotterdam) and APS Fellow Paul A.M. Van Lange (Free University, Amsterdam) have found that superstitious behavior in top athletes positively correlates with the importance of the game and negatively correlates with the degree of control an athlete feels (Schippers & Van Lange, 2005).

*Feelings* of control are not the same as control, of course. Although eating chicken for good luck may not hurt anybody (except the chicken), superstitious thinking about the way the world works undoubtedly has harmful repercussions. Failing to critically examine superstitious feelings about the contagious qualities of misfortune, for example, can serve to further alienate sufferers from disease and members of stigmatized groups whose conditions cannot be transmitted through contact. Rozin and Nemeroff speculate that fear of AIDS contributed to a decline in people's willingness to *donate* blood, due to "backwards" contagion (Rozin & Nemeroff, 1990). It's no coincidence (and certainly no synchronicity) that the System 1 mind that harbors such irrational fears is also the home of our most harmful racial, class, and gender prejudices.

# If You're Feeling Blue . . .

In a memorable scene from *Casablanca*, Humphrey Bogart's piano-playing sidekick Sam sings "When you are blue, just knock on wood." Whether or not it really works, reducing stress does seem to be the reason people engage in the ritual. In general, magical thinking is known to increase in conditions of stress or danger (see Keinan, 2002), and people with a higher need for control may engage in more superstitious behavior under stress than do their more blasé counterparts.

Tel Aviv University psychologist Giora Keinan (2002) measured the knocks on wood made by participants during interviews that included some questions designed to elicit a feeling of tempting fate, like "Have you ever been involved in a fatal road accident?" Half of the participants were interviewed while under a condition of stress, half an hour before taking a test. All the participants also filled out a questionnaire that assessed their overall desire for control over their environment. Half of the participants knocked on wood at least once during the 11-question interview. Keinan also found that there was a greater difference in number of knocks between the high- and low-stress conditions in participants who felt a greater desire for control.

Even when superstitious beliefs and rituals don't directly influence events or outcomes, they actually do have a causal role in at least one important area of our lives; growing evidence shows that they may reduce our stress, and thus have a real (i.e., causal) relationship to our well-being. Health, of course, is another domain, like politics and sports, in which the stakes are high, outcomes uncertain, and a sense of personal control hard to come by, and stress is increasingly being understood as a central factor in health and illness (see "Understanding the Have-Knots," *Observer*, December 2007). The search for explanations and causes has a stress-regulatory function (Keinan & Sivan, 2001) even when those causes are far-fetched. APS Fellow and Charter Member Shelley Taylor showed that breast cancer patients' search for theories about the causes of their illness, and the illusions of control those theories fostered (however accurate or inaccurate), had a favorable influence on their adjustment. As such, she argued that positive self-deception is a worthy goal of therapy (Taylor, 1983; Taylor & Brown, 1988).

A reasoned, realistic, unsuperstitious view of the self and the world doesn't necessarily lead to happiness; if anything, the opposite may be closer to the truth. Superstitious thinking is fostered by positive affect (King et al., 2007); and depression, conversely, can be described as "a loss of positive illusions" (Vyse, 1997, p. 132). Future research on superstition will need to weigh its offenses against reason against its positively self-deceiving, therapeutic properties. In the end, it may be necessary to distinguish between superstitions that ultimately harm ourselves or others, and those that simply help us bird brains make sense of a senseless universe.

# References

Carstensen, L.L., & Mikels, J.A. (2005). At the intersection of emotion and cognition: Aging and the positivity effect. *Current Directions in Psychological Science, 14,* 117–121.

Falk, R. (1989). Judgment of coincidences: Mine versus yours. *American Journal of Psychology, 102,* 477–493.

Hood, B.M., & Bloom, P. (2008). Children prefer certain original objects over perfect duplicates. *Cognition, 106,* 455–462.

Jung, C.G. (1973). *Synchronicity: An acausal connecting principle.* Princeton, NJ: Bollingen. (Original work published 1960)

Kahneman, D., & Tversky, A. (1979). Prospect theory: An analysis of decisions under risk. *Econometrica, 47,* 263–291.

Keinan, G. (2002). The effects of stress and desire for control on superstitious behavior. *Personality and Social Psychology Bulletin, 28,* 102–108.

Keinan, G., & Sivan, D. (2001). The effects of stress and desire for control on the formation of causal attributions. *Journal of Research in Personality, 35,* 127–137.

King, L.A., Burton, C.M., Hicks, J.A., & Drigotas, S.M. (2007). Ghosts, UFOs, and magic: Positive affect and the experiential system. *Journal of Personality and Social Psychology, 92,* 905–919.

Libet, B. (1985). Unconscious cerebral initiative and the role of conscious will in voluntary action. *Behavioral and Brain Sciences, 8,* 529–566.

Pronin, E., Wegner, D.M., McCarthy, K., & Rodriguez, S. (2006). Everyday magical powers: The role of apparent mental causation in the overestimation of personal influence. *Journal of Personality and Social Psychology, 91,* 218–231.

Risen, J.L., & Gilovich, T. (2008). Why people are reluctant to tempt fate. *Journal of Personality and Social Psychology, 95,* 293–307.

Rozin, P., Markwith, M., & Nemeroff, C. (2006). Magical contagion beliefs and fear of AIDS. *Journal of Applied Social Psychology, 22,* 1081–1092.

Rozin, P., & Nemeroff, C. (1990). The laws of sympathetic magic: A psychological analysis of similarity and contagion. In J. Stigler, G. Herdt, & R.A. Shweder (Eds.). *Cultural psychology: Essays on comparative human development* (pp. 205–232). Cambridge, United Kingdom: Cambridge University Press.

Rozin, P., & Nemeroff, C. (2002). Sympathetic magical thinking: The contagion and similarity "heuristics." In T. Gilovich, D.W. Griffin, & D. Kahneman (Eds.), *Heuristics and biases: The psychology of intuitive judgement* (pp.201–216). Cambridge, United Kingdom: Cambridge University Press.

Schippers, M., & Van Lange, P.A.M. (2005). *The psychological benefits of superstitious rituals in top sport* (ERIM Report Series Reference No. ERS-2005-071-ORG). Retrieved September 4, 2008, from http://ssrn.com/abstract=861417

Simon, J. (2008, February 4). *Superstitious McCain won't speculate on the future.* Retrieved September 5, 2008, from http://politicalticker.blogs.cnn.com/2008/02/04/superstitious-mccain-wont-speculate-on-the-future/

Skinner, B.F. (1948). "Superstition" in the pigeon. *Journal of Experimental Psychology, 38,* 168–172.

Stanovich, K.E., & West, R.F. (2002). Individual differences in reasoning. In T. Gilovich, D. Griffin, & D. Kahneman (Eds.), *Heuristics and biases* (pp. 421–440). Cambridge, United Kingdom: Cambridge University Press.

Taylor, S.E. (1983). Adjustment to threatening events: A theory of cognitive adaptation. *American Psychologist, 38,* 1161–1173.

Taylor, S.E., & Brown, J.D. (1988). Illusion and well-being: A social-psychological perspective on mental health. *Psychological Bulletin, 103,* 193–210.

Tversky, A., & Kahneman, D. (1973). Availability: A heuristic for judging frequency and probability. *Cognitive Psychology, 5,* 207–232.

Vyse, S.A. (1997). *Believing in magic: The psychology of superstition.* New York: Oxford University Press.

Wegner, D.M. (2002). *The illusion of conscious will.* Cambridge, MA: MIT Press.

Wegner, D.M. (2003). The mind's best trick: How we experience conscious will. *Trends in Cognitive Sciences, 7,* 65–69.

Wegner, D.M., & Wheatley, T. (1999). Apparent mental causation: Sources of the experience of will. *American Psychologist, 54,* 480–492.

## Critical Thinking

1. What causes people to be superstitious?
2. How does superstition influence our lives?

From *APS Observer,* vol. 21, no. 9, October 2008, pp. 1–7. Copyright © 2008 by American Psychological Society. Reprinted by permission via Copyright Clearance Center.

# The Magical Mystery Four: How Is Working Memory Capacity Limited, and Why?

Working memory storage capacity is important because cognitive tasks can be completed only with sufficient ability to hold information as it is processed. The ability to repeat information depends on task demands but can be distinguished from a more constant, underlying mechanism: a central memory store limited to 3 to 5 meaningful items for young adults. I discuss why this central limit is important, how it can be observed, how it differs among individuals, and why it may exist.

NELSON COWAN

I t may not really be magical, but it is a mystery.[1] There are severe limits in how much can be kept in mind at once (about 3–5 items). When, how, and why does the limit occur?

In a famous paper humorously describing "the magical number seven plus or minus two," Miller (1956) claimed to be persecuted by an integer. He demonstrated that one can repeat back a list of no more than about seven randomly ordered, meaningful items or *chunks* (which could be letters, digits, or words). Other research has yielded different results, though. Young adults can recall only 3 or 4 longer verbal chunks, such as idioms or short sentences (Gilchrist, Cowan, & Naveh-Benjamin, 2008). Some have shrugged their shoulders, concluding that the limit "Just depends" on details of the memory task. Recent research, however, indicates when and how the limit is predictable.

The recall limit is important because it measures what is termed *working memory* (Baddeley & Hitch, 1974; Miller, Galanter, & Pribram, 1960), the few temporarily active thoughts. Working memory is used in mental tasks, such as language comprehension (for example, retaining ideas from early in a sentence to be combined with ideas later on), problem solving (in arithmetic, carrying a digit from the ones to the tens column while remembering the numbers), and planning (determining the best order in which to visit the bank, library, and grocery). Many studies indicate that working memory capacity varies among people, predicts individual differences in intellectual ability, and changes across the life span (Cowan, 2005).

It has been difficult to determine the capacity limit of working memory because multiple mechanisms retain information. Considerable research suggests, for example, that one can retain about 2 seconds' worth of speech through silent rehearsal

(Baddeley & Hitch, 1974). Working memory cannot be limited this way alone, though; in running-span procedures, only the last three to five digits can be recalled (less than 2 seconds' worth). In such procedures, the participant does not know when a list will end and, when it does, must recall several items from the end of the list (Cowan, 2001).

## Understanding Central Capacity Limits

To understand the nature of working memory capacity limits, two distinctions matter. Whereas working memory ability is usually measured in a processing-related, inclusive way, it instead takes storage-specific, central measures to observe capacity limits that are similar across materials and tasks.

The *processing-related* versus *storage-specific* distinction has to do with whether the task under consideration prevents processing strategies that individuals adopt to maximize performance (such as verbally rehearsing items or grouping them together), and whether the task minimizes processes that interfere with storing information in working memory (such as a requirement that the items in storage be rearranged or evaluated while being retained in memory). Storage-specific capacity is a more analytic concept, and the capacity limit stays constant across a much wider variety of circumstances. In a broad sense, working memory ability varies widely depending on what processes can be applied to a given task. To memorize verbal materials, one can try to repeat them in one's mind (rehearse them covertly). One can also try to form chunks from multiple words. For example, to remember to buy bread, milk, and pepper, one can form an image of bread floating in peppery milk. To memorize a sequence of spatial locations, one can envision a pathway formed from the locations. Although we cannot yet make precise predictions about how well working memory will operate in every possible task, we can measure storage-specific capacity by preventing or controlling processing strategies.

That is how one can observe a capacity limit of three to five separate items (Cowan, 2001). In many such studies with rehearsal and grouping curtailed, information was presented (a) in a brief, simultaneous spatial array; (b) in an unattended auditory channel, with attention to the sensory memory taking place only after the sounds ended; (c) during the overt, repetitive pronunciation of a single word by the participant; or (d) in a series with an unpredictable ending, as in running span. In such task conditions, one can observe that a handful of concepts can be held in the conscious mind.

These boundary conditions, in which grouping and rehearsal processes are prevented one way or another, are also of practical use to predict performance when the material is too brief, long, or complex to allow such processing strategies. For example, when trying to comprehend an essay, one might have to hold in mind concurrently the major premise, the point made in the previous paragraph, and a fact and an opinion presented in the cunent paragraph. Only when all of these elements have been integrated into a single chunk can the reader successfully continue to read and understand. Forgetting one of these ideas may lead to a more shallow understanding of the text, or to the need to go back and reread. As Cowan (2001) noted, many theorists with mathematical models of particular aspects of problem solving and thought have allowed the number of items in working memory to vary as a free parameter, and the models seem to settle on a value of about four, where the best fit is typically achieved.

In recent articles, we have shown the constancy of working memory capacity in chunks, by teaching new multi-item chunks. We have presented a set of arbitrarily paired words, such as *desk–ball,* repeatedly and consistently. Concurrently, we have presented other words as singletons. The paired words become new chunks. Young adults can recall three to five chunks from a presented list no matter whether these are learned pairs or singletons. The most precise result was obtained by Chen and Cowan (2009) as illustrated in Figure 1. Ordinarily, the result would depend on the length of the list and of the items, but when verbal rehearsal was prevented by having the participant repeat the word "the" throughout the trial, individuals remembered only about 3 units, no matter whether those were singletons or learned pairs. With similar results across many types of materials and tasks, we believe that there truly is a central working memory faculty limited to 3 to 5 chunks for adults, which can predict mistakes in thinking and reasoning (Halford, Cowan, & Andrews, 2007).

One can ask how individuals differ in working memory ability. They may differ in how much can be stored. However, there are also processes that can influence how effectively working memory is used. An important example is in the use of attention to fill working memory with the items one should be remembering (say, the concepts being explained in a class) as opposed to

1. *Familiarization Instructions*: Learn the pairings.

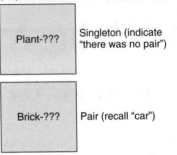

Dog
Brick-Car
Plant
Sink-Ball
Tree-Glass

2. *Training Instructions*: Reproduce the pair.
(Repeated until 100% correct)

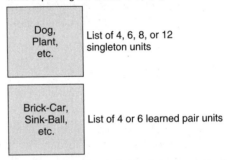

Plant-???    Singleton (indicate "there was no pair")

Brick-???    Pair (recall "car")

3. *List Recall Instructions*: Reproduce the entire list, sometimes while repeating the words "the, the, the . . ." during the entire trial.

Dog,
Plant,
etc.    List of 4, 6, 8, or 12 singleton units

Brick-Car,
Sink-Ball,
etc.    List of 4 or 6 learned pair units

**Figure 1**  Illustration of the three-part method of Chen and Cowan (2009) using word lists. The central capacity limit, which can be observed only if rehearsal is prevented, was about 3 chunks, no matter whether these chunks were singletons or learned word pairs.

filling it with distractions (say, what one is planning to do after class). According to one type of view (e.g., Kane, Bleckley, Conway, & Engle, 2001; Vogel, McCollough, & Machizawa, 2005), low-span individuals remember less because they use up more of their storage capacity holding information that is irrelevant to the assigned task.

Several other recent studies show, however, that this popular view cannot be the whole story and that there are true capacity differences between individuals (Cowan, Morey, AuBuchon, Zwilling, & Gilchrist, 2010; Gold et al., 2006). Cowan et al. compared 7- to 8-year-old and 11- to 12-year-old children and college students, using a version of the array memory procedure illustrated in Figure 2. There were two shapes, but participants were sometimes instructed to retain only items of one shape. To make the task interesting to children, the colored shapes were to be thought of as children in a classroom. When the test probe item was presented, the task was to indicate with a mouse click whether that "child" was in the correct seat, belonged in a different seat, or belonged out (i.e., was missing entirely from the memory array). In the latter case, a click on the door icon sent the "child" to the principal.

We estimated the contents of working memory in several attention conditions. In one condition, objects of one shape were to be attended and the test probe item was of that shape on 80% of the trials. In the remaining 20% of the trials in that condition, an item of the shape to be ignored was nevertheless tested. The test probe sometimes differed in color from the corresponding array item. We scored the proportion of change trials in which the change was noticed (hits) and of no-change trials in which an incorrect response of change was given (false alarms). Hits and false alarms were used in a simple formula to estimate the number of items stored in working memory, taking into account guessing (Cowan, 2001). This value was lower for 7-year olds (about 1.5) than it was for older children or adults (about 3.0), indicating that the age groups differed in storage. There was also an advantage for the test of the shape to be remembered, compared to the shape to be ignored; attention helped greatly. What was noteworthy is that this advantage for the attended shape was just as large in 7-year-olds as it was in adults, provided that the total number of items in the field was small (four). This suggests that simple storage capacity, and not just processing ability, distinguishes young children from adults. Other work suggests that storage and processing capacities both make important, partly separate and partly overlapping contributions to intelligence and development (Cowan, Fristoe, Elliott, Brunner, & Saults, 2006).

The *inclusive* versus *central* distinction has to do with whether we allow individuals to use transient information that is specific to how something sounds, looks, or feels—that is, sensory-modality-specific information—or whether we structure our stimulus materials to exclude that type of information, leaving a residual of only abstract information that applies across modalities (called central information). If one is trying to remember a spoken telephone number, for example, further conversation produced by the same speaker's voice interferes with auditory sensory information and leaves intact only the abstract, central information about the digits in the telephone number. Although it is useful for human memory that people can use vivid memories of how a picture looked or how a sentence sounded, these types of information tend to obscure the finding of a central memory usually limited to 3 to 5 items in adults. That central memory is especially important because it underlies problem solving and abstract thought.

Limits to central memory can be observed better if the contribution of information in sensory memory is curtailed, as shown by Saults and Cowan (2007) in a procedure illustrated in Figure 3. An array of colored squares was presented at the same time as an array of simultaneous spoken digits produced by different voices in four loudspeakers (to discourage rehearsal). The task was sometimes to attend to only the squares or only the spoken digits, and sometimes to attend to both modalities at once. The key finding was that, when attention was directed different ways, a central working memory capacity limit still held. People could remember about 4 squares if asked to attend only to squares, and if they were asked to attend to both squares and digits, they could remember fewer squares, but about 4 items in all. This fixed capacity limit was obtained, though, only if the items to be recalled were followed by a jumble of

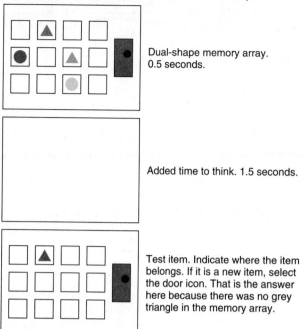

*Instructions for a block of trials:* Attend to colors of the circles, triangles, or both. (In some trial blocks, the shape to be ignored was actually tested on 20% of the trials.)

Dual-shape memory array. 0.5 seconds.

Added time to think. 1.5 seconds.

Test item. Indicate where the item belongs. If it is a new item, select the door icon. That is the answer here because there was no grey triangle in the memory array.

**Figure 2** Illustration of the method of Cowan et al. (2010) using object arrays. For simple materials, the capacity limit increased markedly from age 7 to adulthood, whereas the ability to focus on the relevant items and to ignore irrelevant ones stayed rather constant across that time.

meaningless, mixed visual and acoustic stimuli (a mask) so that sensory memory would be wiped out and the measure of working memory would be limited to central memory. With an inclusive situation (no mask), two modalities were better than one. Cowan and Morey (2007) similarly found that, for the process of encoding (putting into working memory) some items while remembering others, again two modalities are better than one (Cowan & Morey, 2007), whereas modality did not matter for central storage in working memory after encoding was finished.

# Why Is Storage Capacity Limited?

The reasons for the central working memory storage limit of 3 to 5 chunks remain unclear, but Cowan (2005) reviewed a variety of hypotheses. They are not necessarily incompatible; more than one could have merit. There are two camps: (a) capacity limits as weaknesses and (b) capacity limits as strengths.

The capacity-limit-as-weakness camp suggests reasons why it would be biologically expensive for the brain to have a larger working memory capacity. One way this could be the case is if there is a cycle of processing in which the patterns of neural firing representing, say, four items or concepts must fire in turn within, say, every consecutive 100-millisecond period, else not all concepts will stay active in working memory. The representation of a larger number of items could fail because together they take too long to be activated in turn or because patterns

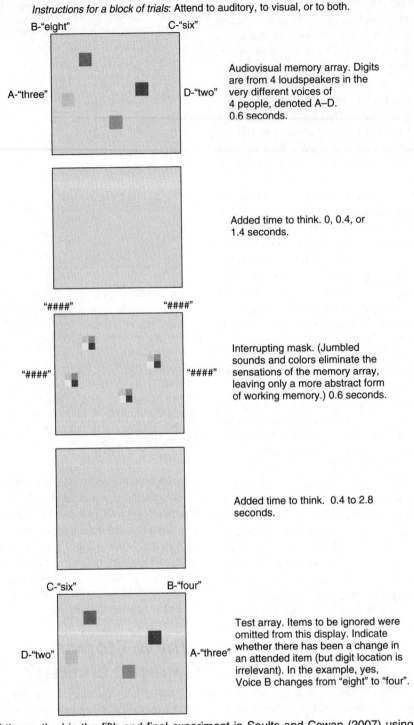

*Instructions for a block of trials*: Attend to auditory, to visual, or to both.

B-"eight"    C-"six"

A-"three"    D-"two"

Audiovisual memory array. Digits are from 4 loudspeakers in the very different voices of 4 people, denoted A–D. 0.6 seconds.

Added time to think. 0, 0.4, or 1.4 seconds.

"####"    "####"

"####"    "####"

Interrupting mask. (Jumbled sounds and colors eliminate the sensations of the memory array, leaving only a more abstract form of working memory.) 0.6 seconds.

Added time to think. 0.4 to 2.8 seconds.

C-"six"    B-"four"

D-"two"    A-"three"

Test array. Items to be ignored were omitted from this display. Indicate whether there has been a change in an attended item (but digit location is irrelevant). In the example, yes, Voice B changes from "eight" to "four".

**Figure 3** Illustration of the method in the fifth and final experiment in Saults and Cowan (2007) using audiovisual arrays. When sensory memory was eliminated, capacity was about 4 items no matter whether these were all visual objects or were a mixture of visual and auditory items.

too close together in time interfere with each other (with, for example, a red square and a blue circle being misremembered as a red circle and a blue square).

If the neural patterns for multiple concepts are instead active concurrently, it may be that more than about four concepts result in interference among them, or that separate brain mechanisms are assigned to each concept, with insufficient neurons at some critical locale to keep more than about four items active at once.

The recommended readings by Cowan (2005), Jonides et al. (2008), and Klingberg (2009) discuss neuroimaging studies showing that one brain area, the inferior parietal sulcus, appears capacity-limited at least for visual stimuli. If capacity is a weakness, perhaps superior beings from another planet can accomplish feats that we cannot because they have a larger working memory limit, similar to our digital computers (which, however, cannot do complex processing to rival humans in key ways).

The capacity-limit-as-strength camp includes diverse hypotheses. Mathematical simulations suggest that, under certain simple assumptions, searches through information are most efficient when the groups to be searched include about 3.5 items on average. A list of three items is well-structured with a beginning, middle, and end serving as distinct item-marking characteristics; a list of five items is not far worse, with two added in-between positions. More items than that might lose distinctiveness within the list. A relatively small central working memory may allow all concurrently active concepts to become associated with one another (chunked) without causing confusion or distraction. Imperfect rules, such as those of grammar, can be learned without too much worry about exceptions to the rule, as these are often lost from our limited working memory. This could be an advantage, especially in children.

# Conclusion

Tests of working memory demonstrate practical limits that vary, depending on whether the test circumstances allow processes such as grouping or rehearsal, focusing of attention on just the material relevant to the task, and the use of modality- or material-specific stores to supplement a central store. Recent work suggests, nevertheless, that there is an underlying limit on a central component of working memory—typically 3 to 5 chunks in young adults. If we are careful about stimulus control, central capacity limits are useful in predicting which thought processes individuals can execute, and in understanding individual differences in cognitive maturity and intellectual aptitude. There are probably factors of biological economy limiting central capacity, but in some ways, the existing limits may be ideal, or nearly so, for humans.

# Recommended Reading

Baddeley, A. (2007). *Working memory, thought, and action.* New York: Oxford University Press. A book providing a thoughtful update of the traditional working memory theory, taken in its broad context, including discussion of the recent episodic-buffer component that may share characteristics with the central-storage-capacity concept.

Cowan, N., & Rouder, J. N. (2009). Comment on "Dynamic shifts of limited working memory resources in human vision." *Science, 323*(5916), 877. An article providing a mathematical foundation for the concept of a fixed capacity limit, and defending that concept against the alternative hypothesis that attention can be spread thinly over all items presented to an individual.

Cowan, N. (2005). (See References). A book presenting the case for a central storage limit in the context of the history of the field, drawing key distinctions and exploring alternative theoretical explanations for the limit.

Jonides, J., Lewis, R. L., Nee, D. E., Lustig, C. A., Berman, M. G., & Moore, K. S. (2008). The mind and brain of short-term memory. *Annual Review of Psychology, 59,* 193–224. A review article broadly overviewing the working memory system, taking into consideration both behavioral and brain evidence and discussing capacity limits along with other possible limitations, such as decay.

Klingberg, T. (2009). The *oveflowing brain: Information overload and the limits of working memory.* New York Oxford University Press. A book broadly and simply discussing recent research on the concept of working memory capacity, emphasizing brain research, working memory training, and practical implications of capacity limits.

# Note

1. To readers in the 26th century or thereafter: The title alludes to *The Magical Mystery Tour,* one of many electromechanically recorded collections of rhythmic, voice-and-instrumental music about life and emotions by the Beatles, a British foursome that had messianic popularity.

# Funding

This research was supported by National Institutes of Health Grant R01 HD-21338.

# References

Baddeley, A. D., & Hitch, G. (1974). Working memory. In G. H. Bower (Ed.), *The psychology of learning and motivation* (Vol. 8, pp. 47–89). New York: Academic Press.

Chen, Z., & Cowan, N. (2009). Core verbal working memory capacity: The limit in words retained without covert articulation. *Quarterly Journal of Experimental Psycholog, 62,* 1420–1429.

Cowan, N. (2001). The magical number 4 in short-term memory: A reconsideration of mental storage capacity. *Behavioral and Brain Sciences, 24,* 87–185.

Cowan, N. (2005). *Working memory capacity.* Hove, East Sussex, England: Psychology Press.

Cowan, N., Fristoe, N. M., Elliott, E. M., Brunner, R.P., & Saults, J. S. (2006). Scope of attention, control of attention, and intelligence in children and adults. *Memory & Cognition, 34,* 1754–1768.

Cowan, N., & Morey, C. C. (2007). How can dual-task working memory retention limits be investigated? *Psychological Science, 18,* 686–688.

Cowan, N., Morey, C. C., AuBuchon, A. M., Zwilling, C. E., & Gilchrist, A. L. (2010). Seven-year-olds allocate attention like adults unless working memory is overloaded. *Developmental Science, 13,* 120–133.

Gilchrist, A. L., Cowan, N., & Naveh-Benjamin, M. (2008). Working memory capacity for spoken sentences decreases with adult aging: Recall of fewer, but not smaller chunks in older adults. *Memory, 16,* 773–787.

Gold, J. M., Fuller, R. L., Robinson, B. M., McMahon, R. P., Braun, E. L., & Luck, S. J. (2006). Intact attentional control of working memory encoding in schizophrenia. *Journal of Abnormal Psychology, 115,* 658–673.

Halford, G. S., Cowan, N., & Andrews, G. (2007). Separating cognitive capacity from knowledge: A new hypothesis. *Trends in Cognitive Sciences, 11,* 236–242.

Kane, M. J., Bleckley, M. K., Conway, A. R. A., & Engle, R. W. (2001). A controlled-attention view of working-memory capacity. *Journal of Experimental Psychology: General, 130,* 169–183.

Miller, G. A. (1956). The magical number seven, plus or minus two: Some limits on our capacity for processing information. *Psychological Review, 63,* 81–97.

Miller, G. A., Galanter, E., & Pribram, K. H. (1960). *Plans and the structure of behavior*. New York: Holt, Rinehart, & Winston, Inc.

Saults, J. S., & Cowan, N. (2007). A central capacity limit to the simultaneous storage of visual and auditory arrays in working memory. *Journal of Experimental Psychology: General, 136,* 663–484.

Vogel, E. K., McCollough, A. W., & Machizawa, M. G. (2005). Neural measures reveal individual differences in controlling access to working memory. *Nature, 438,* 500–503.

# Critical Thinking

1. How does working memory help us manage our everyday lives?
2. What are the limits of working memory?

**Corresponding Author:**—Nelson Cowan, Department of Psychological Sciences, University of Missouri, Columbia, 18 McAlester Hall, Columbia, MO 65211.

From *Current Directions in Psychological Science,* vol. 19, no. 1, February 2010, pp. 51–57. Copyright © 2010 by the Association for Psychological Science. Reprinted by permission of Sage Publications via Rightslink.

# Talk to the Hand

## *New Insights into the Evolution of Language and Gesture*

ERIC WARGO

In his book *Me Talk Pretty One Day,* humorist David Sedaris chronicled his pain at trying to learn French, in France, at age 41. His commiseration with a fellow language student sounds like it could be a dialogue between, say, two australopithecines, dimly anticipating the communicative achievements of their hominid descendents:

> "Sometimes me cry alone at night."
>
> "That be common for I, also, but be more strong, you. Much work and someday you talk pretty. People start love you soon. Maybe tomorrow, okay." (Sedaris, 2000)

Philosophers have always esteemed language among our most defining attributes, and the storytellers of every culture have tried to explain how humans acquired the gift. In Judeo-Christian myth, God granted Man the right to name things as he pleased, and later confused the world's tongues in retribution for human pride—leading to David Sedaris's predicament. Darwin supposed that language's origins were a more gradual and less deliberate outgrowth of animal communication: "Man not only uses inarticulate cries, gestures, and expressions, but has invented articulate language; if, indeed, the word *invented* can be applied to a process, completed by innumerable steps, half-consciously made" (Darwin, 1872/1998).

Accounting for these innumerable steps has been a challenge in the evolutionary psychology of language. What led our ancestors to become articulate? How did we finally learn to, you know, talk pretty?

It is intuitive to look to the vocal calls of primates for clues, and some primatologists still see this form of communication as the likeliest precursor for human language abilities. Yet evidence is accumulating that the "inarticulate cries" of monkeys appear to be controlled by different brain systems than those governing human language ability (Rizzolatti & Arbib, 1998), and psychologists interested in human and ape communication are turning with new interest to the properties of gesture. The story of language's "invention" may turn out to be more complicated than even Darwin could have imagined.

## What is Language?

A language is a system that can express an infinite range of ideas using a finite set of sounds or word elements—a *discrete combinatorial system,* as APS Fellow and Charter Member Steven Pinker, Harvard University, calls it (Pinker, 1994). Simple sound elements like phonemes (for example, the sounds *ba, da,* and *pa;* some researchers even focus on smaller units called *articulatory primitives*—see Poeppel & Monahan, 2008), are combined into words standing for things or actions, which are combined into larger groupings like sentences that express ideas of varying levels of complexity—theoretically, infinite complexity (a language feature known as *recursion*).

The system that enables this infinite recombination from finite raw materials is *grammar,* and it is the element most conspicuously absent from all forms of animal communication. Vervet monkeys, for instance, have what could be called a vocabulary, a handful of distinct warning calls that are tied to specific threats in their environment like leopards, snakes, and eagles (see Cheney & Seyfarth, 2005); but there is no vervet grammar—the monkeys cannot mix and match their calls or use them to express new ideas (but see Zuberbühler, 2005). And as complex as some bird and whale songs are, grammatical rules enabling sentence-like recombination of ideas don't appear to exist in such animals either.

The linguist Noam Chomsky argued that humans uniquely are born with a *universal grammar,* an underlying set of rules that serves as the basis for language acquisition. His classic example was the made-up sentence "Colorless green ideas sleep furiously." It makes no sense—indeed, it consists of self-contradictory ideas—but the brain accepts it because it is grammatical; it obeys the rules of syntax. More recently, Pinker has upheld the Chomskyan view of the innateness of language ability in humans, calling language an "instinct" that humans are born with (Pinker, 1994).

According to Pinker, the instinct for language evolved as an adaptation for social coordination in our hunter-gatherer ancestors (Pinker, 1994), and its deep structure still bears evidence of the fundamental human priorities of manipulating the social and physical environment (Pinker, 2007). Somewhat controversially, Pinker also argues that language is a modular system that evolved independently from other human cognitive abilities—that it is its own unique tool in the toolbox that is the human brain. His view of the modularity of mental adaptations has been compared to that of University of California, Santa Barbara evolutionary psychologists (and APS Fellows) Leda Cosmides and John Tooby, who have likened the mind to a "Swiss Army knife" comprising numerous special-purpose adaptations for solving particular challenges.

Those who argue for a unique language-processing module in the brain make their case in opposition to connectionists, who emphasize that language arises from multiple distributed cognitive abilities and is inseparable from all the other intelligent feats humans can perform. Among those who are passionate about such subtleties, it is a hot debate. Neuroscientists are generally converging on a connectionist view of most cognitive abilities such as object recognition, categorization, and memory (see the April 2008 special issue of *Current Directions in Psychological Science:* "The Interface Between Neuroscience and Psychological Science"). It appears that different aspects of language also are handled by widely distributed, functionally interconnected brain areas. Speech perception and language comprehension, for example, are now known to involve a complex network of brain areas operating in parallel, including a "dorsal pathway" that maps auditory sound representations onto motor representations for producing speech sounds, and a "ventral pathway" that maps speech sound representations onto representations of word concepts (Poeppel & Monahan, 2008; see also Holt & Lotto, 2008).

Different systems also appear to handle semantics (meaning) and syntax (grammar). Recordings of event-related potentials—brain waves recorded with electrodes placed on the scalp—reveal that violations of semantics such as the sentence "He spread his warm bread with socks" causes something in the brain to balk, with a negative potential peaking at 400 milliseconds after the sense-violating word (in this case, the word "socks"; see Hagoort, 2008). However, an entirely different brain wave response betrays the brain's complaint at a violation of syntax. Like Chomsky's observation about colorless green ideas, something about the sentence "The boiled watering can smokes the telephone in the cat" is perfectly acceptable to brain's syntax enforcer even though it makes absolutely no sense. But a violation like "The boiled watering can *smoke* the telephone in the cat" causes a negative-amplitude spike at 600 milliseconds after the offending (grammatically incorrect) word "smoke"—evidence that syntax and sense-making are distinct cognitive functions (see Hagoort, 2008).

## Particularity

Language has been called an instinct because it is so readily learned. Infants quickly begin to acquire language, without being actively taught: At 10 months of age, they know around 50 words (even though they do not say much), but by 30 months, they are already "social sophisticates," speaking in complete sentences with a production vocabulary of 550 words (Golinkoff & Hirsh-Pasek, 2006). Yet while it is instinctively

hungry to acquire language, the newborn brain is also completely unbiased to respond to the particular subset of possible sounds that constitute the spoken language of its parents—that is, when it comes to *phonetics,* it is a blank slate. That changes as the plastic brain quickly rewires (or prunes itself) to recognize only those sounds used in the language being spoken around it; older infants can only discriminate sounds from their own language (see Kraus & Banai, 2007), and adults learning a new language may have difficulty mastering its foreign sound distinctions (e.g., Japanese-speakers often have trouble distinguishing English "l" from "r").

This is one of the most interesting facts about language: you can't learn language without learning *a* language. Thus, while language requires an underlying mechanism (or mechanisms) common to everyone, and while language is used for the same purposes and in the same ways everywhere (i.e., it is a psychological universal), it is also a cultural system whose hallmark is particularity. There is no universal language any more than there is a "typical human." Languages, like people, are unique.

This is not merely an accident of history or evolution. One of the defining features of language, setting it apart from mere communication, is the feature known as *arbitrariness.* The Swiss linguist Ferdinand de Saussure noted that *signifiers* (e.g., words) by and large bear no necessary or logical connection to *signifieds,* or the things they stand for. There is no more reason to designate something you put on your head a "hat" than there is to call it a "chapeau." As such, the connection between the thing you put on your head and the word for it used in your community can only be a learned social convention. This is even true of onomatopoeia—words with a resemblance to natural sounds, the seeming exception to Saussure's rule. A Russian speaker will not recognize the onomatopoetic "bang" as the sound a gun makes, for example; where she grew up, she would have learned this sound as "batz."

The benefit of having to learn your lexicon instead of being born with it already hard-wired is that you are free to use words in novel and creative ways. It is possible to come up with other words for hats, or to lie about hats, or imagine a hat that doesn't exist yet, or wax nostalgic about hats in the past. It would be hard to imagine such human behaviors as tool-making, art, humor, long-term planning, or consciousness of self without the ability to represent abstractions, objects, and states of mind by words and other symbols that can be manipulated independently of what they stand for. The roots not only of abstract thought but also of culture lie in this radical disconnect between words and things.

## Missing Links

On January 21st of this year, Alaskan octogenarian Marie Smith Jones died at her Anchorage home, at age 89. As a result, language conservationists moved her native tongue, Eyak, from the lists of "Endangered" to "Extinct." Smith had been the last living speaker of a language that, in prehistoric times, may have been spoken over much of Alaska's southeastern coast. The minor flurry of news reports of her passing briefly helped publicize the issue of language diversity and its rapid worldwide decline.

Despite the disappearance of languages like Eyak, there are still 6,000 languages spoken in the world today, give or take. They vary widely in the size of their lexicons, but in fundamental respects all these languages are pretty much alike. They are all fully modern and capable of expressing ideas of whatever complexity they are called upon to express. Linguists have observed the emergence of new languages, creoles, out of simplified pidgins that arise in trading communities and other situations when people who don't share a common language live with each other. But even creoles exhibit the complexity and syntactical capabilities of languages having long histories. No anthropologist has ever found, in some remote tribe, an evolutionary "missing link" between modern languages and the more rigid and stereotyped modes of communication used by animals.

Researchers attempting to explain how language could have evolved in humans inevitably return to the linguistic capabilities of other living primates for clues. The obvious social intelligence of apes, in particular, made them appealing candidates in some of the early experimental attempts to assess the language abilities of animals. Apes' vocal tracts cannot produce the sounds needed for spoken language, so in 1967, Beatrice and Allen Gardner (University of Nevada, Reno) tried raising a young chimp, Washoe, to communicate using American Sign Language (ASL), training her using operant conditioning techniques. Washoe's trainers reported that, by the time she died last year at age 42, she had learned around 250 signs and could even apply some of them in novel situations. Koko, a 37-year-old lowland gorilla, has been claimed by Stanford psychologist Francine Patterson to know over 1,000 ASL signs and to recognize over twice that many words of spoken English. Koko has gained a degree of fame for her sign-language abilities, being the subject of television documentaries and even taking part in an online "chat."

But many scientists have rejected the claims of the Gardners, Patterson, and other proponents of animal language, saying that researchers (and an eager public) have projected human-like mentality onto these animals in the absence of compelling evidence that they are doing much more than parroting their trainers or using linguistic signs in relatively rigid, nonlinguistic ways. The only ASL-fluent member of the Gardners' research team, for example, disputed Washoe's use of true ASL signs (see Pinker, 1994). These animals may display remarkable communication abilities, but communication—the ability to affect others' behavior—is not the same thing as language.

The most scientifically compelling case for rudimentary language abilities in apes comes from Kanzi, a bonobo who learned a system of communicating by pressing lexigrams (arbitrary symbols) on a keyboard. Unlike other ape language subjects, Kanzi was not raised by human parents, nor was his "language acquisition" a product of active training—he learned his first keyboard signs passively, as an infant, while his mother was being taught them by researcher Sue Savage-Rumbaugh at Georgia State University's Language Research Center, in the early 1980s. Kanzi, now 27, has shown remarkable abilities to understand spoken language, to link spoken words and things to corresponding lexigrams, and possibly to construct novel

messages from combinations of signs. Savage-Rumbaugh claims that Kanzi is even able to understand the grammatical structure of some sentences (Savage-Rumbaugh, 1989). Whether the finite number of lexigrams available to Kanzi limits his ability to produce sentences as complex as the ones he understands (as Savage-Rumbaugh suggests), or whether there is some more basic linguistic threshold separating his abilities from full-blown language, remains an open question. But the case of Kanzi does appear to refute the notion that apes are only capable of parroting their human companions.

Much has been gained from observing the way primates communicate with each other in their natural environments. Many African monkeys, as well as chimpanzees, have been found to have repertoires of acoustically different alarm calls for different threats. APS Fellow Robert Seyfarth and his University of Pennsylvania colleague and wife Dorothy L. Cheney have found that such calls are highly dependent on social context; vervet monkeys, for example, seldom give an alarm if they are alone, and they are more likely to call in the presence of their own kin than in the presence of unrelated individuals (Cheney & Seyfarth, 2005).

Do monkeys understand the meaning of calls in the same way that humans understand the meaning of words? Is a vervet "leopard" alarm a word for a type of jungle cat, a recommendation ("run!"), or simply a symptomatic expression of a particular flavor of anxiety?

Primate calls are not simply reflexive; a monkey can decide whether or not to make a call based on who else is around. Such "audience effects," displayed by a number of species, are evidence for cognitive control and complexity in communication. But the evidence also suggests that despite the dependence on social context, monkeys lack theory-of-mind ability—the ability to conceptualize what other individuals may be thinking or how their knowledge may be changed by making (or not making) a vocalization. For Cheney and Seyfarth, this inability may be the key thing that distinguishes nonhuman primate communication from human language, and is probably at the root of their inability to generate new signals in creative ways or to utilize signals syntactically (Cheney & Seyfarth, 2005).

An interesting theme emerging in research on primate communication (as well as communication in other vocal animals such as parrots and dolphins) is the extreme asymmetry between vocal production and auditory comprehension. Animals are relatively inflexible and limited in the calls they can produce, yet they are often capable of much greater subtlety when it comes to grasping syntactical (i.e., causal) relationships, understanding the semantic meaning of calls, responding to the pragmatics (intentions and consequences) of calls, and even recognizing calls of other species. For example, Klaus Zuberbühler (University of St. Andrews) has found that Diana monkeys living among chimpanzees often made leopard alarm calls of their own when hearing chimpanzee leopard alarm screams, whereas Diana monkeys with less chimpanzee experience were more likely to hide silently (i.e., from the chimpanzees, who sometimes prey on the monkeys; Zuberbühler, 2005). Ape language experiments (and even everyday experience with pets) reflect the receptiveness and responsiveness to more sophisticated communication than animals are generally able to produce themselves. Zuberbühler suggests that the evolution of language in our species built on a basic competence in comprehension already existing in our primate ancestors.

# How Necessary Was Speech?

The transition from hearing and understanding to actually talking required a revolution not only cognitively (e.g., theory-of-mind ability) but also in controlling the face and mouth. Humans uniquely are able to produce and combine a huge array of subtly distinct sounds (over 100 acoustically unique *phones* are listed in the International Phonetic Alphabet). The difference is partly due to the shape and position of the larynx and to finer motor control of the articulators—lips, tongue, jaw, and other structures that modify sounds. This fine motor control cannot be mastered by monkeys or apes (as the early ape language experiments showed), and it is now known to have a genetic component. In humans, the gene known as FOXP2 controls the facial and mouth motor abilities necessary for speech; damage to this gene causes inability to speak but few or no other cognitive handicaps. The normal human form of this gene dates to a mutation that was established about 200,000 years ago; this may have been a watershed event in the history of human speech (Zuberbühler, 2005).

But speech is not synonymous with language, and may not even be a prerequisite for it.

Most primates have a repertoire of vocal calls, but only we and our closest relatives, the apes, regularly communicate with our hands as well, suggesting that gesture may be a newer evolutionary development than the ability to vocalize. A counterintuitive theory that is gaining ground among researchers in a range of fields—from primatology, neuroscience, and even paleontology—is the notion that the driving force in language evolution may not have been the inarticulate cries of our primate ancestors, but their gestures (Corballis, 2003).

At Emory University, then-PhD-student Amy Pollick and her mentor Frans de Waal coded over 600 hours of videotaped interactions by chimpanzees and their relatively less-studied relatives, bonobos, in different captive groups. The aim was to compare the animals' gestural and vocal/facial communication. They found that the overwhelming majority of signals used to initiate social interactions in both species were either solely gestural or involved a combination of gestures and facial/vocal signals. According to Pollick, this finding was a surprise: Apes scream and hoot at each other a lot, and it would be easy for a casual observer to assume vocalization is these animals' dominant mode of initiating communication.

Ape vocalizations have been relatively less studied than those of monkeys (Zuberbühler, 2005), but recently Zuberbühler and his colleagues have found evidence for cognitive complexity and audience effects in chimpanzee screams. For example, during aggressive encounters, individuals varied their screams depending on the severity of an encounter, their own role in it, and who else was present to hear them; they even exaggerated calls for support (intensifying the severity of a call compared to the real severity of the encounter) if a higher-ranking male was

present (Slocombe & Zuberbühler, 2007). But most research so far shows that chimps' vocal signals are not much more complex than those of monkeys. Sounds are fairly highly stereotyped and are closely tied to particular emotions and situations (Pollick & de Waal, 2007). Social contexts eliciting particular facial/vocal displays in chimps reliably elicit the same displays in bonobos, and vice versa; and most vocalizations don't appear to have a targeted recipient.

By contrast, Pollick and de Waal found a highly nuanced hand-gesture vocabulary in chimps and bonobos, with great situational variation in use of gestures and combination with vocalizations, and a tendency to use gestures dyadically (i.e., more like conversational exchanges). The Emory researchers found that chimp and bonobo gestures were much less tied to particular emotions and situations than their vocalizations were. And hand gestures, even if they clearly evolved from basic object-related manual movements, were much more conventionalized (i.e., less stereotyped) and appeared to be deployed more deliberately—revealing greater cortical control over this mode of communication. Often the meaning of a particular chimp or bonobo gesture could only be extracted from its context.

The Emory researchers also found that, particularly in bonobos but to a lesser extent in chimps, gestures differed between different groups of the same species—evidence that, in these animals, gesture has truly begun to break from biology, becoming cultural. "Far more than facial expressions and vocalizations," they write, "gestures seem subject to modification, conventionalization, and social transmission" (Pollick & de Waal, 2007, p. 8188). Pollick and de Waal speculate that the flexible use of gestures and responsiveness to combined signals that they observed "may have characterized our early ancestors, which in turn may have served as a stepping stone for the evolution of symbolic communication" (p. 8188).

# Talking with Our Hands

Pollick, who now works in Washington, DC as APS's Director of Government Relations, admits that her interest in ape gestures and the evolution of language isn't accidental. She is deaf and from a deaf family, so American Sign Language is, so to speak, her native tongue. "Having grown up with ASL, I was just naturally attuned to issues of communication," Pollick says. "I was also naturally attuned to gesture. All humans gesture, wherever they are, in all cultures. People gesture when they are not visible to the receiver, such as when they talk on the phone. Blind people gesture when talking to other blind people. This led me to think that gesture is deeply ingrained in human communication, and I began to wonder where this came from."

Pollick explains that in order to theorize about the relationship between ape gestures and human language, she drew a stricter distinction between hand gestures and other body movements than previous ape communication researchers had drawn. She also made finer-grained distinctions among different gestures—for example, determining that the meaning of an outstretched hand depended on the angle the hand was rotated at. Chimps, for instance, used an extended, upraised palm (i.e., "gimme") in a variety of situations: to request food, to request sex, to request to be groomed, or to implore the aid of another chimp. Sometimes the gesture was combined with a vocalization such as a scream. Bonobos mainly used the gesture to solicit play.

Humans use the "gimme" gesture too—as well as countless others. Linguists used to ignore the way humans use their hands when communicating, or relegate it to the subordinate category of "body language." But psychological research on human gesture is revealing that, as with chimps and bonobos, when humans talk with their hands it is far more than just an exception or a sideshow to the main attraction.

Important insights into the nature of language have come from studies of signing in the deaf. Linguists agree that human sign languages such as ASL are every bit as "linguistic" as spoken languages are—that is, they possess all the syntactical complexity and are just as flexible and open-ended as their spoken analogues. They are also just as readily learned. University of Toronto psychologist Laura-Ann A. Petitto found that deaf children exposed to ASL or the Quebec sign language, Langue des Signes Quebecoise, learned to sign at the same rate that hearing children acquire spoken language (Petitto, 2000). Other researchers have even suggested that deaf children acquire sign language on a faster developmental schedule than non-deaf learners of spoken language (Meier & Newport, 1990).

If a sign language doesn't happen to be available in a deaf child's environment, she will go ahead and invent one. APS Fellow and Charter Member Susan Goldin-Meadow (University of Chicago) studied profoundly deaf children in the United States and Taiwan who were raised by hearing parents and were unexposed to sign language. Such children spontaneously used gesture to communicate, and their gestures displayed the same structural properties (such as recursion and displaced communication—referring to things not present) that characterize natural spoken languages and sign languages (Goldin-Meadow, 2006).

The sign language instinct appears to exist also in hearing adults who have never learned a sign language. As Pollick notes, most people talk with their hands—that is, gesticulate to provide counterpoint, emphasis, or visual illustration of what they are saying with speech. Goldin-Meadow found that, when gesture accompanies speech, it lacks the fully linguistic properties observed in deaf people's spontaneous signing. In another study by Goldin-Meadow, non-deaf participants were asked to describe an event orally and also to attempt to describe it using only gestures. When they used speech, their hand gestures supported what they were saying imagistically, supporting the main spoken channel of communication by providing a kind of visual aid, but were not by themselves linguistic; however, when they had to describe an event solely through hand gestures, their gestures assumed the linguistic properties the researcher found in her studies with deaf children (Goldin-Meadow, 2006).

Goldin-Meadow's University of Chicago colleague, APS Fellow David McNeill, considers hand gestures to be intrinsic to language, driving thought and speech. Language, he argues, is a dialectic in which images (conveyed by the hands) work with and against speech, the tension between these two modes of thought propelling thought and communication forward. His studies of speakers' hand gestures revealed a temporal structure, distinct from ordinary syntax (sentence structure), in which gestural imagery and spoken content periodically resolved in what he dubs "growth points"—temporal boundaries of unfolding thought sequences that can be detected when a word or phrase synchronizes with gesture in a certain way (McNeill, 2006).

Speakers vary in how they use their hands when they are speaking. In another series of experiments, Goldin-Meadow compared learning and problem-solving ability in speaking children whose gestures matched (i.e., conveyed the same information as) their own or their teachers' verbal explanations of problems with the abilities of children whose gestures conveyed different information than what was being spoken. Children who used mismatching gestures or who were taught by teachers who used mismatching gestures learned faster and were more successful at solving problems than were those whose gestures merely supported the spoken communication. It suggests that this second, silent channel of nonverbal information may be an important helping hand (so to speak) to thought. According to Goldin-Meadow, "A conversation in gesture . . . appears to be taking place alongside the conversation in speech whenever speakers use their hands" (Goldin-Meadow, 2006, p. 37).

## How Did We Get Here?

APS Fellow and Charter Member Michael Corballis (University of Auckland) is a proponent of the gesture-first scenario of language origins, arguing that it makes sense of a wide range of findings in various fields (Corballis, 2003). There is the paleontological evidence, for one thing: Sometime after the human lineage split from that of chimps and bonobos about six million years ago, our australopithecine ancestors became bipedal; whether or not gestural communication was a factor driving this shift, it did free the hands for greater manipulation of the physical environment, and likely facilitated communicative manipulation of the social environment. Australopithecine brains remained ape-like in most respects, as did their vocal tracts and breathing apparatus—meaning they couldn't talk—but expansion of the cortex, including specific brain areas governing language and gesture, is found in their tool-manufacturing descendent *Homo habilis*. Endocasts (casts of brain cases) of 2-million-year-old *H. habilis* skulls reveal an asymmetry that could correspond to expansion of areas on the left side of the brain, such as Broca's area, that have long been associated with language in humans (see Corballis, 2003).

In the 1990s, a group of neuroscientists at the University of Parma, Italy, made a discovery suggesting that the brain area in monkeys corresponding to Broca's area could have served as the platform for the emergence of language out of gesture in our deep primate past (Fogassi & Ferrari, 2007; Rizzolatti & Arbib, 1998). The homologue of Broca's area in the monkey brain, known as area F5, is involved in controlling manual gestures, not vocalizations; it also possesses a *mirror-neuron system*. Mirror neurons fire both when an animal (or person) initiates an action and when the animal perceives another individual make the same action (see "Mirror Neurons: How We Reflect on Behavior" in the May, 2007, issue of the *Observer*). Mirror neuron systems have been proposed as the basis for various forms of learning, social coordination, and even theory-of-mind abilities in animals and humans.

One category of mirror neurons in the monkey F5 fires both when the monkey makes a motor act with its forelimbs and when it hears the sound produced by the same action (e.g., by another monkey, or on a recording); another type of motor neuron in the same area specifically activates during observation of another monkey's mouth-communicative gestures like lip-smacking or tongue protrusion (Fogassi & Ferrari, 2007). Research in humans has revealed similar properties for Broca's area. It activates when people observe goal-related hand or mouth motor movements by other people, for example. And there is evidence for a matching mechanism whereby heard phonemes activate corresponding tongue motor representations in the cortex (Fogassi & Ferrari, 2007).

The neuroscience findings support a longstanding and influential theory of speech perception called the motor theory (Liberman & Mattingly, 1985). In this theory, linguistic primitives (basic elements) are not represented in the cortex as abstract sounds but as the motor signals that one would use to make those sounds. The picture is turning out to be more complicated—speech perception involves many more parts of the brain than just Broca's area. But the common neural basis of manual dexterity and important aspects of language means that the notion that language is a "tool" could be more than just a metaphor. Could tool use and language be flip sides of the same cognitive coin?[1]

## Hand to Mouth

Corballis, like Zuberbühler, sees speech per se as a late development possibly occurring only with the rise of *Homo sapiens* around 170,000 years ago. Yet language, in some form, could well have been around for a long time before that. The beginnings of stone tool manufacture occurred around 2.5 million years ago, followed by a shift from forest dwelling to living and carrying materials on the open savannah around 2 million years ago. These developments hint at a level of abstract thinking and social coordination abilities that could have gone hand in hand (so to speak) with language skills.

One plausible scenario for the transition from gestural to vocal communication is that increased use of the hands for tool making and carrying drove greater use of the face for communication, and this ultimately led to speech. In modern sign languages, manual gestures convey semantic content and facial and body movements act as modifiers. Corballis suggests that facial movements could have become integrated into the manual sign system as carriers of syntax (Corballis, 2003) and this integration could have been an outgrowth of the mechanics of eating—an idea supported by mirror-neuron findings (Fogassi & Ferrari, 2007).

From this gesture–face integration, it would have been a small evolutionary step to add voicing to facial gesture to provide more range of meaning—perhaps made possible by the FOXP2 mutation mentioned earlier, as well as the descent of the larynx and changes to the muscles controlling breathing.[2] Corballis suggests that we should think of speaking not as the production of abstract phonemes but as a kind of noisy gesturing with our mouths (see Corballis, 2003).

Whatever its evolutionary origins, speech has acquired a great deal of autonomy from hand gestures. People can normally communicate on the phone, for example, with little loss of meaning, even if gesturing at the same time helps them think. The autonomy of speech has left many people with the natural impression that our linguistic abilities are more closely akin to animal vocalization than to other forms of communication. Since words and gestures don't fossilize, it may never be possible to answer the question "Where did language come from?" definitively. Pollick acknowledges that the theory that our language abilities evolved from gesture remains a "just-so story," even though the scientific evidence for pieces of the theory is compelling. Only further research, across a range of disciplines, can help settle the question of whether talking pretty piggybacked on gesture or the other way around—or whether language evolved in some completely different way.

## Notes

1. The common neural origins of language and manual dexterity has been used to explain why nine out of ten humans are right-handed (Corballis, 2003). A bias toward right-handedness makes sense if manual dexterity developed in tandem with language ability, both sharing an underlying cortical substrate in the left hemisphere (which controls the right side of the body). However, recent discovery of handedness and hemispherical asymmetries in many other animal species, including many primates, may complicate this picture (see Hopkins & Cantalupo, in press).

2. The descent of the larynx, incidentally, made modern humans uniquely vulnerable to choking. Unlike other animals, we are prevented from breathing and swallowing at the same time, and, thus, are imperiled whenever we eat.

## References

Cheney, D.L., & Seyfarth, R.M. (2005). Constraints and preadaptations in the earliest stages of language evolution. *The Linguistic Review, 22,* 135–159.

Corballis, M.C. (2003). From mouth to hand: Gesture, speech, and the evolution of right-handedness. *Behavioral and Brain Sciences, 26,* 199–260.

Darwin, C. (1998). *The expression of the emotions in man and animals.* New York: Oxford University Press. (Original work published 1872)

Fogassi, L., & Ferrari, P.F. (2007). Mirror neurons and the evolution of embodied language. *Current Directions in Psychological Science, 17,* 136–141.

Goldin-Meadow, S. (2006). Talking and thinking with our hands. *Current Directions in Psychological Science, 15,* 34–39.

Golinkoff, R.M., & Hirsh-Pasek, K. (2006). Baby wordsmith: From associationist to social sophisticate. *Current Directions in Psychological Science, 15,* 30–33.

Hagoort, P. (2008). Should psychology ignore the language of the brain? *Current Directions in Psychological Science, 17,* 96–101.

Holt, L.L., & Lotto, A.J. (2008). Speech perception within an auditory cognitive science framework. *Current Directions in Psychological Science, 17,* 42–46.

Hopkins, W.D., & Cantalupo, C. (in press). Theoretical speculations on the evolutionary origins of hemispheric specialization. Current Directions in Psychological Science.

Kraus, N., & Banai, K. (2007). Auditory-processing malleability: Focus on language and music. *Current Directions in Psychological Science, 16,* 105–110.

Liberman, A.M., & Mattingly, I.G. (1985). The motor theory of speech perception revisited. *Cognition, 21,* 1–36.

McNeill, D. (2006, September). *Gesture and thought.* Paper presented at the Summer Institute on Non-verbal Communication and the Biometrical Principle, Vietri sul Mare, Italy. Downloaded April 2, 2008, from http://mcneilllab.uchicago.edu/pdfs/dmcn_vietri_sul_mare.pdf

Meier, R.P., & Newport, E.L. (1990). Out of the hands of babes: On a possible sign language advantage in language acquisition. *Language, 66,* 1–23.

Petitto, L.A. (2000). On the biological foundations of human language. In H. Lane & K. Emmorey (Eds.), *The signs of language revisited* (pp. 447–471). Mahwah, NJ: Erlbaum.

Pinker, S. (1994). *The language instinct.* New York: HarperCollins.

Pinker, S. (1997). *The stuff of thought.* New York: Viking.

Poeppel, D., & Monahan, P.J. (2008). Speech perception: Cognitive foundations and cortical implementation. *Current Directions in Psychological Science, 17,* 80–85.

Pollick, A.S., & de Waal, F.B.M. (2007). Ape gestures and language evolution. *Proceedings of the National Academy of Sciences, USA, 104,* 8184–8189.

Rizzolatti, G., & Arbib, M.A. (1998). Language within our grasp. *Trends in Neurosciences, 21,* 188–194.

Savage-Rumbaugh, S., Shanker, S.G., & Taylor, T.J. (1998). *Apes, language, and the human mind.* New York: Oxford University Press.

Sedaris, D. (2000). Me talk pretty one day. In *Me talk pretty one day* (pp. 166–173). New York: Little, Brown.

Slocombe, K.E., & Zuberbühler, K. (2007). Chimpanzees modify recruitment screams as a function of audience composition. *Proceedings of the National Academy of Sciences, USA, 104,* 17228–17233.

Zuberbühler, K. (2005). The phylogenetic roots of language: Evidence from primate communication. *Current Directions in Psychological Science, 14,* 126–130.

# Critical Thinking

1. How did language evolve or originate?
2. Which developed first—language or hand gestures?

# Dangerous Distraction

**Psychologists' research shows how cell phones, iPods, and other technologies make us more accident prone and is laying the foundation to make using these gadgets less dangerous.**

Amy Novotney

On a Tuesday evening two years ago, avid cyclists Christy Kirkwood and Debbie Brown were finishing a 13-mile bike ride in Orange County, Calif., when a driver talking on a cell phone swerved into their bike path, knocking Kirkwood off her bike and throwing her 227 feet. The motorist—who had been travelling at 55 mph—continued a short distance before stopping to see what had happened, says University of Utah psychology professor David Strayer, PhD, who served as a consultant on the case.

"The driver thought he'd hit a deer," Strayer recalls.

Kirkwood died from her injuries. Unfortunately, such tragedies have become all too common. In fact, two epidemiological studies—one published in 1997 in *The New England Journal of Medicine* (Vol. 336, No. 7), and another published online in 2005 in the British medical journal *BMJ*—report that talking on the cell phone while driving increases your risk of being in an accident fourfold—an alarming statistic given that 84 percent of Americans own cell phones, according to the Cellular Telecommunications and Internet Association.

In addition, a new report from the AAA Foundation for Traffic Safety finds that more than half of U.S. drivers admit to using a cell phone while driving, at least occasionally. The Human Factors and Ergonomics Society estimates that 2,600 deaths and 330,000 injuries in the United States result each year from driver cell phone use.

Of course, Americans are increasingly using personal digital assistants and other devices that undermine their attention, as well. Last fall, 25 people died and 113 were injured when a commuter train collided head-on with a freight train outside Los Angeles. A National Transportation Safety Board investigation found that text messaging may have played a role: Cell phone records showed the train's engineer had sent a text message 22 seconds before the crash. Last year, Americans sent more than 600 billion text messages—10 times the number they sent three years ago. And 41 percent of us have logged onto the Internet outside our homes or offices, either with a wireless laptop connection or a handheld device, finds a 2007 Pew Internet Project survey.

The problem doesn't just rest with drivers: A 2007 study in *Accident Analysis and Prevention* (Vol. 39, No. 1) by University of South Wales psychologist Julie Hatfield, PhD, found that female pedestrians talking on mobile phones were less likely to look for traffic before stepping into the street and crossed the road more slowly, increasing their risk of colliding with a vehicle.

"As technology and interruption become more and more prevalent, the negative consequences of not paying attention become more pronounced," says Strayer.

With their knowledge of human behavior and cognition, Strayer and other psychologists are exploring the causes of distraction and working to raise awareness of its danger. At the same time, scientists are designing technology that isn't as mentally demanding.

## Limited Capacity

Most people have no problem watching television as they jog on a treadmill or chewing gum while they walk. These are largely effortless tasks that require little sustained attention or thinking. And that may be why many believe they can drive and do any number of secondary tasks as well—from eating or applying makeup to scanning for a song on their MP3 players or talking on cell phones.

But cognitive scientists' research shows the brain has limited bandwidth. Research by psychologists Marcel Just, PhD, and Tim Keller, PhD, of the Center for Cognitive Brain Imaging at Carnegie Mellon University, examined brain activity while participants performed two high-level tasks—responding whether auditorily presented sentences were true or false and mentally rotating three-dimensional objects—both separately and then concurrently. Their findings, published in 2001 in *NeuroImage* (Vol. 14, No. 2), suggest when performing the actions together, brain activation, primarily in the temporal and parietal areas of the cortex, was substantially less than the sum of the activation when participants performed the two tasks alone, even though the tasks drew on different brain regions.

This suggests, Just says, that dual-tasking compels the brain to pull from some shared, limited resource, slowing reaction time.

Another new study he led, published last year in *Brain Research* (Vol. 1, No. 205), examines how this central bottleneck plays out when we're driving. Researchers collected fMRI images of 29 undergraduates as they simulated steering a vehicle along a curving road, either undisturbed or while listening to spoken sentences that they judged as true or false. They found that the listening task reduced driving-related brain activity— the spatial processing that takes place in the parietal lobe—by almost 40 percent.

Just says he expects that such reduction in brain activity occurs no matter where the speech comes from, be it a cell phone, fellow passenger or even a talk radio show.

"Processing spoken language is especially insidious in cars because it's automatic," Just says. "When we ask subjects to ignore what's being said, you can still see the activation associated with the processing of that language."

Meanwhile, new research in the December *Journal of Experimental Psychology: Applied* (Vol. 14, No. 4) shows that cell phone conversations are especially detrimental to driving. The researchers found that cell phone users are more likely to drift out of their lanes and miss their exits than people having in-person conversations. Interestingly, conversations with passengers barely affected any of these three measures. In fact, most passengers took an active role in supporting the driver, often by discussing surrounding traffic. This shared situational awareness may help drivers synchronize an in-vehicle conversation with the processing demands of driving, says study author Frank Drews, PhD, a University of Utah psychology professor.

"If you look at the crash risk, you're actually somewhat less likely to be involved in an accident if you have a passenger than if you're driving by yourself," says Strayer, who collaborated with Drews and colleague Monisha Pasupathi, PhD, on the study.

Human factors experts at the Virginia Tech Transportation Institute (VTTI) have gone a step further to explore how driver inattention leads to collisions. With support from the National Highway Traffic Safety Administration, Virginia Tech researchers tracked driver behavior in 100 vehicles equipped with video and sensor devices for one year. During that time, the vehicles traveled nearly 2 million miles and were involved in 69 crashes and 761 near-crashes. Researchers found that nearly 80 percent of crashes and 65 percent of near-crashes involved driver inattention up to three seconds before the event.

"We were actually able to physically see drivers who were talking on their cell phones, dialing, applying makeup and all the other secondary tasks, and there was no question when it was a contributing factor in the occurrence of a crash," says Charlie Klauer, PhD, a senior research associate at VTTI.

The group recently completed a similar study with 40 teen drivers, who are often the most inexperienced and the earliest adopters of new technologies. Klauer expects the results will show that teens have trouble adapting their behaviors in hazardous driving situations and that distractive devices play an even larger role in teen accidents.

New research also establishes the risks of other technologies:

- Drews's as-yet-unpublished research on text messaging suggests the activity may make motorists even more inattentive: A driver's chance of getting into an accident increases sixfold when he is texting.
- Research by Susan Chisholm, PhD, of the Cognitive Ergonomics Research Lab at the University of Calgary, shows the dangers of mixing digital music players and driving. Her study of 19 drivers age 18 to 22 shows that collisions nearly doubled while people performed such iPod tasks as scanning to find a particular song (*Accident Analysis and Prevention*, Vol. 40, No. 2).
- Research by Hatfield and colleague Timothy Chamberlain reveals that in-car TV screens distract drivers of neighboring cars, resulting in reduced reaction times and impaired lane-keeping.
- There's even concern that car navigation systems may distract the very drivers they are trying to help. In a simulated-driving study published in *Human Factors* (Vol. 46, No. 4), researchers found that when motorists entered information into a touch-screen navigation system, they drove outside lane boundaries 21 percent of the time, as compared with undistracted drivers who strayed only 1.5 percent of the time. Even those providing an address to a speech-recognition system left their lanes 6 percent of the time.

## Psychology's Solutions

Among the ways psychologists are seeking to improve driver safety is developing technological interventions that reduce a driver's workload. Backed by his own research (*Accident Analysis and Prevention*, Vol. 40, No. 2), John D. Lee, PhD, director of human factors research at the University of Iowa's National Advanced Driving Simulator, has found that providing real-time and post-drive feedback to drivers on how well they're doing behind the wheel will help mitigate distraction. With the help of eye-tracking technology, Lee's team has designed an alert system that monitors what motorists are looking at and warns them when their eyes veer away from the road for more than two seconds.

Meanwhile, at the University of Michigan's Transportation Research Institute, scientists have developed a tool to measure traffic conditions, road surface and visibility. Taking into account the driver's experience level, the equipment prevents the driver from receiving phone calls or entering an address into a navigation system when conditions get dangerous.

Early versions of both devices are already in place in some Saabs and Volvos. University of Michigan psychologist Paul Green, PhD, is hopeful that these types of countermeasures will help get motorists' attention back on the road.

"It isn't the solution, it's just a piece of the solution, but it's an interesting one," Green says.

Psychologists are also working to raise awareness about the dangers of distracted driving.

The VTTI researchers, for example, are working with nonprofit organizations, including the Bedford County Combined

Accident Reduction Effort, to get the word out about the effects of distracted driving. Thanks to their efforts, the Bedford County driver's education program encourages parents and teens to use driving contracts that limit cell phone and MP3 player use while driving.

In a national effort, in April the National Highway Traffic Safety Administration published "Driver Distraction: A Review of the Current State of Knowledge," which summarizes research on inattentive driving and examines ways to address the problem through public awareness and legislation. In response to the report, APA Chief Executive Officer Norman B. Anderson, PhD, sent a letter to NHTSA urging the organization to identify areas in need of further research and make recommendations for public outreach efforts.

"Distracted driving is a public health hazard without age barriers that is often misunderstood by not only the public but also by both state and local policymakers," Anderson wrote.

Just agrees, noting that a deeper appreciation for the cognitive strain secondary tasks put on our ability to drive or cross the road might help reduce fatalities.

"I think people are unaware of the fact that using a cell phone has such a massive impact on their performance," he says.

Research that compares and quantifies driver distraction could help. One such study, published in *Human Factors* (Vol. 48, No. 2), suggests that a driver talking on a cell phone is more impaired than one with a blood alcohol level exceeding 0.08.

"Most people wouldn't think of getting in a car with someone who's been drinking, but they don't have a big problem getting into a car with someone who's using their cell phone," Just says.

> ## "Most people wouldn't think of getting in a car with someone who's been drinking, but they don't have a big problem getting into a car with someone who's using their cell phone."
>
> —Marcel Just
> Center for Cognitive Brain Imaging
> at Carnegie Mellon University

Yet efforts to reduce driving while intoxicated went beyond public awareness and increasingly included hefty fines, says Anne McCartt, PhD, vice president of research at the Insurance Institute for Highway Safety. In the case of inattentive drivers, legislation limiting cell phone use may prove effective, she notes. At *Monitor* press time, no state had yet banned all cell phone use by every driver, but 17 states and the District of Columbia do prohibit novice drivers from using cell phones, and six states and D.C. have outlawed drivers from using handheld phones. Seven states bar text messaging, and nine prohibit teens from the activity.

McCartt admits, however, that these laws either are often not enforced enough to change driver behavior, or they exempt hands-free devices without taking into account the research that shows hands-free devices are just as dangerous as hand-held ones. In fact, some psychologists say hands-free exemptions may encourage motorists originally disinclined to use a cell phone while driving to view the activity as safe.

"To some extent, these laws that didn't pay attention to the science may end up actually making the roads a little less safe," Strayer says.

William C. Howell, PhD, chair of the Human Factors and Ergonomics Society's government relations committee, agrees, noting that policymakers may be passing laws to assure the public that they're curing the problem while they are actually misdiagnosing it.

"Not only do we have a bunch of virtually unenforceable and uninformed laws but a false sense that they represent a fix," he says. "Sure, we need to keep up the pressure for more research, but we know enough about how attention works already to guide strategies for addressing the problem in much more promising directions. In other words, our society should be using what's already known more judiciously in dealing with this problem while doing the research necessary to find even more effective approaches."

One way to do this may be to target driver distraction campaigns toward those on the other end of the phone line, says Drews.

"Cell phone conversations take two people," he says. "We need to convince those callers who know that the person they're talking to is driving to ask the driver to pull over or to call them back later."

He says disseminating this message more broadly to the public might help solve the problem more effectively—and may be more economical—than new vehicle technologies or additional legislation.

"It doesn't cost anything," he notes. "They just have to hang up."

## Safety First

Psychologists' research is also informing legislation on the hazards of using these technological devices even when people are not behind the wheel. In 2007, when two pedestrians were killed after being hit while listening to iPods, New York state senator Carl Kruger proposed legislation that would ban the use of handheld devices such as BlackBerrys, iPods and portable video games while crossing streets in major New York cities. Under the bill, pedestrians and bicyclists caught using any kind of electronic device while crossing a street would be hit with a $100 fine. In July, Illinois became the first state to consider a ban on using a cell phone while crossing a street. Neither bill has passed, but several organizations have moved to make pedestrians more aware of the dangers of technologies that divert our attention.

In July, the American College of Emergency Physicians Foundation warned against cell phone use while driving, bicycling, rollerblading or walking, saying they'd noticed a rise in injuries and deaths related to sending texts while engaging in these activities. Also last year, the nonprofit London-based organization Living Streets installed padded lampposts on a busy street in London as part of a safety campaign targeting distracted pedestrians. The move was prompted by a United Kingdom phone survey of 68,000 that found that one in 10 have been injured while walking and texting on their cell phone.

Just says he's not surprised that the use of cell phones while walking has prompted concern.

"Our research extends to other tasks besides driving," Just says. "The reason walking is different, though, is because when you're driving, the person you're most likely to hurt is someone other than yourself."

Psychologists say they hope work like this leads to increased motorist and pedestrian safety, just as campaigns and laws to encourage seat belt use—which has increased every year since NHTSA began collecting data in 1994—led to a steady decrease in passenger fatalities.

# Critical Thinking

1. Can technology be dangerous? If so, how so?
2. What can increase the safety of using advanced technology?

From *Monitor on Psychology* by Amy Novotney, February 2009, pp. 32–36. Copyright © 2009 by American Psychological Association. Reprinted by permission. No further distribution without permission from the American Psychological Association.

# UNIT 6
# Emotion and Motivation

## Unit Selections

## Learning Outcomes

*After reading this Unit, you should be able to:*

- Understand and explain the factors that contribute to how women with families achieve success as leaders.
- Describe the role of the "culture of gender" in how women in different cultures achieve success as leaders.
- Define self-control within the context of everyday life.
- Summarize the key elements of a person's ability to exercise self-control.
- Discuss why eating is a motivated behavior.
- Explain the various ways that mothers might serve as role models to their daughters for eating well.
- Explain both the advantages and disadvantages of anger.
- Identify and discuss factors that cause people to "fly into a rage" and the negative impacts of doing so.

## Student Website
www.mhhe.com/cls

## Internet References

**Emotion**
    www.psychology.org/links/Environment_Behavior_Relationships/Emotion/
**Mind Tools**
    www.helpguide.org/mental/stress_management_relief_coping.htm
**Motivation**
    www.edpsycinteractive.org/topics/motivation/motivate.html

Jasmine's sister was a working mother who always reminded Jasmine about how exciting life on the road as a sales representative was. Jasmine herself stayed home because she wanted to take care of her children, 2-year-old Min, 4-year-old Chi'Ming, and newborn Yuan. One day, Jasmine was having a difficult time with the children. The baby, Yuan, had been crying all day from colic. The other two children had been bickering over their toys. Jasmine, realizing that it was already 5:15 and her husband would be home any minute, frantically started preparing dinner. She wanted to fix a nice dinner so that she and her husband could eat after the children went to bed, then relax and enjoy each other.

This scenario was not to be. Jasmine sat waiting for her no-show husband. When he finally walked in the door at 10:15, Jasmine was furious. His excuse that his boss had invited the whole office for dinner didn't reduce Jasmine's ire. Jasmine reasoned that her husband could have called to say that he wouldn't be home for dinner; he could have taken 5 minutes to do that. He said he did but the phone was busy. Her face was red with rage. She screamed at her husband. Suddenly, bursting into tears, she ran into the living room. Her husband retreated to the safety of their bedroom and the respite that a deep sleep would bring.

Exhausted and disappointed, Jasmine sat alone and pondered why she was so angry with her husband. Was she just tired? Was she frustrated by dealing with young children all day and simply wanted to be around another adult? Was she secretly worried and jealous that her husband was seeing another woman and had lied about his whereabouts? Was she combative because her husband's and her sister's lives seemed so much fuller than her life? Jasmine was unsure of how she felt and why she exploded in such rage at her husband, whom she loved dearly.

This story, while sad and gender stereotypical, is not necessarily unrealistic when it comes to emotions. There are times when we are moved by strong emotions. On other occasions, when we expect to cry, we find that our eyes are dry or simply a little misty. What are these strange things we call emotions? What motivates us to become angry at someone we love?

These questions and others have inspired psychologists to study motivation and emotion. Jasmine's story, besides introducing these topics to you, also illustrates why these two topics are usually interrelated in psychology. Some emotions are pleasant, so pleasant that we are motivated to keep experiencing them.

© Ingram Publishing

Pleasant emotions are exemplified by love, pride, and joy. Other emotions are terribly draining and oppressive—so negative that we hope they will be over as soon as possible. Negative emotions are exemplified by anger, grief, and jealousy. Motivation and emotion and their relationship to each other are the focus of this unit.

# Women at the Top

## *Powerful Leaders Define Success as Work + Family in a Culture of Gender*

How do women rise to the top of their professions when they also have significant family care responsibilities? This critical question has not been addressed by existing models of leadership. In a review of recent research, we explore an alternative model to the usual notion of a Western male as the prototypical leader. The model includes (a) relationship-oriented leadership traits, (b) the importance of teamwork and consensus building, and (c) an effective work–family interface that women with family care responsibilities create and use to break through the glass ceiling. We adopted a cross-cultural perspective to highlight the importance of relational orientation and work–family integration in collectivistic cultures, which supplements models of leadership based on Western men. Our expanded model of leadership operates in the context of a "culture of gender" that defines expectations for women and men as leaders. This complex model includes women in diverse global contexts and enriches our understanding of the interplay among personal attributes, processes, and environments in leadership.

FANNY M. CHEUNG AND DIANE F. HALPERN

There are two very different stories about women's leadership around the world, and depending on which one you choose to tell, and your attitudes toward women in leadership positions, the news is either very good or very bad. Despite the endless blogging and newspaper headlines to the contrary, women are not "opting out" of the workforce to stay home with their babies. The workforce participation of mothers did drop by 2% since its peak in 2000, but as economist Boushey (2005) demonstrated, there was a similar drop in employment for women without children and for all men, which was caused by a general recession from 2001 to 2004. For the first time in U.S. history, women are close to surpassing men in their employment rate, largely because most of the jobs lost in the recent recession have occurred in manufacturing, construction, and finance, where the jobs are largely held by men. The most recently available data show that women now hold 49.1% of jobs in the United States (Rampell, 2009). On the other side of the globe is China, where economic development and culture differ from those in the Western industrialized world but the figure for women's employment is quite similar (45%; "Women Take 45%," 2007). Women are better educated than ever before; they comprise the majority of undergraduate college enrollments in industrialized countries and are catching up in the developing countries (57% in the United States: Peter & Horn, 2005; 44% in China: Department of Population, Social, Science and Technology Statistics, National Bureau of Statistics, 2004). As might be expected from the growing trend of women's higher educational achievement, there are more women than men in mid-level management positions, which has created an overflowing "pipeline" of managers ready for advancement to top-level executive positions in the United States.

Now for the bad news: Despite women's success in education and mid-level management, few women make it to the "O" level—CEO, CFO (chief financial officer), CIO (chief information officer), or CTO (chief technology officer)—in the corporate world or to comparable top levels in noncorporate settings, such as the highest levels of political office or the top rungs of the academic ladder. In the United States, women hold approximately 50% of all management and professional positions, outnumbering "men in such occupations as financial managers; human resource managers; education administrators; medical and health services managers; accountants and auditors; budget analysts; property, real estate, and social and community service managers" (U.S. Department of Labor, Women's Bureau, 2006, para. 12). Despite their middle-management success, only 2% of the Fortune 500 CEOs and 2% of the Fortune 1000 CEOs are women ("Fortune 500 2006: Women CEOs," 2006). Comparable data from the FTSE (Financial Times Stock Exchange) 250 (Singh & Vinnicombe, 2006) show that 2.8% of CEOs for the top 250 companies listed on the London Stock Exchange are women.

A half century after the women's movement, women have only moved to the halfway mark in the corporate world and other organizations in the industrialized Western societies; most are stuck in middle management. Women in other parts of the world are still far from that halfway mark. For example, in China, women make up 16.8% of the heads of government departments and the Communist Party, social organizations, enterprises, and institutions (Department of Population, Social, Science and Technology Statistics,

National Bureau of Statistics, 2004). Even in Hong Kong, which continues to be a more westernized and economically affluent special administrative region after its reunification with China in 1997, women constitute 29.1% of persons employed as managers and administrators (Census and Statistics Department, Government of the Hong Kong Special Administrative Region, 2007). A bevy of commentators have suggested that women are better suited for the "New Economy," with its emphasis on communication and interpersonal skills and the rapid loss of jobs in manufacturing, agriculture, and other job sectors in which physical strength is an asset. Although this may seem like a logical conclusion, there are very few women who have made it to the top leadership positions.

Why are there so few women at the top of the leading organizations given the large numbers that are stalled at middle management? An important clue can be found by taking a closer look at the women who have made it into the rarified atmosphere of life at the top. Almost half of these top executives have no children, and almost half of all women in the United States with salaries greater than $100,000 have no children (Dye, 2005; Hewlett, 2002). Similar data have been found for women who achieve at the highest ranks at research universities, where there have been extensive and eye-opening analyses of the success of women with children. Only one third of all women who began their jobs at research universities without children ever become mothers, and among those who attain tenure, women are twice as likely as their male counterparts to be single 12 years after obtaining their doctorates (Mason & Goulden, 2004). The double standard is alive and well in the workplace. The presence of children signals stability and responsibility for men, who are assumed to be better workers because of their roles as breadwinners. The identical situation for women has the opposite effect.

Recent studies have confirmed the *motherhood wage penalty,* a term that describes the consistent finding that mothers earn less than comparable women without children and less than men in general. By contrast, married men enjoy a *marriage premium,* which refers to one of the most reliable findings in the labor economics literature—the economic advantage that fathers enjoy in the workplace (Hersch & Stratton, 2000). In an experimental investigation of this phenomenon, Correll, Benard, and Paik (2007) responded to a variety of employment advertisements with applications from women that varied according to whether the women had children or were childless. The applications were carefully matched on work-relevant dimensions. Only 3.1% of the mothers were invited for an interview, compared with 6.6% of the identically qualified women who had no children. Discriminatory practices against women were further documented by these researchers when paid undergraduates rated fictitious applicants for employment. Mothers were rated as less competent and were offered a lower starting salary than comparable women without children. The choice for highly successful women has been clear: Choose either a baby or a briefcase.

But what about those women who refused to make such a choice and succeeded at the top of their professions with children and other family care responsibilities? What can we learn from these women who are leading dually successful lives with (by their own description) happy, thriving families and occupational success at the highest levels? While there have been many studies on work–family conflicts for women workers or managers in general, there are few such studies on women leaders in the literature and none that specifically compared women with and without family care responsibilities.

Given the small number of women at the top, most studies on women leaders have relied on in-depth and qualitative interviews. Studies of these exceptional women are not representative of the norm, but they highlight gaps in our understanding of leadership from a gender-sensitive perspective. These studies do not have representative samples, as the population is small, but generally rely on personal networks and snowball techniques in reaching these exceptional targets. For example, Cantor and Bernay (1992) interviewed 25 American women politicians holding high federal, state, and local elected offices; they used structured questions to investigate how these women developed the leadership qualities that enable them to succeed in politics. Cantor and Bernay identified three critical elements in the leadership equation for these women politicians: competent self, creative aggression, and womanpower. Instead of attempting to behave like men in a male environment, these women leaders embraced and integrated typically female qualities, such as tenderness and caring, with assertiveness and achievement orientation. White, Cox, and Cooper (1992) interviewed 48 women executives, entrepreneurs, politicians, and senior professionals in the United Kingdom on their childhoods, education, and work and family histories to examine their career trajectories. Walton's (1997) study of 11 women heads of colleges in the United Kingdom also adopted an interview method to cover a range of themes, including the women's academic career paths, family influences, self-worth, and job satisfaction.

Qualitative studies of women leaders from other ethnic backgrounds have also been conducted in recent years. Gomez and her colleagues (2001) conducted semi-structured, in-depth interviews to investigate the career development of 20 notable Latinas in the United States whose contributions on the local, national, or international level were recognized in their communities. Their study included contextual and cultural variables in addition to personal variables and the family–work interface. The contextual and cultural factors included social movements, economic trends, public policies, and discrimination at the macro level. At the more personal or interpersonal level, the individual's socioeconomic and educational background, social support, availability of mentors, and role models were important factors.

Richie and her colleagues (1997) also used semistructured, in-depth interviews to compare nine high-achieving African women and nine European American women across eight occupational fields in the United States. The interviews covered the participants' work behaviors and attitudes, their sociocultural and personal backgrounds, and the current contextual conditions that led to particular career actions and consequences. The stories told by their participants showed that they achieved career success on their own terms. Their leadership styles were characterized by interconnectedness. Social support provided an important means for them to balance their personal and professional lives. The authors concluded that women's career development differed from men's, and they confirmed "the inappropriateness of applying career theories written by and based on White men to White women and people of color" (Richie et al., 1997, p. 145).

Kawahara, Esnil, and Hsu (2007) interviewed 12 Asian American women leaders who were considered to be high achievers. The themes that were covered in the interviews included the women's personal attributes, leadership styles, support systems, self-worth, and cultural competence. The comments collected from the interviews demonstrated the emphasis on relating to others and creating a harmonious environment, both of which are reflective of collectivistic values. Family and partner support were recognized as playing an important role in these women's achievement.

Studies with women leaders from different ethnic backgrounds highlight the additional context of culture in which women navigate through the *labyrinth,* a term preferred by Eagly and Carli (2007) to the *glass ceiling* metaphor. Culture defines the expectations for women's and men's roles in society and sets the norms and values in social behavior. Cross-cultural studies of top women leaders could provide a richer understanding of the convergent and divergent contextual factors that characterize women's leadership.

Using semi-structured open-ended interviews, we studied 62 women at the top of their professions who either were or had been married and who had significant family care responsibilities (usually children, but we also included care for other family members such as a disabled sibling or parent). Top-level positions included legislators, government ministers, business executives, college presidents, chiefs of police, and other senior-level professionals from China, Hong Kong, and the United States (Halpern & Cheung, 2008). These three societies provide a comparison in terms of cultural context and socioeconomic milieu. Hong Kong is more similar to China in cultural background but at the same time is more similar to the United States in terms of socioeconomic environment, whereas China and the United States are more distinct from one another in both culture and socioeconomic milieu (Watkins, 2006). In addition to describing their career development and leadership styles, these top women leaders in American and Chinese societies described how they created and negotiated a work–family interface. These highly successful women shared their strategies for leading dually successful lives. This study provides a cross-cultural perspective on the key issues for studying women's leadership. We use the lessons we learned from our study to structure the framework of the following review of the research literature on women leaders.

# Integrating Work and Family

Previous research on women in employment has highlighted work–family balance as a major concern (Allen, Herst, Bruck, & Sutton, 2000; Byron, 2005). Working mothers everywhere are known to be short on time, always working a "second shift" after they finish a day at their hectic jobs (Hochschild, 1989). Many countries across the world have conducted time use surveys (United Nations Statistics Division, n.d.). The common finding is that women in paid employment generally spend more hours per day on household duties than do their male counterparts (e.g. Galinsky, 2005). Early studies of work–family balance adopted a scarcity perspective (Greenhaus & Beutell, 1985). It was assumed that the demands of family and work were competing for a finite amount of time, resulting in conflict and stress.

By studying women leaders who managed to maintain their family lives while they advanced in their careers, we identified personal characteristics and strategies that women used to overcome these barriers. As workers in "extreme jobs" that require "24/7" commitment (Hewlett & Luce, 2006), the dually successful top women leaders we interviewed employed many strategies to "make more time." As revealed in our study and other studies of women leaders, these women considered themselves to be experts in multitasking. Because they each lived one life rather than two separate lives at work and at home, they created links between family and work, although they kept their role identities distinct. For example, children went to work with them and often accompanied them on business trips, not only because it allowed the women to spend more time with their children but also because it helped the children understand where their mommies went when they left the house. The women worked from home at least part of the time, often setting rules for switching activities, such as working on Sunday night rather than during the day when they spent the weekend with family, or always being at home for dinner and then working after the children went to bed.

## *Beyond Work–Family Balance*

Recent research on the work–family interface has taken a more balanced view and considered more complex interactions between the work and family domains, which include both negative and positive spillovers in the work–family interface (Rapoport, Bailyn, Fletcher, & Pruitt, 2002). From their meta-analysis reviewing 178 studies on the work–family interface, Ford, Heinen, and Langkamer (2007) found that support from family and work domains was positively related to cross-domain satisfaction. Friedman and Greenhaus (2000) found that when work and family were integrated, the two roles could enhance each other. In integrating these two roles, managing role boundaries was more important than just reducing time at work. Particularly for women, the work–family boundary is more permeable. Thus, we propose that the metaphor of work–family balance be replaced with a metaphor that recognizes the gains that can be achieved by combining or integrating work and family roles (Halpern & Murphy, 2005).

Baltes and Heydens-Gahir (2003) extended a general model of life management strategy to study work–family conflict. They classified the repertoire of adaptive behavior strategies as SOC: selection, optimization, and compensation. The primary focus of *selection* is on the articulation and setting of goals, which give direction to behavior. In our study (Halpern & Cheung, 2008), the top women leaders were very clear about their goals and their priorities. Family and work were both important, and day-to-day decisions were based on family and work needs. They also excelled in the *optimization* strategies through scheduling of time and multitasking. They were flexible in adopting the *compensation* strategy by using alternative means such as outsourcing when time and material resources were limited.

In order to accept the alternative means of fulfilling the demands of a role, many women leaders redefine the structural and personal roles that the workplace and the society have imposed on women (Frone, 2003). In the studies reviewed, most of the women leaders who are married and have families embrace both their family and work roles. However, instead of being superwomen who hold themselves to the highest standards for all of the role-related tasks of being wives and mothers, they adopt different internal and external strategies to redefine their roles. They learn to let go and outsource household tasks just as they would outsource work in a busy office. They recognize that they do not have to do it all by themselves. They alter their internal conceptions of the demands of their work and family roles and define these roles in ways that are meaningful and helpful to them.

Research on work–family balance in Chinese societies suggests a different cultural perspective in understanding the definition of work and family roles. These studies show that work and family are viewed as interdependent domains, unlike the distinct segregation of these two domains in Western concepts of work and family. In individualistic societies, overwork would be considered as taking time away from the family and sacrificing the family for the advancement of one's own career. In collectivistic societies, overwork is likely to be seen as sacrificing oneself for the family, since commitment to work is viewed as a means to ensuring financial security for the family (Yang, Chen, Choi, & Zou, 2000). The needs of the self are subsumed under the needs of the collective. As such, the work–family boundary is more permeable in Chinese societies (Francesco & Shaffer, 2009).

A cross-national comparative study (Spector et al., 2004) involving 15 samples of managers across three culturally distinct regions—Anglo-majority countries (Australia, Canada, England, New Zealand, and the United States), China (Hong Kong, mainland China, and Taiwan), and seven Latin American countries—showed that for the Anglo culture, working long hours was related to work–family stress. For the Chinese and Latin cultures, this was not the case. For the Chinese managers, being married and having children were associated with higher job satisfaction and psychological well-being. A series of studies conducted by Aryee and his colleagues on the work–family interface in Hong Kong (Aryee, Field, & Luk, 1999; Aryee, Luk, Leung, & Lo, 1999) also showed that work and family involvement per se did not lead to work–family conflict. Time conflict did not necessarily lead to strain.

A recent study of working adults in the United States found that women and men with an egalitarian outlook on life, which means they were committed to both their work and their families, reported feeling less guilty when family life interfered with their work than traditional women and men whose commitment was to only one of these spheres of life (Livingston & Judge, 2008). It is interesting to note that these researchers did not find much guilt when work interfered with family life, although one possible explanation for this asymmetry is that few of their participants had partners (36%) or young children (25%). The successful combination of family and work will depend on the obligations people have in both of these spheres.

Past studies of work–life balance rarely included leaders at the top with substantial family care responsibilities and have not considered their responses as a distinct group. Partly it is because this is not an issue that is considered important to men as leaders; partly it is because there are very few top women leaders to be studied. In studies of women leaders, however, we found that the dually successful Western women leaders tended to integrate their work and family roles in the collective unit of the family. Many also regarded family as their priority, and the motivation to succeed at work was to contribute to the well-being of their families and children. In reframing their work as an ally instead of an enemy of the family (Friedman & Greenhaus, 2000), the women leaders in many of the qualitative studies we reviewed reported satisfaction in both domains.

## Redefining Roles

In order to integrate their family roles and work roles, the women leaders in the studies we reviewed redefined their own norms for being a good mother and being a leader, making these roles more compatible than they were under the norms prescribed by the larger society. According to their own definitions, a good mother is highly involved in her children's lives and activities, but she does not need to spend all of her time with them. Typically, the women

leaders in these studies described their devotion to their children and their families. But because they considered family their highest priority, they dedicated themselves to finding solutions to make it work. These solutions included self-enforced standards to ensure that they always had dinner with their families, took the children on any business trip that lasted more than three days, never missed an important event such as a school play or soccer game, and helped with homework every night. For example, in our study (Halpern & Cheung, 2008), one Hong Kong woman executive made a long-distance telephone call to her children every night when she was posted overseas (before Internet communication was widely accessible) and had them fax their homework to her hotel room, which she then faxed back to them after she reviewed it. Several Chinese women leaders talked about going home to eat dinner with their families before leaving for a business dinner or an evening meeting in order to maintain family togetherness. U.S. women leaders talked with pride about never or rarely missing an important event in their children's lives, which they achieved by arranging their work around these events.

These highly successful women also redefined their roles as successful leaders, which included work + family. They worked long hours, but they also managed to leave work for family time. They counted performance and outcome rather than the actual hours at work. Earlier in their careers, some of the women "flew below the radar" and just left work without announcing why to be at after-school events, completing their work later in the evening. Their employers learned that it was their performance that counted. Once they were in positions of leadership, the women leaders had more control over their work schedules, which allowed them to handle dual demands more openly.

Women's dual roles may be viewed as two circles, one representing family and one work. When the demands of a two-circle life are too much for anyone to manage, the total area for both circles needs to be reduced. One way to reduce the total area is to overlap the circles when possible, symbolically blending work and family (see Figure 1). The portion of the family circle that extends beyond the overlap can be reduced with practical strategies such as hiring help to clean the house, prepare meals, and even shop for presents—by outsourcing anything that does not directly contribute to spending time with one's family. In addition, the portion of the circle representing work that is not overlapping with family can also be reduced. Employees can be empowered to do their work without the direct involvement of the women leaders. Many of these high-powered mothers created work-related expectations that also reduced the size of the "work" circle, such as always leaving work at 7:00 or whatever time they routinely set for themselves and scheduling luncheon meetings instead of evening dinners with clients so as to eat dinner with their families.

## Family and Spousal Support

Inevitably, the women leaders interviewed in the various studies all cited the importance of their family support in making it to the top. Having collective identities that emphasized family loyalty, they also fell back on their families to provide support. They relied on some combination of supportive husbands, extended families, and hired help in societies where domestic help was accessible.

The extended family provided much needed help with household chores and child care. Particularly for women from collectivistic societies, proximity to the extended family facilitated their

Distinct Work and Family Domains in a Segregated Model

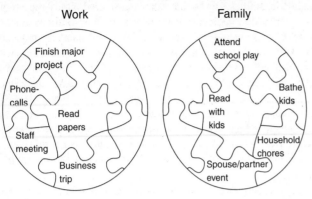

Overlapping Work–Family Domains in an Integrated Model
Work–Family Interface

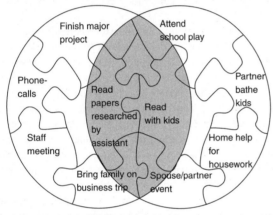

**Figure 1    Segregated Versus Integrated Models of Work–Family Interface**

support networks. Part-time and live-in home help supplemented this network. Even in the United States, home help is not as economically inaccessible to professional women as many people believe. The difficulty lies more in getting reliable and stable home help, as well as in women's personal belief that they have to do everything themselves. In interviews with women leaders, they would talk about child-care arrangements, supervision of domestic helpers, and maintaining emotional labor with the extended family. In studies of male leadership, these arrangements are assumed to be taken care of by someone and are rarely explicitly discussed.

Another distinctive concern for women leaders is their spousal relationships. Studies of marital relationships show that one of the biggest problems for working women is their husbands' lack of support for their careers (Gilbert, 1988; Vannoy-Hiller & Philliber, 1991). In Western studies of mate selection, men prefer to marry down, which usually includes marrying women who are shorter, weigh less, have less education, and earn less than they do (Schoen & Weinick, 1993). So the superior social status of women leaders may pose a threat to their marriages if their husbands are uncomfortable breaking with traditional sex role norms.

The married women leaders in the various studies converged in their appreciation of their husbands' support. Otherwise, their marriages might not have lasted. The supportive husbands were reported to take on a substantial share in housework. More important, they provided emotional support and encouragement. In

our study (Halpern & Cheung, 2008), we specifically addressed the women leaders' relationships with their husbands. Under the strong patriarchal norms in Chinese families, the success of women leaders might have posed a stronger threat to their husbands. However, in this selective sample of women leaders who had stayed married, many described their husbands as their biggest fans, cheerleaders, coaches, and mentors. These husbands were self-assured and confident of themselves. They endorsed egalitarian values toward women. They did not endorse the hierarchical patriarchal norms of marriage and did not feel threatened by the reversed normative roles that put their wives in the limelight and gave them "superior" status.

It is particularly difficult when a family moves for the advancement of the wife's career and the husband takes up the role of the trailing spouse, often with uncertain career prospects at the new location and the loss of a good job at the old location. However, the couples who moved repeatedly to accommodate the wife's promotions considered the sacrifices made by the trailing spouse to be worthwhile. For these couples, the wife's accomplishments and the resources she brought to the marriage were redefined as collective assets to the family instead of threats in a power struggle.

The women leaders who stayed happily married emphasized that they and their husbands grew together in the marriage. They exhibited what marital counselors would call healthy couple behaviors—responsibility, alignment of goals, mutual encouragement and acceptance, commitment to equality in the relationship, empathic listening and open communication, willingness to discuss their relationship, and willingness to engage in joint conflict resolution (Blume, 2006). There was a great deal of give and take, discussion, and negotiation in these marriages. Amidst their busy schedules, our interviewees created the time and space to share their lives with their marital partners. Many of the women mentioned how they designated evenings or weekends for the family or for special dates with their husbands.

# Women's Style of Leadership

Do women lead differently from men? Eagly and Carli (2007) observed that while leadership roles promote similarities in male and female leaders, women generally have a more democratic, participative, and collaborative style of leading. Stern (2008) reviewed studies of high-achieving women and concurred that these women tend to adopt a relational leadership style. They also demonstrate a strong sense of conviction and self-worth. Femininity and leadership are no longer considered incompatible. Virtually all of the women we interviewed believed that their style of leadership as women was better suited for the contemporary workplace. They did not reject femininity or shy away from including family roles as metaphors for their leadership roles. Some of the Chinese women talked about leading like grandmothers or mothers, which included being firm when necessary but always supportive, similar to what Cantor and Bernay (1992) described as "maternal strengths" in the American women politicians. These women were not advocating for a "mushy" or feel-good notion of what a "feminine" approach to leadership might be. Instead, the usual definition they provided included being serious about their work, maintaining the highest personal standards, promoting communication, and being considerate and respectful of their staffs. They also strongly emphasized the notion of a leader as a person of moral character and a role model, which together with a relational orientation have been found to be defining characteristics of leadership in Chinese culture (Smith & Wang, 1996). In Stern's (2008) review of women leaders, making a social contribution and being of service to others were also featured in the women's narratives about their leadership. In Cantor and Bernay's (1992) description of the "womanpower" of women politicians, advancing an agenda of helping others was one of the key motives for their entering politics. Women leaders are particularly conscious of their role in promoting gender equality in their organizations.

In the narratives of women leaders, competition and power are rarely featured. Few of the women leaders in the studies we reviewed mentioned their own power in their narratives about their leadership style or goals. Instead, they emphasized empowering others and creating consensus. They demonstrated what Chin (2007) described as the collaborative process in feminist leadership. Almost all of the women talked about creating flatter organizations and sharing information widely throughout the organization. What emerged is a definition of what is known in the leadership literature as a *transformational* leadership style. Burns (1978) defined transformational leaders as those who "*engage* with others in such a way that leaders and followers raise one another to higher levels of motivation and morality" (p. 20). Over the past 30 years, the concept of transformational leadership has evolved to include leaders who are inspiring, optimistic, moral, and equitable. Judge and Piccolo (2004) built on earlier work in their study of transformational leadership and extended the concept to include charismatic individuals who provide others with inspirational motivation, intellectual stimulation, individual consideration, and a higher purpose in life. This style of leadership is most often contrasted with the more traditional and hierarchically organized transactional style. Transformational leaders transform others by pushing them to assume new points of view and to question their prior assumptions (Goethals, 2005). The perception that women tend to use transformational styles of leadership to a greater extent than do men was confirmed in a meta-analytic review by Eagly, Johannesen-Schmidt, and van Engen (2003) of 45 separate studies. These researchers also found that women leaders tended to engage in more reward-contingency behaviors than men leaders. In other words, the women leaders linked employee rewards to their behaviors in appropriate ways that allowed employees to see the link between their efforts and outcomes at work and the rewards they received. Although the size of the effect that differentiated women from men leaders was small, the meta-analysis showed consistent findings that favored women leaders.

The definition of transformational leadership is more congruent with the interpersonal characteristics associated with women leaders than with the aggressive and hierarchical characteristics associated with male leaders. Women leaders across different studies converge in stressing the importance of communication and team building. In a meta-analytic review of the literature, Lowe, Kroeck, and Sivasubramaniam (1996) found that transformational leadership has a greater association with effective outcomes than does transactional leadership. Logically, then, it might be expected that women, in general, would be more effective leaders because they are more likely to use the style that is associated with better outcomes. The few studies that have examined the effect of having women in top corporate positions confirm this prediction. In one study, researchers sampled over 700 businesses listed in a *Fortune* magazine list of 1,000 businesses (Krishnan & Park, 2005). They found that women constituted 6.7% of the "top

management teams" and 2.8% of the line positions on these teams. (Line positions are those directly related to the profitability of the corporation, as opposed to positions in human resources or communications, which are more likely to be filled by women.) The main finding was a significant positive relationship between the number of women in top management and the financial performance of the company. This is a powerful and important finding. In explaining their results, these researchers noted that differences between female and male leadership styles were crucial, especially women's greater willingness to share information, which can drive better performance throughout the company. It is good for business to keep everyone in the know so they can act with fuller knowledge about the entire company.

## Climbing One Rung at a Time

As Cantor and Bernay (1992) pointed out, most women leaders did not have sandbox dreams of greatness in their childhoods. The women leaders in our study (Halpern & Cheung, 2008) created successful lives for themselves by working hard and working smart. As in Gomez et al.'s (2001) study of Latina leaders, mothers and mentors figured prominently in the women's tales of how they got where they are today. Their mothers played an important role in inspiring them to try their best and in building their self-confidence early in life, and mentors provided an insider's guide to what they needed to know and provided networking opportunities. We note here that although the idea of mentoring is not as well recognized in Asian cultures as it is in the West, the Asian women often acknowledged informal mentoring relationships, without using this particular label.

An important path toward success for most of the contemporary women leaders was through education. The women achieved a high educational level, which built their self-efficacy and provided them upward mobility. Notwithstanding the sociocultural barriers to women's higher education during their lifetimes, the women in the various studies were either encouraged by their families to pursue education as a key to a better life or strived on their own at a later stage in life to get the preparation they needed for advancement. As Fassinger (2005) suggested, high self-efficacy is a key to women's career success.

In Madsen's (2007) study of 10 American women who served as college or university presidents, a pattern of ongoing personal and professional development was identified. These women leaders demonstrated a continuous process of self-monitoring and self-empowerment in taking on challenging responsibilities while inspiring and supporting the people around them.

In Gomez et al.'s (2001) study of 20 Latina leaders, the career–life path of the participants was characterized as an implementation of the self within an immediate context, influenced by their family background, sociopolitical conditions, and cultural environment. Equipped with an ardent sense of self, the participants used social support networks and cognitive reframing to maintain a balanced perspective or to open new doors when confronting challenges.

As in Gomez et al.'s (2001) study, the women we interviewed concurred in acknowledging a pattern of unintended leadership development. In the early stages of their careers, none of the women planned on making it to the top of their professions or, to use Eagly and Carli's (2007) metaphor, making career moves within a labyrinth. They did not strategically plan their routes or attempt to identify the blind alleys at that stage. As many of the women leaders told us, they never thought it would be possible. They found meaningful work that they loved and climbed one rung at a time as they rose to meet new challenges. Few of the women took career breaks or used any family-friendly policies such as part-time employment or flexible scheduling as they moved through the ranks, in part because these options were not generally available at the time. Their stories reflect that they used a blend of "whatever works."

It would be misleading to label circuitous and unplanned routes to the top as serendipity because the opportunities opened for women who were prepared for the uphill climb. The choices the women leaders made earlier in their careers were considered assets rather than losses. Take the example of Sarah Weddington, the former presidential advisor who did not get a job at a high powered law firm when she got out of law school because she was a woman. She ended up with the opportunity to argue the landmark *Roe v. Wade* case in the U.S. Supreme Court and then went on to find jobs in the higher rungs of politics and government. She called it the "step-by-step method of leadership" (Halpern & Cheung, 2008, p. 219). This is similar to the description by Cantor and Bernay (1992) of how women politicians turned what others perceived to be obstacles into possibilities for themselves.

Our sample included two women who became a chief of police and a chief of one of the largest sheriff's departments in the United States, positions that epitomize male leadership. The police chief told us that as she was being promoted within the department, she realized that she would need to have a college degree and a master's degree to make it anywhere near the top, and she had neither. What she did have at the time was a full-time-plus job as a detective with irregular work hours (homicides do not happen within a 9 to 5 day) and young children. She took her time and waited until her children were in high school and then went to college at night, earning both of the necessary degrees and, ultimately, promotion to the top of the force. A number of the women entrepreneurs from China served previously in the People's Liberation Army, a choice that becomes more understandable when one considers that the only alternative they might have had at the time was to be educated by peasants in the countryside, an educational experience that was in accord with the ideology of the Cultural Revolution. Their military training prepared them well for taking the risks they had to take in starting their own businesses later during the new economic reforms in China.

Now that they are in positions of leadership, the successful women leaders are making it easier for the mothers (and others) who are behind them to handle the often competing demands of running a corporation and going home to change diapers and read bedtime stories. As leaders and policymakers, they are competent professionals who overtly demonstrate their care for their employees and clients in their official policies and everyday interactions, thus creating a model of leadership that takes the best parts of both of the traditional roles of leader and mother.

# Cultural Differences and Convergence

The field of cross-cultural leadership has underscored the importance of examining contextual factors when defining leadership (Avolio, 2007). Studies of ethnic women leaders have also highlighted how sociocultural context and cultural identity shape the interpretive lens with which women view the career–life paths they steer (Gomez et al., 2001; Richie et al., 1997).

In cross-cultural psychology, national cultures have been compared in terms of different dimensions of societal norms (Hofstede, 1980). Anglo cultures, like that of the United States, are considered to be individualistic. In these cultures, identity is based in the individual, and emphasis is placed on autonomy and independence. Individuals are supposed to take care of themselves and their immediate families, which consist of the nuclear unit of a couple and their children. In contrast, Asian cultures, like that of the Chinese, are considered to be collectivistic in orientation. Identity is embedded in the social system, an organization, or a group to which the individual belongs. People are born into extended families that take care of them in exchange for their loyalty. Interdependence and harmony among group members are emphasized. As in other societies that emphasize family orientation, the Chinese and the African American women leaders in our study as well as the Latina leaders in Gomez et al.'s (2001) study were more likely to receive social support from their extended families than were the Anglo women leaders.

Culture also defines the social expectations for women's and men's roles. In traditional Chinese culture, women's roles are defined by their different family roles throughout the life stages: daughter, wife, and mother, who should obey, respectively, their father, husband, and son. However, cultural ideologies change with historical events, although there is some lag time before normative attitudes and behaviors change. Socioeconomic and political developments in contemporary China have expanded women's roles. The Communist Party ideology has emphasized liberating Chinese women from their feudalistic oppression as one of the goals of class struggle, and the late Chairman Mao's motto that "women can hold up half the sky" during the 1960s encouraged women to participate in all walks of life. Global campaigns of the women's movement have raised consciousness on gender equality and women's empowerment. There are now legal instruments in China, Hong Kong, and the United States to protect women's rights in employment. However, the structure of the patriarchal family role ascribed to women has moved relatively little despite large changes in the everyday lives of women and men.

Despite great differences in the sociopolitical context during their childhoods, there were striking similarities among the women from China, Hong Kong, and the United States. Many of the mainland Chinese women experienced hardship as they grew up during the Japanese incursion, the Second World War in the 1940s, and the establishment of the People's Republic of China, which was followed by the horrific conditions during the Cultural Revolution, a time when education was denigrated and families were torn apart. The women leaders from Hong Kong had a "foot in two cultures," living first under British rule and, since 1997, under a special administrative region of China which continued to flourish as an international financial center. The leaders from the United States grew up just as opportunities for women opened up as a result of affirmative action and increased legal protection against overt discrimination, although the Equal Rights Amendment failed to gain sufficient support to become national law. Despite the vast sociopolitical differences among these three societies, the culture of gender, with its prescription of appropriate gender roles, exerted a stronger impact on women.

The narratives of the women leaders whom we interviewed (Halpern & Cheung, 2008) highlighted themes that reflected their cultural ideologies. Although all of the women leaders featured their family roles prominently in describing their personal identities, what they considered to be the essential tasks of these roles differed. The American women leaders prided themselves on never missing their children's school plays or soccer games; mothers in Hong Kong put more emphasis on helping their children with their schoolwork. A dominant feature in the Chinese mother's role is overseeing their children's education, with heavy emphasis on supervision of homework and preparation for examinations. Food is another cultural theme that is prominent in the Chinese family. The Chinese mothers from mainland China, Hong Kong, and the United States alike emphasized family dinners as a symbol of family togetherness, describing how they ate with their children before they went out to their own business dinners or went back to work at the office at night. When the hierarchical norms of husband and wife were reversed, the Chinese women leaders were sensitive to how their husbands might lose "face" and took measures to protect against such situations.

Although culture prescribes the expectations for gender roles and behaviors, there are differences within the culture in the way in which individuals play out these roles. We recognize that there are also ethnic, regional, and class differences within the larger cultural group. For example, some of the American women leaders relied on live-in helpers, with fewer of them relying on their extended families for help with child care than the women in mainland China and Hong Kong. The physical distance for the U.S. women from their extended families may have been a barrier that made using this resource a rare occurrence.

## The Culture of Gender

When we began our study, we thought there would be many differences between the Chinese and American women leaders in how they managed the combination of top-level work and a successful family life. We expected that the American women leaders would segregate their work and family roles more distinctly, as suggested by Western theories and research on work–family conflict. However, the cultural differences we found relate more to the contents rather than the structure of the role ideology. There was more convergence in the way that these women leaders interwove work and family roles on their paths to the top. Even though they subscribed to gender roles, the Chinese and the American women leaders alike defied the constraints of sexism, which is pervasive across culture. They embraced the multifaceted roles involved in being women. With their growing confidence in their own identities, they did not need to conform to the roles and behaviors of men in order to become leaders. Unlike Western men, they did not segregate their work roles and family roles into distinct domains that could result in conflict. Instead, they integrated their work and family roles in ways that enabled them to harmonize both. Their successful strategies can inform our understanding of the work–family interface. A recent study of working adults in the Netherlands also found that women were more likely to use strategies that facilitated the combination of work and family than were men (van Steenbergen, Ellemers, & Mooijaart, 2007). Instead of viewing the combination of these two spheres of life as necessarily negative, the women found ways to benefit from combining their dual roles, which was a consistent theme among our sample of women leaders and other studies of women leaders with families.

In hindsight, one reason for the cross-cultural similarities is that all of the women share what we are calling "the culture of gender." Notwithstanding the cultural differences found according

to the usual understanding of culture, there are pancultural gender role norms that create opportunities and constraints for all women leaders (Inglehart & Norris, 2003). In every society, gender norms prescribe the roles and behaviors that differentiate the experiences of women and men. There are restrictions inherent in the roles of women that make it difficult for them to achieve at high levels in demanding careers. Across national boundaries, women leaders are exposed to similar stereotypes that form sexist prejudice in organizations and to the same media that scutinize their physical appearance, clothing, and family responsibilities with a magnifying glass while portraying their male counterparts as dealing with substantive issues. Reviewing the culture of gender helps us to expand our understanding of leadership, which includes not only individual traits and behaviors but also the process of integrating work and family as two major domains in a leader's life.

## An Alternative Model of Leadership

Leadership studies have moved beyond the "trait" and "situation" approaches to more integrated theories of leadership that include the contributions of relationships, contexts, and culture (Avolio, 2007). We note here that in all the qualitative studies of women leaders, researchers relied on the women's tales of their success and how they perceived the interplay among their life roles. The use of semi-structured interviews led the participants to respond to particular aspects of their careers in ways they chose to recall. Families, employers, and employees may have perceived the lives of these women very differently, but we were more concerned with how the women explained their own choices and actions. They were (mostly) pleased with their success at work and at home, which led us to label them as dually successful.

The success stories of the women leaders in various studies show us not only a fuller picture of how women can attain leadership but also how gender can inform leadership research. The study of women's leadership styles and their integration of work and family roles have enriched our understanding of the interplay of personal attributes, processes, and environment in a complex model of leadership that includes women in diverse global contexts. Their exceptional experiences guide us to consider an alternative model to the usual notion of a Western male as the prototypical leader in an organizational setting. This alternative model encompasses a fuller picture of leaders as human beings who steer their lives successfully (Figure 2). It includes the multiple roles of leaders in a complex world. It shows the developmental steps taken by the leaders navigating through their life courses, which are shaped by sociopolitical conditions and current contexts. These contexts may facilitate greater access to education and mentoring for women, which in turn build up their self-efficacy. Flexible working conditions and social support make it possible for women to combine work and family. These steps are not meant to be rigid sequences but are intended to illustrate the incremental and interactional nature of leadership development. The model strengthens the consideration of the interpersonal and relational dimensions of leadership. The transformational leadership style creates a flatter organization in a global work context. This model also recognizes the importance of the integration of different domains of a leader's life. The interplay of these domains varies during different developmental stages of the

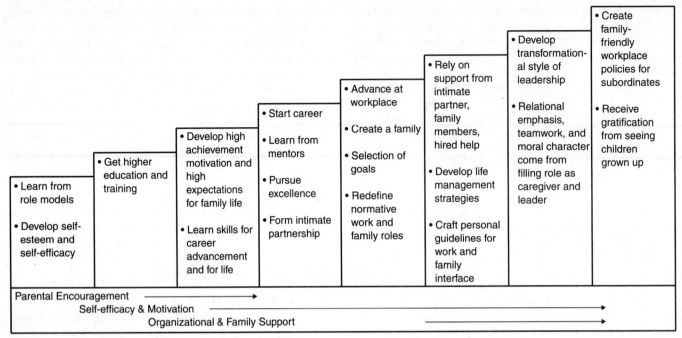

**Figure 2** Step-by-Step Model of Leadership Development Incorporating Work and Family Roles

leader's life course. We suggest that filling family roles such as those of mothers and caregivers, becoming leaders at work, and making these roles compatible have helped women to cultivate the transformational style of leadership.

We base our suggestions on the lessons we learned from the successful women leaders who have families, which is an unusual group. We do not intend to paint an overly rosy picture of these women's lives. They had their share of hardship and strain at work and at home. But they have managed to steer through the labyrinth despite the barriers. We did not speak to their family members and get their perspectives. That will be a direction for future studies. We also recognize that women leaders without families may face convergent and divergent issues, and so do men leaders with and without families. What we are suggesting is that a more comprehensive and inclusive model takes into account the gaps in existing models. Future research could compare how women at different stages of the career development and family life cycles construe their life purposes in incremental steps, and how powerful men and women define their success as work + family in a model of transformational leadership.

# References

Allen, T. D., Herst, D. E. L., Bruck, C. S., & Sutton, M. (2000). Consequences associated with work-to-family conflict: A review and agenda for future research. *Journal of Occupational Health Psychology, 5,* 278–308, doi:101037/1076-8998.5.2.278

Aryee, S., Field, D., & Luk, V. (1999). A cross-cultural test of a model of work–family interface. *Journal of Management, 25,* 491–511. doi: 10.1177/014920639902500402

Aryee, S., Luk, V., Leung, A., & Lo, S. (1999). Role stressors, interrole conflict, and well-being: The moderating effect of spousal support and coping behaviors among employed parents in Hong Kong. *Journal of Vocational Behavior, 54,* 259–278. doi:10.1006/jvbe. 1998.1667

Avolio, B. J. (2007). Promoting more integrative strategies for leadership theory-building. *American Psychologist, 62,* 25–33. doi:10.1037/0003-066X.62.1.25

Baltes, B. B., & Heydens-Gahir, H. A. (2003). Reduction of work–family conflict through the use of selection, optimization, and compensation behaviors. *Journal of Applied Psychology, 88,* 1005–1018. doi:10.1037/0021-9010.88.6.1005

Blume, R. (2006). *Becoming a family counselor: A bridge to family therapy theory and practice.* Hoboken, NJ: Wiley.

Boushey, H. (2005, November). *Are women opting out? Debunking the myth* [Briefing paper]. Retrieved from the Center for Economic and Policy Research website: www.cepr.net/documents/publications/opt_out_2005_11_2.pdf

Burns, J. M. (1978). *Leadership.* New York, NY: Harper & Row.

Byron, K. (2005). A meta-analytic review of work–family conflict and its antecedents. *Journal of Vocational Behavior, 67,* 169–198. doi:10.1016/j.jvb.2004.08.009

Cantor, D. W., & Bernay, T. (1992). *Women in power: The secrets of leadership.* Boston, MA: Houghton Mifflin.

Census and Statistics Department, Government of the Hong Kong Special Administrative Region. (2007). *Women and men in Hong Kong: Key statistics.* Hong Kong, China: Author. Retrieved from www.censtatd.gov.hk/products_and_services/products/publications/statistical_report/social_2007_data/index_cd_B1130303_dt_back_yr_2007.jsp

Chin, J. L. (2007). Overview: Women and leadership: Transforming visions and diverse voices. In J. L. Chin, B. Lott, J. K. Rice, & J. Sanchez-Hucles (Eds.), *Women and leadership: Transforming visions and diverse voices* (pp. 1–17). Oxford, England: Blackwell.

Correll, S. J., Benard, S., & Paik, I. (2007). Getting a job: Is there a motherhood penalty? *American Journal of Sociology, 112,* 1297–1338. doi:10.1086/511799

Department of Population, Social, Science and Technology Statistics, National Bureau of Statistics. (2004). *Women and men in China:*

*Facts and figures 2004*. Beijing, China: Author. Retrieved from www.stats.gov.cn/english/statisticaldata/otherdata/men&women_en.pdf

Dye, J. L. (2005, December). *Fertility of American women: June 2004* (Current Population Reports, P20-555). Retrieved from U.S. Census Bureau website: www.census.gov/prod/2005pubs/p20-555.pdf

Eagly, A. H., & Carli, L. L. (2007). *Through the labyrinth: The truth about how women become leaders.* Boston, MA: Harvard Business School Press.

Eagly, A. H., Johannesen-Schmidt, M. C., & van Engen, M. (2003). Transformational, transactional, and laissez-faire leadership styles: A meta-analysis comparing women and men. *Psychological Bulletin, 95,* 569–591. doi:10.1037/0033-2909.129.4.569

Fassinger, R. (2005). Theoretical issues in the study of women's career development: Building bridges in a brave new world. In W. B. Walsh & M. L. Savickas (Eds.), *Handbook of vocational psychology: Theory, research, and practice* (3rd ed., pp. 85–126). Mahwah, NJ: Erlbaum.

Ford, M. T., Heinen, B. A., & Langkamer, K. L. (2007). Work and family satisfaction and conflict: A meta-analysis of cross-domain relations. *Journal of Applied Psychology, 92,* 57–80. doi:10.1037/0021-9010.92.1.57

Fortune 500 2006: Women CEOs for Fortune 500 companies. (2006, April 17). *Fortune, 153*(7). Retrieved from http://money.cnn.com/magazines/fortune/fortune500/womenceos/

Francesco, A. M., & Shaffer, M. A. (2009). Working women in Hong Kong: *Neuih keuhng yahn* or oppressed class? In F. M. Cheung & E. Holroyd (Eds.), *Mainstreaming gender in Hong Kong society* (pp. 311–334). Hong Kong, China: Chinese University Press.

Friedman, S. D., & Greenhaus, J. H. (2000). *Work and family—Allies or enemies? What happens when business professionals confront life choices.* New York, NY: Oxford University Press.

Frone, M. R. (2003). Work–family balance. In J. C. Quick & L. E. Tetrick (Eds.), *Handbook of occupational health psychology* (pp. 143–162). Washington DC: American Psychological Association.

Galinsky, E. (2005). *Overwork in America: When the way we work becomes too much.* New York, NY: Families and Work Institute.

Gilbert, L. A. (1988). *Sharing it all: The rewards and struggles of two-career families.* New York, NY: Plenum Press.

Goethals, G. R. (2005). Presidential leadership. *Annual Review of Psychology, 56,* 545–570. doi:10.1146/annurev.psych.55.090902.141918

Gomez, M. J., Fassinger, R. E., Prosser, J., Cooke, K., Mejia, B., & Luna, J. (2001). Voces abriendo caminos (Voices forging paths): A qualitative study of the career development of notable Latinas. *Journal of Counseling Psychology, 48,* 286–300. doi:10.1037/0022-0167.48.3.286

Greenhaus, J. H., & Beutell, N. J. (1985). Sources of conflict between work and family roles. *Academy of Management Review, 10,* 76–88.

Halpern, D. F., & Cheung, F. M. (2008). *Women at the top: Powerful leaders tell us how to combine work and family.* New York, NY: Wiley/Blackwell.

Halpern, D. F., & Murphy, S. E. (Eds.). (2005). *From work–family balance to work–family interaction: Changing the metaphor.* Mahwah, NJ: Erlbaum.

Hersch, J., & Stratton, L. S. (2000). Household specialization and the male marriage wage premium. *Industrial and Labor Relations Review, 54,* 78–94. doi:10.2139/ssrn.241067

Hewlett, S. A. (2002). Executive women and the myth of having it all. *Harvard Business Review, 80,* 66–73.

Hewlett, S. A., & Luce, C. B. (2006). Extreme jobs: The dangerous allure of the 70-hour work week. *Harvard Business Review, 84,* 49–59.

Hochschild, A. R. (1989). *The second shift.* London, England: Penguin.

Hofstede, G. (1980). *Culture's consequences: International differences in work-related values.* Beverly Hill, CA: Sage.

Inglehart, R., & Norris, P. (2003). *Rising tide: Gender equality and cultural change around the world.* New York, NY: Cambridge University Press.

Judge, T. A., & Piccolo, R. F. (2004). Transformational and transactional leadership: A meta-analytic test of their relative validity. *Journal of Applied Psychology, 89,* 901–910. doi:10.1037/0021-9010.89.5.755

Kawahara, D. M., Esnil, E. M., & Hsu, J. (2007). Asian American women leaders: The intersection of race, gender, and leadership. In J. L. Chin, B. Lott, J. K. Rice, & J. Sanchez-Hucles (Eds.), *Women and leadership: Transforming visions and diverse voices* (pp. 297–313). Malden, MA: Blackwell.

Krishnan, H. A., & Park, D. (2005). A few good women—on top management teams. *Journal of Business Research, 58,* 1712–1720. doi:10.1016/j.jbusres.2004.09.003

Livingston, B. A., & Judge, T. A. (2008). Emotional responses to work–family conflict: An examination of gender role orientation among working men and women. *Journal of Applied Psychology, 93,* 207–211. doi:10.1037/0021-9010.93.1.207

Lowe, K. B., Kroeck, K. G., & Sivasubramaniam, N. (1996). Effectiveness correlates of transformational and transactional leadership: A meta-analytic review of the MLQ literature. *The Leadership Quarterly, 7,* 385–425. doi:10.1016/S1048-9843(96)90027-2

Madsen, S. R. (2007). Women university presidents: Career paths and educational backgrounds. *Academic Leadership, 5,* 11–16.

Mason, M. A., & Goulden, M. (2004, November–December). Do babies matter (Part II)?: Closing the baby gap. *Academe, 90*(6) 10–15. Retrieved from http://ucfamilyedge.berkeley.edu/babies%20matterII.pdf

Peter, K., & Horn, L. (2005). *Gender differences in participation and completion of undergraduate education and how they changed over time* (NCES 2005–169). Retrieved from National Center for Education Statistics website: http://nces.ed.gov/pubs2005/2005169.pdf

Rampell, C. (2009, February 5). As layoffs surge, women may pass men in job force. *New York Times.* Retrieved from www.nytimes.com/2009/02/06/business/06women.html

Rapoport, R., Bailyn, L., Fletcher, J. K., & Pruitt, B. H. (2002). *Beyond work–family balance: Advancing gender equity and workplace performance.* San Francisco, CA: Jossey-Bass.

Richie, B. S., Fassinger, R. E., Linn, S. G., Johnson, J., Prosser, J., & Robinson, S. (1997). Persistence, connection, and passion: A qualitative study of the career development of highly achieving African American–Black and White women. *Journal of Counseling Psychology, 44,* 133–148. doi:10.1037/0022-0167.44.2.133

Schoen, R., & Weinick, R. M. (1993). Partner choice in marriage and cohabitations. *Journal of Marriage and the Family, 55,* 408–414. doi:10.2307/352811

Singh, V., & Vinnicombe, S. (2006). *The Female FTSE Report 2006: Identifying the new generation of women directors.* Retrieved from www.som.cranfield.ac.uk/som/dinamic-content/research/documents/ftse2006full.pdf

Smith, P. B., & Wang, Z. M. (1996). Chinese leadership and organizational structures. In M. B. Bond (Ed.), *The handbook of Chinese psychology* (pp. 322–337). Hong Kong, China: Oxford University Press.

Spector, P. E., Cooper, C. L., Poelmans, S., Allen, T. D., O'Driscoll, M., Sanchez, J. I., . . . Lu. L. (2004). A cross-national comparative study of work–family stressors, working hours, and well-being: China and Latin America versus the Anglo world. *Personnel Psychology, 57,* 119–142. doi:10.1111/j.1744-6570.2004.tb02486.x

Stern, T. (2008). Self-esteem and high-achieving women. In M. A. Paludi (Ed.), *The psychology of women at work: Challenges and solutions for our female workforce. Vol. 3. Self, family and social affects* (pp. 25–53). Westport, CT: Praeger.

United Nations Statistics Division. (n.d.). Allocation of time and time use. Retrieved from http://unstats.un.org/unsd/demographic/sconcerns/tuse/

U.S. Department of Labor, Women's Bureau. (2006). *Quick facts on women in the labor force in 2006.* Retrieved from www.dol.gov/wb/factsheets/Qf-laborforce-06.htm

Vannoy-Hiller, D., & Philliber, W. W. (1991). *Equal partners: Successful women in marriage.* Newbury Park, CA: Sage.

van Steenbergen, E. F., Ellemers, N., & Mooijaart, A. (2007). How work and family can facilitate each other: Distinct types of work–family facilitation and outcomes for women and men. *Journal of Occupational Health Psychology, 12,* 279–300. doi:10.1037/1076-8998.12.3.279

Walton, K. D. (1997). UK women at the very top: An American assessment. In H. Eggins (Ed.), *Women as leaders and managers in higher education* (pp. 70–90). Bristol, PA: Open University Press.

Watkins, K. (2006). *Human development report 2006. Beyond scarcity: Power, poverty and the global water crisis.* New York, NY: United Nations Development Programme. Retrieved from http://hdr.undp.org/en/media/HDR06-complete.pdf

White, B., Cox, C., & Cooper, C. (1992). *Women's career development: A study of high flyers.* Cambridge, MA: Blackwell.

Women take 45% workforce in China. (2007, May 18). *People's Daily Online.* Retrieved from http://english.people.com.cn/200705/18/eng20070518_375703.html

Yang, N., Chen, C. C., Choi, J., & Zou, Y. (2000). Sources of work–family conflict: A Sino-U.S. comparison of the effects of work and family demands. *Academy of Management Journal, 43,* 113–123. doi:10.2307/1556390

# Critical Thinking

1. What appear to be the key factors related to how women with families achieve success as leaders?

2. What is the "culture of gender" and how does it influence women in different culture to achieve success in leadership?

**FANNY M. CHEUNG,** Department of Psychology, The Chinese University of Hong Kong; **DIANE F. HALPERN,** Department of Psychology Claremont McKenna College.

The Halpern and Cheung (2008) interview study was partly funded by the Bureau of Educational and Cultural Affairs of the U.S. Department of State and by the Council for International Exchange of Scholars in a grant to Fanny M. Cheung under the 2004 Fulbright New Century Scholars Program.

Correspondence concerning this article should be addressed to Fanny M. Cheung, Department of Psychology, The Chinese University of Hong Kong, Shatin, Hong Kong, or Diane F. Halpern, Department of Psychology, Claremont McKenna College, 850 Columbia Avenue, Claremont, CA 91711. E-mail: fmcheung@cuhk.edu.hk or diane.halpern@claremontmckenna.edu

# Resisting Temptation

Eric Wargo

Every year the holidays put us grownups through the same wringer. Sometime late in December, we remember that the "holiday spirit" is really not about eager anticipation and indulgence; it is about controlling ourselves, resisting temptations, mastering our urges. All that food, occasions to drink a little or a lot too much, the pressure cooker of families and relatives . . . so many opportunities to say, do, or consume things we might regret.

And now comes January, that cold month when we all lay in our warm beds and reconsider our resolutions. Get up early and go to the gym before work? I must have been drunk when I resolved to do that.

The problem of how we master our impulses and follow through on our goals is not new, of course—it has engaged philosophers for as long as there have been people in togas. Controlling our passions and cravings was emphasized by the ancient Stoics and Buddhists, for example, and virtue derived from self-restraint is a cornerstone of the Judeo-Christian tradition. In one way or another, all cultures have regarded the ability to discipline ourselves as central to what defines us as human. Animals appear to obey their appetites in the moment; people—at least, adult people—can say "no" to what may be immediately tempting, for the sake of the greater material rewards or moral virtue that come from reining ourselves in.

Yet most of us fail to rein ourselves in as much as we would like, at least in some part of our lives. In one way or another, failures of willpower are at the root of countless problems in our society—obesity, addictions, violence, relationship problems, consumer debt, to name just a few. For this reason, the science of willpower—as a subset of the larger domain of self-regulation (see Baumeister & Vohs, 2004)—is emerging as a major priority in the psychological sciences. Where does willpower come from? Why do some people have more of it than others? How can it be strengthened?

## Hot Marshmallows

The litmus test of how much willpower you have is whether you can resist a marshmallow. At least, this is the paradigm in the classic deferral-of-gratification studies conducted at Stanford in the early 1970s by current APS President Walter Mischel (see Mischel, 1996). In one version of his famous experiment, four-year-olds were left in a room with a bell, with which they could summon an experimenter who, they were promised, would give them a single marshmallow. But they were also told that if they could hold out and wait for the experimenter to return on his own, they would receive two marshmallows. In other variants, the children had the first marshmallow in front of them from the start and had to resist this immediate temptation if they were to reap the larger reward. In such studies, some kids managed to wait up to 20 minutes for the grand prize of two marshmallows, and some caved early for the lesser reward.

The principle underlying the challenge faced by those four-year-olds is sometimes called *temporal discounting:* To a small child, one marshmallow right away may seem more valuable than two marshmallows in some indefinite future. Transposed to adult behavior, it is easy to see how temporal discounting leads otherwise rational people to compromise their long-term health and happiness for short-term gains. That big-screen TV on sale in Best Buy might seem more tangibly rewarding as you stand gazing at it than some vague future free of credit card payments. Or tonight's dessert special—chocolate mousse cake—may seem more important (as you observe another lucky diner savor it) than a slimmer waistline down the road.

A single marshmallow, like a single trip to the gym or a single impulse purchase, may seem trivial, but over the course of life, our successes and failures in the area of self-mastery add up to predict a lot about our success and failure in many areas. People high in self-control are healthier, have better relationships, and are more successful in school and work than those low in the trait. The children in Mischel's marshmallow study, for example, were tracked through adolescence, and the researchers found that the four-year-olds who successfully delayed gratification to reap a larger reward were better adjusted later and scored higher on their SATs, than did those who hadn't been able to hold out (Mischel, 1996).

Sigmund Freud thought that young children developed the capacity for deferring gratification by forming mental images of desired stimuli (the mother's breast was Freud's exemplar, but you could think in terms of marshmallows too); they endured frustration and laid the foundations for later self-mastery by enjoying their mental pictures in place of the real objects they represented. Mischel used his sweet-treat paradigm to test Freud's theory and found that the Viennese psychoanalyst was only partly right. Keeping a reward in mind, and thereby maintaining an expectation of it, did seem to be important. But some mental marshmallows worked considerably better than others.

Specifically, encouraging kids to create vivid, highly arousing mental images of the sweet, gooey treat led them quickly unto temptation, whereas encouraging them to form abstract, non-arousing (or "cold") cognitive representations (thinking of the marshmallows as "puffy clouds," for instance) facilitated waiting. Children who were able to wait for two marshmallows did so by distracting themselves from the aversive wait by thinking about something else instead—or, in some versions of the experiment, by forming arousing, or "hot," mental images of alternative, unavailable rewards, such as a warm fresh pretzel.

Mischel's discovery leads to real-life strategies for self-control: Viewing temptations abstractly—"cooling" immediate stimuli—helps redress the here-and-now bias produced by temporal discounting, enabling us to take a longer-term perspective. By the same token, making long-term priorities "hot" adds weight to those goals, helping them defeat our short-term impulses.

Many psychologists view self-control in terms of the interplay of two distinct self-regulation systems, one that is planful and takes more mental effort, and one that is quick and impulsive and responsive to stimuli in the moment. In the model proposed by Mischel and APS Fellow Janet Metcalfe (Columbia), the more emotional "hot" system dukes it out with the reasoned and rational "cool" system (Metcalfe & Mischel, 1999). These systems are part of a larger cognitive-affective processing system—a constellation of goal representations, expectations about our self-efficacy and competence (i.e., it matters for our willpower if we believe we have it), and situational appraisals that interact and moderate each other (Mischel & Ayduk, 2004). Research in neuroscience is lending support to such dual-process theories by showing the brain systems involved in both impulsivity and self-control.

# Willpower in the Brain

Most Psychology 101 students know the story of Phineas Gage, the Vermont railroad worker who received the first known prefrontal lobotomy when an explosively propelled iron rod passed clear through the front of his head, destroying parts of his frontal lobe. That Gage survived this freak accident at all is miraculous, particularly considering it happened in 1848. But it was the dramatic change in his behavior after his accident that earned Gage his permanent place in psychology textbooks. Once an "efficient and capable" foreman, his accident rendered him, according to his physician, irreverent, profane, impatient, obstinate, vacillating, and unable to follow through with his plans. He became an impulsive and ineffectual shadow of his former self–in short, "no longer Gage."

Gage's accident was hardly a controlled experiment, and some of the anecdotal evidence in the case is now viewed with a critical eye by scientists. But the take-home point has held for over a century and a half: Be careful when tamping dynamite with an iron rod. The other take-home point has been pretty much just as durable, at least in psychology: Willpower and other executive faculties like decision making have a lot to do with the *prefrontal cortex,* or PFC.

Neuroimaging and other tools are rapidly adding to our understanding of the various executive processes that unfold in the human forebrain. The front-most or anterior portion of the PFC, which is implicated in working memory capacity, is linked to the kinds of deferral of gratification tasks studied by Mischel. This may be because overriding temporal discounting requires keeping long-term goals in mind (see Shamosh et al., 2008). Other major structures within the PFC include the dorsolateral PFC, associated with forethought and inhibition of impulses, and the ventromedial PFC, involved in regulating emotions and sensitivity to punishment and reward. The latter area is what was probably damaged in Gage's case (see Wagar & Thagard, 2004).

Information about punishment and reward is vital to making sound decisions. Patients with damage to the ventromedial PFC have trouble taking the long view and considering the future consequences of immediate payoffs—what University of Iowa neurologist Antoine Bechara and his colleagues have called "myopia for the future" (Bechara, Tranel, & Damasio, 2000). This is shown in a risk-decision paradigm known as the Iowa Gambling Task, in which participants overturn cards from an array of decks that vary in the size of the monetary rewards offered. Some of the decks appear highly rewarding at first but also contain catastrophic losses that ultimately bankrupt players who preferentially choose them. People with ventromedial PFC damage tend to persist in picking from these high-payout but ultimately treacherous bad decks. Bechara (2005) suggests that failures of willpower such as drug addiction can be understood as a failure of the prefrontal, long-term reward/punishment system to suppress an impulsive, short-term reward/punishment system involving the brain's limbic system, particularly the amygdala.

Whether the cool-headed prefrontal system is able to override our emotional, amygdala-based impulses depends on various factors. Age is one of them: The ventromedial PFC matures later than other brain systems (it is still developing in early adulthood); as a result, children and adolescents also perform poorly on the Iowa Gambling Task (Hooper, Luciana, Conklin, & Yarger, 2004), and generally make poorer decisions than adults do (see Reyna & Farley, 2006). Stress is another factor: Exposure to stressors such as loud noises, crowds, bureaucratic frustrations, or being discriminated against has been found to reduce people's performance in subsequent self-control tasks (see Muraven & Baumeister, 2000).

# Flex Your Muscles

One of the main limits on willpower, though, turns out to be . . . willpower. Exerting self-control in one domain makes it harder to exert self-control in another, at least right away. Over the past decade and a half, a large number of studies have shown that executive processes by which we control our impulses behave a lot like muscles that get tired through use.

In a study led by APS Fellow Roy Baumeister (Florida State University), a group of hungry participants was forbidden from eating freshly baked cookies sitting on a plate in front of them and made to eat radishes instead. These participants gave up faster on a subsequent frustrating task than did a control group who had been freely allowed to indulge their sweet tooth (Baumeister, Bratslavsky, Muraven, & Tice, 1998). And in a study led by Mark Muraven (SUNY-Albany), participants made to suppress all thoughts of a white beer for five minutes consumed more beer afterwards in a "taste test" than did those in a control group, even though they knew they would subsequently be taking a driving test (Muraven, Collins, & Neinhaus, 2002).

Numerous variants of this paradigm—making a group of participants exercise restraint in one situation and then comparing their performance with that of a control group in a subsequent self-control task—have shown the same pattern: Self-control is a limited resource that can be drained through exertion (Baumeister, Vohs, & Tice, 2007). Baumeister and colleagues call this fatigued state "ego-depletion," and it is a significant discovery because it explains why many of our specific willpower failures occur when our strength has been taxed by other self-control demands. Refraining from blowing up at one's boss during the day may make it hard to resist a big meal of comfort food that evening. The constant effort of sticking to a diet may cause us to make more impulsive purchases at the mall.

The muscle that controls willpower does much more than just keep our impulses in check. It is part of a larger set of executive functions involved in self-monitoring, coping with stressors, weighing alternatives, and making decisions, all of which draw on the same limited energy source. In a recent series of studies led by Kathleen Vohs (University of Minnesota), participants who were asked to choose among various consumer products subsequently showed diminished pain tolerance and consumed less of a nasty-tasting vinegar drink (even though they were paid a nickel per ounce consumed); college students asked to choose among various college courses subsequently studied less for a math test, opting to play video games or read magazines instead (Vohs et al., 2008). Non-ego-depleted persons are also better at logical reasoning and intelligent thought (see Baumeister, Vohs, & Tice, 2007) and at dealing with setbacks that are unexpected (see Baumeister, 2008).

It is even possible to become ego-depleted by watching *other people* exert willpower. In a new study by psychologists at Yale and UCLA, participants were asked to put themselves in the shoes of a fictional hungry waiter or waitress in a gourmet restaurant who was forbidden from eating on the job. They then viewed pictures of various products like watches, cars, and appliances and rated how much they would be willing to spend for them. Exercising vicarious self-control led people to be willing to spend more on the consumer goods, as compared with a control group (Ackerman, Goldstein, Shapiro, & Bargh, in press).

Impulse purchases and eating binges may let us know our willpower is tired, yet until recently psychologists have not known how to assess self-control effort independently of such behavioral indicators. But based on the fact that self-regulation overlaps with brain systems governing the autonomic, "fight-or-flight" stress response, University of Kentucky psychologist Suzanne Segerstrom hypothesized that physiological responses shared with stress might also work as a measure of effort at self-regulation. In 2007, she and her collaborator Lise Solberg Nes published the results of a study showing that participants' heart-rate variability (speeding and slowing of heartbeats), a common stress response, also increased when participants resisted cookies in favor of carrots and when they worked at solving tough anagrams (Segerstrom & Solberg Nes, 2007). Although people often know it when they are stressed, they generally aren't directly aware of exerting self-regulatory exertion, especially for such trivial stakes as a cookie. The new finding points to one way future researchers may directly measure flexing and fatigue of the willpower muscle.

But the $64,000 question is this: If willpower acts like a muscle, can we strengthen it through exercise? Evidence so far suggests the answer is yes: Using self-control in specific areas such as spending or exercise can gradually increase one's resistance to ego-depletion, even in unrelated self-control tasks (Baumeister, Gailliot, DeWall, & Oaten, 2006). For example, in one study, participants suppressed all thoughts of a white beer during an initial task subsequently gave up sooner on a strenuous handgrip task. They all then returned to the lab two weeks later to undergo the same two ordeals; however, in the intervening time, one group engaged in some form of self-regulatory exercise—tracking their food consumption, controlling their mood, or working on their posture. On their second lab visit, those who had exercised in the interim were not as worn out by not thinking of a white beer. Other studies have shown the same benefit of doing daily exercises like using one's nondominant hand for routine tasks or working to improve one's language (such as trying not to curse).

## Free Will Hunting

Psychological scientists have often shied away from using terms like "will" or "willpower," preferring the less philosophically or morally loaded "self-control" or the broader "self-regulation." Since the Enlightenment, science has generally accepted that our bodies, and our brains, are machines, subject to the laws of mechanistic causality. If mental processes unfold like clockwork, where could will—that is, free personal choice—enter in?

Attempts to reconcile free will with mechanistic determinism tend to result in the *homuncular fallacy:* Medieval physicians blamed certain mental and physical ailments on homunculi, miniature people working mischief inside our heads and bodies; such a "mini-me" has served psychologists and logicians as an apt metaphor for the hall of mirrors that often results when attempting to explain unconstrained choice in a deterministic universe: If I'm not the one consciously deciding my destiny, something inside of me is. But if I'm just the vehicle for an inner decider, then how does the decider decide? And how is that decided? Simply, how can you account for free will without endlessly deferring the question to a homunculus inside a homunculus inside a homunculus, on to infinity? Just thinking about it is enough to make your homunculus spin.

Twentieth-century psychology tended to deal with the homunculus problem by severely restricting the scope of free will. Freud, for example, argued that much of what we think of as willed behavior is actually governed by instincts and drives that we are unaware of. But to many of his critics, an unconscious self (especially one that expresses not-ready-for-prime-time desires through dreams, symptoms, and slips of the tongue) sounds like just another homunculus, not a real solution to the problem of personal agency. The more empirically grounded Behaviorists of the 1950s, such as B.F. Skinner, advocated that we stoically banish the notion of freedom altogether: Human behavior was purely mechanistic, as obedient to discernible causal laws as any other physical process, and we would create a better world if we gave up our childish belief in free will.

Findings in the neurosciences and cognitive science have lent considerable tacit support to this position. The neurobiologist Benjamin Libet found that motor actions subjects experienced as being consciously willed were actually initiated in the brain as much as a half second prior to subjects' awareness of their own intention (Libet, 1985). APS Fellow and Charter Member John Bargh (Yale) has conducted numerous studies showing the degree to which our actions are governed by automatic, non-conscious processes (see Bargh & Chartrand, 1999; Bargh & Williams, 2006). In light of these kinds of findings, some researchers, like APS Fellow Daniel M. Wegner (Harvard), argue that the feeling of conscious will is an illusion that arises when our automatically guided actions happen to coincide with our internal monitoring of them (Wegner, 2002).

One problem with eliminating free will from the picture is that with it goes the concept of personal responsibility, the philosophical underpinning of modern societies and the root of all ethics. For medieval theologians, human freedom was what makes humans capable of salvation—we can choose rightly and wrongly, and thereby help determine our fate not only here on earth but also in the hereafter. Jean-Paul Sartre went so far as to maintain that every second of our lives we are "radically free" to choose our destiny, fully responsible for every single thing we do, say, or think. (The French philosopher would have little patience for my excuses for not going to the gym.) In 2006, an anonymous editorial-writer in *The Economist* worried what would happen if neuroscience, by exposing the mechanisms of decision making, caused the ideas of free will and responsibility to disappear (Free to Choose?, 2006).

Bearing out such fears, recent research suggests that a world that disbelieved in free will would be a worse place, not better. In a study by Vohs and APS Fellow Jonathan W. Schooler (University of California, Santa Barbara) participants who read a passage about free will's nonexistence by the biologist Francis Crick (the discoverer of DNA) were more likely to cheat on a subsequent arithmetic task than were controls who read a neutral essay (Vohs & Schooler, 2008). In another study, participants read a series of passages that either affirmed or denied the existence of free will and then answered a set of GRE questions; they checked their own answers and rewarded themselves monetarily for their number correct. Again, there was a significant effect: Belief in determinism promoted cheating.

Are the notions of free will—and by extension willpower—simply convenient illusions that somehow keep us from misbehaving?

# Sweet Freedom

Ironically, it may be the empirical mindset of psychology that rescues free will from oblivion. Complete determinism is just as unproven and scientifically unprovable as complete freedom

is, Baumeister (2008) points out. Moreover, the fact that belief in and desire for freedom are enduring and universal features of human societies makes little sense if there is not some way in which free will is a relevant and useful construct. Baumeister argues that it is most productive to think of it as a continuum: Some people have it more than others, sometimes we are able to hold out for two marshmallows and sometimes we aren't, and it's the difference that is revealing and informative in a science of mind.

The ability to exercise conscious will over our impulses, Baumeister argues, was a late-evolving system that conferred enormous advantages on our ancestors by enabling them to live in complex cultural groups. The executive gray matter occupying the proud position over our eyes expanded rapidly after our hominid ancestors rose up on two feet and began making tools, communicating, and cooperating for the common good. Other social animals exert self-control too, but submitting that control to conscious, reasoned guidance—what most people mean by free will—seems to be a hallmark of humans, whose intricate, rule-bound societies far surpass in complexity those of other species. Yet free action was, and remains, limited by its high energetic costs, as revealed by the ego-depletion research already mentioned.

Recent research by one of Baumeister's students, Matt Gailliot (University of Amsterdam), has revealed just how apt the term *willpower*—once regarded by psychologists as merely a metaphor or folk concept—really is. The brain is powered by glucose, the same thing that powers your muscles. And though the brain makes up only 2 percent of the body's mass, it consumes an amazing 75 percent of the glucose in the blood; executive functions like reasoning, decision making, and impulse control may be especially demanding (Gailliot, 2008). Increased blood glucose has been linked to improved executive processing, working memory, and reaction time; low blood glucose or problems utilizing it have been linked to such self-control problems as aggression and criminality, impulsivity, poor attentional and emotional control, trouble coping with stress, and difficulty quitting smoking.

While working with Baumeister at Florida State University, Gailliot conducted a series of studies showing just what a glucose guzzler willpower can be (Gailliot et al., 2007). Participants in ego-depletion experiments were found to have significantly lower blood sugar following willpower-demanding tasks. And those who replenished their blood sugar with a sweetened drink after exercising self-control in an initial task were better able to master temptation in a subsequent task than a control group of subjects who instead quenched their thirst with an artificially sweetened beverage. Gailliot has also gone on to examine the role of glycogen, the chemical form in which glucose is stored in the body and brain for future use (Gailliot, 2008). The brain's glycogen stores become recharged during sleep and gradually become depleted over the course of the day. It is likely that this pattern partly accounts for the diminished willpower (and other aspects of executive functioning) commonly experienced in the evening. (Other factors that can drain glycogen stores are stress, alcohol, and possibly even high summer temperatures.)

The seeming irony for dieters in the willpower–blood glucose link is not lost on Gailliot and his colleagues: Future research will need to examine if there is a Catch-22 effect whereby limiting sugar intake through dieting could actually impede our ability to resist, say, sugary food (there's something else to make your homunculus spin). In any case, the authors emphasize that the lesson in their research is *not* to start sucking down soda or candy bars in an effort to boost willpower: Such foods give a quick, temporary boost to blood sugar, which is why the researchers used sweet drinks for their laboratory studies, but the effect is short lived. Over time, high sugar consumption can lead to insulin resistance or even diabetes, conditions in which the ability to metabolize glucose is seriously impaired (Taubes, 2007), with all the willpower problems that may entail. Fortunately, the glucose fuel needed for the body and brain are metabolized from many other, better food sources; protein and complex carbohydrates (e.g., vegetables and fruit) maintain a steady supply of glucose throughout the day and are surely a better bet for optimal brainpower and willpower (Gailliot et al, 2007).

## Saving Gas

Willpower is a highly energy-demanding process in an already energy-hungry organ, so it makes sense that we only use it when we have to (Baumeister, 2008). Most of the time, for many of our daily-life activities, relatively automatic processes and reflexive responses to situational cues are good enough to guide us.

Given willpower's scarcity, an effective strategy for following through on your New Year's resolutions may be to circumvent it altogether. APS Fellow and Charter Member Peter M. Gollwitzer (NYU) has studied the difference between mere goals (such as "I want to lose weight") and *implementation intentions,* which actually specify a plan of action ("When the waiter comes, I'm going to order a salad"; Gollwitzer, Fujita, & Oettingen, 2004). The latter prove to be much more effective in helping us keep our promises to ourselves. Implementation intentions help us notice opportunities for working toward our objectives (e.g., the waiter taking my order) and even anticipate likely obstacles, prescribing ways of dealing with them. In a number of experiments, Gollwitzer has found that creating mental links between situational cues and predecided courses of action—"if–then plans"—helps enlist the force of habit to alleviate willpower's brain burden, allowing a predetermined behavior to unfold without too much effortful deliberation.

Whether we view willpower in terms of its muscle-like qualities or in terms of competing (e.g., hot vs. cold) circuits in a complex cognitive control system, a positive message in the psychological science of willpower is that self-mastery, however limited, is also responsive to intervention and improvement. By adjusting how we think of the things that tempt us in the short term and the goals we are striving for in the long, we can alter the balance of these influences. We can also build self-control the same way we build our biceps, not only improving its strength but also intelligently allocating it to high-priority challenges rather than wasting it on things that are less important. Future research may show that we can even optimize our willpower through diet. And knowing willpower's limitations helps point us in the direction of strategies that can help our goals run off as planned even if our inner decider is fatigued.

This leaves us with no more excuses. I'm off to the gym.

## References

Ackerman, J.M., Goldstein, N.J., Shapiro, J.R., & Bargh, J.A. (in press). You wear me out: The vicarious depletion of self-control. *Psychological Science.*

Bargh, J.A., & Chartrand, T.L. (1999). The unbearable automaticity of being. *American Psychologist, 54,* 462–479.

Bargh, J.A., & Williams, E.L. (2006). The automaticity of social life. *Current Directions in Psychological Science, 15,* 1–4.

Baumeister, R.F. (2008). Free will in scientific psychology. *Perspectives on Psychological Science, 3,* 14–19.

Baumeister, R.F., & Vohs, K.D. (2004). *Handbook of self-regulation: Research, theory, and applications.* New York: Guilford.

Baumeister, R.F., Vohs, K.D., & Tice, D.M. (2007). The strength model of self-control. *Current Directions in Psychological Science, 16,* 351–355.

Bechara, A. (2005). Decision making, impulse control and loss of willpower to resist drugs: A neurocognitive perspective. *Nature Neuroscience, 8,* 1458–1463.

Bechara, A., Tranel, D., & Damasio, H. (2000). Characterization of the decision-making deficit of patients with ventromedial prefrontal cortex lesions. *Brain, 123,* 2189–2202.

Free to choose? Modern neuroscience is eroding the idea of free will. (2006, December 19). *The Economist, 381,* 16–18.

Gailliot, M.T. (2008). Unlocking the energy dynamics of executive functioning: Linking executive functioning to brain glycogen. *Perspectives on Psychological Science, 3,* 245–263.

Gailliot, M.T., Baumeister, R.F. DeWall, C.N., Maner, J.K., Plant, E.A., Tice, D.M., et al. (2007). Self-control relies on glucose as a limited energy source: Willpower is more than a metaphor. *Journal of Personality and Social Psychology, 92,* 325–336.

Gollwitzer, P.M., Fujita, K., & Oettingen, G. (2004). Planning and the implementation of goals. In R.F. Baumeister & K.D. Vohs (Eds.), *Handbook of self-regulation: Research, theory, and applications* (pp. 211–228). New York: Guilford.

Hooper, C.J., Luciana, M., Conklin, H.M., & Yarger, R.S. (2004). Adolescents' performance on the Iowa Gambling Task: Implications for the development of decision-making and ventromedial prefrontal cortex. *Developmental Psychology, 40,* 1148–1158.

Libet, B. (1985). Unconscious cerebral initiative and the role of conscious will in voluntary action. *Behavioral and Brain Sciences, 8,* 529–566.

Metcalfe, J., & Mischel, W. (1999). A hot/cool system analysis of delay of gratification: Dynamics of willpower. *Psychological Review, 106,* 3–19.

Mischel, W. (1996). From good intentions to willpower. In P.M. Gollwitzer and J.A. Bargh (Eds.), *The psychology of action.* (pp. 197–218). New York: Guilford.

Mischel, W., & Ayduk, O. (2004). Willpower in a cognitive-affective processing system: The dynamics of delay of gratification. In R.F. Baumeister & K.D. Vohs (Eds.), *Handbook of self-regulation: Research, theory, and applications* (99–129). New York: Guilford.

Muraven, M., & Baumeister, R.F. (2000). Self-regulation and depletion of limited resources: Does self-control resemble a muscle? *Psychological Bulletin, 126,* 247–259.

Muraven, M., Collins, R. L., Neinhaus, K. (2002). Self-control and alcohol restraint: An initial application of the self-control strength model. *Psychology of Addictive Behaviors, 16,* 113–120.

Reyna, V.F., & Farley, F. (2006). Risk and rationality in adolescent decision making: Implications for theory, practice, and public policy. *Psychological Science in the Public Interest, 7,* 1–44.

Segerstrom, S.C., & Solberg Nes, L. (2007). Heart rate variability reflects self-regulatory strength, effort, and fatigue. *Psychological Science, 18,* 275–281.

Shamosh, N.A., DeYoung, C.G., Green, A.E., Reis, D.L., Johnson, M.R., Conway, A.R.A., et al. (2008). Individual differences in delay discounting: Relation to intelligence, working memory, and anterior prefrontal cortex. *Psychological Science, 19,* 904–911.

Taubes, G. (2007). *Good calories, bad calories.* New York: Knopf.

Vohs, K.D., Baumeister, R.F., Schmeichel, B.J., Twenge, J.M., Nelson, N.M., & Tice, D.M. (2008). Making choices impairs subsequent self-control: A limited-resource account of decision making, self-regulation, and active initiative. *Journal of Personality and Social Psychology, 94,* 883–898.

Vohs, K.D., & Schooler, J.W. (2008). The value of believing in free will: Encouraging a belief in determinism increases cheating. *Psychological Science, 19,* 49–54.

Wagar, B.M., & Thagard, P. (2004). Spiking Phineas Gage: A neurocomputational theory of cognitive–affective integration in decision making. *Psychological Review, 111,* 67–79.

Wegner, D.M. (2002). *The illusion of conscious will.* Cambridge, MA: MIT Press.

## Critical Thinking

1. How does self-control work?

2. How does self-control operate in the context of everyday life?

3. What are the key elements of a person's ability to exercise self-control?

From *APS Observer,* January 2009. Copyright © 2009 by American Psychological Society. Reprinted by permission via Copyright Clearance Center.

# A Nurturing Relationship
## *Mothers as Eating Role Models for Their Daughters*

**Recognizing that moms can have a huge impact on children's food habits goes a long way toward helping to break familial cycles of disordered eating behavior and dieting.**

KINDY R. PEASLEE

Confirming the reality of the previous dialogue, a recent *Teen People* magazine survey of 1,000 teens showed that 39% worry about weight. Many factors influence whether an adolescent will develop a positive or negative body image. When we look back in time at the evolution of the changing body shape and size of American women and girls, we see actresses' sizes decreasing and real women's sizes increasing. Regardless of the reason, the common trend points to a slenderizing standard of the female ideal. In a culture in which girls are bombarded with skinny, glossy, and superficial images, moms need to be a mirror their daughters can look into and see a reflection of understanding, reassurance, wisdom, and love.

## The Biological Connection

Last September, I attended the Mother-Daughter Role Modeling Summit in New York City (www.mother-daughter.org/summit.html). This research presentation was organized to explore a mother's impact as a healthy behaviors role model for her daughter. Special guests included Joan Lunden, former cohost of ABC's *Good Morning America*, and her daughter. Both participate in a campaign to challenge mothers to pass on a new legacy of making better food and beverage choices, promoting positive self-esteem, and supporting physical activity to their daughters. The campaign aims to educate mothers about their influence in shaping their daughters' eating habits, dieting behaviors, and self-image.

As the first female role model, a mother's choice about what she eats and drinks impacts her daughter's choices and how she feels about her body. The mother-child bond is the first primary relationship we experience, and it powerfully impacts what we believe about ourselves. The evidence shows that, unintentionally, mothers often model both positive and negative behaviors.

## Remember . . . Daughter See, Daughter Do . . .

"Mom, I am so fat! I look awful. I can't go to school today," my daughter, Kristin, pleaded.

"You are not fat. You look fine." I tried to answer calmly and confidently. We'd had this conversation before.

"I am fat. Look at my legs. I'd be fine if I could just cut my body off from the waist down. I feel awful," Kristin groaned. "Nothing I wear looks right. Isn't there a pill or something I can take to lose weight? I mean it. I can't go to school!"

Fear gripped my heart and stopped me dead in my tracks. I didn't know what to say. As a therapist, I was all too aware of the potential for eating disorders, as well as the epidemic of dieting among adolescent girls. "You are not fat, "I answered firmly.

"You just don't get it, Mom! You don't understand!" Kristin headed for her room, tears beginning to stream down her face.

"Maybe we can take an aerobics class together after school," I called after her, grasping at anything to turn the conversation in a more positive direction.

"I knew it!" Kristin cried harder. "You think I'm fat too!"

—Excerpt taken from the first chapter of *Mom, I Feel Fat! Becoming Your Daughter's Ally in Developing a Healthy Body Image.* Author Sharon Hersh shares a maddening moment that occurred with her daughter and planted a seed for her book.

"Mothers, especially, are very influential," says Debra Waterhouse, MPH, RD, presenter at the summit and author of *Outsmarting the Mother-Daughter Food Trap: How to Free*

*Yourself From Dieting—and Pass on a Healthier Legacy to Your Daughter.* Mothers "unknowingly pass the torch" to their daughters, says Waterhouse. She surveyed more than 100 mothers who had good and seemingly innocent food intentions toward feeding their preadolescent daughters, yet these good intentions still ultimately led to unhealthy eating behaviors for their daughters. Mothers were limiting junk food in their daughters' diets, putting them on low-fat diets, making sure no sweets were in the house, and not allowing for snacking between meals. Waterhouse discourages mothers from restricting their daughters' food intake, reminding them that daughters will react in one of two ways: rebelling and overeating when mom is not looking, or accepting and not eating at all when mom isn't looking.

"More mothers are dieting; more daughters are dieting. More mothers are disordered eaters; more daughters are disordered eaters. More mothers are overweight; more daughters are overweight. This sequence is not coincidental," says Waterhouse. She explains that if a mom is a disordered eater, she is more likely to try to control her daughter's eating, and her daughter is more likely to become a disordered eater and be overweight. However, if a mom is an intuitive eater, she is more likely to trust her daughter's eating decisions, and her daughter is more likely to become an instinctive eater and maintain a comfortable weight.

In her book, Waterhouse shares many mother and daughter examples. One is of a 26-year-old daughter who remembers, "My mother dieted every January and June, so I thought that it must be a normal part of womanhood to vow a 20 pound weight loss with each New Year's resolution and the same 20 pound loss with each presummer diet." Another daughter, aged 35, says, "My mother once told me that I had long, lovely legs and a short, fat waist. Twenty years later, I still like my legs but curse my waist each and every day." Once a mother's words are spoken, they are seldom forgotten. Perhaps your own mother's statements echo in your mind even now as an RD counseling others about nutrition and body image. Do any of these well-meaning comments sound familiar? "You're getting a little chunky, aren't you?" "Pull in your stomach and stand up straight. You'll look thinner." "Only wear dark colors. They will hide your fat." Or, "I want you to have a normal life, so please lose some weight."

# The Legacy of Dieting

Every day, more than 56% of U.S. women are on diets. Parents, especially mothers, can do much to spare their children a lifelong struggle with eating and weight. In her counseling, author and therapist Sharon Hersh challenges moms to examine their own beliefs and prejudices about their weight and appearance. Her suggestion to mothers is to pull out photos of themselves at different ages. What photos are they drawn to? Why? Organize the photos chronologically. How has their body changed? When did they become aware of their body? When did they like their body or not like it? What was going on in their life then? Hersh believes that as a mother, it is important to communicate acceptance and respect to your own body regardless of weight,

which will reduce some pressure daughters may feel to change their bodies. Do not model or encourage dieting. Accept and talk about the fact that diets don't work and the dangers of altering one's body through dieting.

Moms preoccupied with dieting who try to influence their daughters' weight and eating habits may actually place them at risk for developing negative eating behaviors, such as the lack of response to internal cues to hunger and satiety.[1,2] Mothers who use pressure or coercive feeding strategies are more likely to have daughters who are picky eaters or at risk for obesity. Girls whose mothers criticize their eating habits or weight may develop lasting problems with body image and self-esteem. Restriction only cries out for self-indulgence.[3,4]

Yet, girls may still choose to diet even without a mother's dieting influence. Cheryl Rice, a nurse from upstate New York, was fortunate to grow up with a mother who didn't diet. However, she started dieting in high school and college and put pressure on herself to diet. Her mother never criticized her daughter's weight. Rice remembers that even her father never made negative comments on what she feels was her "chunky body type" growing up. It was only in later years, when her mom was in her 60s, that mother and daughter attended TOPS (Taking Pounds Off Sensibly) weight loss classes.

# Role Modeling

"In order for role modeling to occur, the child must observe the model's behavior, have the ability to perform the behavior, and be motivated to perform the behavior," says Leann Birch, PhD, director of the Center for Childhood Obesity Research at Penn State University and one of the research presenters at the summit. "Same-sex models are more likely to be imitated. Mothers are more influential than fathers on their daughters." Mothers are strong influencers because they still have the primary responsibility for making food available in a family and providing food experiences for a baby during pregnancy and breast-feeding.

Mothers also play a role in modeling physical activity to their daughters. "Being a soccer mom isn't confined to a minivan: Moms can play or coach," says Christina Economos, PhD, assistant professor and New Balance Chair in Childhood Nutrition at the Friedman School of Nutrition Science and Policy at Tufts University. Economos, who presented research on physical activity topics at the summit, says that by modeling and engaging in the activity themselves, mothers with high levels of healthy activity were less overweight than mothers with lower levels of activity. The percentage of highly active girls was significantly higher when at least one parent provided physical activity support.[5] Recommendations from the American Academy of Pediatrics encourage parents to become good role models by increasing their own level of physical activity and incorporating an activity that family members of all ages and abilities can do together— not only daughters.[6]

As far as positive role modeling with eating behaviors, moms with a higher fruit and vegetable intake have daughters who consume more fruits and vegetables. Family meals provide opportunities for children to observe parental fruit and

# For Your Clients: Top 10 Do's and Don'ts for Moms

## Do's

1. **Appreciate your body.** If you appreciate your body, your daughter will learn to appreciate hers as well. Focus on your favorite features instead of complaining about what's less desirable.
2. **Consume a variety of fruits, vegetables, lean meats, low-fat milk, and whole grains daily.** Studies show that mothers who model healthy eating habits, such as drinking milk, are more likely to have daughters who do. If you want your daughter to fill her glass with milk instead of soda, you need to do the same.
3. **Serve milk at every meal.** Studies indicate that teens who drink milk instead of sugary sodas tend to weigh less and have less body fat. Drinking three glasses of low-fat milk per day is a healthy habit to promote strong bones and a lean, toned body.
4. **Be physically active and enjoy it.** Mothers who value the importance of exercise positively influence an active lifestyle in their daughters. Studies show that inactive mothers tend to have inactive daughters.
5. **Eat family meals at home.** Sharing meals together at home provides multiple opportunities for you to model healthy behaviors. Your own food and beverage choices may be more influential than any other attempt you make to control what your daughter eats and drinks.

## Don'ts

1. **Do not criticize your daughter's body.** Compliment her positive attributes and teach by example. Research suggests that girls whose mothers criticize their eating habits or weight may develop lasting problems with body image and self-esteem.
2. **Do not be self-critical.** Studies have found a mother's concern about her own weight, dieting practices, and overeating are transmitted to her daughter. Mothers may unknowingly pass on poor body image and weight worries to their daughters.
3. **Do not let sugary beverages dominate.** Soft drinks and sugary fruit drinks are the No. 1 source of calories in a teen's diet. Plus, they're void of the vital nutrients your daughter needs. If you limit your intake, your daughter will likely do the same.
4. **Do not talk about your dieting.** Instead of talking about dieting around your daughter, educate her on foods that provide important nutrients she needs for building strong bones and a healthy body.
5. **Do not use pressure.** Pressuring your daughter to eat certain foods will likely backfire. Research suggests that modeling the desired behavior is a more effective approach for encouraging healthy choices.

Source: www.mother-daughter.org/dos_donts.html

# RDs as Role Models

- Educate mothers on the impact they have in shaping their daughters' eating habits, dieting behaviors, and self-image.
- Council parents about the importance of family meals at home and eating the foods and drinking the beverages they want their children to consume.
- Educate adolescent girls on the dangers of unhealthy dieting, the unrealistic thin ideal, and the realities of maturing female bodies.
- Discourage mothers from using pressure or restrictive feeding practices with their daughters. Encourage a role model approach, making healthful foods available.
- Ensure that parents are involved in childhood obesity prevention and treatment programs.
- Emphasize the importance of teachers, coaches, and principals to serve as positive role models for students and incorporate body image, self-esteem, and eating disorder prevention into health curricula.

vegetable consumption. When fruits and vegetables are available at home and adolescents are involved in meal preparation, they have lower intakes of fat and higher intakes of fruits, vegetables, folate, and vitamin A. Interestingly, mothers who pressure their daughters to eat are more likely to have picky eaters who consume significantly fewer fruits and vegetables than nonpicky eaters.[7,8]

Tamara Vitale, MS, RD, a department of nutrition and food sciences professor at Utah State University, raised two daughters (now aged 27 and 31) and taught them that healthy food doesn't taste bad. Both daughters say they still remember their mom teaching them how easy it is to make roasted vegetables and other fresh foods from scratch, which taste better than convenience foods. Even though most of their friends thought vegetables were gross, they remember always having vegetables on their plates—to them, eating vegetables wasn't a big deal. Vitale says both are now excellent cooks, at healthy weights, and one daughter is now passing the legacy of healthy eating onto her 11-month-old son, who eats a wide variety of healthy whole foods.

Vitale's older daughter, a vegetarian since the age of 12, says she remembers, "My mom told me that I could be a vegetarian as long as I figured out how to get protein, etc, from other foods; that empowered me to understand about food choices." Vitale says that now, whenever her daughters come home for a visit, they request a "10-a-day meal" (meaning lots of vegetables).

In our diet-crazed culture, this inspiring story about daughters experiencing healthy role modeling shows how children's balanced mealtime experience will affect their food choices for the rest of their lives. The rewards of knowing you are teaching your daughters how to eat for enjoyment is a true legacy to leave. We can be the next generation of women to be aware of our spoken and unspoken influence and, as mothers, be motivated to become healthier role models for our daughters.

As dietitians, let's continue to live and teach a nondiet lifestyle and stop the dieting mentality. Daughters also have a role to play and can help and encourage their mothers to live a diet-free life. Let's be the women who leave a new legacy for our daughters by ending the negative link between mothers, daughters, and dieting to bring about a healthier generation of daughters.

# Resources
## Websites
### Finding Balance

Check out a newly launched video-on-demand resource website for eating and body image issues. www.findingbalance.com

### F.I.T. Decisions

F.I.T. (Future Identity of Teens) hosts Girls Only!, a weekend conference for teenage girls to teach them how to live healthful, balanced lives. Nationally known speakers, drama skits, fashion shows, kick boxing, and snacks are part of the all-day workshop. www.fitdecisions.org

### HUGS International, Inc.

HUGS for Better Health website features resources on how to build a nondiet lifestyle. www.hugs.com

### Remuda Ranch

Remuda Ranch is an eating disorder treatment center devoted to the unique needs of women and girls and integrates specialized therapies such as art, equine, body image, and movement program components as part of the recovery treatment. www.remudaranch.com

# Books

Brumberg JJ. *The Body Project: An Intimate History of American Girls.* New York: Random House; 1997.

Gaesser G. *Big Fat Lies: The Truth About Your Weight and Your Health.* Carlsbad, Calif.: Gürze; 2002.

Hersh S. *Mom, I Feel Fat! Becoming Your Daughter's Ally in Developing a Healthy Body Image.* Colorado Springs, Colo.: Waterbrook Press; 2001.

Hutchinson MG. *200 Ways to Love the Body You Have.* Freedom, Calif.: Crossing Press; 1999.

Jantz GL. *Hope, Help & Healing for Eating Disorders: A New Approach to Treating Anorexia, Bulimia, and Overeating.* Colorado Springs, Colo.: Waterbrook Press; 2002.

Rhodes C. *Life Inside the 'Thin' Cage: A Personal Look into the Hidden World of the Chronic Dieter.* Colorado Springs, Colo.: Waterbrook Press; 2003.

Tribole E, Resch E. *Intuitive Eating: A Recovery Book for the Chronic Dieter.* New York: St. Martin's Press; 1996.

# Critical Thinking

1. How do healthy eating behaviors affect one's quality of life?

2. In what ways do mothers serve as role models for their daughters' eating behavior?

**KINDY R. PEASLEE**, RD, is the founder of Kindy Creek Promotions, an upstate New York-based marketing firm specializing in the promotion of natural and organic food and beverage products. She can be reached at kindy@kindycreek.com. Visit her recipe website for parents: www.healthy-kid-recipes.com

For references, view article on our archive at www.TodaysDietitian.com.

# Why So Mad?

## *Why Everyone Is So Angry and Why We Must Calm Down*

Andrew Santella

You are better than this. You are not a hostile person, not a picker of fights. You're a Boy Scout troop leader, Friend of the Library, PTA volunteer. Last year, you even called in and donated money during a National Public Radio fund drive.

And yet you have these moments when the worst parts of your nature come to the fore. Moments when the world seems to be conspiring against you and the frustration builds inside you and the frustration turns to rage.

This morning, for example, you were running late for an 8:30 meeting and you just wanted to get your latte and bagel from Starbucks and run. Of course the guy in front of you in line had to spend 10 minutes talking to the woman behind the counter about that most fascinating of topics, the weather. You're ashamed to admit it now, but you were on the verge of balling up your $10 bill, throwing it across the counter, and screaming for service.

Actually, the whole day has been a little like this. At work, you had a tense exchange with your boss about what he called "peculiarities" in your expense account.

Then, on your way home, as you were inching toward a tollbooth on 294, it happened again. You had 20 minutes to get home, pick up your daughter, and drive her over to her dance lessons. No chance, right? The traffic was going nowhere when suddenly, thank God, another lane opened up. You went for it. So did the guy in your blind spot. A Hummer, cutting right across your bow like you weren't even there. And off you went, laying on the horn, screaming some embarrassingly unoriginal obscenities, spittle flying, face contorted. If you could have caught a peek of yourself in the rearview at that moment, you would have seen a person who appeared utterly insane.

Here's the thing—and maybe you'll find this comforting or maybe you'll find it frightening. There are a lot of you out there.

Rage seems to be all the rage lately. Look around; it's not difficult to conclude that the world is getting angrier and angrier. Our politics are angry, dominated by Bush-haters and Clinton-haters and even Nader-haters. Our popular music is angry, spiked with misogynistic rants and paranoid fantasies. Our highways run like rivers of anger. As Peter Wood points out in his book *A Bee in the Mouth: Anger in America Now* (Encounter, 2007), automakers are even making angrier-looking cars, with grills that seem to snarl at whatever gets in their way.

Are we really that angry? It's not an easy question to answer. There simply aren't a lot of practical ways to measure how pissed off people are. Judging by the space on the nation's bookshelves taken up by books about anger, we seem to be living in a golden age of Wrath Lit. You can find books about the perils of anger, books about how anger can work for you, and books that relate personal battles with rage.

Does this Wrath Lit explosion indicate a growing level of anger in the world or just a greater interest in the topic? Are we really angrier or just trying harder than ever to understand our anger? For that matter, is there more anger being released into our world or are our camera-phones just capturing more episodes of angry behavior and websites such as YouTube making them more accessible?

> **It's not just that people have such fury, it's that they are so proud of their rage, so eager to broadcast it, so determined to assert their rage as a badge of their identity. I'm pissed off, therefore I matter.**

"Have rates of public rage from seemingly normal people gone up, or has our awareness of it gone up?" Colorado State University psychologist Jerry Deffenbacher asks. "We don't know. But there are a lot of angry people out there."

Not even episodes of road rage are easy to quantify. In 1997 the American Automobile Association Foundation for Traffic Safety released a study that detailed an increase in road rage incidents of as much as 7 percent each year since 1990. Media outlets, already awash in trend stories about the road rage phenomenon, reported the study widely. *USA Today* described "an 'epidemic' of aggressive driving."

Then a piece by Michael Fumento in the *Atlantic Monthly* punched holes in the AAA study, arguing that any increase in reported incidents of road rage was the result of increased awareness. The newly coined road rage label had become a convenient way to describe episodes that might not have been reported at all in the past. The article quoted one researcher saying, "You get an epidemic by the mere coining of a term."

Barry Glassner, in his book *The Culture of Fear* (Basic, 2000), asked why journalists became so interested in the road rage "epidemic," when—even using AAA's numbers—angry drivers accounted for no more than one in a thousand roadway deaths between 1990 and 1997.

If measuring road rage is problematic, what about violent crime? Surely statistics on assaults, batteries, and murders would help measure a welling of anger in the world. Here, too, there is a problem. As Deffenbacher points out, violent crime figures seem to be going down.

Even though taking stock of our rage on the road and our angry assaults on others proves frustrating, it is possible to quantify one particular kind of anger epidemic, directed at one particular kind of victim. Call it Vending Machine Madness. A 1988 article in the *Journal of the American Medical Association* reported 15 serious injuries, three fatal, as a result of irate men rocking vending machines that had taken their money without giving them snacks.

How did it come to this? It's the kind of question that comes to you as you sit in your car in line at the tollbooth once you have emerged from your meltdown and regained some self-control. Is there something in the way we live our lives—maybe the frantic pace we set, maybe our relentless emphasis on personal fulfillment—that is bringing our rage to the surface? Or is it, as Wood suggests, that we have made a virtue of expressing our anger, so appearing pissed off, defiant, and aggressive is all just part of being authentic, keeping it real? Or, as Glassner argues, do Americans just have a knack for pessimistic panic-mongering so that we see crises wherever we look?

Certainly you've never thought you might need help. You are familiar with the anger management industry that has sprung up to provide that help, but the whole process makes too easy a target for it to be taken seriously. After all, you've seen the Adam Sandler–Jack Nicholson comedy *Anger Management.*

Then you remember to think about spouses trapped in angry, maybe violent, marriages, about kids being warped by a parent's misplaced rage. Ask one of them if the world is getting angrier or if they might not welcome some help for the scariest people in their worlds.

If that's a little too much for you, just ask one of those poor mopes lying flattened under a snack machine.

As one of the seven deadly sins, anger holds an exalted place but is a bit of a misfit in the group. It is the only one of the seven that doesn't pay off in our self-interest.

For people who have never been unusually prone to anger, that makes the emotion difficult to understand. There's no obvious payoff to a fit of anger. Only an outburst, hurt feelings, or, worse yet, violence. Hardly ever any real resolution to the problem that started the whole thing. Where's the temptation in that?

Lust we can understand. Gluttony we can understand. They may be wrong and hurtful, but we can acknowledge that it's sometimes hard to ignore that extra slice of pizza, hard to say no to the noontime quickie.

In *The Enigma of Anger* (Jossey-Bass, 2002), Garret Keizer writes that his anger "has more often distressed those I love and who love me than it has afflicted those at whom I was angry."

Knowing that anger doesn't always pay doesn't necessarily make it easier to control, which may help explain why anger is so prominent in our lives. The Christian religious tradition centers on a God who, when provoked, turned people to salt, drowned entire armies, and sent floods and pestilence as tokens of his wrath. The most famous episode of anger in the New Testament is Jesus lashing out at the money changers in the temple. It might be the most modern scene in the Gospels.

We're also deeply suspicious of our anger. The Romans preached self-control, and Renaissance essayist Michel de Montaigne advised marshaling anger and using it wisely. He urged people to "husband their anger and not expend it at random for that impedes its effect and weight. Heedless and continual scolding becomes a habit and makes everyone discount it."

That advice recognizes one of the paradoxes of anger: It's often destructive, it's often a waste, but every once in a while it works. It can fuel our drive to achieve, help us maintain our self-respect, stop the world from walking all over us.

The trick, apparently, is getting angry at the right times and not getting angry at the wrong ones. Sounds easy, right? Mark Twain suggested this: "When angry, count to four. When very angry, swear."

Wood, in *A Bee in the Mouth,* argues that one of the most telling signs of a national problem with anger is the hostile tone of our political discourse. He calls it a new style of anger. "For the first time in our political history," Wood writes, "declaring absolute hatred for one's opponent has become a sign not of sad excess, but of good character." As an example of political discourse that delights in its own vitriol, he cites Jonathan Chait's 2003 essay in the *New Republic,* which begins, "I hate President George W. Bush." Such language is typical of what Wood calls our "angriculture." It's not just that people have such fury, Wood argues, it's that they are so proud of their rage, so eager to broadcast it, so determined to assert their rage as a badge of their identity. I'm pissed off, therefore I matter.

Wood recognizes the vein of anger that has always run through American history, but he may not do full justice to the venom and the power of historical fury. Contemporary wrathmongers like Ann Coulter are loud and all too visible. But compare her to self-appointed avenger Preston Brooks, the South Carolinian who took a cane to Massachusetts senator Charles Sumner on the Senate floor in 1856. Clearly, extreme fury is nothing new in American politics.

---

**The *Journal of the American Medical Association* reported 15 serious injuries, three fatal, as a result of irate men rocking vending machines that had taken their money without giving them snacks.**

---

Often it changed our world for the better. American history owes a great deal to the motivational power of wrath. The abolition movement was largely fueled by rage, and so was the women's suffrage movement.

The abortion clinic bombers and schoolhouse shooters of recent decades may be the most violent examples of contemporary American rage. But don't forget strident bloggers, finger-pointing cable-news hosts, brawling professional athletes, bullying grade schoolers, and those Little League parents who go after umpires, veins bulging. It's likely that more often than not, anger plays itself out on the home front. The wife-beaters and screamers-at-kids are probably doing more damage with their anger than any of the more visibly angry people. Once you start looking for anger, you see it everywhere.

Then again, maybe we're not angry enough. Given war, environmental crisis, and economic injustice, maybe we should be out in the streets in force, demanding change. *New York Times* columnist Bob Herbert recently declared that the "anger quotient is much too low."

Too angry? Not angry enough? Not one of the sources I consulted suggested that we, as a society, have arrived at precisely the appropriate level of anger for our circumstances. Like perfect happiness, this "anger quotient" must be an elusive target.

So is there any hope for you and your anger? Is there any reason to believe that someday you will be able to survive the afternoon commute without screaming or tailgating or displaying choice fingers?

One option, of course, is to seek out some help with anger management. The very phrase has become such a familiar part of our lives—how often does a day pass without hearing of some offender being sentenced to attend anger management sessions?—that it's easy to forget that it is a relatively recent coinage. Raymond W. Novaco may have been the first to use the term, in his seminal 1975 work *Anger Control* (Lexington), but the term didn't begin appearing in the popular media until well into the 1980s.

## Anger is often destructive, it's often a waste, but every once in a while it works.

One of the first and most influential popular books on anger was Carol Tavris' 1982 *Anger: The Misunderstood Emotion* (Simon & Schuster). Her book was a response to the then-popular "ventilationist" strategies that suggested that loudly articulating our anger would free us emotionally. Tavris insisted on a more subtle and complex approach to anger, one that even acknowledged its constructive aspects.

"I have watched people use anger, in the name of emotional liberation, to erode affection and trust, whittle away their spirits in bitterness and revenge, diminish their dignity in years of spiteful hatred," she wrote. "And I watch with admiration those who use anger to probe for truth, who challenge and change the complacent injustices of life."

Two decades later, researchers were still probing for the constructive aspects of anger. A January 2000 article in the journal *Health Psychology* suggested that calmly discussing angry feelings and working toward solutions with others can have health benefits. But the emphasis, the researchers pointed out, must be on solving problems, not merely venting feelings.

Anger management specialists usually work from a menu of strategies that include everything from deep-breathing exercises to muscle relaxation techniques to visualization exercises that help people regain their calm. Other interventions stress cognitive approaches that aim to change unhelpful patterns of thinking. And there are, as always, pharmaceutical options. Emil Coccaro, chair of psychiatry at the University of Chicago, has explored using Prozac to treat explosively angry people.

Psychologist Deffenbacher urges, among other things, using humor to defuse anger. The idea is that the next time you find yourself tempted to call someone a dumbass, you can merely picture that person as, say, a burro wearing a dunce cap. The image might be amusing enough to get you through your angry moment.

Whatever successes anger management professionals can claim, they are clearly dealing with new realities that make it all too easy to vent rage. John Duffy, a Chicago-area psychologist and life coach, says many of the teenagers he works with use text messaging and social networking sites such as MySpace to lash out at classmates or authority figures who have crossed them. This spring the *New York Times* reported on the popularity among high school students of "hit lists"—sometimes posted online, sometimes scrawled on a school wall—of people an angry student would like to harm. Part of the appeal is being able to spew bitter thoughts at targets without having to confront them and deal with them as human presences. Just as road ragers may find it easier to flip someone off when the gesture is mediated by a windshield, information technologies allow us to vent at a digital remove.

Anger has been called a sin. It has been called an emotion. Former secretary of state Alexander Haig once called it a "management vehicle."

One thing anger cannot be called, not yet anyway, is a mental disorder. *The Diagnostic and Statistical Manual of Mental Disorders,* psychiatry's official guidebook to mental illness, offers multiple varieties of depressions, anxieties, and phobias, but no specific category of disorders for which anger is the defining characteristic. The closest it comes is a mention of intermittent explosive disorder, which is marked by "aggressive impulses that result in serious assaultive acts" in which the aggressiveness "is grossly out of proportion" to the immediate provocation.

Anger experts want more. "We need probably a half-dozen anger disorders," says Deffenbacher. Such an array, he argues, would help legitimize the study of anger, and help researchers to understand it better and doctors to improve their interventions.

Not everyone agrees. Some people argue that making anger a disorder would give domestic abusers a get-out-of-jail-free card, allowing them to plead that they were at the mercy of an illness when they lashed out. Others simply object to the idea of labeling more and more behaviors as disorders, which they say only feeds the therapeutic and pharmaceutical industries.

Deffenbacher and other specialists in anger, however, say that recognizing dysfunctional anger as a disorder would help more troubled people recognize their problems and seek help. That argument should not be dismissed too easily. For most angry people, the real problem is not their anger. The problem is the endless series of people and things that keep provoking their anger. "Want me to stop being angry?" the angry guy asks. "Then tell the world to leave me alone."

Even the most patient of us can put together a long list of things that piss us off in the course of a day. What does it for you? People who fail to say "excuse me" when they run over your foot with their baby stroller? Drivers who drift across your lane when they make a left-hand turn in front of you? Bellicose vice presidents of the United States? Litterers who toss cigarette butts and Big Gulp cups out of car windows? Movie theater talkers? Cell phone loudmouths? E-mail nonresponders? Wiseass journalists?

What if they could all be convinced to disappear? What if all the things that pushed your buttons just went away? You're a decent person. At the core, your nature is good. Remember how you stayed late to clean up after the book group meeting last week, even though it wasn't your turn? If you could just avoid the jerks, the rude bastards, how much calmer would you be?

In *The Enigma of Anger,* Keizer writes about Abbot Ammonas, who lived in the fourth century as a hermit in a remote and desolate region of Egypt. Keizer points out that Ammonas, while doing his monkly spiritual exercises, never ceased praying to be delivered from his anger. Which raises the question: What exactly does a hermit have to get angry about?

Ammonas, whatever hardships he had to endure in the desert, was spared "Dixie" ringtones, telemarketers, and traffic jams. He was spared Bill O'Reilly. Yet he continued to struggle with his anger.

Maybe Ammonas' problem was that he was left, in the end, with the one thing that not even you—well-meaning and kindhearted as you are—can escape.

Your own angry self.

## Critical Thinking

1. What are the advantages and disadvantages of anger?
2. What causes people to "fly into a rage"? What are the consequences of such an emotion?

**ANDREW SANTELLA** (www.andrewsantella.com) has written for the *New York Times Book Review, Slate,* and *GQ.* Reprinted from *Notre Dame* (Summer 2007), a quarterly magazine produced by the University of Notre Dame.

# UNIT 7
# Development

## Unit Selections

## Learning Outcomes

*After reading this Unit, you should be able to:*

- Explain how infants learn about their world.

- Explain the nature of the human mind in middle-aged people.

- Evaluate recent evidence that shows that the Internet has positive effects on the social development of adolescents.

- Explain the Internet-enhanced self-disclosure hypothesis.

- Describe the key elements of a successful marital or intimate relationship.

- Discuss the warning signs that a marital or intimate relationship is in trouble.

- Assess the theory that the United States is a "death-denying society."

- Explain the most effective approach to interacting with a person who has recently experienced death of a friend or significant other.

## Student Website
www.mhhe.com/cls

## Internet References

**Developmental Psychology**
psychology.about.com/od/developmentalpsychology/Developmental_Psychology.htm
**Puberty and Adolescence**
www.nlm.nih.gov/medlineplus/ency/article/001950.htm
**Social Psychology of Aging**
www.trinity.edu/MKEARL/gersopsy.html

The Garcias and the Szubas are brand new parents; in fact, they are still at the hospital with their newborns. When the babies are not in their mothers' rooms, both sets of parents wander down to the hospital's neonatal nursery where pediatric nurses care for both babies—José Garcia and Kimberly Szuba. Kimberly is alert, active, and often cries and squirms when her parents watch her. On the other hand, José is quiet, often asleep, and less attentive to external commotion when his parents view him in the nursery.

Why are these babies so different? Are the differences gender-related? Will these differences disappear as these children develop, or will they be expressed even more prominently? What does the future hold for each child? Will Kimberly excel at sports and José excel at art? Can Kimberly overcome her parents' poverty and succeed in a professional career? Will José become a doctor like his mother or a pharmacist like his father? Will both of these children escape childhood disease, maltreatment, and the other misfortunes sometimes visited upon North American children?

Developmental psychologists are concerned with all of the Kimberlys and Josés of our world. Developmental psychologists study age-related changes in language, motor and social skills, cognition, and physical health. Developmental psychologists are interested in the common skills shared by all children, as well as the differences among children, and the events that create these differences.

For just a moment, think back over your developmental path. What kind of person are you? What sorts of skills do you possess? Are you artistic? Are you athletic? Do you enjoy reading? Do you speak more than one language? Are you outgoing or shy? What about your personal values such as integrity and honor—how did you acquire these values? Did you have to work hard at becoming the person you are now, or did you just sort of become who you are naturally?

Think now about the present and the future. How are you changing as a college student—is college shaping the way you think and challenging your values and beliefs? Will you ever stop developing or changing or growing or looking at the world in new ways?

In general, developmental psychologists are concerned with the forces that guide and direct development over the course of a lifetime. Some developmental theorists argue that the forces that shape a child are found in the environment, such as social class, quality of available stimulation, parenting style, and so

© The McGraw-Hill Companies, Inc./John Flournoy, photographer

on. Other theorists insist that genetics and related physiological factors such as hormones underlie human development. A third set of psychologists believe that a combination or interaction of all these factors are responsible for development. In this unit, we explore what developmental psychologists can tell us about human growth and change over lifespan.

# A Learning Machine
## *Plasticity and Change throughout Life*

Leah Nelson

Drawing together five psychological scientists unlikely to cross paths outside of a conference, one of the APS 18th Annual Convention's themed programs, "Plasticity & Change: A Lifelong Perspective," showcased extraordinary research from various areas, all suggesting that the brain is almost infinitely adaptable from earliest infancy through latest adulthood. Although their research approached the topic from different angles, each presenter demonstrated the brain's extraordinary capacity to bend, stretch, expand, and specialize itself in response to challenges.

Gregg Recanzone, University of California, Davis, kicked off the discussion with a talk on animal models of adult neural plasticity. His findings indicate that the brain can be trained to increase its sensitivity to various stimuli. In one experiment, Recanzone exposed adult owl monkeys to two tones and decreasing the difference between them over time. After several weeks of training at this relatively simple task, their auditory sensitivity sharpened to a point at which they were able to easily discriminate between tones that were indistinguishable at the beginning of training. This increased sensitivity, Recanzone found, corresponded with a functional reorganization of the cerebral cortex—meaning that the activity of large populations of neurons in the monkeys' brains adapted. This evidence of plasticity in animal subjects' brains, Recanzone said, suggests that long-term levels of performance may be related to changes in neural activity.

## Purposes of Plasticity

As a "learning machine," said the next presenter, Michael Merzenich of the University of California at San Francisco, the brain "has the incredible task . . . of recapitulating what we've learned in the history of our species." Merzenich has recently been researching plasticity among the elderly. Adult brains, he said, use plasticity for "purposeful" reasons, based on specific needs. For example, a professional musician might find it useful to train her brain to recognize absolute pitches, while a mechanic's brain would be better served by expanding its sensitivity to the precise differences among types of rumbles from a troubled car's insides. In contrast, during the "critical period" of childhood, the brain experiences "anything-goes plasticity," adapting itself to sort and interpret a huge variety of incoming data from the world. As individuals master major skill sets, massive cortical changes occur, said Merzenich. It is only after the development of *selective attention control*—the ability to sort and focus on preferred input—that plasticity shifts into a more purpose-driven, adult mode.

Like the adult monkeys' brain in Recanzone's experiment, the adult human brain can be trained to accommodate new skills. Merzenich said that his research is about "shaping the machinery of your brain . . . to develop the capacities of your life." As people grow older, he said, their brains become "noisier" because they are filled with more information, the management of which causes them to slow down. Increased noise degrades brains' learning-control machinery. But these changes are reversible, Merzenich said. In one experiment, he used adaptive computer games to rejuvenate the learning machinery of elderly subjects. His findings are striking: Through auditory training, people between the ages of 70 and 95 were able to recover the cortical plasticity of people 10 to 15 years younger than they. Visual training resulted in increased plasticity equivalent to that of brains 25 years younger. Countering conventional wisdom, which says that brains simply slow down with age, Merzenich said that it is "very easy to change cortical dynamics by training."

## The Logic of Imagination

Merzenich focused on the elderly; Alison Gopnik of the University of California, Berkeley talked about plasticity in children's brains. In "The Logic of Imagination: How Children Change the World," she offered insight on the potential connection between children's imaginative capacity and the patterns of human evolution. "Everything in the environment we live in now was completely imaginary at one point in time," she said. "The deepest part of our human nature is that we are trying to escape human nature."

Evolution, Gopnik said, requires that we discover new things about how the world works and use this knowledge to imagine new things, to change the world based on our imaginings. Cognitive stretches are made possible by the brain's ability to create abstract representations of the world, imagine things that don't exist yet in those representations, and build them. Our ability to develop coherent theories about how things work—or might work—is what allows us to turn imagined worlds into real ones. Gopnik proposed that young children behave like scientists exploring the world for the first time: making predictions, testing them, comparing data, and forming new theories. She discussed an experiment in which young subjects were encouraged to hypothesize about the nature of an object that seemed to respond to both physical stimuli and vocal requests. Based on their knowledge of the world, the children all assumed initially that the object could not respond to their vocal commands. When it appeared to do just that, the children were able to override their assumptions and theorize that the object did in fact understand them. "Children do seem to begin with assumptions about how the world works, but can very rapidly use data to learn," Gopnik said. "Children are able to use this powerful computational machinery to imagine new things in the world, and they can use that new information to do new things in the world. . . . What children are doing is discovering new things about the world, and later on using that machinery to change the world." Like little scientists—and like every human who has ever imagined and invented anything new—children hypothesize, experiment, and make changes based on new data. Their ability to reshape their assumptions according to reality and then reshape reality based on their imaginings reflects the course of human evolution as a whole. It is the capacity for plasticity that makes it possible for children to learn and for the species to evolve, build, change, and grow.

## Controlling Desires

In "Delay of Gratification Over Time: Mechanisms and Developmental Implications," Columbia University's Walter Mischel discussed another outcome of imaginative ability. With temptations of every kind constantly surrounding us, he asked, how do we learn to delay gratification? He proposed that the brain can conceive of two representations of every object—a "cool" representation of its abstract aspects and a "hot" representation of its rewarding traits. Anticipatory responses, such as salivation at the thought of delicious food, are "hot." Delayed gratification, said Mischel, an APS Fellow, is possible because we can also conceive of that same food in abstract terms—as fattening, for example, or likely to give us a stomach ache.

From birth, children want instant gratification. But by stretching their brains to encompass abstract concepts and counterfactuals, they are able to train themselves to control their desires. "What's important is what kids are doing in their heads," Mischel explained. He described an experiment in which children were shown a real cake and a picture of a cake. When he told the children to imagine that the real cake was only a picture, they reported "cool" reactions and a decreased desire to eat the dessert. When the children were asked to imagine that the picture was a real cake, they had "hot" reactions even though they knew the cake wasn't really there. The degree of a child's power to delay gratification at an early age is a good predictor of later coping ability. Early delay skills protect against later vulnerability, Mischel said, so training children in "cooling strategies," like using their imaginations, can have a significant payoff later in life. "Delay makes it possible for people to cool it if and when they want to," Mischel said.

## Effects of Deprivation

The symposium's final presenter, Sir Michael Rutter of King's College, underscored the limits of cortical plasticity with a somber report on "Long-Term Effects of Early Institutional Deprivation: Findings from an Adoption Study and Implications of Causal Mechanisms." Rutter and his associates followed the behavioral development of children who were adopted from Romanian orphanages by UK families after the fall of the Ceausescu regime. After evaluating them at the time of adoption, they studied a sample of such children at ages four, six, and eleven years, deploying a battery of cognitive and psychological tests to construct a theory about the results of profound deprivation followed by above-average living environments.

Some of their findings surprised them. "Like much of science, one has a mix of the expected and the totally unexpected," Rutter said. At arrival, most of the children tested as mentally retarded, but by age eleven, they were nearly normal. Variations tended to correlate to the amount of time spent in deprived conditions: Children who had been in orphanages for less than six months recovered most completely, while those who were there longer displayed more severe and longer-lasting deficits. What surprised researchers was that the nature of the deficits varied among the children: Instead of consistently suffering a similar set of problems, each child showed a different pattern of disturbance. This finding suggested to Rutter that plasticity must vary from child to child—that individual brains will respond to similar extreme circumstances in completely different ways. Unable to find a strong connection between adaptive ability and the characteristics of the households that adopted the children, Rutter concluded that, although psychosocial deprivation was the main risk factor for all the deficits the children displayed, its effects are neither universal nor fixed—a challenge to what some developmental theories would predict most researchers would expect. "Whatever theoretical explanation we end up with," Rutter concluded, "we'll have to account for these huge individual differences." Rutter also delivered the Keynote Address at the APS annual meeting.

The five presenters were delighted at the similarities they saw among their diverse fields. "We should change the way we do business," said Mischel. "Psychological science is at the point that it should become a big science. We should think about the way that chemistry and physics became great sciences. The time of each person in his own lab should maybe be over."

## Critical Thinking

1. How do infants learn about their world?
2. What does it mean to say that the human brain shows plasticity and resiliency over the lifespan?

LEAH NELSON is a writer who lives in New York.

From *APS Observer*, August 2006, pp. 27–28. Copyright © 2006 by American Psychological Society. Reprinted by permission via the Copyright Clearance Center.

# The Mind at Midlife

Longstanding beliefs say the adult brain is best in its youth, but research now suggests otherwise. The middle-aged mind preserves many of its youthful skills and even develops some new strengths.

MELISSA LEE PHILLIPS

Ask those who've entered the thick of middle age what they think about their mental capacities and you're likely to hear a slew of complaints—their brains don't work as quickly as they used to, they're distractable and unfocused, and they can never remember anyone's name.

While some of these complaints reflect real declines in brain function in our middle years, the deficiencies of a middle-aged brain have likely been overstated by anecdotal evidence and even by some scientific studies.

Contrary to its reputation as a slower, duller version of a youthful brain, it seems that the middle-aged mind not only maintains many of the abilities of youth but actually acquires some new ones. The adult brain seems to be capable of rewiring itself well into middle age, incorporating decades of experiences and behaviors. Research suggests, for example, the middle-aged mind is calmer, less neurotic and better able to sort through social situations. Some middle-agers even have improved cognitive abilities.

"There is an enduring potential for plasticity, reorganization and preservation of capacities," says cognitive neuroscientist Patricia Reuter-Lorenz, PhD, of the University of Michigan in Ann Arbor.

Researchers now have an unprecedented wealth of data on the aging brain from the Seattle Longitudinal Study, which has tracked the cognitive abilities of thousands of adults over the past 50 years. These results show that middle-aged adults perform better on four out of six cognitive tests than those same individuals did as young adults, says study leader Sherry Willis, PhD, of the University of Washington in Seattle.

While memorization skills and perceptual speed both start to decline in young adulthood, verbal abilities, spatial reasoning, simple math abilities and abstract reasoning skills all improve in middle age.

Cognitive skills in the aging brain have also been studied extensively in pilots and air-traffic controllers. Again, older pilots show declines in processing speed and memory capacity, but their overall performance seems to remain intact. In a study published in *Neurology* (Vol. 68, No. 9) in 2007, researchers tested pilots age 40 to 69 as they performed on flight simulators. Older pilots took longer to learn to use the simulators but did a better job than their younger colleagues at achieving their objective: avoiding collisions.

Many middle-aged people are convinced that they're just not as mentally skilled or even as intelligent as they used to be, Willis says. But it's possible that's an illusion arising from the aspects of cognition that do suffer in middle age.

"They may get the sense they're cognitively slow just because they're perceptually slow or slow with psychomotor skills," she says, when in reality their brains are performing most tasks remarkably well.

> **"This time of life brings so many new opportunities to invest in your own cognitive and physical resources, so you can buffer against the effects of older age."**
>
> —Patricia Reuter-Lorenz University of Michigan in Ann Arbor

## Changing Strategies

Researchers used to believe that brain activity would slow down with aging so that older brains would show less activity overall than younger ones. But functional neuroimaging studies have overturned that assumption.

For example, psychologist Cheryl Grady, PhD, of the University of Toronto, and her colleagues have found that older adults use more of their brains than young adults to accomplish certain tasks. In a study published in the *Journal of Neuroscience* (Vol. 3, No. 2) in 1994, Grady reported that performing a face-matching task activates mainly the occipital visual areas in younger adults, but older adults use these areas as well as the prefrontal cortex. (Both groups of adults are equally skilled at the task.)

Several groups, including Grady's, have also found that older adults tend to use both brain hemispheres for tasks that only activate one hemisphere in younger adults. Younger adults show similar bilateralization of brain activity if the task is difficult enough, Reuter-Lorenz says, but older adults use both hemispheres at lower levels of difficulty.

The strategy seems to work. According to work published in *Neuroimage* (Vol. 17, No. 3) in 2002, the best-performing older adults are the most likely to show this bilateralization. Older adults who continue to use only one hemisphere don't perform as well.

Reuter-Lorenz finds these changes with age encouraging, as they show that the middle-aged brain is capable of altering how it does things in order to accomplish the task at hand. "Compensation through some brain mechanisms may make up for losses in others," she says.

Grady cautions that many studies on the middle-aged brain are preliminary, as this age group "hasn't been studied very much. It certainly hasn't been studied enough." Most functional imaging studies, for example, tend to recruit college students and retirees as study subjects, Grady says. Cognitive characteristics of in-between ages are often simply extrapolated from the two ends of the spectrum.

While a linear continuum may be accurate for many traits, it may not always be a valid assumption. Grady's own work on brain activation during memory tasks, for example, suggests that the middle-aged pattern does fall between those of a young adult and an elderly person.

For example, the amount of white matter in the brain, which forms the connections among nerve cells, seems to increase until age 40 or 50 and then falls off again. "So that suggests that there are some developmental changes that really don't hit their peak until somewhere in middle age," Grady says.

## At Least the Glasses are Rose-Colored

Emotions and social interactions—even personality—may systematically change as people enter middle age. Many studies have found that people become calmer and less neurotic as they age. "There's a quieting of emotional storms," Reuter-Lorenz says.

Work by cognitive psychologist Mara Mather, PhD, of the University of Southern California in Los Angeles, has found that older adults tend to focus more on positive information and less on negative information than their younger counterparts. In 2004, she and her colleagues reported in *Psychological Science* (Vol. 15, No. 4) that the amygdala in older adults actually responds less to negative stimuli (such as unpleasant pictures) than it does in young adults. Starting around age 40, people also show a better memory for positive images than for negative ones, and this trend continues until at least age 80.

This "positivity effect" is seen even more strongly in people who are doing exceptionally well cognitively, Mather says, "so it doesn't seem to be something that just goes along with cognitive decline; it seems to be something that's an active process."

These findings fit with many self-reports from middle-aged and older individuals, Mather says. Older adults rank emotional stability and positive affect as more important than younger adults do, and they say that they're better at regulating their own emotions than they were in their youth.

Although scientifically analyzing such qualities as judgment and wisdom is considerably more difficult than measuring psychomotor speed or memory storage capacity, some researchers are trying to do just that. Research over the past several years has reported that middle-aged people are much more expert at many social interactions—such as judging the true intentions of other human beings—than are those either younger or older.

And work by David Laibson, PhD, at Harvard University, found that adults in midlife show better economic understanding and make better financial decisions than either younger or older adults. In fact, the average person's financial judgment seems to peak at 53.

## Variability and Influences

One of the middle-aged mind's most striking features may not be any one feature or ability, but rather the variation in cognitive skills that's found in this age group. Although differences in cognition obviously exist among individuals at all ages, these differences seem to increase in middle age.

For example, memory and attention frequently suffer in middle age, but some individuals' abilities actually improve in midlife. In Willis's Seattle study, most participants' ability to remember lists of words declined in middle age, but about 15 percent performed better on this task than they did as young adults.

"If you study a wide range of abilities, you begin to realize how very complex cognitive decline is and how many individual differences there are," Willis says.

This variation in behavioral performance is also reflected in expression of genes related to learning and memory. In a study published in *Nature* in 2004 (Vol. 429, No. 6,994), the brains of adults under age 40 consistently showed little damage and high levels of expression of these genes, while brains from those over 73 showed lots of damage and low gene expression. But in the middle-aged group, results varied widely. Some middle-aged brains were already shutting down, whereas others were indistinguishable from a 30-year-old brain.

"It's a very interesting and heterogeneous group," Grady says. With more study of middle age in general—especially of those who seem to glide through those years with cognitive abilities intact or even improving—scientists hope to enable many more people to preserve cognitive health into old age.

So far, research suggests that remaining cognitively impressive with age comes from adopting certain behaviors as well as possessing some genetic luck, Willis says. For example, researchers have identified several gene variants that are risk factors for early memory problems. But people who show cognitive improvement in midlife also tend to be more physically, cognitively and socially active than those who don't fare as well.

"Instead of a crisis, middle age should be thought of as a time for a new form of self-investment," Reuter-Lorenz says. "This time of life brings so many new opportunities to invest in your own cognitive and physical resources, so you can buffer against the effects of older age."

# Critical Thinking

1. What are the characteristics of mental life during middle age?

2. Describe the ways in which modern research is shedding new light on our beliefs about cognitive functioning during middle age.

# Social Consequences of the Internet for Adolescents

## A Decade of Research

Adolescents are currently the defining users of the Internet. They spend more time online than adults do, and they use the Internet for social interaction more often than adults do. This article discusses the state of the literature on the consequences of online communication technologies (e.g., instant messaging) for adolescents' social connectedness and well-being. Whereas several studies in the 1990s suggested that Internet use is detrimental, recent studies tend to report opposite effects. We first explain why the results of more recent studies diverge from those of earlier studies. Then, we discuss a viable hypothesis to explain the recent findings: the Internet-enhanced self-disclosure hypothesis. Finally, we discuss some contingent factors that may deserve special attention in future research.

PATTI M. VALKENBURG AND JOCHEN PETER

When online communication technologies, such as e-mail and chat rooms, became popular in the 1990s, several authors believed that these technologies would reduce adolescents' social connectedness and well-being. Social connectedness refers to adolescents' relationships with others in their environment (e.g., friends, family members). At the time, it was assumed that (a) the Internet motivates adolescents to form superficial online relationships with strangers that are less beneficial than their real-world relationships (e.g., Nie, 2001) and (b) time spent with online strangers occurs at the expense of time spent with existing relationships (Kraut et al., 1998), so that (c) adolescents' social connectedness and well-being are reduced (e.g., Kraut et al., 1998).

This reduction hypothesis received considerable empirical support in the second half of the 1990s. Several studies in the early years of the Internet, conducted among adolescents and adults, demonstrated that Internet use was negatively related to social connectedness and well-being. For example, a longitudinal study by Kraut et al. (1998) showed that Internet use reduced adolescents' social connectedness and well-being within a period of 1 year. In addition, Nie (2001) demonstrated that adults who spent more time on the Internet spent less time with friends. Finally, Mesch (2001) found that adolescents who had fewer friends, particularly fewer "friends who always listened to them," were more likely to be Internet users.

However, while these reduction effects were demonstrated consistently in the early stages of Internet adoption, at least two changes in Internet use may render such effects less likely now. First, in the second half of the 1990s, it was hard to maintain one's existing social network on the Internet because the greater part of this network was not yet online. For example, in the study by Mesch (2001), only 11% of adolescents were online. In the Kraut et al. (1998) study, none of the respondents had Internet access before they participated in the study.

At the time, online contacts were separated from offline contacts. But at present, the vast majority of adolescents in Western countries have access to the Internet (e.g., Lenhart & Madden, 2007). At such high access rates, a negative effect of the Internet on social connectedness is less likely because adolescents have more opportunities to maintain their social network through this medium.

Second, communication technologies that were popular among adolescents in the 1990s, such as MUDs (Multi-User Dungeons) and public chat rooms, were typically used for communication between strangers. However, in recent years, several communication technologies, such as Instant Messaging (IM) and social networking sites like Facebook, have been developed that encourage adolescents to communicate with existing friends. European and U.S. studies have shown that 84% (e.g., Gross, 2004) to 88% (e.g., Valkenburg & Peter, 2007a) of adolescents use use IM for communication with existing friends.

## A Time-Related Shift from Negative to Positive Internet Effects

Obviously, when media use changes, its outcomes may change. Because adolescents now predominantly use the Internet to maintain their existing friendships, the condition for negative effects of the Internet on social connectedness and well-being no longer exists. It is no surprise, therefore, that most recent Internet studies have demonstrated that adolescents' online communication stimulates, rather than reduces, social connectedness and/or well-being. For example, in a 2-year follow-up study based on their initial sample of Internet novices, Kraut et al. (2002) found that Internet use improved social connectedness and well-being. Several other recent studies have demonstrated significantly positive relationships between online communication (mostly IM) and adolescents' social connectedness and/or well-being (e.g., Bessière, Kiesler, Kraut, & Boneva, 2008; Valkenburg & Peter, 2007a). However, these positive results are only found for adolescents who use the Internet predominantly to maintain existing friendships (Bessière et al., 2008). When they use it primarily to form new contacts and talk with strangers, the positive effects do not hold (Bessière et al., 2008; Valkenburg & Peter, 2007b).

## Identifying Underlying Processes

Although changes in Internet use may plausibly explain changes in the social effects of the Internet, the question remains *why* online communication is positively related to social connectedness and well-being. Unfortunately, earlier studies on the effects of the Internet have typically investigated direct relationships between the independent variables (i.e., different types of Internet use) and dependent variables (i.e., social connectedness or well-being) without exploring the processes that may underlie these relationships. In the past years, we have conducted several studies to identify the underlying processes of the relationship between the Internet and social connectedness. On the basis of these studies, we have formulated a hypothesis that may explain the Internet's positive effects—the Internet-enhanced self-disclosure hypothesis. This hypothesis states that the positive effects of the Internet on social connectedness and well-being can be explained by enhanced online self-disclosure. Online self-disclosure refers to online communication about personal topics that are typically not easily disclosed, such as one's feelings, worries, and vulnerabilities. The three assumptions of our hypothesis are summarized in Figure 1.

## Assumption 1: Online Communication Stimulates Online Self-Disclosure

The first assumption of our hypothesis is that online communication stimulates online self-disclosure. This assumption is based on earlier computer-mediated communication (CMC) theories in general and on Walther's (1996) hyperpersonal communication theory in particular. According to hyperpersonal communication theory, CMC is typically characterized by reduced visual, auditory, and contextual cues (e.g., social status cues). An important consequence of these reduced cues is that CMC interactants become less concerned about how others perceive them and, thus, feel fewer inhibitions in disclosing intimate information. In other words, their communication becomes hyperpersonal—that is, unusually intimate. These liberating processes are particularly relevant to adolescents, for whom shyness and self-consciousness are inherent to their developmental stage.

The assumption that CMC stimulates self-disclosure has received ample support. A series of studies have shown that CMC and online communication result in more and/or more intimate self-disclosures (e.g., Tidwell & Walther, 2002; Valkenburg & Peter, in press). In fact, the finding that online communication enhances self-disclosure is one of the most consistent outcomes in CMC research.

## Assumption 2: Online Self-Disclosure Enhances Relationship Quality

A second assumption of our hypothesis is that Internet-enhanced online self-disclosure enhances the quality of adolescents' relationships (see Figure 1). It is long-standing wisdom in interpersonal communication that offline, face-to-face self-disclosure is an important predictor of adolescents' friendships (Berndt, 2002). Several studies have demonstrated that face-to-face self-disclosure is related to the closeness and quality of adolescent friendships (e.g., McNelles & Connolly, 1999). Adolescents identify the mutual disclosure of intimate topics as a vital characteristic of high-quality friendships and as one of those friendships' highest rewards (Buhrmester & Prager, 1995).

There is also evidence that *online* self-disclosure is related to friendship formation (McKenna & Bargh, 2000) and to the quality of existing friendships (Valkenburg & Peter, 2007a). A recent longitudinal study showed that, within 1 year, adolescents' online self-disclosure resulted in higher-quality friendships (Valkenburg & Peter, in press). This study also found that the direct relationship between online communication and the quality of friendships disappeared when online self-disclosure was added to the analysis. The disappearance of this direct effect implies that online self-disclosure mediates the relationship between online communication and the quality of friendships. It also means that it is not just online communication (or mere exposure to IM) that leads to higher-quality friendships; Internet-enhanced self-disclosure accounts for the positive effect of online communication on the quality of friendships.

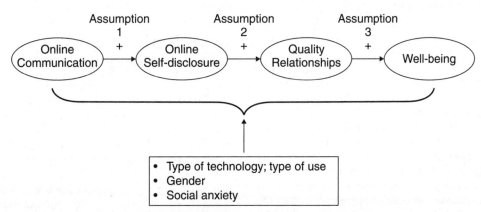

**Figure 1 The Internet-enhanced self-disclosure hypothesis.** Assumption 1 is that online communication stimulates online self-disclosure. Assumption 2 is that this higher online self-disclosure leads to higher-quality relationships, which in turn (Assumption 3) increase adolescents' well-being. This stimulation effect depends, however, on (a) the type of technology that is used, (b) the user's gender, and (c) the user's level of social anxiety. All three assumptions of the internet-enhanced self-disclosure hypothesis have been confirmed in several studies.

# Assumption 3: High-Quality Relationships Promote Well-Being

The final assumption is that Internet-enhanced self-disclosure indirectly promotes adolescents' well-being—specifically, by enhancing the quality of their relationships (see Figure 1). This assumption is based on the repeated finding that the quality of adolescents' friendships is a powerful predictor of their well-being (Erdley, Nangle, Newman, & Carpenter, 2001). High-quality friendships can form a powerful buffer against stressors in adolescence, and adolescents with high-quality friendships are often happier than adolescents without such friendships (Hartup & Stevens, 1997).

However, although there is evidence that online self-disclosure enhances the quality of adolescent friendships (e.g., Valkenburg & Peter, in press) and that the quality of friendships promotes well-being (e.g., Erdley et al., 2001), it is unclear whether the quality of adolescents' friendships mediates, and thus accounts for, the relationship between online self-disclosure and well-being. However, a recent study did provide circumstantial evidence for our final assumption (Valkenburg & Peter, 2007b). It was demonstrated that the quality of adolescents' friendships mediated the relationship between their online communication with existing friends and their well-being: Online communication stimulated the quality of adolescent's friendships, and via this route, it improved adolescents' well-being, measured with the five-item satisfaction-with-life scale developed by Diener, Emmons, Larsen, and Griffin (1985).

# Who Benefits Most from the Effects of Online Communication?

The effects of the Internet may be contingent upon many factors, such as the type of technology, the adolescent who is using the technology, and his or her social environment. Although the literature on Internet effects has rapidly grown in the past decade, knowledge about the factors that may influence any Internet effect is still scarce. At least three moderating factors deserve more attention. These factors, which are presented at the bottom of Figure 1, have not yet been investigated in an integrated effects model. Therefore, their function in the effects model cannot yet be decisively specified.

## Type of Technology, Type of Use

Online communication and online self-disclosure can stimulate adolescents' social connectedness and, thereby, their well-being. However, several studies have found that this positive Internet effect holds only when (a) adolescents predominantly talk with their existing friends (Bessière et al., 2008; Valkenburg & Peter, 2007a) or (b) when they use IM (Valkenburg & Peter, 2007b). IM is a text-based technology that is predominantly used to talk with existing friends. Therefore, self-disclosure via IM inherently means self-disclosure to existing friends. Communication technologies that are predominantly used to communicate with strangers (e.g., chat in a public chatroom) or more solitary forms of Internet use (e.g., surfing) have no effects or even negative effects on social connectedness and well-being (Bessière et al., 2008; Valkenburg & Peter, 2007b). Future research should, therefore, differentiate between types of Internet use and formulate hypotheses that are based on the functions that these technologies have for adolescents.

## Gender

Adolescent boys seem to benefit more from online communication with existing friends than girls do. About one in three adolescents are able to self-disclose better online than they are offline. This holds more for boys than for girls (Schouten, Valkenburg, & Peter, 2007). Especially in early and middle adolescence, adolescents are inhibited in disclosing themselves in face-to-face settings. At this stage, IM may be particularly helpful to encourage self-disclosure. In face-to-face settings, adolescent boys generally have more difficulty self-disclosing to friends than girls do (McNelles & Connolly, 1999). Therefore, boys especially benefit from online communication to stimulate their self-disclosure and, thereby, their social connectedness and well-being (Schouten et al., 2007).

## Social Anxiety

In the 1990s, it was often believed that the Internet would especially attract socially anxious adolescents. Social anxiety implies that one is worried about the self and consequently is inhibited in face-to-face social interactions. There are two hypotheses on the relationship between social anxiety and online communication. The social compensation hypothesis assumes that it is mainly socially anxious adolescents who turn to online conversation. The reduced audiovisual cues of the Internet may help these adolescents overcome the inhibitions they typically experience in real-life interactions. The opposite hypothesis—the rich-get-richer hypothesis—states that it is primarily socially competent adolescents who use the Internet for online communication. These adolescents, who already have strong social skills, may consider the Internet as just another venue to get in touch with peers (Kraut et al., 2002).

Most studies seem to support the rich-get-richer hypothesis rather than the social compensation hypothesis (for a summary, see Valkenburg & Peter, 2007a). Adolescents who are socially competent in offline settings also more often use online communication technologies, such as IM, to stay in touch with these friends. These adolescents typically also often use other communication technologies, such as social networking sites and text messaging through their cell phones (Bryant, Sanders-Jackson, & Smallwood, 2006). However, in comparison with their socially competent peers, socially anxious adolescents do more often prefer online self-disclosure to offline self-disclosure. Because socially anxious adolescents are inhibited in face-to-face social interactions, they may prefer a more protected environment in which they feel less inhibited to reveal their concerns. The Internet provides them with such an environment. The reduced auditory and visual cues of online communication diminish the constraints that socially anxious adolescents typically experience in offline settings (Schouten et al., 2007). Furthermore, because socially anxious adolescents often prefer settings in which their interactions can be prepared ahead of time, they find the control over message construction, which is possible in online communication, more important than less socially anxious adolescents do (Schouten et al., 2007).

# Conclusions and Future Research

Based on the evidence presented in this article, it is plausible to assume that online self-disclosure accounts for the positive relationship between online communication and social connectedness. However, Internet research is still young and does not yet allow us to draw decisive conclusions. Several alternative explanations may be possible. For example, in comparison with face-to-face communication, online communication may result in greater positivity of interaction, in enhanced liking of online partners, and in more breadth of interaction. These processes may all qualify as alternative explanations for the positive relationship between Internet use and social connectedness found in recent studies. In addition, other moderators may have to be added to our model. For example, in face-to-face interactions, self-disclosure is often only effective for the development of close friendships when the communication partner is responsive and supportive. It is important to investigate whether these results also hold for online self-disclosure.

We hope that future research will pay attention to additional variables that may explain the social consequences of the Internet and that they will compare the validity of our hypothesis with that of other explanatory hypotheses. Future research should also investigate the simultaneous effect of different communication technologies. Most research has focused on the effects of IM and chat in public chat rooms. However, the advent of IM and chat technologies coincided with all kinds of other technologies, such as text messaging through cell phones. For an encompassing view on the differential effects of current communication technologies, it is important to compare the effects of these different technologies.

The positive effect of online communication with existing friends may be attributed to enhanced online self-disclosure. However, the same liberating or disinhibiting mechanisms of online communication that have led to the positive outcomes that were the focus of this paper can also have negative consequences for adolescents. For example, flaming (hostile and insulting interactions between Internet users), online harassment, and cyberbullying may all be associated with the disinhibition that results from the reduced auditory and visual cues in CMC. Our article must not be misunderstood simply as a glorification of the Internet. There is definitely a need for more research to identify the conditions under which adolescents may experience potential positive or adverse effects of different forms of online communication and how adolescents can be educated about such effects.

## Recommended Reading

McKenna, K.Y.A., & Bargh, J.A. (2000). (See References). A useful reference on the special attributes of the Internet and their possible social consequences.

Valkenburg, P.M., & Peter, J. (in press). (See References). A longitudinal study that found support for the Internet-enhanced self-disclosure hypothesis (available online at www.cam-ascor.nl/images/documents/2008__valkenburg__peter_JOC_IM.pdf).

Wallace, P.M. (1999). *The psychology of the Internet*. Cambridge, UK: Cambridge University Press. Rather dated but still useful to understand the psychology of the Internet.

## References

Berndt, T.J. (2002). Friendship quality and social development. *Current Directions in Psychological Science, 11,* 7–10.

Bessière, K., Kiesler, S., Kraut, R., & Boneva, B.S. (2008). Effects of Internet use and social resources on changes in depression. *Information, Communication, and Society, 11,* 47–70.

Bryant, J.A., Sanders-Jackson, A., & Smallwood, A.M.K. (2006). IMing, text messaging, and adolescent social networks. *Journal of Computer-Mediated Communication, 11(2),* article 10. Retrieved January 2, 2009, from http://jcmc.indiana.edu/vol11/issue2/ bryant.html

Buhrmester, D., & Prager, K. (1995). Patterns and functions of self-disclosure during childhood and adolescence. In K.J. Rotenberg (Ed.), *Disclosure processes in children and adolescents.* Cambridge, UK: Cambridge University Press.

Diener, E., Emmons, R.A., Larsen, R.J., & Griffin, S. (1985). The satisfaction with life scale. *Journal of Personality Assessment, 49,* 71–75.

Erdley, C.A., Nangle, D.W., Newman, J.E., & Carpenter, E.M. (2001). Children's friendship experiences and psychological adjustment. *New Directions for Child and Adolescent Development, 91,* 5–24.

Gross, E.F. (2004). Adolescent Internet use: What we expect, what teens report. *Journal of Applied Developmental Psychology, 25,* 633–649.

Hartup, W.W., & Stevens, N. (1997). Friendships and adaptation in the life course. *Psychological Bulletin, 121,* 355–370.

Kraut, R., Kiesler, S., Boneva, B., Cummings, J., Helgeson, V., & Crawford, A. (2002). Internet paradox revisited. *Journal of Social Issues, 58,* 49–74.

Kraut, R., Patterson, M., Lundmark, V., Kiesler, S., Mukopadhyay, T., & Scherlis, W. (1998). Internet paradox: A social technology that reduces social involvement and psychological well-being? *American Psychologist, 53,* 1017–1031.

Lenhart, A., & Madden, M. (2007). T*eens, Privacy & Online Social Networks.* Washington, DC: Pew Internet & American Life Project.

McKenna, K.Y.A., & Bargh, J.A. (2000). Plan 9 from cyberspace: The implications of the Internet for personality and social psychology. *Personality and Social Psychology Review, 4,* 57–75.

McNelles, L.R., & Connolly, J.A. (1999). Intimacy between adolescent friends: Age and gender differences in intimate affect and intimate behaviors. *Journal of Research on Adolescence, 9,* 143–159.

Mesch, G. (2001). Social relationships and Internet use among adolescents in Israel. *Social Science Quarterly, 82,* 329–340.

Nie, N.H. (2001). Sociability, interpersonal relations and the Internet: Reconciling conflicting findings. *American Behavioral Scientist, 45,* 420–435.

Schouten, A.P., Valkenburg, P.M., & Peter, J. (2007). Precursors and underlying processes of adolescents' online self-disclosure: Developing and testing an "Internet-attribute-perception" model. *Media Psychology, 10,* 292–314.

Tidwell, L.C., & Walther, J.B. (2002). Computer-mediated communication effects on disclosure, impressions, and interpersonal evaluations. *Human Communication Research, 28,* 317–348.

Valkenburg, P.M., & Peter, J. (2007a). Preadolescents' and adolescents' online communication and their closeness to friends. *Developmental Psychology, 43,* 267–277.

Valkenburg, P.M., & Peter, J. (2007b). Online communication and adolescents' well-being: Testing the stimulation versus the displacement hypothesis. *Journal of Computer Mediated Communication, 12(4),* article 2. Retrieved January 2, 2009, from http://jcmc.indiana.edu/vol12/issue4/valkenburg.html

Valkenburg, P.M., & Peter, J. (in press). The effects of instant messaging on the quality of adolescents' existing friendships: A longitudinal study. *Journal of Communication.*

Walther, J.B. (1996). Computer-mediated communication: Impersonal, interpersonal, and hyperpersonal interaction. *Communication Research, 23,* 3–43.

## Critical Thinking

1. What evidence exists that supports the idea that the internet has positive effects on the social development of adolescents?

2. What is the Internet-enhanced self-disclosure hypothesis?

# Making Relationships Work

## A Conversation with Psychologist John M. Gottman

**The best science we have on relationships comes from the most intense relationship of all—marriage. Here's what we know about it.**

*Harvard Business Review*

It has become common to extol the value of human relationships in the workplace. We all agree that managers need to connect deeply with followers to ensure outstanding performance, and we celebrate leaders who have the emotional intelligence to engage and inspire their people by creating bonds that are authentic and reliable. There's a large and fast-growing support industry to help us develop our "softer" relationship skills; many CEOs hire executive coaches, and libraries of self-help books detail how best to build and manage relationships on the way to the top.

Despite all the importance attached to interpersonal dynamics in the workplace, however, surprisingly little hard scientific evidence identifies what makes or breaks work relationships. We know, for instance, that the personal chemistry between a mentor and his or her protégé is critical to that relationship's success, but we don't try to work out what the magic is, at least not in any rigorous way. The absence of hard data and painstaking analysis exacts a heavy price: When relationships sour, as they easily can, there's little guidance on what you can do to patch things up. Even the best human resources officers may not know how or when to stage an intervention. If companies were more effective in helping executives handle their relationships through difficult times, they would see the company's productivity soar and find it much easier to retain leadership talent.

**Good relationships aren't about clear communication–they're about small moments of attachment and intimacy.**

But if there's little research on relationships at work, some is beginning to emerge on relationships at home. That's good news because the way that people manage their work relationships is closely linked to the way they manage their personal ones. People who are abusive at home, for example, are likely to be abusive at work. If you believe that—as most psychologists do—then the relevance of the work of those who study relationships at home immediately becomes obvious.

Few people can tell us more about how to maintain good personal relationships than John M. Gottman, the executive director of the Relationship Research Institute. At the institute's Family Research Laboratory—known as the Love Lab—Gottman has been studying marriage and divorce for the past 35 years. He has screened thousands of couples, interviewed them, and tracked their interactions over time. He and his colleagues use video cameras, heart monitors, and other biofeedback equipment to measure what goes on when couples experience moments of conflict and closeness. By mathematically analyzing the data, Gottman has generated hard scientific evidence on what makes good relationships.

HBR senior editor Diane Coutu went to the Seattle headquarters of the Relationship Research Institute to discuss that evidence with Gottman and to ask about the implications of his research for the work environment. As a scientist, he refuses to extrapolate beyond his research on couples to relationships in the workplace. The media have sensationalized his work, he says. However, he was willing to talk freely about what makes for good relationships in our personal lives.

Successful couples, he notes, look for ways to accentuate the positive. They try to say "yes" as often as possible. That doesn't mean good relationships have no room for conflict. On the contrary, individuals in thriving relationships embrace conflict over personality differences as a way to work them through. Gottman adds that good relationships aren't about clear communication—they're about small moments of attachment and intimacy. It takes time and work to make such moments part of the fabric of everyday life. Gottman discusses these and other nuances of his wisdom, acquired from experience and research, in this edited version of Coutu's conversation with him.

**You're said to be able to predict, in a very short amount of time and with a high degree of accuracy, whether couples will stay together for the long term. How do you manage that?**

Let me put it this way: If I had three hours with a couple, and if I could interview them and tape them interacting–in positive ways as well as in conflict–then I would say that I could predict a couple's success rate for staying together in the next three to five years with more than 90% accuracy. I've worked with 3,000 couples over 35 years, and the data support this claim, which have now been replicated by other scientists.

**Could you train me to decide whether I should hire Dick or Jane?**

I know this question has come up in the media, which have tried to sex up my work. But the reliability you see in my research has to do with studying relationships specifically. Just to predict whether an interviewee would be a good fit for a job—you couldn't do it. At least I know *I* couldn't do it. I rely on my research to be able to look at *couples*. And even with couples, I need to witness a sample interaction. The more emotional and the more realistic the situation is, the better I am at predicting with a high level of accuracy.

For instance, one test we've used for years is the "paper tower task." We give couples a bunch of materials, such as newspaper, scissors, Scotch tape, and string. We tell them to go build a paper tower that is freestanding, strong, and beautiful, and they have half an hour to do it. Then we watch the way the couples work. It's the very simple things that determine success. One time we had three Australian couples do the task. Beforehand, we had the couples talk on tape about each other and about a major conflict in their relationship that they were trying to resolve. So we had some data about how relatively happy or unhappy they were. When one couple who came across as happy started building their paper tower, the man said, "So, how are we going to do this?" The woman replied, "You know, we can fold the paper, we can turn the paper, we can make structures out of the paper." He said, "Really? Great." It took them something like ten seconds to build a tower. The wife in an unhappily married couple started by saying, "So how are we going to do this?" Her

husband said, "Just a minute, can you be quiet while I figure out the design?" It didn't take much time to see that this couple would run into some difficulties down the line.

**Your work depends heavily on your interviewing technique. How did you develop it?**

My hero was Studs Terkel. I think he's by far the greatest interviewer ever. Bill Moyers is good. Barbara Walters is very good, too, but Terkel is amazing. In one interview, he went into a woman's attic and said to her, "Give me a tour, tell me what's up here." He had a big cigar in his mouth, but he was really interested. Acting as the tour guide, she said, "Well, I don't talk much about this doll." Terkel pointed out that it was not a new doll. "No," she said, "my first fiancé gave me this doll, before he was killed in a car accident. He was the only man I've ever loved." Surprised, Terkel remarked, "You're a grandmother; you must have married." She replied, "Yeah, and I love my husband, but just not like I loved Jack." The woman then launched into a great monologue, prompted by Terkel. We studied his tapes and based our interview technique on his approach.

**What's your biggest discovery?**

It sounds simple, but in fact you could capture all of my research findings with the metaphor of a saltshaker. Instead of filling it with salt, fill it with all the ways you can say yes, and that's what a good relationship is. "Yes," you say, "that is a good idea." "Yes, that's a great point, I never thought of that." "Yes, let's do that if you think it's important." You sprinkle yeses throughout your interactions—that's what a good relationship is. This is particularly important for men, whose ability to accept influence from women is really one of the most critical issues in a relationship. Marriages where the men say to their partners, "Gee, that's a good point" or "Yeah, I guess we could do that" are much more likely to succeed. In contrast, in a partnership that's troubled, the saltshaker is filled with all the ways you can say no. In violent relationships, for example, we see men responding to their wives' requests by saying, "No way," "It's just not going to happen," "You're not going to control me," or simply "Shut up." When a man is not willing to share power with his wife, our research shows, there is an 81% chance that the marriage will self-destruct.

---

**When a man is not willing to share power with his wife, our research shows, there is an 81% chance that the marriage will self-destruct.**

**Does that mean that there's no room for conflict in a good relationship?**

Absolutely not. Having a conflict-free relationship does not mean having a happy one, and when I tell you to say yes a lot, I'm not advising simple compliance. Agreement is not the same as compliance, so if people think they're giving in all the time, then their relationships are never going to work. There are conflicts that you absolutely must have because to give in is to give up some of your personality.

Let me explain by illustrating from personal experience. My wife is very bad at just sitting still and doing nothing. A couple of years ago I gave her a book called *The Art of Doing Nothing.* She never read it. She always has to be up and about doing things. I'm not like that. I don't multitask the way she does; if I take a day off, I want it to be a day off. I want to play music; I want to have a sense of leisure. We fight about this difference all the time. She wants me to do stuff around the house, and I want her to take it easy. And it's worth fighting about this because it's an important personality difference between us. I don't want to adopt her style, and she doesn't want to adopt mine.

Another common issue in many relationships is punctuality. People have huge differences in their attitudes toward it and fight about it constantly. And they should—because unless you do, you can't arrive at an understanding of your differences, which means you can't work out how to live with them.

**What else do people in relationships fight about?**

I actually analyzed about 900 arguments last summer. With the help of the lab staff, I interviewed people about their fights—we saw them fighting in the lab and then outside the lab, and we talked about the issue. What we learned from measuring all these interactions is that most people fight about nothing. Their fights are not about money, or sex, or in-laws—none of that stuff. The vast majority of conflicts are about the *way* people in the relationship fight. One fight we studied was about a remote control. The couple was watching television, and the man said, "OK, let me see what's on," and started channel surfing. At one point the woman said, "Wait, leave it on that program, it's kind of interesting." He replied, "OK, but first let me see what else is on." She kept objecting until he finally said, "Fine, here!" and handed her the remote. She bristled and said, "The way you said 'fine,' that kind of hurt my feelings." He shot back with, "You've always got to have it your way." It may seem really elementary, but that's what people fight about. Unfortunately, most of these issues never get resolved at all. Most couples don't go back and say, "You know, we should really discuss that remote control issue." They don't try to repair the relationship. But repair is the sine qua non of relationships, so everybody needs to know how to process those regrettable moments.

I want to stress that good relationships are not just about knowing when to fight and how to patch things up. We also need humor, affection, playing, silliness, exploration, adventure, lust, touching—all those positive emotional things that we share with all mammals. Something that's been so hard for me to convey to the media is that trivial moments provide opportunities for profound connection. For example, if you're giving your little kid a bath and he splashes and you're impatient, you miss an opportunity to play with him. But if you splash back and you clean up later, you have some fun together and you both get really wet, laugh, and have a beautiful moment. It's ephemeral, small, even trivial—yet it builds trust and connection. In couples who divorce or who live together unhappily, such small moments of connection are rare.

**We can't splash around at work. Are there equivalent ways to achieve connections there?**

There are many similar things you can do in a work environment. You can go into your friend David's office and say, "How's little Harry doing?" And he might say, "You know, he really likes his new school. He's excited by it, and in fact you know what he's doing now . . .?" The conversation might take five or ten minutes, but you've made a connection. This goes for the boss, too. A lot of times the person who's running an organization is pretty lonely, and if somebody walks into her office and doesn't talk about work but instead asks about her weekend, the message is, "Hey, I like you. I notice you independent of your position." Within organizations, people have to see each other as human beings or there will be no social glue.

**What about intimate relationships at work–thumbs up or down?**

That can be really problematic. Marriage researcher Shirley Glass did some terrific work on friendship in the work-place. She gave this wonderful example of a man who hadn't had sex for a long time. He and his wife had a new baby and were fighting a lot. Then after work one day, he and his coworkers went out to celebrate a really successful quarter at the company. Everybody had a good time. People eventually started to go home, but this man and a female coworker lingered. They were talking about the excellent fourth quarter earnings, and she said, "You know, George, this is the happiest I've seen you in months." Nothing untoward was happening, but he was enjoying the conversation in a way that he hadn't with his wife in a long time. So on the way home, he thought to himself, "You know, we laughed and shared a lot, and it was kind of intimate, and I should really go home and say, 'Nancy, I'm really kind of worried because I just had a conversation with a woman at work, and I felt closer to her than I've felt to you in months, and it scares the hell out of me, and we need to talk.' " But he knew exactly how his wife would react. She'd tell him to grow up and would say, "Hey, I have this baby sucking at my teats and now you're being a baby, too. I don't need this kind of crap from you, so just suck it up and get on with it. You're a new father, and quit having those conversations with that woman at work." So he decided not to share the experience with his wife because, he thought, "Nothing really happened anyway." But something did happen, and now he's got a secret. That's the beginning of betrayal.

### Is there no difference between an emotional and a physical affair?

I honestly don't think so. I've seen this in my clinical work and in my research. Most affairs are not about sex at all; they're about friendship. They're about finding somebody who finds you interesting, attractive, fascinating. This can be on a physical or an emotional level–it all boils down to the same thing.

### What contributes to a successful long-term relationship?

Look for the positive in each other. Robert Levenson, of the University of California at Berkeley, and I are in the 18th year of a 20-year longitudinal study in the San Francisco Bay area. We have two groups of couples who were first assessed when they were in their forties and sixties and are now, respectively, in their sixties and eighties. The surprising thing is that the longer people are together, the more the sense of kindness returns. Our research is starting to reveal that in later life your relationship becomes very much like it was during courtship. In courtship you find your new partner very charming and positive. It was all so new then. You de-emphasized the negative qualities and magnified the positive ones. In the long term, the same thing happens. You say, "She's a wonder woman. She can get us through anything." For instance, my wife and I have just moved out of the house we lived in for 14 years, and she orchestrated the entire thing. She was amazing. My genius was to sit back and say nothing. In good relationships, people savor the moments like this that they have together.

### Is there such a thing as an ideal relationship?

I don't really know. Somebody I admired a long time ago was Harold Rausch, now retired, from the University of Massachusetts, who studied relationships and decided there was an optimal level of intimacy and friendship— and of conflict. He called couples who had achieved those levels "harmonious." He said that couples who preferred some emotional distance in their relationships were psychologically brittle and not very oriented toward insight and deep understanding. Rausch identified another

type of couple—those who fought a lot and were really passionate—and he said they're messed up, too.

We studied those three groups of couples as well, and our research showed that they could all be successful. The people who wanted more distant relationships and friendships valued loyalty, commitment, and dedication but weren't so interested in intimacy. Still, they could have very happy marriages. You might think, "OK, they don't fight a lot in order to avoid conflict, and maybe that's bad for the kids." It turns out that wasn't true at all. We followed the kids' emotional and intellectual development, and a distant relationship between the parents turned out to be fine for the children. Our research showed that bickering a lot can be fine, too, provided that both people in the relationship agree to it. People have different capacities for how much intimacy and passion they want and how much togetherness they want. The problem is when there's a mismatch.

## Within organizations, people have to see each other as human beings or there will be no social glue.

### Are the short-term factors for success in relationships different from the factors that make for long-term success?

We face this question about short- and long-term success when we study adolescents and their relationships. We don't necessarily want a 14-year-old's dating relationship to last, but we'd like it to be a positive experience, and we'd like to facilitate our kids' growth and not lead them down a negative path. Whether we look at teenagers or at older couples, it turns out again and again that respect and affection are the two most important things. Whatever your age, there are so many ways you can show respect for your partner. Express interest in the story she's telling at dinner, pay him compliments, listen to her ideas, ask him to watch a *Nova* special with you so that you can discuss it later. The possibilities abound.

### What other advice emerges from your study of good relationships?

I think that men need to learn how to embrace their wives' anger. This message is particularly pertinent today because women are now being educated and empowered to achieve more economically, politically, and socially. But our culture still teaches women that when they assert themselves they are being pushy or obnoxious. Women who get angry when their goals are blocked are labeled as bitchy or rude. If men want to have a good relationship with women, they have to be sensitive to the changing dimensions of power and control in the Western world. And they have to accept the asymmetry in our relationships for the time being.

The good news is that embracing your wife's anger just a little bit can go a long way toward unleashing feelings of appreciation and affection.

I had this funny experience when I sold my book *The Seven Principles for Making Marriage Work* to my publisher. I met with the head of the marketing department, a young guy who leaned back in his chair as if he were not at all impressed by any of my work. He pointed his finger at me and said, "All right, tell me one thing in the next 30 seconds that I can do to improve my marriage right now!" I told him that if I were to pick just one thing it would be to honor his wife's dreams. The guy jumped up, put on his coat, and left the room. I found out months later that he had immediately hopped on the subway to Brooklyn, where he surprised his wife, who was at home with a young baby. Her mouth dropped when he asked her what her dreams were. He told me later that she said she thought he would never ask.

### What would you suggest we be on guard against in relationships?

What I call the Four Horsemen of the Apocalypse—criticism, defensiveness, stonewalling, and contempt—are the best predictors of breakup or continued misery. Readers familiar with my work will remember that I consider contempt to be the worst: It destroys relationships because it communicates disgust. You can't resolve a conflict with your partner when you're conveying the message that you're disgusted with her. Inevitably, contempt leads to greater conflict and negativity. Our research also shows that people in contemptuous relationships are more likely to suffer from infectious illnesses—flu, colds, and so on—than other people. Contempt attacks the immune system; fondness and admiration are the antidotes.

### Are you in a successful relationship?

Yes, my wife and I have just celebrated our 20th wedding anniversary, but we both had disastrous first marriages. Mine failed because my first wife and I had opposite dreams. I really love children and wanted to be a father, but she wasn't so sure and that was a deal breaker. Could a therapist have saved that relationship? I don't think so. My need to be a father was too great. And I'm so glad I became a dad. It's the most important thing I've ever done.

## Critical Thinking

1. What are the key elements of a successful marital or intimate relationship?
2. What are the primary warning signs that a marital or intimate relationship is at risk?

# Blessed Are Those Who Mourn— and Those Who Comfort Them

**In our death-denying society, all too often the message is: Get over it and get back to normal. The fact is, the bereaved's "normal" never will be the same.**

DOLORES PUTERBAUGH

Disbelief is the first thing you feel. The news does not make any sense. There is some mental scrambling around for an anchor. Is this real? How could this be? There is sadness and surprise and, perhaps hidden in the back of your mind, a sense of relief that it did not happen to you.

A friend, coworker, or extended family member has lost a loved one. Perhaps it was after a long illness, or maybe it was sudden and even violent: a crime, an accident, or suicide. The deceased may have been very old or an infant, perhaps not even yet born. Your friend's life has been irreparably changed, and you have an important role to play—even if you are "just" a coworker.

We live in a death-denying society. Most companies offer little time off for survivors, with many people using vacation days or even unpaid leave to accommodate vigils, funeral, and initial recovery. The physically and emotionally wounded survivors return to school or work within days, and often the expectation is that they will be "back to normal." The fact is, their "normal" has changed forever. Bereavement is a ripping away of part of one's heart. A hospice nurse told me the thing that strikes her most about bereavement counseling is that people always are taken by surprise at how powerful it is; the societal message of "getting over it" has infected most individuals.

Since we all will go through this—not once, but many times—it makes sense to figure out what to do to be helpful. Perhaps this will come back around to us, or perhaps we will just have the satisfaction of knowing that we tried to be supportive of a friend in need.

In *Healing Grief at Work: 100 Practical Ideas After Your Workplace Is Touched by a Loss,* clinician Alan Wolfelt reveals the experience of a client whose coworkers announced, one year after her child's death, that it was time to put away the picture on her desk and move on with her life. Knowing that this is shockingly inappropriate still does not provide guidance on how to behave. Of course, you would like to think you are more compassionate than that, but how can one act on that compassion?

Some simple aspects to being appropriately supportive are: be physically present; do not assume the "expert's" position; be a friend.

If a coworker has lost a loved one, you might not think it appropriate to go to the vigil or the funeral. Go! The vigil, visitation, and funerals, as well as the meal afterwards, not only are for the deceased—they are for the mourners, who need affirmation of their loss, recognition of their status as mourners, and support in their time of pain. Make sure you sign the guest book, greet the family, and participate in the rites whenever appropriate. Religious rites exist to help honor the deceased person and to provide comfort to the bereaved; every faith has developed rites to be celebrated in community, not alone. As part of the community of survivors, your role is to offer support.

In the weeks after the loss, continue to provide a physical presence. You may be rebuffed; deal with it and keep trying. This is not a time to keep score over whose turn it is to call whom, or who is next to invite whom to lunch. Prepare meals; invite the mourners over for food or call and invite yourself (with a prepared meal) over to their house. Show up with cleaning supplies or with a box of tissues. It can mean a lot to someone if you are able to help with the tasks that the deceased used to do. The survivor may be too upset or physically incapable of taking over the deceased's chores. Asking for help is difficult for most people, so volunteer your services.

Losing someone we love creates a tremendous void inside. The mourner may feel completely without anchor. This individual cannot be expected to hold up his or her end of the relationship with you at present. Saying, "Call me if you want to talk," is not good enough; be the one who calls and says, "How are you?" or "What about going out for breakfast on Saturday?" Evenings and weekends usually are hardest for those in mourning; make yourself available and be specific with your invitations.

Mourners often complain to me that friends, coworkers, and extended family analyze their (the mourners') grief process and mental health. This is not useful feedback. A common intervention by nonmourners is to provide unsolicited instruction on what stage of grief the mourner is experiencing. Some friends attempt to provide comfort by trying to put the loss into perspective. Another common error is to give mental health diagnoses and recommendations. Not only is this presumptuous, but it is self-aggrandizing on the friends', coworkers', or extended family's part. It is as if to say, "Let's look at you as a case study."

In a similar vein, more misused than any other expert is Elisabeth Kubler-Ross, whose 1969 work, *On Death and Dying,* was based on intensive interviews with the terminally ill and their families. She identified specific stages that occurred between the terminal diagnosis and death: denial and isolation; anger; bargaining; depression; acceptance; and hope. In the first stage, the reality is not accepted; the patient believes this is not happening. In the second stage, the reality begins to set in, but there is anger. From a psychological standpoint, anger is the emotion that accompanies the desire to change a situation; the dying person wants to fight the terminal condition. Next comes bargaining, generally with God: if you cure me, I'll never ———— or I'll always ————. This normal reaction can become paralyzing if the ill person is burdened with an ill-formed theology that believes in a higher power who doles out earthly experiences based on behavior. When bargaining fails, a depressed state of helplessness often ensues. It is beneficial if the dying are able to reach a stage of acceptance and hope. With all due respect to Kubler-Ross and her landmark work with the dying, many researchers and clinicians believe we cannot transfer her stages of dying on those in grief.

These normal reactions to terrible news often have been used to provide a template for grief. However, other researchers and specialists in the field offer different structures for making sense of the mourning process. J.W. Worden identified four primary tasks of grieving that assure a healthy outcome: accepting the fact of the death; working through the pain of the grief; adjusting to a world without the deceased; and renegotiating the internal relationship with the deceased so that the survivor can move forward with life.

Friends and coworkers should—at all costs —avoid announcing to the bereaved what stage, phase, or task they believe the mourner is experiencing at present, or should be. There are not very many "shoulds," if any, in grieving. Each person's experience of grief is unique and even experienced counselors are hesitant to assess any judgment on where someone "should" be at a given point in their grief. There are some specific things that must happen for a grief to become integrated into the person, but these happen gradually, with some overlapping, regressing, patience, and considerable pain.

# Gaining Perspective

Another error often made by those trying to comfort grieving persons is attempting to put things into perspective. Survivors have been told to be grateful that someone who died unexpectedly "went quickly without suffering," while those whose loved ones died in hospice care are informed that they are fortunate that there was an opportunity to "say goodbye." Others who

nursed dying loved ones for weeks, months, or even years have confided that friends are less sympathetic because they presume they "had a chance to prepare and could do their grieving in advance." Each person's experience of grief is unique, shaped by the relationship as well as their history, spirituality, and physical, emotional, and mental resources. Friends and family should refrain from rating someone else's grief.

This also is not a time to diagnose. As a mental health professional, I sometimes am asked about this: When is grieving "depression"? This question most often comes from friends of a survivor. My response is that it is normal to feel depressed after a tremendous loss. For some months, the bereaved can expect to have disruptions in sleep, appetite, and energy. Some people will sleep often; a bereavement counselor with more than 20 years in the field describes the experience of grief like recovering from major surgery: sleep and healthy foods are imperative parts of healing; take naps every day, she recommends. Others may suffer lack of sleep. They feel exhausted and crave the escape of sleep, but are restless. Some lose their appetite while others may gain weight by eating for comfort. Concentration may be very poor, and short-term memory temporarily may become impaired. Most mourners can benefit from carrying a small notebook and writing down all tasks, even the simplest, for a few months after the death.

Some mourners will suffer a terrifying inertia. Taking the initiative to call you will be overwhelming. Simple tasks often take twice as long as usual. Doing any chores around the house will feel exhausting, and it especially can be difficult to take over the things that the deceased used to do. Others may fly into a frenetic pace, using busyness as a kind of drug to keep the emotional darkness at bay.

It is important to take some kind of action if the person shows signs of suicidal planning, such as talking about "when I'm gone," giving away personal items, and suddenly seeming upbeat (a sign that he or she has come to a decision about how to handle things—by dying). In this case, immediately go to other family members, clergy, or consult a mental health professional on what to do.

This is not a time to preach. Even ordained clergy assert that it is not recommended at this juncture to teach the mourning about your particular theology of life and death. Accept them where they are and help them find comfort within their own tradition. Encourage and let yourself be part of the rituals of grieving: prayer services, memorial Masses, candles, planting trees, or otherwise offering memorial are important means to express formally the process of separation and loss.

Being a good friend, coworker, or family member to someone who is mourning is simple, but not always easy. In many ways, you should continue whatever your relationship was before the death. If you had lunch together, continue to have lunch together; if you rotated card games at one another's home, keep up the routine.

Do not be afraid to say the deceased person's name. If tears come, it is not because you reminded the mourner of the dead person. He or she was in no danger of forgetting! Most people want to hear people talk about the person they love. They want to hear the funny stories and warm memories you may have, or be given the opportunity to share some of their own. Let them tell you the same stories over and over. This narration of the life they shared is part of the healing process. Ask to see photo albums and to hear the tales of times past. Listen to the story of the death and surrounding experiences as often as you have to. They are integrating the story of the person they love and have lost into their life in the present.

Mourners may ask if they are "going crazy" based on poor concentration, edginess, thinking they see or hear the deceased, and either great tearfulness or an inability to cry. It would help if friends and coworkers were patient and accepting of these aspects to grief.

Keep in mind the anniversaries of the death and, if you were close to the people, any significant dates such as birthdays or wedding anniversaries. Monthly anniversaries of the death are very difficult and mourners are well aware of these dates. Send a card, bring in flowers, or invite your friend over for a meal.

Holidays will be terribly difficult: Do not wait until the last minute to invite someone in mourning over for Thanksgiving, a concert, and other holiday (or nonholiday) religious or social activities. If the person is "taken" for Thanksgiving, ask them for the next day. That typical four-day holiday weekend can be torture if it seems like everyone else is with people they love.

## Let's Talk—Or Not

For many, talking about their feelings is difficult. Our voyeuristic television shows may indicate otherwise, but it often is hard to discuss one's innermost feelings. Activities done side-by-side, rather than face-to-face, may encourage gradual conversation and sharing of thoughts, feelings, and memories surrounding the deceased's life, death, and the survivor's life since the death. Fishing, walking, and long drives are great ways to let someone have an opportunity for private conversation.

When conversation can occur, hold back trite sayings such as "He's in a better place," or "She's your guardian angel," or (perhaps worst of all), "It was God's will." Without intimate familiarity with the mourner's theology, you risk hurting that individual terribly. People in mourning do not need fortune telling about their future prospects ("You'll have other children" or "You're young . . . you'll find someone else"). They do not need to be advised about having a "stiff upper lip" or "toughing it out."

Do not singlehandedly take on responsibility to spare this person from grief. If you are very close with the individual in mourning, be sure you have a support system of your own. Spending a lot of time with someone who is grieving can be upsetting. You may find yourself recalling your own grief experiences and feelings of loss. Share these, at first, with someone else in your circle rather than with the bereaved. They are not ready to commiserate until later in the process.

Most important, do not take a grieving person's anger, tears, rebuffs, or rejection personally. It will be healthier for you and more helpful for your friend if you bear in mind that terrible pain sometimes interferes with polite behavior. Respect people's desire for some time and privacy but do not give up, walk away, or leave them alone.

## Critical Thinking

1. Is it true that the United States is a "death-denying society"? Please explain.

2. What is the most effective approach to interacting with a person who has recently experienced the death of a friend or significant other?

**DOLORES PUTERBAUGH** is a psychotherapist in private practice in Largo, Fla.

# UNIT 8

# Personality Processes

## Unit Selections

## Learning Outcomes

*After reading this Unit, you should be able to:*

- Evaluate the notion that personalities are permanent.

- Summarize the role of beliefs in shaping or changing our personalities.

- Evaluate the contribution of evolutionary psychology to the study of intelligence.

- Define and explain the Savanna Principle and how it relates to intelligence research.

- Explain the steps people might consider for changing or improving their personalities.

- Understand the nature of optimism and how it can be learned.

## Student Website

www.mhhe.com/cls

## Internet References

**Great Ideas in Personality**
www.personalityresearch.org
**The Personality Project**
personality-project.org/personality.html

Sabrina and Sadie are identical twins. When the girls were young, their parents tried very hard to treat them equally. They dressed them the same, fed them same meals, and allowed them to play with the same toys. Each had a kitten from the same litter. Whenever Sabrina received a present, Sadie received one, too, and vice versa. Both girls attended dance school and completed early classes in ballot and tap dance. In elementary school, the twins were both placed in the same class with the same teacher. The teacher also tried to treat them the same.

In junior high school, Sadie became a tomboy. She loved to play rough-and-tumble sports with the neighborhood boys. On the other hand, Sabrina remained indoors and practiced the piano. Sabrina was keenly interested in hobbies such as painting, needlepoint, and crocheting. Sadie was more interested in reading novels, especially science fiction, and watching adventure programs on television.

As the twins matured, they decided it would be best to attend different colleges. Sabrina went to a small, quiet college in a rural setting, and Sadie matriculated at a large public university. Sabrina majored in English, with a specialty in poetry; Sadie switched majors several times and finally decided on a psychology major.

Why, when these twins were exposed to the same early childhood environment, did their interests, personalities, and paths diverge later? What makes people—even identical twins—so unique, so different from one another? The study of individual differences is the domain of personality psychology.

The psychological study of personality has included two major thrusts. The first has focused on the search for the commonalties of human behavior and personality. Its major question is, "How are humans, especially their personalities, affected by specific events or activities?" The second has focused on discovering the bases on which individuals differ in their responses

© Bananastock

to events. In its early history, this specialty was called genetic psychology because most people assumed that individual differences resulted from differences in inheritance. By the 1950s, the term *genetic psychology* had given way to the more current term: the *psychology of individual differences.*

Today, most psychologists accept the principle that both genes and the environment are important determinants of any type of behavior, whether it be watching adventure movies or sitting quietly and reading or caring for the elderly. Modern researchers devote much of their efforts to discovering how the two sources of influence interact to produce a unique individual. Thus, the focus of this unit is on personality characteristics and the differences and similarities among individuals.

# Can Personality Be Changed?
## *The Role of Beliefs in Personality and Change*

CAROL S. DWECK

James Springer and James Lewis were identical twins separated shortly after birth and reared apart. Yet both married and divorced women names Linda, and then married women named Betty. They had similar interests. James #1 enjoyed carpentry and James #2 enjoyed mechanical drawing, and both showed similar levels of sociability, flexibility, and self-control on personality tests.

When Barbara Herbert and Daphne Goodship, also identical twins, were reunited at age 39, each arrived wearing a beige dress and a brown velvet jacket. Each had the eccentric habit of pushing up her nose and each giggled more than anyone else she knew.

These dramatic examples might lead people to believe that personality is encoded in our genes and impossible to change. If such specific things as the velvet jacket or such broad things as sociability are programmed in, it might imply that everything in between is too. However, more and more research is suggesting that this is not the case. Far from being simply encoded in the genes, much of personality is a flexible and dynamic thing (Mischel & Shoda, 1995) that changes over the life span and is shaped by experience (Roberts, Walton, & Viechtbauer, 2006). What is more, we are beginning to understand how to change it.

Studies of twins often highlight (a) specific preferences and habits and (b) broad traits of personality and temperament (but see Roberts et al., 2006, for data on how much even these broad aspects of personality change over time). However, they often neglect the levels in between, and yet these are arguably the most important part of who we are.

What is this "in-between" part of personality? Several prominent theorists of personality propose that all (Mischel & Shoda, 1995) or much (McAdams, 1995) of the action takes place below the level of broad traits. Mischel and Shoda place such things as goals and construals at this level, and McAdams places such things as personal strivings and coping strategies there. In this paper, I focus on core beliefs or belief systems that, I will show, can organize and shape people's goals and strivings, as well as their construals of

and reactions to the environment, to create consistent patterns of experience and actions. Indeed, Allport (1964) defined personality in terms of consistent patterns of experience and action that are evident across multiple situations or life contexts. As such, beliefs, with their power to mold experience and action, are central to this definition of personality. Moreover, showing that belief interventions do, in fact, change such consistent patterns of experience and action will be central to the case that personality can be changed.

People's beliefs include their mental representations of the nature and workings of the self, of their relationships, and of their world. From infancy, humans develop these beliefs and representations, and many prominent personality theorists of different persuasions acknowledge that they are a fundamental part of personality. For example, Mary Rothbart, the eminent temperament researcher, argues that personality contains much more than temperament and patterns of habitual behavior; importantly, it also includes the way one perceives self, others, and events (Rothbart & Ahadi, 1994). Jack Block, often seen as a trait theorist, proposes that models of the self and the self's relationship to the world create the "organizing, motivating, and life-defining contexts within which the individual acts," and suggests that a central part of personality development is the encoding of internal models, schemas, and premise systems from socialization experiences (Block, 1993).

Focusing on people's beliefs, as opposed to their simple preferences and habits or broad personality traits, helps us answer in more precise ways questions like: What personality factors allow people to function well in their lives—that is, to grow and learn, sustain satisfying relationships, achieve well in school and careers, be caring toward others, or recover from setbacks? This is because beliefs can typically be defined very precisely, measured very simply, and altered through interventions to reveal their direct impact. In contrast, broad personality traits can be assessed, but they contain no implications for how you might change them.

Beliefs are not necessarily easy to change, but they tell you where to begin.

To illustrate these points, I will use recent research that examines two very basic beliefs: people's beliefs about whether their attributes can be developed or not and people's beliefs about whether others will accept them or not. In describing this research, I will underscore the idea that beliefs and their impact are part of personality, that they underlie important aspects of adaptive functioning, and that they have unique implications for interventions.

## Self-Theories: Beliefs about the Malleability of Personal Attributes

My research shows that acquired beliefs play a critical role in how well people function. These are people's self-theories. Some people have a *fixed* (or "entity") theory, believing that their qualities, such as their intelligence, are simply fixed traits. Others have a *malleable* (or incremental) theory, believing that their most basic qualities can be developed through their efforts and education. Research shows that people with a malleable theory are more open to learning, willing to confront challenges, able to stick to difficult tasks, and capable of bouncing back from failures (Dweck, 1999). These qualities lead to better performance in the face of challenges such as difficult school transitions (Blackwell, Trzesniewski, & Dweck, 2007), demanding business tasks (e.g., negotiations; Kray & Haselhuhn, 2007), and difficulties in relationships (e.g., dealing with conflict; Kammrath & Dweck, 2006). All of us would agree that these are a key part of how people function.

However, a malleable theory can be taught. When it is, people show increased motivation to learn and they perform better on challenging tasks. How is the malleable theory taught? In a study by Aronson, Fried, and Good (2002) with college students at a rigorous university, students in the experimental group were shown a film that highlighted how the brain is capable of making new connections throughout life and how it grows in response to intellectual challenge. They also wrote a letter to a struggling younger student emphasizing that the brain is malleable and that intelligence expands with hard work. At the end of that semester, the college students who had learned about malleable intelligence (compared to two control groups that did not) showed greater valuing of academics, enhanced enjoyment of their academic work, and higher grade-point averages.

Blackwell, Trzesniewski, and Dweck (2007) conducted a malleable-intelligence intervention with students making the difficult transition to junior high school (see also Good, Aronson, & Inzlicht, 2003). Both the experimental and control groups received an 8-session workshop built around

study skills, but the malleable-intelligence group also learned that the brain is like a muscle that gets stronger with use and that the brain forms new connections every time learning occurs. The students in the control group, despite the excellent tutoring in study skills, showed little improvement in motivation and no improvement in grades. Those in the malleable-intelligence group, however, showed significant improvement in grades and significantly greater changes in their motivation (e.g., showing greater conscientiousness in their homework and studying, and putting more effort into their classroom learning).

More recently, we have been developing and testing a computer-based version of this workshop (called "Brainology"). After a pilot study in 20 New York City schools, virtually every student (anonymously) reported important changes in such things as their study habits and persistence in the face of obstacles. Many reported picturing their neurons forming new connections as they studied and learned.

People can also learn these self-theories from the kind of praise they receive (Mueller & Dweck, 1998). Ironically, when students are praised for their intelligence, they move toward a fixed theory. Far from raising their self-esteem, this praise makes them challenge-avoidant and vulnerable, such that when they hit obstacles their confidence, enjoyment, and performance decline. When students are praised for their effort or strategies (their process), they instead take on a more malleable theory—they are eager to learn and highly resilient in the face of difficulty.

Thus self-theories play an important (and causal role) in challenge seeking, self-regulation, and resilience, and changing self-theories appears to result in important real-world changes in how people function.

## Relationship Beliefs: Expectations of Acceptance or Rejection

Fifty years ago, John Bowlby proposed that infants form internal working models of how relationships work and that these internal working models serve as prototypes for subsequent relationships. An important implication was that "insecure" models might not allow children to recognize consistent, available, and affectionate caretakers should they come on the scene.

Infant-attachment researchers have long been able to measure the quality of parent–infant relationships and have assumed that internal working models accompany them, but they had not measured working models in infants. In new research, Susan Johnson, Frances Chen, and I (Johnson, Dweck, & Chen, 2007) have provided the first evidence for internal working models of relationships in infants. We began by assessing 12- to 16-month-old infants' relationships with their mothers. That is, using the standard "strange situation" paradigm (in which the infant and mother are separated and reunited to see whether the infant uses the mother as a secure base in times of stress), infants were classified as securely or insecurely attached. Later, in an infant-habituation paradigm, these same infants were shown a film in which a large "mother" ball and a small "baby" ball were headed up a series of steps. Although the mother climbed easily, the baby was unable to follow her and began to cry. Infants were shown this film repeatedly until their interest waned. On the test trials, they were then shown two different endings, one in which the mother returns to the crying baby and another in which she continues up the steps on her own leaving the baby at the bottom.

Which ending "surprised" them and caused them to look longer? Infant-cognition researchers have long used recovery of looking time as evidence that infants see the new stimulus as a violation of their expectations. In this study, the securely attached infants looked longer when the mother kept going, but the insecurely attached infants made no such discrimination and, if anything, were slightly more "surprised" when the mother came back. Thus infants with secure and insecure attachment relationships had formed different expectations about whether a caretaker would be responsive to a child's needs.

These expectations of positive or negative responses from others have been shown to lie at the heart of adult relationships as well. Geraldine Downey and her colleagues, for example, have demonstrated that people who anxiously expect negative responses from others have more fragile relationships, perceive rejection in ordinary behavior, respond to conflict and rejection in ways that undermine their relationships, and become less engaged with and do less well in their academic institutions over time (e.g, Pietrzak, Downey, & Ayduk, 2005). Adult-relationship researchers have shown not only that these expectations consistently predict how well people function in relationships and interpersonal settings, but also that these beliefs are malleable (Baldwin & Dandeneau, 2005; Mikulincer & Shaver, 2007).

Expectations of rejection can be particularly harmful for minority students as they try to fit into historically White institutions. Thus, Walton and Cohen (2007) developed an experimental intervention aimed at African American students and designed to increase their expectations of acceptance. Participants, first-year college students, were taught that doubts about belonging in college are common at first but short-lived. They were presented with survey statistics, as well as personal testimonies from upperclassmen, and they wrote a speech (delivered to a video camera) explaining why people's perceptions of acceptance

might change over time. Students in the control group engaged in similar activities but with respect to their political beliefs.

Changing Black students' expectations of acceptance had dramatic effects. First, compared to the control group, Black students in the experimental group took many more challenging courses (57% vs. 36%). Second, students in the experimental group were more resilient. On days of high adversity, they showed no change in their motivation, compared to those in the control group, who showed a substantial drop. Next, students in the experimental group were much more likely to reach out to professors (sending 3 times as many e-mails to them and going to office hours more often), and they studied significantly more hours per day. Finally, students in the experimental group showed an increase in grades in the semester following the intervention, whereas students in the control group showed a decrease.

## Small Intervention, Large Impact

The self-theories interventions and the expectation-of-acceptance intervention both yielded surprisingly large changes with seemingly modest input, and contrast with many large, costly interventions that yielded little or nothing. They follow in the footsteps of earlier attribution interventions, which changed people's explanations for events and by doing so changed their reactions to them. These interventions all speak to the effectiveness of targeting beliefs that lie at the heart of important motivational, self-regulatory, and interpersonal patterns.

What's more, in these interventions, the changes cut across many of the broad traits that are often thought to be relatively stable: openness to experience (e.g., challenge-seeking), conscientiousness (e.g., hours studied), sociability (e.g., reaching out to others), and negative affectivity (e.g., resilient vs. negative reactions to setbacks). Indeed, feeding up from the in-between level, this may be one of the mechanisms for change in these broader traits (Roberts et al., 2006).

## Impact of Socialization and Experience

Beliefs also have unique implications for understanding the impact of experience on personality and functioning. As research has shown, experience plays a key role in shaping self-theories and expectations of positive responsiveness, as well as attributions. Indeed, many of our experiences may be packaged and carried forward in the form of these kinds of beliefs or mental representations.

Several striking examples have emerged from developmental research on attributions. The effect of domestic violence, abuse, or maternal depression on the development of subsequent depression in children is significantly influenced by the attributions children make for those events (e.g., Garber, Keiley, & Martin, 2002; Grych, Fincham, Jouriles, & McDonald, 2000). When those events are packaged with negative self-attributions or self-blame, children later show a greater vulnerability to depression. Children who are faced with similar negative life events but who understand or explain them in different ways are not as vulnerable.

## Conclusion

We have looked at the in-between part of personality by examining acquired—and changeable—beliefs. We have seen that they underlie many patterns of adaptive functioning, and that they have unique implications for understanding personality development and personality change. The most important next step for personality researchers is to identify other core beliefs or belief systems that can vary across individuals (or cultures)— beliefs about the self, others, relationships, and the world—and that are responsible for important, consistent patterns of experience and action. Another key step is to continue to show how these beliefs feed into broader personality "traits" and contribute to their malleability.

Perhaps it was inevitable that James Springer and James Lewis would love carpentry and mechanical drawing or that Barbara Herbert and Daphne Goodship would giggle. It is possible that some consistent patterns, such as these, are less reliant on experience. However, it is not inevitable that people will function poorly in important areas of their lives. Beliefs matter, beliefs can be changed, and when they are, so too is personality.

## Recommended Reading

Aronson, J., Fried, C., & Good, C. (2002). (See References). An excellent example of research showing how short, targeted interventions can yield striking changes in patterns of cognition, affect, and behavior.

Mikulincer, M., & Shaver, P.R. (2007). (See References). A comprehensive overview of theory, methods, and findings in the area of adult attachment, showing the widespread effects of relationship schemas.

Molden, D.C., & Dweck, C.S. (2006). Finding "meaning" in psychology: A lay theories approach to self-regulation, social perception, and social development. *American Psychologist, 61,* 192–203. A review of research on the ways in which implicit theories create patterns of goals, construals, emotions, and behavior across a variety of domains.

Pietrzak, J., Downey, G., & Ayduk, O. (2005). (See References). A fine review of theory and research on how learned expectations of rejection lead people to process and react to interpersonal cues in ways that undermine their interpersonal relationships.

Walton, G.M., & Cohen, G.L. (2007). (See References). A compelling research article showing how inducing expectations of interpersonal acceptance promotes marked changes in motivation and behavior.

## References

Allport, G.W. (1964). *Pattern and growth in personality.* New York: Holt.

Aronson, J., Fried, C., & Good, C. (2002). Reducing the effects of stereotype threat on African American college students by shaping theories of intelligence. *Journal of Experimental Social Psychology, 38,* 113–125.

Baldwin, M.W., & Dandeneau, S.D. (2005). Understanding and modifying the relational schemas underlying insecurity. In M. Baldwin (Ed.), *Interpersonal cognition* (pp. 62–84). New York: Guilford.

Blackwell, L., Trzesniewski, K., & Dweck, C.S. (2007). Implicit theories of intelligence predict achievement across an adolescent transition: A longitudinal study and an intervention. *Child Development, 78,* 246–263.

Block, J. (1993). Studying personality the long way. In D.C. Funder, R.D. Parke, C. Tomlinson-Keasey, & J. Block (Eds.), *Studying lives through time: Personality and development* (pp. 9–41). Washington, DC: American Psychological Association.

Dweck, C.S. (1999). *Self-theories: Their role in motivation, personality and development.* Philadelphia: Taylor and Francis/ Psychology Press.

Garber, J., Keiley, M.K., & Martin, N.C. (2002). Developmental trajectories of adolescents' depressive symptoms: Predictors of change. *Journal of Consulting and Clinical Psychology, 70,* 79–95.

Good, C., Aronson, J., & Inzlicht, M. (2003). Improving adolescents' standardized test performance: An Intervention to reduce the effects of stereotype threat. *Journal of Applied Developmental Psychology, 24,* 645–662.

Grych, J.H., Fincham, F.D., Jouriles, E.N., & McDonald, R. (2000). Interparental conflict and child adjustment: Testing the mediational role of appraisals in the cognitive-contextual framework. *Child Development, 71,* 1648–1661.

Johnson, S., Dweck, C.S., & Chen, F. (2007). Evidence for infants' internal working models of attachment. *Psychological Science, 18,* 501–502.

Kammrath, L., & Dweck, C.S. (2006). Voicing conflict: Preferred conflict strategies among incremental and entity theorists. *Personality and Social Psychology Bulletin, 32,* 1497–1508.

Kray, L.J., & Haselhuhn, M. (2007). Implicit theories of negotiating ability and performance: Longitudinal and experimental evidence. *Journal of Personality and Social Psychology, 93,* 49–64.

McAdams, D. (1995). What do we know when we know a person? *Journal of Personality, 63,* 365–396.

Mikulincer, M., & Shaver, P.R. (2007). *Attachment in adulthood: Structure, dynamics, and change.* New York: Guilford.

Mischel, W., & Shoda, Y. (1995). A cognitive-affective systems theory of personality: Reconceptualizing the invariances in personality and the role of situations. *Psychological Review, 102,* 246–268.

Mueller, C.M., & Dweck, C.S. (1998). Intelligence praise can undermine motivation and performance. *Journal of Personality and Social Psychology, 75,* 33–52.

Pietrzak, J., Downey, G., & Ayduk, O. (2005). Rejection sensitivity as an interpersonal vulnerability. In M. Baldwin (Ed.), *Interpersonal cognition* (pp. 62–84). New York: Guilford.

Roberts, B.W., Walton, K.E., & Viechtbauer, W. (2006). Patterns of mean-level change in personality traits across the life course: A meta-analysis of longitudinal studies. *Psychological Bulletin, 132,* 1–25.

Rothbart, M.K., & Ahadi, S.A. (1994). Temperament and the development of personality. *Journal of Abnormal Psychology, 103,* 55–66.

Walton, G.M., & Cohen, G.L. (2007). A question of belonging: Race, fit, and achievement. *Journal of Personality and Social Psychology, 92,* 82–96.

## Critical Thinking

1. What is the argument for saying that personalities are "permanent"?
2. How do one's beliefs shape or alter one's personality?

**CAROL S. DWECK,** Department of Psychology, Jordan Hall, Stanford University, Stanford, CA 94305; e-mail: dweck@stanford.edu.

**Acknowledgments**—This paper is based on a keynote address delivered at the 2007 Annual Convention of the Association for Psychological Science, Washington, DC.

# Evolutionary Psychology and Intelligence Research

SATOSHI KANAZAWA

E volutionary psychology and intelligence research have largely stood separately despite the fact that both of these subfields of psychology take biological and genetic influences on human behavior and cognition seriously. In some sense, this is understandable. Evolutionary psychology focuses on universal human nature, which is shared by all humans, or on sex-specific male human nature and female human nature, which are shared by all men and all women, respectively. In contrast, intelligence research (psychometrics) is part of differential psychology, which focuses on what makes individuals different from each other. Psychometrics is concerned with accurate measurement of intelligence precisely because individuals vary in their level of intelligence largely (though not entirely) because of their different genetic makeup.

Yet, as Tooby and Cosmides (1990a) articulated, the concept of universal human nature is not inimical to or incompatible with individual differences (in intelligence or other traits). Although individual differences have yet to be fully integrated into evolutionary psychology (Buss, 1995; Nettle, 2006), some evolutionary psychologists have incorporated heritable or reactively heritable (Tooby & Cosmides, 1990a) individual differences in personality (Buss, 1991; MacDonald, 1995; Nettle, 2005), sociosexuality (Gangestad & Simpson, 1990, 2000), and attachment and reproductive strategies (Belsky, Steinberg, & Draper, 1991; Buss & Greiling, 1999). Scarr (1995), and J. M. Bailey (1998) called for the incorporation of behavior genetics into evolutionary psychology in order to emphasize heritable individual and group differences and provide a fuller explanation of human behavior.

In this article, I follow the lead of earlier evolutionary psychologists who have attempted to incorporate individual differences. I seek to integrate evolutionary psychology, on the one hand, and intelligence research in particular and differential psychology in general, on the other. I aim to incorporate individual differences in general intelligence and other traits into universal human nature. I suggest how and when evolutionary constraints on the human brain, universally shared by all humans, may interact with general intelligence, such that more intelligent individuals have fewer such constraints than less intelligent individuals. I suggest that general intelligence is both a domain-specific evolved psychological mechanism *and* an individual-difference variable. I derive a novel hypothesis, called the Savanna–IQ Interaction Hypothesis, from the intersection of evolutionary psychology and intelligence research and discuss its implications. Among other things, this hypothesis suggests one possible explanation for why general intelligence is correlated with the Big Five personality factor Openness to Experience; at the same time, it calls for a refinement of the concept of novelty. I conclude with several illustrations of how and when more intelligent individuals are more likely than less intelligent individuals to acquire and espouse evolutionarily novel values.

## The Savanna Principle

Adaptations, physical or psychological, are designed for and adapted to the conditions of the environment of evolutionary adaptedness, not necessarily to the current environment (Tooby & Cosmides, 1990b). This is easiest to see in the case of physical adaptations, such as the vision and color recognition system.

What color is a banana? A banana is yellow in the sunlight and in the moonlight. It is yellow on a sunny day, on a cloudy day, and on a rainy day. It is yellow at dawn and at dusk. The color of a banana appears constant to the human eye under all these conditions despite the fact that the actual wavelengths of the light reflected by the surface of the banana under these varied conditions are different. Objectively, bananas are not the same color all the time. However, the human eye and color recognition system can compensate for these varied conditions because they all occurred during the course of the evolution of the human vision system, and humans can perceive the objectively varied colors as constantly yellow (Cosmides & Tooby, 1999, pp. 17–19; Shepard, 1994).

So a banana looks yellow under all conditions *except in a parking lot at night.* Under the sodium vapor lights commonly used to illuminate parking lots, a banana does not appear natural yellow. This is because the sodium vapor lights did not exist in the ancestral environment, during the course of the evolution of the human vision system, and the visual cortex is therefore incapable of compensating for them.

The same principle holds for psychological adaptations. Pioneers of evolutionary psychology (Crawford, 1993; Symons, 1990; Tooby & Cosmides, 1990b) all recognized that the evolved psychological mechanisms are designed for and adapted to the conditions of the environment of evolutionary adaptedness, not necessarily to the conditions of the current environment. I systematized these observations into what I called the *Savanna Principle* (Kanazawa, 2004a): The human brain has difficulty comprehending and dealing with entities and situations that did not exist in the ancestral environment. Burnham and Johnson (2005, pp. 130–131) referred to the same observation as the *evolutionary legacy hypothesis,* whereas Hagen and Hammerstein (2006, pp. 341–343) called it the *mismatch hypothesis.*

The Savanna Principle can explain why some otherwise elegant scientific theories of human behavior, such as the subjective expected utility maximization theory or game theory in microeconomics, often fail empirically, because they posit entities and situations that did not exist in the ancestral environment. For example, nearly half the players of one-shot Prisoner's Dilemma games make the theoretically irrational choice to cooperate with their partner (Sally, 1995). The Savanna Principle suggests that this may possibly be because the human brain has difficulty comprehending completely anonymous social exchange and absolutely no possibility of knowing future interactions (which together make the game truly one-shot; Kanazawa, 2004a, pp. 44–45). Neither of these situations existed in the ancestral environment; however, they are crucial for the game-theoretic prediction of universal defection.

Fehr and Henrich (2003) suggested that one-shot encounters and exchanges might have been common in the ancestral environment. In their response to Fehr and Henrich, Hagen and Hammerstein (2006) pointed out that even if one-shot encounters were common in the ancestral environment, anonymous encounters could not have been common, and the game-theoretic prediction of defection in one-shot games requires both noniteration and anonymity. A lack of anonymity can lead to reputational concerns even in nonrepeated exchanges.

As another illustration of the Savanna Principle, individuals who watch certain types of TV shows are more satisfied with their friendships, just as they would be if they had more friends or socialized with them more frequently (Derrick, Gabriel, & Hugenberg, 2009; Kanazawa, 2002). This may possibly be because realistic images of other humans, such as found in television, movies, videos, and photographs, did not exist in the ancestral environment, where all realistic images of other humans *were* other humans. As a result, the human brain may have implicit difficulty distinguishing "TV friends" (the characters repeatedly seen on TV shows) and real friends.

Most evolutionary psychologists and biologists concur that humans have not undergone significant evolutionary changes in the last 10,000 years, since the end of the Pleistocene Epoch, because the environment during this period has not provided a stable background against which natural and sexual selection can operate over many generations (A. S. Miller & Kanazawa, 2007, pp. 25–28). This is the assumption behind the Savanna Principle. More recently, however, some scientists have voiced opinions that human evolution has continued and even accelerated during the Holocene Epoch (Cochran & Harpending, 2009; Evans et al., 2005). Although these studies conclusively demonstrate that new alleles have indeed emerged in the human genome since the end of the Pleistocene Epoch, the implication and importance of such new alleles for evolutionary psychology are not immediately obvious. In particular, with the sole exception of lactose tolerance, it is not clear whether these new alleles have led to the emergence of new evolved psychological mechanisms in the last 10,000 years.

# The Evolution of General Intelligence

General intelligence refers to the ability to reason deductively or inductively, think abstractly, use analogies, synthesize information, and apply it to new domains (Gottfredson, 1997; Neisser et al., 1996). The *g* factor, which is often used synonymously with general intelligence, is a latent variable that emerges in a factor analysis of various cognitive (IQ) tests. They are not exactly the same thing. *g* is an *indicator* or *measure* of general intelligence; it is not general intelligence itself. As a measure of reasoning ability, general intelligence is what Cattell (1971) called "fluid intelligence" ($Gf$), not what he called "crystallized intelligence" (*Gc*), which, while influenced by general intelligence, is a measure of acquired knowledge.

The concept of general intelligence poses a problem for evolutionary psychology (Chiappe & MacDonald, 2005; Cosmides & Tooby, 2002; G. F. Miller, 2000a). Evolutionary psychologists contend that the human brain consists of domain-specific evolved psychological mechanisms, which evolved to solve specific adaptive problems (problems of survival and reproduction) in specific domains. If the contents of the human brain are domain specific, how can evolutionary psychology explain general intelligence?

In contrast to views expressed by G. F. Miller (2000b); Cosmides and Tooby (2002), and Chiappe and MacDonald (2005), I proposed that what is now known as general intelligence may have originally evolved as a domain-specific adaptation to deal with evolutionarily novel, nonrecurrent problems (Kanazawa, 2004b). The human brain consists of a large number of domain-specific evolved psychological mechanisms to solve recurrent adaptive problems. In this sense, our ancestors did not really have to *think* in order to solve such recurrent problems. Evolution has already done all the thinking, so to speak, and equipped the human brain with the appropriate psychological mechanisms, which engender preferences, desires, cognitions, and emotions and motivate adaptive behavior in the context of the ancestral environment.

Even in the extreme continuity and constancy of the ancestral environment, however, there were likely occasional problems that were evolutionarily novel and nonrecurrent, problems that required our ancestors to think and reason in order to solve. Such problems may have included, for example, the following:

1. Lightning has struck a tree near the camp and set it on fire. The fire is now spreading to the dry underbrush. What should I do? How can I stop the spread of the fire? How can I and my family escape it? (Since lightning never strikes the same place twice, this is guaranteed to be a nonrecurrent problem.)

2. We are in the middle of the severest drought in a hundred years. Nuts and berries at our normal places of gathering, which are usually plentiful, are not growing at all, and animals are scarce as well. We are running out of food because none of our normal sources of food are working. What else can we eat? What else is safe to eat? How else can we procure food?

3. A flash flood has caused the river to swell to several times its normal width, and I am trapped on one side of it while my entire band is on the other side. It is imperative that I rejoin them soon. How

can I cross the rapid river? Should I walk across it? Or should I construct some sort of buoyant vehicle to use to get across it? If so, what kind of material should I use? Wood? Stones?

To the extent that these evolutionarily novel, nonrecurrent problems happened frequently enough in the ancestral environment (a different problem each time) and had serious enough consequences for survival and reproduction, then any genetic mutation that allowed its carriers to think and reason would have been selected for, and what we now call "general intelligence" could have evolved as a domain-specific adaptation for the domain of evolutionarily novel, nonrecurrent problems, which did not exist in the ancestral environment and for which there are therefore no dedicated modules.

From this perspective, general intelligence may have become universally important in modern life (Gottfredson, 1997; Herrnstein & Murray, 1994; Jensen, 1998) only because our current environment is almost entirely evolutionarily novel. The new theory suggests, and empirical data confirm, that more intelligent individuals are better than less intelligent individuals at solving problems only if they are evolutionarily novel. More intelligent individuals are not better than less intelligent individuals at solving evolutionarily familiar problems, such as those in the domains of mating, parenting, interpersonal relationships, and wayfinding (Kanazawa, 2004b, 2007), unless the solution involves evolutionarily novel entities. For example, more intelligent individuals are no better than less intelligent individuals in finding and keeping mates, but they may be better at using computer dating services. Three recent studies, employing widely varied methods, have all shown that the average intelligence of a population appears to be a strong function of the evolutionary novelty of its environment (Ash & Gallup, 2007; D. H. Bailey & Geary, 2009; Kanazawa, 2008).

My theory (Kanazawa, 2004b) builds on and shares common themes with earlier evolutionary theories of intelligence, which posit climatic, ecological, and social novelties as the main forces behind the evolution of intelligence. Jerisen (1973) employed the concept of the encephalization quotient (EQ) to explain the evolution of intelligence of species as a function of the novelty of their ecological niches. Dunbar's (1998) and Humphrey's (1976) social brain hypothesis and Byrne and Whiten's (1988) machiavellian intelligence hypothesis both explain the evolution of intelligence as a consequence of having to deal with and potentially deceive a large number of conspecifics in the group. Geary's (2005) motivation-to-control theory explains the expansion of the human brain as a result of the human need to control, first its physical environment and then the social environment of fellow humans.

Gottfredson (1997) argued that other humans provide the greatest complexities in social life, which select for greater intelligence. Social relationships, while themselves evolutionarily familiar and recurrent, may occasionally add novelty and complexity that requires general intelligence to deal with.

## "Intelligences"

In recent years, psychologists have discussed various forms of intelligence or "intelligences," such as emotional intelligence (Mayer, Salovey, & Caruso, 2008; Salovey & Mayer, 1990), social intelligence (Kihlstrom & Cantor, 2000; Marlowe, 1986), mating intelligence (Geher & Miller, 2007), and Gardner's (1983) notion of multiple intelligences, which include linguistic, logical-mathematical, bodily-kinesthetic, spatial, musical, interpersonal, and intrapersonal intelligences. There is no question that these are all important intrapersonal and interpersonal skills and abilities that individuals need in their daily lives. Further, it seems reasonable to suggest that there are individual differences in such skills and abilities in the realm of interpersonal relations.

However, it is not at all clear what we gain by referring to such skills, competences, and abilities as "intelligences." The concept of intelligence in its historical origin in psychology was purely cognitive (Spearman, 1904). I personally would have preferred to keep it that way; however, the tide appears to have turned against my purist position. Whether to call these intrapersonal and interpersonal competencies "intelligences" or "skills," however, is a purely semantic matter without any necessary substantive implications. At any rate, in this article, I focus exclusively on purely cognitive general intelligence and not on other forms of intelligence, for two reasons. First, this is how most intelligence researchers and psychometricians define the concept of intelligence. Although educational, social, clinical, and industrial/organizational psychologists may refer to other "intelligences" as predictors of individual performance, intelligence researchers are nearly unanimous in their exclusive focus on cognitive general intelligence (Jensen, 1998). Second, as mentioned above, the concept of *general* intelligence presents a particular theoretical problem for evolutionary psychology's modular view of the human brain. Such a modular view can easily accommodate other "intelligences" as separate domain-specific modules, but it has more difficulty incorporating *general* intelligence with its seeming domain generality.

Other people and interactions with them (including mating) are "entities and situations" that we are certain existed during the entire period of human evolution. The theory of the evolution of general intelligence would therefore predict that general intelligence would not increase or correlate with emotional intelligence, social intelligence, or mating intelligence, each of which independently evolved to solve evolutionarily familiar problems in a given domain (Mayer, Salovey, Caruso, & Sitarenios, 2001, pp. 236–237). Several studies demonstrate that general intelligence is uncorrelated (or sometimes even negatively correlated) with measures of emotional, social, and mating intelligence (Davies, Stankov, & Roberts, 1998; Derksen, Kramer, & Katzko, 2002; Ford & Tisak, 1983; Fox & Spector, 2000; Kanazawa, 2007; Marlowe & Bedell, 1982).

There is some contrary evidence, however. Mayer, Roberts, and Barsade (2009) explicitly defined emotional intelligence as an application of general intelligence to the domain of emotions, and Roberts, Zeidner, and Matthews's (2001) study shows that measures of emotional intelligence are significantly and moderately *positively* correlated with general intelligence (as measured by the Air Force Qualifying Test). The question of whether emotional, social, and mating intelligences are "really" intelligences and how cognitive they are is difficult to answer definitively because, as Mayer et al. (2008) noted, there is a very wide spectrum of approaches to these other "intelligences." Some of them take cognitive intelligence seriously, others do not.

# Is Evolutionary Novelty a Domain?

The theory of the evolution of general intelligence as a domain-specific adaptation is subject to two contradictory criticisms. The first criticism is that the domain of evolutionary novelty, which encompasses all entities and situations that did not exist in the ancestral environment, is too large and undefined, and thus a set of potentially indefinite evolutionarily novel problems presents the same "frame problem" that inspired Tooby and Cosmides (1992) to advocate the domain-specific view of the human mind. The second criticism is that evolutionarily novel problems in the ancestral environment and throughout human evolutionary history have by definition been few and far between, and thus they could not have exerted sufficient selection pressure to lead to the evolution of general intelligence as a domain-specific adaptation.[1]

## Is the Domain of Evolutionary Novelty Too Large?

Evolutionarily novel problems have two characteristics in common: They are unanticipated by evolution (and thus there are no dedicated modules to solve them), and they are solvable by logical reasoning. Technically, all adaptive problems, evolutionarily novel or otherwise, are in principle logically solvable. Given sufficient time and data, for example, men, collectively and over time, can eventually figure out that women with symmetrical facial features are genetically healthier and that those with low waist-to-hip ratios are more fecund, so they should find them more desirable as mates. However, for such evolutionarily familiar and recurrent problems like mate selection, evolution short-circuits the long process of trial and error and simply equips men with the module that inclines them to find women with symmetrical features and low waist-to-hip ratios sexually attractive without really knowing why. For other, evolutionarily novel, nonrecurrent problems, however, evolution has not had time or opportunity to equip humans with such dedicated modules, and they therefore have to "figure out" the problems anew and on their own by logic and reason.

What defines the domain of evolutionarily novel problems, along with their being novel and unanticipated by evolution, is their logical solvability, and it is therefore no larger nor any less defined than other domains, such as cheater detection, language acquisition, and face recognition. After all, potential cheaters may be any kind of exchange partner, and potential deception may occur in any situation. But cheaters all have one thing in common: violation of social contract. Similarly, potential first language to be acquired by a newborn baby may come in any form; there are a nearly infinite number of natural human languages. Yet they all have key features in common, what Chomsky (1957) calls the deep structure of grammar. Hence a developmentally normal human baby, equipped with the language acquisition device, can acquire any human language as its native language, however diverse and varied on the surface such languages may be. Similarly, all evolutionarily novel problems, infinite though they may be in potential number, have certain features in common that define them, chief among which is their logical solvability.

It is not that evolution can anticipate a whole host of evolutionarily novel problems in the future (any more than it could have anticipated the emergence of new human languages such as English or German). It is just that people who have been able to solve (rare and nonrecurrent) evolutionarily novel problems in the past genetically pass on the same ability to their descendants, who can then use it to solve other evolutionarily novel problems in the future, because all evolutionarily novel problems share the common characteristic of logical solvability.

All evolved psychological mechanisms (or modules) are content rich (Tooby & Cosmides, 1992). The contents of general intelligence as a domain-specific adaptation are a set of tools that allow its possessors to arrive at logical conclusions. Such a set of logical tools may include the principle of transitivity (If A then B, and if B then C, then it follows that if A then C); what is now known as Mills's methods of induction (such as the method of difference and the method of concomitant variation); syllogism and deductive reasoning (although deduction begins with a universally true major premise, which is unlikely to have been available to our ancestors); analogy; abstraction, and so forth. In general, intelligent people are those who can use these logical tools and reason correctly and efficiently.

## Is the Domain of Evolutionary Novelty Too Small?

A second criticism of the theory avers that evolutionarily novel, nonrecurrent problems could not have arisen frequently enough in the ancestral environment to exert sufficient selection pressure to lead to the evolution of general intelligence or any other adaptation. Selection pressure, however, is a multiplicative function of the frequency of the problem and the magnitude of the selective force. Even a very weak selective force could lead to an evolved adaptation if the adaptive problem in question happens frequently enough over the course of human evolution to accumulate its small effects. Conversely, even a very infrequent adaptive problem can exert sufficient selection pressure if the magnitude of the selective force (the negative consequences of failing to solve the adaptive problem) is sufficiently great.

To take an extreme example for illustrative purposes, suppose a widespread drought or massive flash flood (of a kind used in the examples of evolutionarily novel problems above) on average happens once a century (roughly five generations), but, every time it happens, it kills everyone below the median in logical thinking and reasoning ability. So the adaptive problem happens very infrequently, but the selective force is very strong. In this scenario, in only one millennium (a blink of an eye on the evolutionary time scale), the average intelligence of the population becomes greater than the top 0.1% of the original population. This is equivalent to the current population of the United States, with the mean IQ of 100, changing to a new population 10 centuries later with a mean IQ of 146. From our current perspective, the average person then will be a genius. Even if the selective force was much weaker (one tenth of the original scenario above) and the adaptive problem only wiped out the bottom 5% in logical reasoning (allowing the top 95% of the population to survive each drought or flood every century), it would still take only 13,500 years to achieve a comparable effect on the average intelligence of the population and shift it upward by more than three standard deviations.

It would therefore appear that even an infrequent adaptive problem can produce sufficient selection pressure if the selective force is sufficiently strong. It would not be unreasonable to speculate that *some* (different) novel and nonrecurrent problem happened once a century during the evolutionary past that required our ancestors to think and reason to solve and that killed off the bottom 5% of the population in such an ability. General intelligence as a domain-specific adaptation would then have evolved relatively rapidly, in less than 15,000 years.

# Is General Intelligence a Domain-Specific Adaptation or an Individual-Difference Variable?

Some critics (Borsboom & Dolan, 2006) contend that general intelligence could not be an adaptation because it is an individual-difference variable. Adaptations are universal and constant features of a species shared by all its members; in contrast, there are obviously heritable individual differences in general intelligence, whereby some individuals are more intelligent than others. These critics argue that adaptations and heritable individual differences are mutually exclusive.

These criticisms betray profound misunderstanding of the nature of adaptations. A trait could simultaneously be an evolved adaptation and an individual-difference variable. In fact, *most adaptations exhibit individual differences.* Full-time bipedalism is a uniquely human adaptation, yet some individuals walk and run faster than others. The eye is a complex adaptation, yet some individuals have better vision than others. Language is an adaptation, yet some individuals learn to speak their native language at earlier ages and have greater linguistic facility than others.

Individual differences in general intelligence and other adaptations are what Tooby and Cosmides (1990a) called random quantitative variation on a monomorphic design. "Because the elaborate functional design of individuals [e.g., general intelligence as a domain-specific adaptation] is largely monomorphic [shared by all members of a species], our adaptations do not vary in their architecture from individual to individual (*except quantitatively* [emphasis added])" (Tooby & Cosmides, 1990a, p. 37).

Intraspecific (interindividual) differences in such traits pale in comparison to interspecific differences. Carl Lewis and I run at a virtually identical speed compared with cheetahs or sloths. Similarly, Einstein and I have virtually identical intelligence compared with cheetahs or sloths. It is therefore possible for a trait to be both universal and species-typical (exhibiting virtually no variation in the architecture in a cross-species comparison) *and* to manifest vast individual differences in quantitative performance among members of a single species. General intelligence may be one such trait.

Tooby and Cosmides (1990a, pp. 38–39) made this exact point, using "a complex psychological mechanism regulating aggression" (p. 38) as their example. They contended that this mechanism is an adaptation, even though there are heritable individual differences in the mechanism's threshold of activation (i.e., whether one has a "short fuse" or not). Tooby and Cosmides suggested that a complex psychological mechanism regulating aggression "is (by hypothesis) universal and therefore has zero heritability" (p. 38) even though "the *variations* in the exact level at which the threshold of activation is set are probably not adaptations" (p. 39).

The ability to run bipedally, faster than a sloth but slower than a cheetah, is a trait that is universally shared by all normally developing humans; it is a species-typical adaptation with zero heritability. But the exact speed at which a human can run is a heritable individual-difference variable and is therefore not an adaptation. Similarly, I propose that general intelligence is an adaptation and has zero heritability (in the sense that all humans have the ability to think and reason), even though the exact level of an individual's general intelligence ("IQ") is not an adaptation and is a highly heritable individual-difference variable. And Tooby and Cosmides (1990a, p. 57) contended that "nonadaptive, random fluctuations in the monomorphic design of a mental organ can give rise to heritable individual differences *in nearly every manifest feature of human psychology* [emphasis added]." One would therefore expect some individual differences in general intelligence as a domain-specific adaptation.

Explicitly recognizing that general intelligence can simultaneously be a domain-specific, species-typical adaptation *and* an individual-difference variable allows us to integrate evolutionary psychology—the study of species-typical evolved psychological mechanisms—and intelligence research—the study and measurement of heritable individual differences in general intelligence. Further, Tooby and Cosmides's (1990a) notion of the random quantitative (but heritable) variations on a monomorphic design would allow us to study individual differences in other evolved psychological mechanisms.

For example, the cheater detection module was among the first evolved psychological mechanisms to be discovered (Cosmides, 1989). It is clearly an adaptation, in that all human beings have the evolutionarily given and innate ability to detect when they might be cheated out of a fair exchange in a social contract. But are there individual differences in how well individuals can detect cheaters? Are some individuals inherently better at it than others? If so, are such individual differences heritable? Are some individuals genetically predisposed to fall victim to cons and scams?

Theory of mind is another evolved psychological mechanism; adult humans have the ability to infer the mental states of others. However, we already know that some individuals with pathological conditions (autism, Asperger's syndrome) have a weakened or absent capacity for theory of mind (Baron-Cohen, 1995). Can developmentally typical individuals also vary in their theory of mind? Dunbar (2005) suggested that there are individual differences in higher order theory of mind ("I think that you think that Sally thinks that Anne thinks that . . .") and that good writers like Shakespeare are rare because great dramas like *Othello* require writers to possess a sixth-order theory of mind. If individuals can vary in their capacity for higher order theory of mind, it seems reasonable to suggest that they might also vary in their capacity for first-order theory of mind, with some being better than others at accurately inferring the mental states of another person. If so, can such individual differences in the evolved psychological mechanism of theory of mind be heritable, since we already know that autism and Asperger's syndrome may be heritable (A. Bailey et al., 1995; Folstein & Rutter, 1988)?

Incorporating individual differences, not only in general intelligence but in other evolved psychological mechanisms, will allow us to pursue these and other questions at the new frontier where evolutionary psychology meets differential psychology.

## How General Intelligence Modifies the Evolutionary Limitations of the Human Brain

The logical conjunction of the Savanna Principle and the theory of the evolution of general intelligence suggests a qualification of the Savanna Principle. If general intelligence evolved to deal with evolutionarily novel problems, then the human brain's difficulty in comprehending and dealing with entities and situations that did not exist in the ancestral environment (proposed in the Savanna Principle) should interact with general intelligence such that the Savanna Principle will hold stronger among less intelligent individuals than among more intelligent individuals. More intelligent individuals should be better able than less intelligent individuals to comprehend and deal with evolutionarily novel (but *not* evolutionarily familiar) entities and situations.

Thus, the Savanna–IQ Interaction Hypothesis (Kanazawa, 2010) suggests that less intelligent individuals have greater difficulty than more intelligent individuals with comprehending and dealing with evolutionarily novel entities and situations that did not exist in the ancestral environment; in contrast, general intelligence does not affect individuals' ability to comprehend and deal with evolutionarily familiar entities and situations that existed in the ancestral environment.

Evolutionarily novel entities that more intelligent individuals are better able to comprehend and deal with may include ideas and lifestyles, which form the basis of their values and preferences; it would be difficult for individuals to prefer or value something that they cannot truly comprehend. Hence, applied to the domain of preferences and values, the Savanna–IQ Interaction Hypothesis suggests that more intelligent individuals are more likely than less intelligent individuals to acquire and espouse evolutionarily novel preferences and values that did not exist in the ancestral environment but that general intelligence has no effect on the acquisition and espousal of evolutionarily familiar preferences and values that existed in the ancestral environment (Kanazawa, 2010).

## General Intelligence and Openness to Experience

Research in personality psychology has shown that one of the five-factor personality model factors—Openness to Experience—is significantly positively (albeit moderately) correlated with intelligence (Ackerman & Heggestad, 1997). The similarity and overlap between intelligence and openness are apparent from the fact that some researchers call this personality factor "intellect" rather than "openness" (Goldberg, 1992; McRae, 1994). Although it is widely accepted by personality psychologists that intelligence and openness covary across individuals, it is not known why (Chamorro-Premuzic & Furnham, 2006). The Savanna–IQ Interaction Hypothesis can potentially provide one explanation for why more intelligent individuals are more open to new experiences and are therefore more prone to seek novelty. It is instructive to note from this perspective that only the actions, ideas, and values facets of openness to experience are significantly correlated with general intelligence, not the fantasy, esthetics, and feelings facets (Gilles, Stough, & Loukomitis, 2004; Holland, Dollinger, Holland, & MacDonald, 1995).

At the same time, the Savanna–IQ Interaction Hypothesis suggests a possible need to refine the concept of novelty and to distinguish between *evolutionary novelty* (entities and situations that did not exist in the ancestral environment) and *experiential novelty* (entities and situations that individuals have not personally experienced in their own lifetimes). Although the five-factor personality model does not specify the type of novelty that open individuals are more likely to seek, the Savanna–IQ Interaction Hypothesis suggests that more intelligent individuals are more likely to seek only evolutionary novelty, not necessarily experiential novelty.

For example, all those who are alive in the United States today have lived their entire lives in a strictly monogamous society, and despite recent news events, very few contemporary Americans have any personal experiences with polygyny. Therefore monogamy is experientially familiar for most Americans, whereas polygyny is experientially novel. The five-factor model may therefore predict that more intelligent individuals are more likely to be open to polygyny as an experientially novel idea or action.

In contrast, humans have been mildly polygynous throughout their evolutionary history (Alexander, Hoogland, Howard, Noonan, & Sherman, 1979; Leutenegger & Kelly, 1977), and socially imposed monogamy is a relatively recent historical phenomenon (Kanazawa & Still, 1999). Therefore polygyny is evolutionarily familiar, whereas monogamy is evolutionarily novel. The Savanna–IQ Interaction Hypothesis would therefore predict that more intelligent individuals are more likely to be open to monogamy and less open to polygyny. In fact, the evidence suggests that more intelligent men are more likely to value monogamy and sexual exclusivity than are less intelligent men (Kanazawa, 2010).

As another example, for most contemporary Americans, traditional names derived from the Bible, such as John and Mary, are experientially more familiar than untraditional names such as OrangeJello and LemonJello (Levitt & Dubner, 2005). So the five-factor model may predict that more intelligent individuals are more likely to give their children untraditional names such as Orange Jello and LemonJello than are less intelligent individuals. From the perspective of the Savanna–IQ Interaction Hypothesis, however, both John and OrangeJello are equally evolutionarily novel (because the Bible itself and all the traditional names derived from it are evolutionarily novel), so it would not predict that more intelligent individuals are more likely to give their children untraditional names. In fact, there is no evidence at all that more intelligent individuals are more likely to prefer untraditional names for their children (Fryer & Levitt, 2004; Lieberson & Bell, 1992).

The Savanna–IQ Interaction Hypothesis underscores the need to distinguish between evolutionary novelty and experiential novelty. It can potentially explain why more intelligent individuals are more likely to seek evolutionary novelty but not necessarily experiential novelty. It further suggests that the established correlation between openness and intelligence may be limited to the domain of evolutionary novelty, not necessarily experiential novelty, but the current measures of openness do not adequately address this proposal.

# Empirical Illustrations

The Savanna–IQ Interaction Hypothesis, derived from the intersection of evolutionary psychology and intelligence research, suggests one potential way to account for some known individual differences. I discuss just a few of them here for illustrative purposes.

## TV Friends

Consistent with the Savanna Principle, I (Kanazawa, 2002) and Derrick et al. (2009) showed that individuals who watch certain types of TV shows are more satisfied with their friendships, which suggests that they may possibly have implicit difficulty distinguishing evolutionarily novel realistic images of actors they repeatedly see on TV and their real friends. My reanalysis of the same data from the General Social Surveys shows, however, that this seeming difficulty in distinguishing between "TV friends" and real friends appears to be limited to men and women with below-median intelligence (Kanazawa, 2006). Those who are above the median in intelligence do not report greater satisfaction with friendships as a function of watching more TV; only those below the median in intelligence do. This finding seems to suggest that the evolutionary constraints on the brain suggested by the Savanna Principle, whereby individuals have implicit difficulty recognizing realistic electronic images on TV for what they are, appear to be weaker or altogether absent among more intelligent individuals.

## Political Attitudes

It is difficult to define a whole school of political ideology precisely, but one may reasonably define *liberalism* (as opposed to *conservatism*) in the contemporary United States as the genuine concern for the welfare of genetically unrelated others and the willingness to contribute larger proportions of private resources for the welfare of such others. In the modern political and economic context, this willingness usually translates into paying higher proportions of individual incomes in taxes toward the government and its social welfare programs.

Defined as such, liberalism is evolutionarily novel. Humans (like other species) are evolutionarily designed to be altruistic toward their genetic kin (Hamilton, 1964a, 1964b), their repeated exchange partners (Trivers, 1971), and members of their deme (a group of intermarrying individuals) or ethnic group (Whitmeyer, 1997). They are not designed to be altruistic toward an indefinite number of complete strangers whom they are not likely ever to meet or exchange with. This is largely because our ancestors lived in small bands of 50–150 genetically related individuals, and large cities and nations with thousands and millions of people are themselves evolutionarily novel.

An examination of the 10-volume compendium *The Encyclopedia of World Cultures* (Levinson, 1991–1995), which describes *all* human cultures known to anthropology (more than 1,500) in great detail, as well as extensive primary ethnographies of traditional societies (Chagnon, 1992; Cronk, 2004; Hill & Hurtado, 1996; Lee, 1979; Whitten, 1976), reveals that liberalism as defined above is absent in these traditional cultures. Although sharing of resources, especially food, is quite common and often normatively prescribed among hunter-gatherer tribes, and although trade with neighboring tribes often takes place (Ridley, 1996), there is no evidence that people in contemporary hunter-gatherer bands *freely* share resources with *members of other tribes*. Because all members of a hunter-gatherer tribe are genetic kin or at the very least repeated exchange partners (friends and allies for life), sharing of resources among them does not qualify as an expression of liberalism as defined above. Given its absence in the contemporary hunter-gatherer tribes, which are often used as modern-day analogs of our ancestral life, it may be reasonable to infer that sharing of resources with total strangers that one has never met or is not ever likely to meet—liberalism—was not part of our ancestral life. Liberalism may therefore be evolutionarily novel, and the Savanna–IQ Interaction Hypothesis would predict that more intelligent individuals are more likely to espouse liberalism as a value than are less intelligent individuals.

Analyses of large representative American samples from the National Longitudinal Study of Adolescent Health (Add Health) and the General Social Surveys confirm this prediction (Kanazawa, 2010). Net of age, sex, race, education, earnings, and religion, more intelligent individuals are more liberal than their less intelligent counterparts. For example, among the Add Health respondents, those who identify themselves as "very liberal" in early adulthood have a mean childhood IQ of 106.4, whereas those who identify themselves as "very conservative" in early adulthood have a mean childhood IQ of 94.8. Even though past studies show that women are more liberal than men (Lake & Breglio, 1992; Shapiro & Mahajan, 1986; Wirls, 1986), and Blacks are more liberal than Whites (Kluegel & Smith, 1986; Sundquist, 1983), the analyses show that the effect of intelligence on liberalism is twice as large as the effect of sex or race.

## Choice Within Genetic Constraints: Circadian Rhythms

Choice is not incompatible with or antithetical to genetic influence. As long as heritability ($h^2$) is less than 1.0, individuals can still exercise some choice within broad genetic constraints. For example, political ideology has been shown to be partially genetically influenced; some individuals are genetically predisposed to be liberal or conservative (Alford, Funk, & Hibbing, 2005; Eaves & Eysenck, 1974). Nonetheless, individuals can still choose to be liberal or conservative within broad genetic constraints, and, as discussed above, more intelligent individuals are more likely to choose to be liberal than are less intelligent individuals.

Another example of choice within genetic constraints is circadian rhythms—whether one is a morning person or a night person. Virtually all species in nature, from single-cell organisms to mammals, including humans, exhibit a daily cycle of activity called circadian rhythm (Vitaterna, Takahashi, & Turek, 2001). The circadian rhythm in mammals is regulated by two clusters of nerve cells called the suprachiasmatic nuclei (SCN) in the anterior hypothalamus (Klein, Moore, & Reppert, 1991). Geneticists have by now identified a set of genes that regulate the SCN and thus the circadian rhythm among mammals (King & Takahashi, 2000). "Humans, however, have the unique ability to cognitively override their internal biological clock and its rhythmic outputs" (Vitaterna et al., 2001, p. 90).

Although there are some individual differences in the circadian rhythm, whereby some individuals are more nocturnal than others, humans are basically a diurnal (as opposed to nocturnal) species. Humans rely very heavily on vision for navigation but, unlike genuinely nocturnal species, cannot see in the dark or under little lighting, and our ancestors did not have artificial lighting during the night until the domestication of fire. Any human in the ancestral environment up and about during the night would have been at risk of predation by nocturnal predators.

Once again, ethnographic evidence from traditional societies available in *The Encyclopedia of World Cultures* (Levinson, 1991–1995) and extensive ethnographies (Chagnon, 1992; Cronk, 2004; Hill & Hurtado, 1996; Lee, 1979; Whitten, 1976) suggest that people in traditional societies usually rise shortly before dawn and go to sleep shortly after dusk in order to take full advantage of the natural light provided by the sun. There is no indication that there are any sustained nocturnal activities, other than occasional conversations and singing, in these tribes. It is therefore reasonable to infer that our ancestors must also have limited their daily activities to daylight, and sustained nocturnal activities are largely evolutionarily novel. The Savanna–IQ Interaction Hypothesis would therefore predict that more intelligent individuals are more likely to be nocturnal than are less intelligent individuals.

Analysis of a large representative sample from Add Health confirms this prediction (Kanazawa & Perina, 2009). Net of age, sex, race, marital status, parenthood, education, earnings, religion, current status as a student, and number of hours worked in a typical week, more intelligent children grow up to be more nocturnal as adults than do less intelligent children. Compared with their less intelligent counterparts, more intelligent individuals go to bed later on weeknights (when they have to get up at a certain time the next day) and on the weekend (when they do not), and they wake up later on weekdays (but not on the weekend, for which the positive effect of childhood IQ on nocturnality is not statistically significant). For example, those with childhood IQs of less than 75 go to bed around 11:42 p.m. on weeknights in early adulthood, whereas those with childhood IQs of over 125 go to bed around 12:30 a.m..

# Conclusion

This article seeks to integrate evolutionary psychology—the study of universal human nature—and intelligence research—the study and measurement of individual differences in intelligence. Tooby and Cosmides's (1990a) notion of random quantitative variation on a monomorphic design allows us to view general intelligence as both a domain-specific evolved adaptation (monomorphic design) and an individual-difference variable (random quantitative variation). Such random quantitative variation can also be highly heritable.

Although I have focused on general intelligence and psychometrics in this article, the proposed approach can integrate evolutionary psychology and any aspect of differential psychology. Aggression, theory of mind, the cheater detection mechanism, and some personality traits could all simultaneously be evolved psychological mechanisms and individual-difference variables.

The Savanna–IQ Interaction Hypothesis, which derives from the intersection of evolutionary psychology and intelligence research, suggests that more intelligent individuals are better able to comprehend and deal with evolutionarily novel entities and situations than are less intelligent individuals, but general intelligence does not affect individuals' ability to comprehend and deal with evolutionarily familiar entities and situations. The hypothesis suggests a new way to view some individual differences, such as the extent to which individuals implicitly confuse "TV friends" and real friends, political attitudes on the liberal–conservative continuum, and circadian rhythms, even when these traits are under some genetic control. As long as heritability ($h^2$) is less than 1.0, there is room for some individual choice.

The general approach proposed in this article will allow genuine integration of evolutionary psychology, on the one hand, and intelligence research in particular and differential psychology in general, on the other. It would simultaneously allow evolutionary psychologists to study a much wider range of psychological traits than hitherto possible and intelligence researchers and differential psychologists to make use of the theories and concepts of evolutionary psychology.

# Notes

1. I thank Jeremy Freese and Todd K. Shackelford, respectively, for articulating these views to me.

# References

Ackerman, P. L., & Heggestad, E. D. (1997). Intelligence, personality, and interests: Evidence for overlapping traits. *Psychological Bulletin, 121,* 219–245. doi:10.1037/0033–2909.121.2.219

Alexander, R. D., Hoogland, J. L., Howard, R. D., Noonan, K. M., & Sherman, P. W. (1979). Sexual dimorphisms and breeding systems in pinnipeds, ungulates, primates, and humans. In N. A. Chagnon & W. Irons (Eds.), *Evolutionary biology and human social behavior: An anthropological perspective* (pp. 402–435). North Scituate, MA: Duxbury Press.

Alford, J. R., Funk, C. L., & Hibbing, J. R. (2005). Are political orientations genetically transmitted? *American Political Science Review, 99,* 153–167.

Ash, J., & Gallup, G. G., Jr. (2007). Paleoclimatic variation and brain expansion during human evolution. *Human Nature, 18,* 109–124. doi:10.1007/s12110–007–9015-z

Bailey, A., Le Couteur, A., Gottesman, I., Bolton, P., Simonoff, E., Yuzda, E., & Rutter, M. (1995). Autism as a strongly genetic disorder: Evidence from a British twin study. *Psychological Medicine, 25,* 63–77. doi:10.1017/S0033291700028099

Bailey, D. H., & Geary, D. C. (2009). Hominid brain evolution: Testing climatic, ecological, and social competition models. *Human Nature, 20,* 67–79. doi:10.1007/s12110–008–9054–0

Bailey, J. M. (1998). Can behavior genetics contribute to evolutionary behavioral science? In C. Crawford & D. L. Krebs (Eds.), *Handbook of evolutionary psychology: Ideas, issues, and applications* (pp. 211–233). Mahwah, NJ: Erlbaum.

Baron-Cohen, S. (1995). *Mind blindness: An essay on autism and theory of mind.* Cambridge, MA: MIT Press.

Belsky, J., Steinberg, L., & Draper, P. (1991). Childhood experiences, interpersonal development, and reproductive strategy: An evolutionary theory of socialization. *Child Development, 62,* 647–670. doi:10.1111/j.1467–8624.1991.tb01558

Borsboom, D., & Dolan, C. V. (2006). Why g is not an adaptation: A comment on Kanazawa (2004). *Psychological Review, 113,* 433–437. doi:10.1037/0033–295X.113.2.433

Burnham, T. C., & Johnson, D. D. P. (2005). The biological and evolutionary logic of human cooperation. *Analyse & Kritik, 27,* 113–135.

Buss, D. M. (1991). Evolutionary personality psychology. *Annual Review of Psychology, 42,* 459–491. doi:10.1146/annurev.ps.42.020191.002331

Buss, D. M. (1995). Evolutionary psychology: A new paradigm for psychological science. *Psychological Inquiry, 6,* 1–30.

Buss, D. M., & Greiling, H. (1999). Adaptive individual differences. *Journal of Personality, 67,* 209–243. doi:10.1111/1467–6494.00053

Byrne, R., & Whiten, A. (1988). *Machiavellian intelligence: Social expertise and the evolution of intellect in monkeys, apes, and humans.* Oxford, England: Oxford University Press.

Cattell, R. B. (1971). *Abilities: Their structure, growth, and action.* Boston, MA: Houghton Mifflin.

Chagnon, N. (1992). *Yanomamö* (4th ed.). Fort Worth, TX: Harcourt Brace Jovanovich.

Chamorro-Premuzic, T., & Furnham, A. (2006). Intellectual competence and the intelligent personality: A third way in differential psychology. *Review of General Psychology, 10,* 251–267. doi:10.1037/1089–2680.10.3.251

Chiappe, D., & MacDonald, K. (2005). The evolution of domain-general mechanisms in intelligence and learning. *Journal of General Psychology, 132,* 5–40.

Chomsky, N, (1957). *Syntactic structures.* The Hague, The Netherlands: Mouton.

Cochran, G., & Harpending, H. (2009). *The 10,000 year explosion: How civilization accelerated human evolution.* New York, NY: Basic Books.

Cosmides, L. (1989). The logic of social exchange: Has natural selection shaped how humans reason? Studies with the Wason selection task. *Cognition, 31,* 187–276. doi:10.1016/0010–0277(89)90023–1

Cosmides, L., & Tooby, J. (1999). *What is evolutionary psychology?* Unpublished manuscript, Center for Evolutionary Psychology, University of California, Santa Barbara.

Cosmides, L., & Tooby, J. (2002). Unraveling the enigma of human intelligence: Evolutionary psychology and the multimodular mind. In R. J. Sternberg & J. C. Kaufman (Eds.), *The evolution of intelligence* (pp. 145–198). Mahwah, NJ: Erlbaum.

Crawford, C. B. (1993). The future of sociobiology: Counting babies or proximate mechanisms? *Trends in Ecology and Evolution, 8,* 183–186. doi:10.1016/0169–5347(93)90145-F

Cronk, L. (2004). *From Mukogodo to Maasai: Ethnicity and cultural change in Kenya.* Boulder, CO: Westview.

Davies, M., Stankov, L., & Roberts, R. D. (1998). Emotional intelligence: In search of an elusive construct. *Journal of Personality and Social Psychology, 75,* 989–1015. doi:10.1037/0022–3514.75.4.989

Derksen, J., Kramer, I., & Katzko, M. (2002). Does a self-report measure for emotional intelligence assess something different than general intelligence? *Personality and Individual Differences, 32,* 37–48. doi:10.1016/S0191–8869(01)00004–6

Derrick, J. L., Gabriel, S., & Hugenberg, K. (2009). Social surrogacy: How favored television programs provide the experience of belonging. *Journal of Experimental Social Psychology, 45,* 352–362. doi:101016/j.esp.2008.12.003

Dunbar, R. I. M. (1998). The social brain hypothesis. *Evolutionary Anthropology, 6,* 178–190.

Dunbar, R. I. M. (2005). Why are good writers so rare? An evolutionary perspective on literature. *Journal of Cultural and Evolutionary Psychology, 3,* 7–21. doi:10.1556/JCEP.3.2005.1.1

Eaves, L. J., & Eysenck, H. J. (1974). Genetics and the development of social attitudes. *Nature, 249,* 288–289. doi:10.1038/249288a0

Evans, P. D., Gilbert, S. L., Mekel-Bobrov, N., Vallender, E. J., Anderson, J. R., Vaez-Azizi, L. M., . . . Lahn, B. T. (2005, September 9). *Microcephalin,* a gene regulating brain size, continues to evolve adaptively in humans. *Science, 309,* 1717–1720. doi:10.1126/science.1113722

Fehr, E., & Henrich, J. (2003). Is strong reciprocity a maladaptation? On the evolutionary foundations of human altruism. In P. Hammerstein (Ed.), *Genetic and cultural evolution of cooperation* (pp. 55–82). Cambridge, MA: MIT Press.

Folstein, S. E., & Rutter, M. L. (1988). Autism: Familial aggregation and genetic implications. *Journal of Autism and Developmental Disorders, 18,* 3–30. doi:10.1007/BF02211815

Ford, M. E., & Tisak, M. S. (1983). A further search for social intelligence. *Journal of Educational Psychology, 75,* 196–206. doi:10.1037/0022–0663.75.2.196

Fox, S., & Spector, P. E. (2000). Relations of emotional intelligence, practical intelligence, general intelligence, and trait affectivity with interview outcomes: It's not all just 'G.' *Journal of Organizational Behavior, 21,* 203–220. doi:10.1002/(SICI)1099–1379(200003)21:2<203::AID-JOB38>3.0.CO;2-Z

Fryer, R. G., Jr., & Levitt, S. D. (2004). The causes and consequences of distinctly Black names. *Quarterly Journal of Economics, 119,* 767–805.

Gangestad, S. W., & Simpson, J. A. (1990). Toward an evolutionary history of female sociosexual variation. *Journal of Personality, 58,* 69–96. doi:10.1111/j.1467–6494.1990.tb00908

Gangestad, S. W., & Simpson, J. A. (2000). The evolution of human mating: Trade-offs and strategic pluralism. *Behavioral and Brain Sciences, 23,* 573–644. doi:10.1017/S0140525X0000337X

Gardner, H. (1983). *Frames of mind: The theory of multiple intelligences.* New York, NY: Basic Books.

Geary, D. C. (2005). *The origin of mind: Evolution of brain, cognition, and general intelligence.* Washington, DC: American Psychological Association.

Geher, G., & Miller, G. (Eds.). (2007). *Mating intelligence: Sex, relationships, and the mind's reproductive system.* Mahwah, NJ: Erlbaum.

Gilles, G. E., Stough, C., & Loukomitis, S. (2004). Openness, intelligence, and self-report intelligence. *Intelligence, 32,* 133–143.

Goldberg, L. R. (1992). The development of markers for the big-five factor structure. *Psychological Assessment, 4,* 26–42.

Gottfredson, L. S. (1997). Why g matters: The complexity of everyday life. *Intelligence, 24,* 79–132. doi:10.1016/S0160–2896(97)90014–3

Hagen, E. H., & Hammerstein, P. (2006). Game theory and human evolution: A critique of some recent interpretations of experimental games. *Theoretical Population Biology, 69,* 339–348. doi:101016/j.tpb.2005.09.005

Hamilton, W. D. (1964a). The genetical evolution of social behavior. I. *Journal of Theoretical Biology, 7,* 1–16. doi:10.1016/0022–5193(64)90038–4

Hamilton, W. D. (1964b). The genetical evolution of social behavior. II. *Journal of Theoretical Biology, 7,* 17–52. doi:10.1016/0022–5193(64)90039–6

Herrnstein, R. J., & Murray, C. (1994). *The bell curve: Intelligence and class structure in American life.* New York, NY: Free Press.

Hill, K., & Hurtado, A. M. (1996). *Ache life history: The ecology and demography of a foraging people.* New York, NY: Aldine.

Holland, D. C., Dollinger, S. J., Holland, C. J., & MacDonald, D. A. (1995). The relationship between psychometric intelligence and the five-factor model of personality in a rehabilitation sample. *Journal of Clinical Psychology, 51,* 79–88. doi:10.1002/1097–4679(199501)51:1<79::AID-JCLP2270510113>3.0CO;2-P

Humphrey, N. K. (1976). The social function of the intellect. In P. P. G. Bateson & R. A. Hinde (Eds.), *Growing points in ethology* (pp. 303–317). New York, NY: Cambridge University Press.

Jensen, A. R. (1998). *The g factor: The science of mental ability.* Westport, CT: Praeger.

Jerisen, H. (1973). *Evolution of the brain and intelligence.* New York, NY: Academic Press.

Kanazawa, S. (2002). Bowling with our imaginary friends. *Evolution and Human Behavior, 23,* 167–171. doi:10.1016/S1090–5138(01)00098–8

Kanazawa, S. (2004a). The Savanna Principle. *Managerial and Decision Economics, 25,* 41–54. doi:10.1002/mde.1130

Kanazawa, S. (2004b). General intelligence as a domain-specific adaptation. *Psychological Review, 111,* 512–523. doi:10.1037/0033–295X.111.2.512

Kanazawa, S. (2006). Why the less intelligent may enjoy television more than the more intelligent. *Journal of Cultural and Evolutionary Psychology, 4,* 27–36. doi:10.1556/JCEP.4.2006.1.2

Kanazawa, S. (2007). Mating intelligence and general intelligence as independent constructs. In G. Geher & G. Miller (Eds.), *Mating intelligence: Sex, relationships, and the mind's reproductive system* (pp. 283–309). Mahwah, NJ: Erlbaum.

Kanazawa, S. (2008). Temperature and evolutionary novelty as forces behind the evolution of general intelligence. *Intelligence, 36,* 99–108. doi:10.1016/j.intell.2007.04.001

Kanazawa, S. (2010). Why liberals and atheists are more intelligent. *Social Psychology Quarterly, 73,* 33–57. doi:10.1177/0190272510361602

Kanazawa, S., & Perina, K. (2009). Why night owls are more intelligent. *Personality and Individual Differences, 47,* 685–690. doi:10.1016/j.paid.2009.05.021

Kanazawa, S., & Still, M. C. (1999). Why monogamy? *Social Forces, 78,* 25–50.

Kihlstrom, J. F., & Cantor, N. (2000). Social intelligence. In R. J. Sternberg (Ed.), *Handbook of intelligence* (pp. 359–379). Cambridge, England: Cambridge University Press.

King, D. P., & Takahashi, J. S. (2000). Molecular genetics of circadian rhythms in mammals. *Annual Review of Neuroscience, 23,* 713–742. doi:10.1146/annurev.neuro.23.1.713

Klein, D. C., Moore, R. Y., & Reppert, S. M. (1991). *Suprachiasmatic nucleus: The mind's clock.* New York, NY: Oxford University Press.

Kluegel, J. R., & Smith, E. R. (1986). *Beliefs about inequality: Americans' view of what is and what ought to be.* New York, NY: Aldine.

Lake, C. C., & Breglio, V. J. (1992). Different voices, different views: The politics of gender. In P. Ries & A. J. Stone (Eds.), *The American woman, 1992–93: A status report* (pp. 178–201). New York, NY: Norton.

Lee, R. B. (1979). *The !Kung San: Men, women, and work in a foraging society.* Cambridge, England: Cambridge University Press.

Leutenegger, W., & Kelly, J. T. (1977). Relationship of sexual dimorphism in canine size and body size to social, behavioral, and ecological correlates in anthropoid primates. *Primates, 18,* 117–136. doi:10.1007/BF02382954

Levinson, D. (Ed.). (1991–1995). *Encyclopedia of world cultures* (Vols. *1–10*). Boston, MA: G. K. Hall.

Levitt, S. D., & Dubner, S. J. (2005). *Freakonomics: A rogue economist explores the hidden side of everything.* London, England: Penguin.

Lieberson, S., & Bell, E. O. (1992). Children's first names: An empirical study of social taste. *American Journal of Sociology, 98,* 511–554. doi:10.1086/230048

MacDonald, K. (1995). Evolution, the five-factor model, and levels of personality. *Journal of Personality, 63,* 525–567. doi:101111/j.1467–6494.1995.tb00505.x

Marlowe, H. A., Jr. (1986). Social intelligence: Evidence for multidimensionality and construct independence. *Journal of Educational Psychology, 78,* 52–58. doi:10.1037/0022–0663.78.1.52

Marlowe, H. A., & Bedell, J. R. (1982). Social intelligence: Further evidence for the independence of the construct. *Psychological Reports, 51,* 461–462.

Mayer, J. D., Roberts, R. D., & Barsade, S. G. (2009). Human abilities: Emotional intelligence. *Annual Review of Psychology, 59,* 507–536. doi:10.1146/annurev.psych.59.103006.093646

Mayer, J. D., Salovey, P., & Caruso, D. R. (2008). Emotional intelligence: New ability or eclectic traits? *American Psychologist, 63,* 503–517. doi:10.1037/0003–066X.63.6.503

Mayer, J. D., Salovey, P., Caruso, D. R., & Sitarenios, G. (2001). Emotional intelligence as a standard intelligence. *Emotion, 1,* 232–242. doi:10.1037/1528–3542.1.3.232

McRae, R. R. (1994). Openness to experience: Expanding the boundaries of Factor V. *European Journal of Personality, 8,* 251–272. doi:10.1002/per.2410080404

Miller, A. S., & Kanazawa, S. (2007). *Why beautiful people have more daughters.* New York, NY: Penguin.

Miller, G. F. (2000a). How to keep our metatheories adaptive: Beyond Cosmides, Tooby, and Lakatos. *Psychological Inquiry, 11,* 42–46.

Miller, G. F. (2000b). Sexual selection for indicators of intelligence. In G. R. Bock, J. A. Goode, & K. Webb (Eds.), *The nature of intelligence* (pp. 260–275). New York, NY: Wiley.

Neisser, U., Boodoo, G., Bouchard, T. J., Jr., Boykin, A. W., Brody, N., Ceci, S. J., . . . Urbina, S. (1996). Intelligence: Knowns and unknowns. *American Psychologist, 51,* 77–101. doi:10.1037/0003–066X.51.2.77

Nettle, D. (2005). An evolutionary approach to the extraversion continuum. *Evolution and Human Behavior, 26,* 363–373. doi:10.1016/j.evolhumbehav.2004.12.004

Nettle, D. (2006). The evolution of personality variation in humans and other animals. *American Psychologist, 61,* 622–631. doi:10.1037/0003–066X.61.6.622

Ridley, M. (1996). *The origins of virtue: Human instincts and the evolution of cooperation.* New York, NY: Viking Press.

Roberts, R. D., Zeidner, M., & Matthews, G. (2001). Does emotional intelligence meet traditional standards for an intelligence? Some new data and conclusions. *Emotion, 1,* 196–231. doi:10.1037/1528–3542.1.3.196

Sally, D. (1995). Conversation and cooperation in social dilemmas: A meta-analysis of experiments from 1958 to 1992. *Rationality and Society, 7,* 58–92. doi:10.1177/1043463195007001004

Salovey, P., & Mayer, J. D. (1990). Emotional intelligence. *Imagination, Cognition and Personality, 9,* 557–568.

Scarr, S. (1995). Psychology will be truly evolutionary when behavior genetics is included. *Psychological Inquiry, 6,* 68–71. doi:10.1207/s15327965pli0601_13

Shapiro, R. Y., & Mahajan, H. (1986). Gender differences in policy preferences: A summary of trends from the 1960s to the 1980s. *Public Opinion Quarterly, 50,* 42–61. doi:10.1086/268958

Shepard, R. N. (1994). Perceptual-cognitive universals as reflections of the world. *Psychonomic Bulletin & Review, 1,* 2–28.

Spearman, C. (1904). General intelligence, objectively determined and measured. *American Journal of Psychology, 15,* 201–293. doi:10.2307/1412107

Sundquist, J. L. (1983). *Dynamics of the party system* (Rev. ed.). Washington, DC: Brookings Institution.

Symons, D. (1990). Adaptiveness and adaptation. *Ethology and Sociobiology, 11,* 427–444. doi:10.1016/0162–3095(90)90019–3

Tooby, J., & Cosmides, L. (1990a). On the universality of human nature and the uniqueness of the individual: The role of genetics and adaptation. *Journal of Personality, 58,* 17–67.

Tooby, J., & Cosmides, L. (1990b). The past explains the present: Emotional adaptations and the structure of ancestral environments. *Ethology and Sociobiology, 11,* 375–424. doi:10.1016/0162–3095(90)90017-Z

Tooby, J., & Cosmides, L. (1992). The psychological foundations of culture. In J. H. Barkow, L. Cosmides, & J. Tooby (Eds.), *The adapted mind: Evolutionary psychology and the generation of culture* (pp. 19–136). New York, NY: Oxford University Press.

Trivers, R. L. (1971). The evolution of reciprocal altruism. *Quarterly Review of Biology, 46,* 35–57.

Vitaterna, M. H., Takahashi, J. S., & Turek, F. W. (2001). Overview of circadian rhythms. *Alcohol Research and Health, 25,* 85–93.

Whitmeyer, J. M. (1997). Endogamy as a basis for ethnic behavior. *Sociological Theory, 15,* 162–178. doi:10.1111/0735–2751.00030

Whitten, N. E., Jr. (1976). *Sacha Runa: Ethnicity and adaptation of Ecuadorian jungle Quichua.* Urbana: University of Illinois Press.

Wirls, D. (1986). Reinterpreting the gender gap. *Public Opinion Quarterly, 50,* 316–330.

## Critical Thinking

1. What is the Savanna Principle?

2. Describe the way in which the Savanna Principle may be used to conduct research on intelligence

# Second Nature

**Your personality isn't necessarily set in stone with a little experimentation, the ornery and bleak can reshape their temperaments and inject pluck and passion into their lives.**

KATHLEEN MCGOWAN

Call it the cult of the ugly duckling. We devour stories of personal transformation: the uptight guy who learns to cut loose, the wallflower who becomes the life of the party. It's the staple of self-help books and romantic comedies—as well as the primary reason that people drag themselves to high-school reunions. ("Can you believe that guy who never talked is now a real estate mogul?") But psychologists have long believed that major personality makeovers are impossible. In fact, the big themes of personality—whether you are shy or outgoing, relaxed or a worrywart—seem to be scripted at a very young age.

Recently, however, personality researchers have begun looking more closely at the smaller ways we can and do change. Positive psychologists, who investigate human talents, have identified 24 character strengths—familiar qualities we admire, such as integrity, loyalty, kindness, vitality—and are limning them to find out why these faculties come so naturally to some people. What they're discovering is that many of these qualities amount to habitual ways of responding to the world—habits that can be learned.

"The evidence is good that most of these things can be changed," says Christopher Peterson, professor of psychology at the University of Michigan. "That doesn't mean it's easy. It doesn't come in a flash." Psychologists talk about personality change the way doctors talk about the biological set point for weight: Nature designed some of us to be heavy, and others to be slim. It's not impossible to alter your weight, but it requires going against your own grain.

But eventually, the new way of being can come to feel like second nature. Peterson cites himself as an example. Inherently introverted, he realized early on in his career as an academic that his reticence would prove disastrous in the lecture hall. So he learned to be more outgoing, to crack jokes, and to entertain big classes full of psychology students. "Do I still have an introverted temperament? Yes, in that if I'm in a big crowd, I get anxious," he says. "But my behavior is consistently extroverted, because I've worked to make it that way. Now, it's very spontaneous."

Whether Peterson's personality has truly changed is almost beside the point. He may not be an extrovert, technically speaking, but he behaves like one, and is treated like one. Tweaking the way you interpret and react to the world can be a transformative experience, freeing you up to act in new ways. At first, it feels awkward, even bizarre. But with new behaviors come new experiences, creating a feedback loop that, over time, reinforces the transition.

Some sought-after qualities are easier to develop than others. Courage, joy, passion, and optimism are among the more amenable to cultivation, but each requires mastering a different—and sometimes surprising—set of skills. To bring more joy and passion into your life, you must paradoxically be more open to experiencing sadness, anxiety, and fear. Learning to think like an optimist, it turns out, is less important than acting like one. And being courageous has nothing to do with how afraid you are: It's a matter of how strongly you feel about your goals. Cultivating these characteristics puts you on the road to that blend of happiness, satisfaction, and purpose that is the height of human functioning, what positive psychologists call "the good life."

## Optimism: Make the Road by Walking

When David Fajgenbaum was 18 years old, he had a horrible shock. Just as he was gearing up for his new life at Georgetown University, his mother was diagnosed with brain cancer. Instead of jumping into the freshman whirlwind of libraries, parties, and football games, he spent every weekend at home with his family. "I had three feelings: I felt alone, I felt helpless, and I felt guilty for being at school," he says now.

Before his mother's death, an idea struck him: To honor her, he'd reach out to others who were going through the same thing. Back on campus, he quickly found that beyond ordinary counseling, the university had no services for grieving students. So Fajgenbaum launched a support group, Students of Ailing Mothers and Fathers.

The project snowballed. Both affected students and their friends wanted to do something useful to combat their terrible feelings of helplessness, and so the group organized fundraisers for research money, and began helping younger kids in high schools. The organization now has more than 20 chapters, and even earned a "Brick" award, a national prize for youth service.

Even after his mother died, Fajgenbaum did not withdraw. Instead, he spent three to four hours every day building his group. "I invested everything I had in it" Fajgenbaum says now. "And it's the most rewarding thing, to honor somebody and at the same time be able to have an impact." He took action despite his own pain—a mainstay of the optimistic mind-set.

Optimists seem to be sprinkled with fairy dust. They suffer less and recover quicker. They're healthier and better-liked and have stronger marriages and more fun. It's enough to make the rest of us gloomy—except that psychologists believe that a lot of these qualities stem from cognitive habits that can be learned. More than any other major personality trait, optimism is a matter of practice.

### More than any other major personality trait, optimism is a matter of practice.

The key to increasing optimism lies in understanding its true nature. It's not relentless cheer or "positive thinking." It has more to do with how you behave, says Suzanne Segerstrom, an associate professor of psychology at the University of Kentucky in Lexington. "I think an optimistic outlook can be cultivated, but it's even better to cultivate optimistic behavior—engagement and persistence toward one's goals," she says.

Anticipating a better future, an optimist takes the steps necessary to create it. If Fajgenbaum, now 23, were more pessimistic, he'd probably have given up when he found out that Georgetown didn't have the support networks he sought, figuring that it was impossible for him, a bereaved freshman, to do anything about it. Instead, he resolved to build them himself.

Pessimists are skeptical that their own actions can lead to good results and tend to overlook positive outcomes when they do occur. To overcome this stumbling block, Segerstrom recommends in her recent book, *Breaking Murphy's Law: How Optimists Get What They Want from Life—and Pessimists Can Too*, that you train yourself to pay attention to good fortune. Keep a log in which you write down three positive things that come about each day. This will help you convince yourself that favorable outcomes actually happen all the time, making it easier to begin taking action.

Keep a journal, too, but don't write down your darkest thoughts and fears. Instead, envision a future that you desire and describe how it could evolve out of your present circumstances. By clarifying exactly what you'll need to do to get what you want, you can create your own map to a more hopeful state of mind.

Then, with the pump primed, it'll be easier to make small moves that lead to gratifying results, building further enthusiasm

that will protect you from setbacks. Fajgenbaum was a finalist for the Rhodes scholarship, but didn't get the award. Never mind. He's now finishing his master's degree in public health at Oxford—thanks to a different award—and after that, will go on to medical school at the University of Pennsylvania to study oncology. He thinks he has a shot at curing cancer. The rest of us might call that Pollyannaish, but he's just calling it his life's work.

## Passion: Taking the Plunge

You know it when you see it. Someone who is fully engaged, deeply involved, totally dedicated—a person brimming with passion. But you've probably never seen it take the form of a 525-foot dive straight down into the depths of the ocean. Tanya Streeter, 35, is the Tiger Woods of freediving, the sport of plunging deep into the water without tanks or other breathing equipment. Beginning in 1998, she set nine world records, often besting both men and women. An average person can hold her breath for one minute. Streeter can do it for six.

The physical stamina required for this sport is intense. But the psychological demands were even more overwhelming—and for Streeter, that was the allure. Sure, she was terrified some of the time. Who wouldn't be? But she learned to untangle her fears from her judgment of what her body and mind could do. "In my career as a competitive freediver, there was a limit to what I could do—but it wasn't anywhere near where I thought it was" she says. "When I did my first deep dive, it was 100 feet. I thought I'd never go any farther."

### Passions don't arrive like bolts out of the blue. They build slowly, through the process of gradual mastery.

By 2003, Streeter had smashed every record she worked against, and saw no point in rehashing old glories. So she switched to another extreme sport: television hosting. She'd always been passionate about the ocean. Now, she had the opportunity to promote conservation and environmentalism using her celebrity and her amazing swimming skills to introduce viewers to the wonders of the sea.

### We spend so much time experimenting with foods, with ways to organize our houses, and so little time experimenting with all the ways we can act as a person.

Streeter was not a natural in front of the camera. The first day of filming her first ocean documentary, she was painfully self-conscious. "I was horrible," she says. "I sucked." When it was over, she strapped on her fins and took off for a reef for a good cry. But as she's become better at hosting, she's enjoyed it more and more. "It's just so difficult to be relaxed and calm and who you are on camera," she says. "That's the endless—and the most satisfying—challenge."

It's tempting to brand Streeter as a fundamental go-getter, born with fire in her belly. But finding a pursuit that pushes your buttons can infuse anyone with sudden zeal for life. The secret about consuming passions, though, is that while they appear effortless, they require discipline and ability. If they were easy, they wouldn't be so rewarding. Such passions—anything from becoming an opera aficionado to a black belt in karate—tend to be "very open-ended in the amount of skill or knowledge required," says psychologist Paul Silvia of the University of North Carolina at Greensboro. The Holy Grail comes in moments of "flow," when you are so absorbed in what you're doing that you lose yourself. This, in turn, generates feelings of mastery, well-being, and enduring satisfaction.

Many people have at least one such passion. Streeter already has two. But for those who are seeking this sense of fulfillment, there are a few tricks, suggests Todd Kashdan, a psychologist at George Mason University. The first step is to commit to learning a bit about a subject. Passions don't arrive like bolts out of the blue. They build slowly, through the process of gradual mastery. "Passion and interest, the research is clear, come out of practice and expertise," says Peterson.

As a greenhorn, you also have to put up with feeling like an idiot—to tolerate and laugh at your own ignorance. "You must be willing to accept the discomfort and negative feelings that come your way," says Kashdan.

In fact, those butterflies in your stomach will probably be the first sign that you've hit upon a potential pursuit, says Streeter. "The thing that scares you the most tends to be the most fulfilling," she says. "It doesn't have to be something great. It has to be something that you aren't sure you can do."

## Joy: The Art of Loving Life

Mauro Zappaterra was in the fast lane of the fast track, among the elite of young physician-scientists. After grueling training at Harvard Medical School, in January of 2004 he plunged into the research he'd been longing to do, the project that would earn him his PhD.

The problem: He was miserable. "I've always been really excited about life," he says. "And then I got to the lab, and it wasn't working" His research didn't mesh with his curiosity about healing, which was what had brought him into medicine. And he was preoccupied with the future. His girlfriend urged him to take some time off, but "vacation" and "break" are foreign concepts to MD/PhD students. Finally, he did—and it was a transforming experience. During eight months in Santa Fe, Zappaterra soaked up everything he could about healing techniques not taught at Harvard: polarity therapy, meridians, trauma resolution. "I was interested in how compassion, healing, and medicine could be intertwined," he says.

When he got back from Santa Fe, Zappaterra switched labs to study how cerebrospinal fluid nourishes and protects the developing nervous system. This cutting-edge research project also connects to his ongoing training in craniosacral therapy, an alternative medical practice in which the cranial bones, spine, and connective tissue are subtly contacted to bring harmony to the nervous system and thereby treat pain, stress, and injuries.

He also vowed to live more fully in the present moment, and to look for the joy in everything, including failure, disappointment, and sickness. He used meditation, focusing methods, and techniques learned from craniosacral therapy to reach his goals. That's when Zappaterra stumbled upon one of the counterintuitive realities of personality change: The kind of joy he found was often quiet and reflective rather than loud and exuberant. The way Zappaterra, now 32, describes it today, it's as if he feels all of his feelings more deeply, and takes pleasure even from sadness. "I can be joyous, even when I'm not in a joyful mood," he says. In the lab, failure is a constant. For every experiment that goes well, 99 don't work at all. But Zappaterra now believes that these frustrations and setbacks help him learn—about both his research and himself.

---

**Bad things will come find you. . . . For the positive stuff, you have to open the door, go hunt for it, and find it.**

---

Essentially, what he trained himself to do is what Loyola University psychologist Fred Bryant calls "savoring": the art of managing positive feelings. Whereas coping well means dealing successfully with problems and setbacks, savoring—glorying in what goes right—is an equally crucial emotional competence. "If all you're doing is trying to get by, trying to avoid the bad, you're missing half of life," says Bryant, author of *Savoring: A New Model of Positive Experience.* Although people tend to think that taking pleasure in good things comes naturally, it's really a skill. "Bad things will come and find you, knock down your door, and make you deal with them," he adds. "The positive stuff ain't like that. You have to open the door, go hunt for it, and find it."

To heighten joy in life, Bryant suggests that when something good happens, you make time to pay attention to it. Share the experience: The happiest people celebrate triumphs with others. Take a "mental photograph" in which you describe the positive event and its circumstances to yourself in great detail.

Joy can also be held back by rigidity. Kashdan recommends scrutinizing the prohibitions and barriers that structure your life. "The way to living a more zestful life is to be guided and flexible rather than governed," says Kashdan. Zappaterra's turnaround came when he realized that he needed to take time off, even though it violated the creed of MD/PhD students.

Try paying more attention to your mind-set, Kashdan adds. Are you concentrating on avoiding failure or looking forward to an opportunity to do something well? "The protection mode—focusing on being safe—might get in the way of your reaching your goals." For example, are you hoping to get through a business lunch without embarrassing yourself, or are you thinking about how riveting the conversation might be? That slight difference in mentality "changes how you think, how you feel, what parts of the brain light up," says Kashdan. It subtly inflects your interactions with the world, and is one simple way to have more fun with what you already do.

As with other changes, learning to be more joyous does not come quickly. When Zappaterra got back from Santa Fe, he planted a dozen seeds from a split-leaf philodendron, a slow-growing houseplant that eventually produces huge, glossy leaves. Zappaterra tended the seedlings as a daily reminder of how long it takes to make a real change in a human life. Nearly three years later, he's learned to get better at seeing the good in things. And he's enjoying his big, beautiful plants.

# Courage: Doing the Right Thing

Usually, we think of courage as physical bravery—the backbone it takes to face enemy fire or stand up to a dictator. But ordinary life demands its own style of bravery, more humble and harder to spot. Day-to-day courage might involve confronting a bullying boss. It could mean stepping up to take responsibility for a mistake. For industrial engineer Kenneth Pedeleose, it meant speaking out against something he thought was wrong.

Pedeleose, an analyst at the Defense Contract Management Agency, which monitors federal military contracts, was stationed at a plant in Marietta, Georgia, where military cargo planes were being built. His job was to oversee the contracts, and he didn't like what he saw: high prices for spare parts ($714 for rivets and $5,217 for brackets) on one project and serious safety violations on another. In 2002, he and other engineers went "public" sending a report to the Congress members making decisions about military operations.

The Department of Defense launched a major investigation of the project, and an inspector general's report later substantiated many of Pedeleose's allegations. The agency found it would be too dangerous to use these planes for their main purpose: dropping equipment and troops into hostile areas. In 2006 the contract was restructured to include more oversight and accountability—and lower prices.

Was Pedeleose honored for his vigilance? Not exactly. He was labelled a whistleblower, suspended twice in the past four years, and had to fight to get his back pay reinstated (he won). The experience was stressful and draining, he says. Pedeleose estimates he has spent 2000 hours over the years uncovering fraud and abuse, and defending himself against retaliation. Nonetheless, he is now working on his fifth report, which he also plans to send to Congress.

"What I saw sickened me," he says now. "If I could have stopped an airplane from crashing, and I just sat back and didn't do anything about it, I couldn't have looked at myself in the mirror." Pedeleose was in the position to make a difference, and had the knowledge and the authority to call attention to the wrongs he had witnessed. Another key: He prepared his case meticulously, marshalling all the facts and documenting every allegation. "Bravery would play into it, but I calculated it so I had a high chance of success. It means more when you can prove what you're saying."

Pedeleose's story illuminates a widely misunderstood truth about courage: It is motivated not by fearlessness, but by a strong sense of duty. People who behave bravely often say they were afraid at the time, finds Cynthia Pury, a psychologist at Clemson University. But their principles forced them to take action. Her survey research revealed that whether a student acted courageously had more to do with how strongly he or she felt about the situation than with how frightening it was.

Pury believes that people can learn to become more courageous. Many of her students described doing the same things before they took action. Faced with a risky situation, they first tried to calm themselves down. They prepared for the situation, looking for a way to mitigate the danger, just as Pedeleose did by documenting his allegations. And they focused on what they were trying to accomplish, and how important it was. "I don't think any intervention about courage is going to go that far unless you help people decide what's important," she says.

"Being courageous is really a large number of moments in which, in the face of feeling uncomfortable, you still went forward," says Kashdan. Set up small behavioral experiments for yourself, he suggests. Try a few episodes of sticking your neck out. "We spend so much time experimenting with foods, with different ways to organize our houses, and so little time experimenting with all the ways we can act as a person." Flexibility is the hallmark of psychological health, and it can be energizing and even thrilling to step out of your habits.

Over the long term, picking up a new character trait may help you inch toward being the person you want to be. And in the short term, the effort itself could be surprisingly rewarding, a kind of internal adventure—a way to see the world from a different angle—without ever leaving home.

# Critical Thinking

1. Can people improve their personalities? If so, what are the steps people might take to change their personalities?

2. What is optimism?

3. Is optimism learned or does it have a biological basis?

---

**KATHLEEN MCGOWAN** is a former senior editor at *PT* and a freelance science writer living in New York City.

# UNIT 9
# Social Processes

## Unit Selections

## Learning Outcomes

*After reading this Unit, you should be able to:*

- Explain the ethical problems that the original Milgram study posed for psychology and for science.

- Describe the ways in which modern psychologists have tried to reconcile these problems in replicating Milgram's work.

- Define false confession and explain the factors that cause it.

- Summarize the ways in which confessions, false or otherwise, corrupt other evidence available in court cases.

- Explain the argument that humans are "wired to connect."

- Describe the ways in which modern technology is influencing the ways that humans connect to one another and evaluate whether these influences are having positive or negative effects on our ability to relate socially to one another.

## Student Website
www.mhhe.com/cls

## Internet References

**Nonverbal Behavior and Nonverbal Communication**
www3.usal.es/~nonverbal
**The Social Psychology Network**
www.socialpsychology.org

We humans are particularly social creatures, as are many of the other species with whom we share this planet. We tend to assemble in groups, some large and some small. We form friendships with all sorts of people. Many of these relationships develop naturally from shared interests and common goals. Some of these friendships are long-lasting and endure all sorts of hardships. Other kinds of friendships are shorter-term that are often soon forgotten. On special occasions we form highly unique relationships in which we fall in love with another person and decide to commit the rest of our lives, or at least a large chunk of it, to being this person's most intimate companion. And then there are families, the most common of all groups and perhaps the most interesting social unit full of fascinating dynamics that emerge as children are born, grow up, and form families of their own.

The responsibility for understanding the complicated facets of human social behavior fall to social psychologists. These psychologists, like most research-focused behavioral scientists, have been trained to apply rigorous experimental methods to discovering, understanding, and explaining how people interact with one another. During the past century, social psychologists have studied some of the most pressing and fascinating social behaviors of the day. For example, social psychologists have examined, and indeed continue to study, discrimination and prejudice, conformity, and obedience to authority. In addition to these high-profile issues, social psychologists have studied the more positive side of human social behavior such as liking and loving, attitude formation and change, attribution, and group behavior and decision making.

In the past few decades, psychologists have become more aware of the impact of culture on human social relationships and have turned their attention to exploring differences among cultures with respect to social development, social perception,

© McGraw-Hill Companies

social influence, and social change. As we move deeper into the 21st century, and the world seemingly becomes smaller and smaller, the demand for social psychologists to provide explanations for both positive and negative social behaviors that are impacted by cultural influences will only become greater.

Thus, as you study social psychology in your introductory psychology course, apply the principles you are learning not just to better understanding your own social behavior, but also ask yourself how these principles might (or might not) generalize to the social behavior of individuals from different cultures. Doing so might put you in a better position to understand the whys and wherefores of social behavior that would seem, on the surface anyway, to be so radically different from your own. In this unit, we explore the fascinating field of social psychology.

# Replicating Milgram

Last month, we featured IRB best practices ("IRBs: Navigating the Maze" November 2007 Observer), and got the ball rolling with strategies and tips that psychological scientists have found to work. Here, we continue the dissemination effort with the second of three articles by researchers who share their experiences with getting their research through IRB hoops. Jerry Burger from Santa Clara University managed to do the seemingly impossible—he conducted a partial replication of the infamous Milgram experiment. Read on for valuable advice, and look for similar coverage in upcoming Observers.

JERRY BURGER

"It can't be done."

These are the first words I said to Muriel Pearson, producer for ABC News' *Primetime,* when she approached me with the idea of replicating Stanley Milgram's famous obedience studies. Milgram's work was conducted in the early 1960s before the current system of professional guidelines and IRBs was in place. It is often held up as the prototypic example of why we need policies to protect the welfare of research participants. Milgram's participants were placed in an emotionally excruciating situation in which an experimenter instructed them to continue administering electric shocks to another individual despite hearing that person's agonizing screams of protest. The studies ignited a debate about the ethical treatment of participants. And the research became, as I often told my students, the study that can never be replicated.

Nonetheless, I was intrigued. Although more than four decades have passed since Milgram conducted his research, his obedience studies continue to occupy an important place in social psychology textbooks and classes. The haunting black-and-white images of ordinary citizens delivering what appear to be dangerous, if not deadly, electric shocks and the implications of the findings for atrocities like the Holocaust and Abu Ghraib are not easily dismissed. Yet because Milgram's procedures are clearly out-of-bounds by today's ethical standards, many questions about the research have gone unanswered. Chief among these is one that inevitably surfaces when I present Milgram's findings to students: Would people still act that way today?

The challenge was to develop a variation of Milgram's procedures that would allow useful comparisons with the original investigations while protecting the well-being of the participants. But meeting this challenge would raise another: I would also need to assuage the apprehension my IRB would naturally experience when presented with a proposal to replicate the study that can never be replicated.

I went to great lengths to recreate Milgram's procedures (Experiment Five), including such details as the words used in the memory test and the experimenter's lab coat. But I also made several substantial changes. First, we stopped the procedures at the 150-volt mark. This is the first time participants heard the learner's protests through the wall and his demands to be released. When we look at Milgram's data, we find that this point in the procedure is something of a "point of no return." Of the participants who continued past 150 volts, 79 percent went all the way to the highest level of the shock generator (450 volts). Knowing how people respond up to this point allowed us to make a reasonable estimate of what they would do if allowed to continue to the end. Stopping the study at this juncture also avoided exposing participants to the intense stress Milgram's participants often experienced in the subsequent parts of the procedure.

Second, we used a two-step screening process for potential participants to exclude any individuals who might have a negative reaction to the experience. Potential participants were asked in an initial phone interview if they had ever been diagnosed with a psychiatric disorder; if they were currently receiving psychotherapy; if they were currently taking any medications for emotional difficulties; if they had any medical conditions that might be affected by stress; if they ever had any problems with alcohol or drug use; and if they had ever experienced serious trauma, such as child abuse, domestic violence, or combat. Individuals who responded "yes" to any of these questions (about 30 percent) were excluded from the study. During the second step in the screening process, participants completed measures of anxiety and depression and were interviewed in person by a licensed clinical psychologist. The clinicians were shown the anxiety and depression data and were allowed to interview participants for as long as needed (about 30 minutes on average). The clinicians were instructed to err on the side of caution and to exclude anyone who they judged might have a negative reaction to the experiment procedures. More than 38 percent of the interviewed participants were excluded at this point.

Third, participants were told at least three times (twice in writing) that they could withdraw from the study at any time and still receive their $50 for participation. Fourth, like Milgram, we administered a sample shock to our participants (with their consent). However, we administered a very mild 15-volt shock rather than the 45-volt shock Milgram gave his participants. Fifth, we allowed virtually no time to elapse between ending the session and informing participants that the learner had received no shocks. Within a few seconds after ending the study, the learner entered the room to reassure the participant he was fine. Sixth, the experimenter who ran the study also was a clinical psychologist who was instructed to end the session immediately if he saw any signs of excessive stress. Although each of these safeguards came with a methodological price (e.g., the potential effect of screening out certain individuals, the effect of emphasizing that participants could leave at any time), I wanted to take every reasonable measure to ensure that our participants were treated in a humane and ethical manner.

Of course, I also needed IRB approval. I knew from my own participation on the IRB that the proposal would be met with concern and perhaps a little fear by the board's members. I work at a relatively small university, and our IRB consists of individuals from a variety of academic backgrounds. I knew that few members would be comfortable or confident when assessing a potentially controversial proposal from another discipline. Given the possibility of a highly visible mistake, the easy response would have been to say "no." To address these concerns, I created a list of individuals who were experts on Milgram's studies and the ethical questions surrounding this research. I offered to make this list available to the IRB. More important, Steven Breckler, a social psychologist who

currently serves as the executive director for science at the American Psychological Association, graciously provided an assessment of the proposal's ethical issues that I shared with the IRB.

In the end, all the extra steps and precautions paid off. The IRB carefully reviewed and then approved the procedures. More than a year after collecting the data, I have no indication that any participant was harmed by his or her participation in the study. On the contrary, I was constantly surprised by participants' enthusiasm for the research both during the debriefing and in subsequent communications. We also produced some interesting findings. Among other things, we found that today people obey the experimenter in this situation at about the same rate they did 45 years ago. ABC devoted an entire 60-minute *Primetime* broadcast to the research and its implications. Finally, it is my hope that other investigators will use the 150-volt procedure and thereby jumpstart research on some of the important questions that motivated Stanley Milgram nearly half a century ago.

# Critical Thinking

1. What ethical problems did the original Milgram study pose for psychology?

2. How have modern psychologists tried to reconcile these ethical problems in replicating Milgram's work?

---

**JERRY BURGER** is a professor of psychology at Santa Clara University. His research interests include social influence, particularly compliance, and the perception of and motivation for personal control.

---

From *APS Observer,* December 2007. Copyright © 2007 by American Psychological Society. Reprinted by permission via Copyright Clearance Center.

# The Psychology and Power of False Confessions

IAN HERBERT

On July 8, 1997, Bill Bosko returned to his home in Norfolk, Virginia, after a week at sea to find his wife murdered in their bedroom. A few hours later, Bosko's neighbor, Danial Williams was asked to answer questions at the police station. And after eight hours there, Williams confessed to the rape and murder of Michelle Moore-Bosko.

Five months later, because of inconsistent physical evidence, the Norfolk police became convinced that Williams did not act alone and turned their attention to Joseph Dick, Williams' roommate. Dick confessed as well. He later pled guilty, testified against two other co-defendants, named five more accomplices who were never tried, and publicly apologized to the victim's family. "I know I shouldn't have done it," Dick said just before the judge gave him a double life sentence. "I have got no idea what went through my mind that night—and my soul."

Dick now says that all of that is untrue, and he has a team of lawyers who believe him. In 2005, the Innocence Project filed a petition on behalf of Williams, Dick, and the other two members of the group called the "Norfolk Four." They petitioned Virginia Governor Tim Kaine for clemency on the basis of new physical evidence, and in August 2009, the outgoing governor issued conditional pardons, which set the men free but forced them to be on parole for the next 20 years. It was a decision that Kaine struggled with, and he granted conditional pardons because he said the men failed to fully prove their innocence. "They're asking for a whole series of confessions . . . to all be discarded," Kaine said on a radio show in the fall of 2008. "That is a huge request."

We know that false confessions do happen on a fairly regular basis. Because of advances in DNA evidence, the Innocence Project has been able to exonerate more than 200 people who had been wrongly convicted, 49 of whom had confessed to the crime we now know they didn't commit. In a survey of 1,000 college students, four percent of those who had been interrogated by police said they gave a false confession.

## But Why?

False confessions seem so illogical, especially for someone like Joseph Dick of the Norfolk Four, who got a double life sentence after confessing. Why do people confess to crimes they didn't commit? Some do it for the chance at fame (more than 200 people confessed to kidnapping Charles Lindbergh's baby), but many more do it for reasons that are far more puzzling to the average person. In the November 2004 issue of *Psychological Science in the Public Interest,* APS Fellow Saul Kassin looked at the body of research and described how the police are able to interrogate suspects until they confess to a crime they didn't commit.

Generally, it starts because people give up their Miranda rights. In fact, Richard A. Leo found that a majority of people give up the right to remain silent and the right to an attorney. In fact, according to self-report data, innocent suspects gave up their rights more often than guilty suspects (most told Leo either that this was because they felt that they didn't have anything to hide because they were innocent or that they thought it would make them look guilty).

Once a suspect starts talking, the police can use a variety of techniques to make the accused feel as though they are better off confessing than continuing to deny (these include promises of leniency and threats of harsher interrogation or sentences). If a suspect feels like a conviction is inevitable no matter what he or she says, confessing may seem like a good idea.

But, in some cases, the accused comes to believe that he or she actually did commit the crime. It's been shown repeatedly that memory is quite malleable and unreliable. Elizabeth Loftus has repeatedly shown that the human brain can create memories out of thin air with some prompting. In a famous series of experiments, Loftus, APS Past President, was able to help people create memories for events that never happened in their lives simply through prompting. She helped them "remember" being lost in a shopping mall when they were children, and the longer the experiment went on, the more details they "remembered." The longer police interrogate a suspect, emphatic about his guilt and peppering their interrogation with details of the crime, the more likely a suspect is to become convinced himself.

Joseph Dick claims that this is what happened to him. His confession, testimony, and apology to the family were not lies, he maintains, but rather the product of a false memory. "It didn't cross my mind that I was lying," he said. "I believed what I was saying was true."

## 'Corrupting the Other Evidence'

Despite the evidence that false confessions are a regular occurrence, most jurors struggle with the concept just like Kaine did with the Norfolk Four. Confessions are difficult to discount, even if they appear to be coerced. Years ago, Kassin noticed that cases with confessions have an unusually high conviction rate, and since then he has dedicated his life to studying why that happens and what can be done about it.

In a 1997 study, Kassin and colleague Katherine Neumann gave subjects case files with weak circumstantial evidence plus either a confession, an eyewitness account, a character witness, or no other evidence. Across the board, prospective jurors were more likely to vote guilty if a confession was included in the trial, even when they were told that the defendant was incoherent at the time of the confession and immediately recanted what he said.

Kassin and Neumann also did two simultaneous studies to further explore the power of confessions. In one, they had people watch a trial and turn a dial to rate the extent to which evidence convinced them the defendant was guilty or innocent. The other asked potential jurors after the trial which evidence was most powerful. In both the mid-trial and post-trial ratings, jurors saw the confession as the most incriminating. Other studies have shown that conviction rates rise even when jurors see confessions as coerced and even when they say that the confession played no role in their judgment. "I don't honestly think juries stand a chance in cases involving confessions," Kassin says. "They're bound to convict."

Kassin says he doesn't blame jurors. He travels around the country lecturing on the psychology of false confessions and he says "the most common reaction I get from a lay audience is, 'Well, I would never do that. I would never confess to something I didn't do.' And people apply that logic in the jury room. It's just that basic belief that false confessions don't occur." What's more, the evidence juries are given in conjunction with the false confessions is very damning, Kassin says. False confessions of guilt often include vivid details of how a crime was committed—and why. Confessions sometimes even come with an apology to the family. It's no wonder jurors have trouble discounting them.

What confessions rarely include is an explanation of why the person confessed. In most states, police are not required to videotape the interrogations, just the confessions. So juries don't get to see any potential police coercion and they don't get to see the police planting those vivid details in the minds of the suspects.

And that may be just the tip of the iceberg. Kassin believes that confessions can have a dramatic impact on trials even if they never make it into a courtroom. They can influence potential eyewitnesses, for example, and taint other kinds of evidence.

Kassin recently teamed up with psychologist Lisa Hasel to test the effect of confessions on eyewitnesses. They brought subjects in for what was supposed to be a study about persuasion techniques. The experimenter briefly left the room and, during that time, someone came in and stole a laptop off the desk. The subjects were then shown a lineup of six suspects, none of whom was the actual criminal, and they were asked to pick out which member of the lineup, if any, committed the crime. Two days later, the witnesses were brought back for more questioning. Those who had identified a suspect were told that the person they identified had confessed, another person had confessed, all suspects continued to deny their involvement, or that the identified suspect had continued to deny his involvement. Those who had (correctly) said none of the people in the lineup committed the crime were told either that all suspects denied the crime, that an unspecified suspect had confessed, or that a specific suspect had confessed.

The results show that confessions can have a powerful effect on other evidence. Of the people who had identified a subject from the original lineup, 60 percent changed their identification when told that someone else had confessed. Plus, 44 percent of the people who originally determined that none of the suspects in the lineup committed the crime changed their mind when told that someone had confessed (and 50 percent changed when told that a specific person had confessed). When asked about their decision, "about half of the people seemed to say, 'Well, the investigator told me there was a confession, so that must be true.' So they were just believing the investigator," Hasel said. "But the other half really seemed to be changing their memory. So that memory can never really be regained once it's been tainted." What's more, people who were told that the person they wrongly pinpointed as the culprit had confessed saw their confidence levels soar. After that confirmation, they remembered the crime better and were more sure about details. The implications for inside the courtroom are obvious if eyewitnesses who incorrectly picked someone out of a lineup can become so sure of their choice after learning that the person confessed. "It is noteworthy that whereas physical evidence is immutable (once collected and preserved, it can always be retested), an eyewitness's identification decision cannot later be revisited without contamination," Kassin and Hasel write.

Kassin and Hasel suspect that false confessions may also affect the memories of people who are potential alibis for defendants. Kassin worked on the actual case of John Kogut, who was accused of raping and murdering a 16-year-old girl. Kogut was at a party for his girlfriend at the time the crime was committed, and he had multiple alibi witnesses. But after 18 hours of interrogation, Kogut confessed to the grisly crime. "After he confessed to the crime, [the witnesses] started dropping off one-by-one," Hasel said. "'You know, maybe I saw him earlier in the night but not later; maybe I saw him later in the night but not earlier; it must have been a different night, I must be wrong.'" Kassin and Hasel are currently working on an experiment similar to their eyewitness study to test this theory on a broad basis.

This phenomenon may be explained by the same Loftus research about creating false memories that may have lead to the false confession in the first place. So it is plausible that eyewitnesses or alibi witnesses might begin to remember things differently when told about something as powerful as a confession. But what about scientific evidence? At least confessions can't change something as concrete as DNA evidence or fingerprints, right? Even that belief may be untrue.

In 2006, University College London psychologist Itiel Dror took a group of six fingerprint experts and showed them samples that they themselves had, years before, determined either to be matches or non-matches (though they weren't told they had already seen these fingerprints). The experts were now given some context: either that the fingerprints came from a suspect who confessed or that they came from a suspect who was known to be in police custody at the time the crime

was committed. In 17 percent of the non-control tests, experimenters changed assessments that they had previously made correctly. Four of the six experts who participated changed at least one judgment based on the new context. "And that's fingerprint judgments," Kassin said. "That's not considered malleable. And yet there was some degree of malleability and one of the ways to influence it was to provide information about the confession."

The practical importance of this research extends well beyond the laboratory. In a white paper set to be published in *Law and Human Behavior* in 2010, Kassin and four other prominent confession experts make recommendations, including, most notably, mandatory taping of all interrogations in capital cases. Kassin has begun to research this idea. His preliminary data illustrates that, shown two versions of known false confessions (one that just included the confession or another that included the entire interrogation), subjects were significantly less likely to vote guilty when shown the entire interrogation. "The information that the jury doesn't have and needs is how did this guy come to confess and then, when he did confess, how did he know all this information about the crime if he in fact wasn't there," Kassin says. "So yes, I think videotaping is probably the single best protection to be afforded to a defendant."

That would help defendants who were coerced into confessing by police, but would do nothing to help those who lost alibi witnesses or were convicted with the help of eyewitness testimony because of knowledge of a confession. To combat that problem, Hasel and much of the scientific community argues for double-blind testing when handling evidence, meaning that the police officer handling the lineup doesn't know which member of the lineup is the suspect. "So they can't consciously or unconsciously direct [witnesses] to a particular person," she says.

And she wants to investigate whether judges and jurors can understand this topic of evidence dependence—the idea that a confession contaminates other evidence. If jurors are told that a false confession may have tainted other evidence, are they able to look at it objectively and make their own judgment? Can judges grasp its ramifications on appeals? Kassin believes that, because of the persuasive potency of confessions and evidentiary dependence, it's not good enough for judges to look at the other evidence and determine that a jury would have convicted even without the coerced confession.

"If it turns out that the confession corrupted the other evidence, then there is no such thing as harmless error,"

Kassin said. "I don't think you can look at that other evidence once there is a confession out of the box because once the confession is out there, it corrupts all that other evidence."

## Critical Thinking

1. What is a false confession and what causes it?
2. How do confessions, false or otherwise, corrupt other evidence available in court cases?

# We're Wired to Connect

## Our brains are designed to be social, says bestselling science writer Daniel Goleman—and they catch emotions the same way we catch colds.

MARK MATOUSEK

Have you ever wondered why a stranger's smile can transform your entire day? Why your eyes mist up when you see someone crying, and the sight of a yawn can leave you exhausted? Daniel Goleman, PhD, has wondered, too, and just as he helped revolutionize our definition of what it means to be smart with his 1995 blockbuster, *Emotional Intelligence,* the two-time Pulitzer nominee and former science reporter for *The New York Times* has dropped a bombshell on our understanding of human connection in his startling new book, *Social Intelligence* (Bantam).

For the first time in history, thanks to recent breakthroughs in neuroscience, experts are able to observe brain activity while we're in the act of feeling—and their findings have been astonishing. Once believed to be lumps of lonely gray matter cogitating between our ears, our brains turn out to be more like interlooped, Wi-Fi octopi with invisible tentacles slithering in all directions, at every moment, constantly picking up messages we're not aware of and prompting reactions—including illnesses—in ways never before understood.

"The brain itself is social—that's the most exciting finding," Goleman explains during lunch at a restaurant near his home in Massachusetts. "One person's inner state affects and drives the other person. We're forming brain-to-brain bridges—a two-way traffic system—all the time. We actually catch each other's emotions like a cold."

The more important the relationship, the more potent such "contagion" will be. A stranger's putdown may roll off your back, while the same zinger from your boss is devastating. "If we're in toxic relationships with people who are constantly putting us down, this has actual physical consequences," Goleman says. Stress produces a harmful chemical called cortisol, which interferes with certain immune cell functions. Positive interactions prompt the body to secrete oxytocin (the same chemical released during lovemaking), boosting the immune system and decreasing stress hormones. As a doting grandparent himself (with author-therapist wife Tara Bennett-Goleman), the author often feels this felicitous rush. "I was just with my two-year-old granddaughter," he says. "This girl is like a vitamin for me.

Being with her actually feels like a kind of elixir. The most important people in our lives can be our biological allies."

The notion of relationships as pharmaceutical is a new concept. "My mother is 96," Goleman goes on. "She was a professor of sociology whose husband—my father—died many years ago, leaving her with a big house. After retiring at 65, she decided to let graduate students live there for free. She's since had a long succession of housemates. When she was 90, a couple from Taiwan had a baby while they were living there. The child regarded her as Grandma and lived there till the age of two. During that time, I swore I could see my mother getting younger. It was stunning." But not, he adds, completely surprising. "This was the living arrangement we were designed for, remember? For most of human history there were extended families where the elderly lived in the same household as the babies. Many older people have the time and nurturing energy that kids crave—and vice versa. If I were designing assisted-living facilities, I'd put daycare centers in them and allow residents to volunteer. Institutions are cheating children," he says. "And we older people need it, too."

## Positive interactions can boost the immune system: "The most important people in our lives can be our biological allies."

Young or old, people can affect our personalities. Though each of us has a distinctive temperament and a "set point of happiness" modulating our general mood, science has now confirmed that these tendencies are not locked in. Anger-prone people, for example, can "infect" themselves with calmness by spending time with mellower individuals, absorbing less-aggressive behavior and thereby sharpening social intelligence.

A key to understanding this process is something called mirror neurons: "neurons whose only job is to recognize a smile and make you smile in return," says Goleman (the same goes for frowning and other reactions). This is why, when you're smiling, the whole world does indeed seem to smile with you. It also explains the Michelangelo phenomenon, in which long-term partners come to resemble each other through facial-muscle mimicry and "empathic resonance." If you've ever seen a group with a case of the giggles, you've witnessed mirror neurons at play. Such mirroring takes place in the realm of ideas, too, which is why sweeping cultural ideals and prejudices can spread through populations with viral speed.

This phenomenon gets to the heart of why social intelligence matters most: its impact on suffering and creating a less crazy world. It is critical, Goleman believes, that we stop treating people as objects or as functionaries who are there to give us something. This can range from barking at telephone operators to the sort of old-shoe treatment that long-term partners often use in relating to each other (talking at, rather than to, each other). We need, he says, a richer human connection.

Unfortunately, what he calls the "inexorable technocreep" of contemporary culture threatens such meaningful connection. Presciently remarking on the TV set in 1963, poet T.S. Eliot noted that this techno-shredder of the social fabric "permits millions of people to listen to the same joke at the same time, and yet remain lonesome." We can only imagine what the dour writer would have made of Internet dating. And as Goleman points out, this "constant digital connectivity" can deaden us to the people around us. Social intelligence, he says, means putting down your BlackBerry, actually paying full attention—showing people that they're being experienced—which is basically what each of us wants more than anything. Scientists agree that such connection—or lack of it—will determine our survival as a species: "Empathy," writes Goleman, "is the prime inhibitor of human cruelty."

And our social brains are wired for kindness, despite the gore you may see on the nightly news. "It's an aberration to be cruel," says Goleman. Primitive tribes learned that strength lay in numbers, and that their chances of surviving a brutal environment increased exponentially through helping their neighbors (as opposed to, say, chopping their heads off). Even young children are wired for compassion. One study in Goleman's book found that infants cry when they see or hear another baby crying, but rarely when they hear recordings of their own distress. In another study, monkeys starved themselves after realizing that when they took food, a shock was delivered to their cage mate.

Perhaps the most inspiring piece of the social-intelligence puzzle is neuroplasticity: the discovery that our brains never stop evolving. "Stem cells manufacture 10,000 brain cells every day till you die," says Goleman. "Social interaction helps neurogenesis. The brain rises to the occasion the more you challenge it."

## Critical Thinking

1. What is the argument that humans are "wired to connect"?

2. How has modern technology influenced the ways that humans connect to one another? Are these influences positive or negative in terms of our ability to relate socially to one another?

---

**MARK MATOUSEK** is the author of *The Art of Survival* (Bloomsbury).

# UNIT 10
# Psychological Disorders

## Unit Selections

## Learning Outcomes

*After reading this Unit, you should be able to:*

- Define Attention Deficit Disorder and describe its key symptoms.

- Explain how Attention Deficit Disorder develops.

- Describe the (a) importance of recent research showing that parents do not realize the nature of the stress that their children experience and (b) how men and women tend to differ in experiencing stress.

- Review and explain effective strategies for coping with stress.

- Explain the relationship between poverty and the development of psychological problems in children.

- Describe the interventions that might help low-income children cope with the stressors they experience.

- Understand and explain the factors that lead people to stigmatize individuals who suffer from mental disorders.

- Review and evaluate the suggestions that psychologists have for reducing the stigma associated with mental disorders.

- Summarize what we know about the development of ADHD in preschoolers.

- What can psychologists do to identify and treat ADHD in preschoolers?

## Student Website
www.mhhe.com/cls

## Internet References

**American Association of Suicidology**
www.suicidology.org
**Ask NOAH About: Mental Health**
www.noah-health.org/en/mental
**Mental Health Net Disorders and Treatments**
www.mentalhelp.net
**National Clearinghouse for Alcohol and Drug Information**
ncadi.samhsa.gov
**National Women's Health Resource Center (NWHRC)**
www.healthywomen.org

Jay and Harry were two brothers who owned a service station. Harry and Jay had a good working relationship. Harry was the "up-front" man. Taking customer orders, accepting payments, and working with parts distributors, Harry was the individual who dealt most directly with the public, delivery personnel, and other people accessing the station. Jay worked behind the scenes. While Harry made the mechanical diagnoses, Jay was the mastermind who did the corrective work. Some of his friends thought Jay was a veritable mechanical genius; he could fix anything. Preferring to spend time by himself, Jay had always been a little odd and a bit of a loner. Jay's friends thought his emotions had always been inappropriate and more intense than other people's emotional states, but they passed it off as part of his eccentric talent. On the other hand, Harry was the stalwart of the family. He was the acknowledged leader and decision maker when it came to family finances.

One day Jay did not show up for work on time. When he finally did appear, he was dressed in the most garish outfit and was laughing hysterically and talking to himself. At first, Harry suspected that his brother had taken some illegal drugs. However, Jay's condition persisted and, in fact, worsened. Out of concern, his family took him to their physician, who immediately sent Jay and his family to a psychiatrist. After several visits, the doctor informed the family that Jay suffered from schizophrenia. Jay's maternal uncle had also been schizophrenic. The family somberly left the psychiatrist's office and went to the local pharmacy to fill a prescription for anti-psychotic medication.

What caused Jay's drastic change in mental health? Was Jay destined to be schizophrenic because of his family tree? Did competitiveness with his brother and the feeling that he was less revered than Harry cause his descent into mental disorder? How can psychiatrists and clinical psychologists make accurate diagnoses? Once a diagnosis of mental disorder is made, can the individual ever completely recover?

Mental disorders affect millions of people throughout the world. As hinted with the short story about Jay and Harry, mental disorders impact every aspect of an individual's life, but especially work, family, and friendships. Because of the detrimental impact of mental disorders on the individual, they have been a focal point of psychological research for decades. This important work has revealed the likely origins or causes of mental

© Tristan Savatier/Getty Images

disorders and has led to breakthroughs in the care and treatment of people with mental disorders. This unit emphasis the questions that psychologists have attempted to address in their quest to understand fully the nature of mental illness.

# A New Approach to Attention Deficit Disorder

**It's not a simple behavior disorder but rather a complex syndrome of impairments in the management system of the brain.**

THOMAS E. BROWN

As burgeoning numbers of children and adolescents are being diagnosed with attention deficit disorders, parents are increasingly asking teachers, "Do you think my child has ADD or ADHD?" Some insist that their child receive multiple accommodations for presumed ADD/ADHD. Many teachers and school administrators are uncertain about how to respond. They are also unsure about which interventions are appropriate when a student appears to be impaired by attention disorders but the parents are skeptical or refuse to consider that possibility.

A recent study conducted by the U.S. Centers for Disease Control found that approximately 7.8 percent of U.S. children ages 4–17 are currently diagnosed with Attention Deficit Disorder (ADD) or Attention Deficit/Hyperactivity Disorder (ADHD) (*Journal of the American Medical Association, 2005*). This means that most teachers are likely to have at least a couple of students with ADD/ADHD[1] in every class they teach. However, few educators are familiar with major findings from recent scientific studies of attention deficit disorders or with the implications of these findings for schools.

For decades, most educators, physicians, psychologists, and parents have thought of ADD as a cluster of behavior problems, a label for children who can't sit still, won't stop talking, and often are disruptive in class. Discussion has centered mainly on controversy over whether children with this diagnosis should be treated with stimulant medication, which, paradoxically, calms down overactive bodies and brains. However, recent research offers a new way of understanding this disorder and a different view of how medication treatment actually works in the brain.

## The Symphony of the Brain

Few researchers still think of ADD as a simple behavior disorder. Increasingly, specialists are recognizing that it is a complex syndrome of impairments in development of the brain's cognitive management system, or executive functions. The disorder affects one's ability to

- Organize and get started on tasks.
- Attend to details and avoid excessive distractibility.
- Regulate alertness and processing speed.
- Sustain and, when necessary, shift focus.
- Use short-term working memory and access recall.
- Sustain motivation to work.
- Manage emotions appropriately.

One way to imagine the cluster of cognitive functions involved in the new model of ADD is to visualize a symphony orchestra composed of talented musicians. Regardless of their expertise, the musicians need a competent conductor who will select the piece to play, make sure they start at the same time and stay on tempo, fade in the strings and then bring in the brass, and manage them as they interpret the music. Without an effective conductor, the symphony will not produce good music.

In individuals with ADD, the parts of the brain that correspond to the individual musicians often work quite well. The problem is with the conductor, with those executive functions that, in a healthy individual, work together to accomplish a task. ADD impairs neural circuits that function as the conductor of the symphony.

Take James, for example. He's a bright 6th grader who enthusiastically participates in class discussions that relate to science or social studies. He often contributes examples from shows he has watched on the Discovery Channel or History Channel or from the many books he has read. However, he rarely completes homework assignments, can't keep track of his papers or books, and often claims that he can't recall what he has just finished hearing or reading in class.

Julie has her own set of challenges with accomplishing school tasks. A quiet, intelligent 9th grader, she was on the honor roll every year—until she got to high school. Halfway through freshman year, she is in danger of failing most of her major classes because of missing homework and low test grades. Her parents say that although she spends many hours each night doing homework, she loses track of what she needs to hand in for each class. As she works to catch up on overdue work in one course, she falls behind in others. She also studies hard for tests and knows all the answers when others quiz her on the material, but on the following day when she takes the test, she's unable to recall most of the information. Both James and Julie display executive function impairment.

## The Six Executive Functions

One model describing the executive functions emerged from my research with children, adolescents, and adults. Although each of the six components of the model has a single-word label, they are not unitary variables like height, weight, or blood pressure. Instead, each is like a basket containing a cluster of related cognitive functions. The six executive functions that work together in various combinations are

- *Activation:* organizing, prioritizing, and activating for work.
- *Focus:* focusing, sustaining, and shifting attention to tasks.
- *Effort:* regulating alertness and sustaining effort and processing speed.
- *Emotion:* managing frustration and modulating emotions.
- *Memory:* using working memory and accessing recall.
- *Action:* monitoring and self-regulating action.

In daily life, these clusters of cognitive functions operate, often without our conscious involvement, in integrated and dynamic ways to accomplish a wide variety of tasks. They do not continually work at peak efficiency for

any of us; everyone has difficulty with some of them from time to time. However, those diagnosed with ADD—James and Julie, for example—are substantially more impaired in their ability to use these executive functions than are most other people of the same age and developmental level.

---

**Approximately 7.8 percent of U.S. children ages 4–17 are currently diagnosed with ADD or ADHD.**

---

We no longer see ADD as an all-or-nothing concept. It's not like pregnancy, where one either is or isn't pregnant, with nothing in between. Diagnosing ADD is more like distinguishing clinical depression from normal fluctuations in mood. Although everyone feels sad from time to time, treating a person for depression only makes sense when he or she is significantly impaired by depressive symptoms over a substantial period of time. Similarly, the diagnosis of ADD/ADHD is not warranted for people who have occasional difficulty with the relevant symptoms but rather for those who are significantly impaired by the cluster of ADD symptoms over a longer period of time.

## Differences in Development

As teachers know, a student's capacity to exercise these various self-management functions develops slowly from early childhood through late adolescence or early adulthood. We hold different expectations for 8-year-olds than for 5-year-olds in their capacity to sustain attention, follow directions, remember information, and so on. We also know that within any given age group, some children develop these abilities more quickly and in more refined ways than others do. A diagnosis of ADD/ADHD is appropriate only when the individual's impairment is significantly greater than that of most other children of the same age and developmental level.

Scientific evidence has now demonstrated that although some basic elements of executive functions emerge during early childhood, these complex self-management networks are not fully developed until the late teens or early twenties (Brown, 2005). Accordingly, most governments will not allow their citizens to drive a motor vehicle until they are at least 16 years old. This is not because the drivers' legs are too short for their feet to reach the pedals; rather, it is because the crucial executive functions of the brain that enable an individual to manage the complexities and high-stakes responsibilities of driving a car do not develop sufficiently until middle or late adolescence.

Because normal development of executive functions is not complete until late adolescence or early adulthood, it is not always possible to identify, during childhood, students with impairments in these functions. For some students, ADD impairments become obvious during preschool. These students may be wildly hyperactive or unable to sit still or follow even the most basic directions. Other students may learn and behave quite well during elementary school, showing signs of ADD impairments only when middle school challenges their self-management abilities as they leave behind a classroom in which a single teacher has helped guide their executive functions.

Some students do not manifest their ADD impairments in noticeable ways until they encounter the more demanding world of high school, where they may be unable to cope with the ongoing conflicts and demands of study, classroom performance, homework in several subjects, and family and social interactions. Other students with ADD do not have noticeable symptoms until even later. Their parents may have built such successful compensatory scaffolding around them that their ADD impairments do not become apparent until the scaffolding is suddenly removed—as when the student moves away from home to attend a college or university.

## Why Here and Not There?

The most perplexing aspect of an ADD diagnosis is the situational specificity of the symptoms. Every child, adolescent, and adult with ADD whom I have ever seen has a few types of activity in which they effectively exercise cognitive functions that are quite impaired in almost every other circumstance.

Take Larry, for example, a high school junior who was the goaltender for his ice hockey team. His parents brought him in for evaluation the day after the team won the state championship. As they described his performance, it was clear that he was an extraordinary goalie who kept careful track of the puck throughout each game. He was bright; his IQ was in the very superior range. However, he was always in trouble with his teachers. They reported that although he occasionally made impressively perceptive comments in class, most of the time he was distracted and "out to lunch," unable to follow the class discussion. "If you can pay attention so well when you're playing hockey," they would ask him, "then why can't you pay attention in class?"

Not all individuals with ADD focus best in sports; some get intensely involved in such activities as playing video games, drawing, building with Legos, or completing mechanical tasks. All seem to have a few specific activities in which they can focus well and for long periods of time. Yet they have difficulty focusing on many other tasks that they recognize are important and that they want to do well, such as completing an essay or preparing for a major exam. People often see ADD as a problem of willpower: "You can do it here," they say. "Why can't you do it there?" ADD is *not* a problem of willpower, however. It is a chronic impairment in the chemistry of the management system of the brain.

## A Word about Medications

Evidence now shows that ADD is a highly heritable disorder, with impairments related to problems in the release and reloading of two crucial neurotransmitter chemicals made in the brain: dopamine and norepinephrine. These chemicals play a crucial role in facilitating communication within neural networks that orchestrate cognition. A massive body of evidence indicates that 8 of 10 individuals with the disorder experience significant improvement in their functioning when treated with appropriately fine-tuned medications. These treatments can compensate for inefficient release and reloading of essential neurotransmitters at countless synaptic connections in the brain.

However, ADD is not like a strep infection, where you can take a course of antibiotics and knock out the infection. It's more like a vision problem: Appropriately prescribed eyeglasses can improve impaired vision, but not cure it. Similarly, medications for ADD may help alleviate symptoms, but only for those hours of the day when the medication is active in the brain. During these times, some students under treatment can perform most self-management tasks quite well. For others, medication alone is not sufficient.

Approximately 50 percent of students with ADD have one or more specific learning disorders. If students with concurrent ADD and learning disabilities do not receive adequate treatment for their ADD impairments, it is unlikely that they will benefit from special education instruction because they will not be in a state that makes them available to learn. But medication alone will not alleviate their learning disability problems. Students with both ADD and learning disabilities often require accommodations or special education services.

## The Difficulties of Diagnosis

When we considered ADD/ADHD a simple behavior disorder, it was easy to diagnose. Teachers could readily spot students who were chronically inattentive, restless, and impulsive in the classroom and on the playground. However, the new model of ADD—as a developmental impairment of executive functions—requires a different kind of evaluation, an approach that can pick up more subtle cognitive impairments. These may or may not be accompanied by hyperactivity or other readily observable symptoms. For example, a student may appear to be paying attention in class when he is actually drifting off and thinking of unrelated things. Another student may diligently read her assignment but then be unable to recall what she's just read.

To begin with, the most important assessment element is an individual clinical interview to query the student about a variety of daily cognitive functions. This requires a clinician who is well trained to recognize ADD and differentiate it from other learning, emotional, and behavioral problems. The evaluating clinician also needs to gather information from parents and teachers that describes the student's strengths and impairments as he or she encounters such tasks as keeping track of assignments, doing homework, reading for understanding, organizing thoughts for writing projects, and socially interacting both in and out of school. Rating scales—such as the Conners Rating Scale, Behavior Assessment System for Children (BASC), or Brown ADD Scales—can be helpful in gathering data for evaluation, but none is sufficient in itself for making or ruling out a diagnosis of ADD.

Nor can standard IQ scores or achievement test scores help an evaluator diagnose ADD. However, IQ index scores on the Wechsler Intelligence Scale for Children (WISC-IV) or Wechsler Adult Intelligence Scale (WAIS-III) can suggest ADD impairments if the student's score for the Working Memory and/or Processing Speed Index is one standard deviation or more below that student's index score for Verbal Comprehension or Perceptual Organization. Any student who underachieves in school and displays such discrepancies between basic cognitive abilities and indices of executive functions should be carefully evaluated for possible ADD.

**ADD impairs the neural circuits that function as the conductor of the symphony of the brain.**

Three specific groups of students with ADD tend to be overlooked: bright students, female students, and students under stress. Adults often think that very bright students who underachieve are lazy, the assumption being that one cannot be bright and, at the same time, have significant ADD impairments. In fact, individuals with ADD are found at all IQ levels. Female students with ADD may be difficult to spot because they generally don't call attention to themselves with dramatic, disruptive behavior. Finally, adults often explain away the achievement problems of students coming from families with multiple social stressors, such as divorce, unemployment, poverty, and multiple relocations. Teachers may assume that poor achievement is just the student's reaction to these difficulties. They may not realize that ADD is more common in families under psychosocial stress.

## Importance of Early Identification

When a student with or without hyper-activity or behavior problems chronically underachieves, educators should consider evaluating the student for ADD/ADHD. To start the process, school staff should systematically gather relevant information from teachers and the school psychologist about specific impairments observed in the student's academic work, classroom performance, or social interactions. They should present this information to parents with suggestions about how the parents can arrange for an appropriate evaluation to identify causes of the student's chronic difficulties and possible options for intervention.

Before school staff can adequately assist parents in identifying students for a possible ADD/ADHD evaluation, however, teachers, school psychologists, and administrators need to develop a solid understanding of the new model for attention deficit disorders. Resources are available online at http://help4ADHD.org, a website funded by the U.S. Centers for Disease Control, or in the *CHADD Educator's Manual* available at http://chadd.org

Early identification of students with ADD is important because appropriate interventions can prevent a student from becoming demoralized by repeated experiences of frustration and failure. With appropriate intervention, most students with ADD/ADHD can achieve at the level of their abilities.

## Note

1. I use the terms ADD and ADHD interchangeably in this article.

# References

Brown, T. E. (2005). *Attention deficit disorder: The unfocused mind in children and adults.* New Haven, CT: Yale University Press.

*Journal of the American Medical Association.* (2005, November 9). 18, 2293–2295.

# Critical Thinking

1. What is attention deficit disorder and what are its primary symptoms?

2. How does an individual acquire or develop attention deficit disorder?

**Thomas E. Brown** is Associate Director of the Yale Clinic for Attention and Related Disorders, Department of Psychiatry, Yale University School of Medicine. He is the author of *Attention Deficit Disorder: The Unfocused Mind in Children and Adults* (Yale University Press, 2005) and the developer of the Brown ADD Scales for Children, Adolescents, and Adults (Psychological Association, 1996, 2001); www.drthomasebrown.com.

# The Kids Aren't All Right

**New data from APA's Stress in America survey indicate parents don't know what's bothering their children.**

CHRISTOPHER MUNSEY

There's a disconnect between what children say they're worrying about and what their parents think is stressing them, a gap that could have long-term implications for children's mental and physical health, according to APA's latest Stress in America research.

Children age 8 to 17 say they worry about doing well in school, getting into good colleges and their family's finances. They also report suffering headaches, sleeplessness and upset stomachs.

But these stresses and symptoms are going largely unnoticed by parents, survey findings show.

In fact, more than one in three children report experiencing headaches in the past month, but only 13 percent of parents think their children experience headaches as a result of stress. In addition, while 44 percent of children report sleeping difficulties, only 13 percent of parents think their kids have trouble sleeping.

The survey also found that about one-fifth of children reported they worry a great deal or a lot, but only 3 percent of parents rate their children's stress as extreme (an 8, 9 or 10 on a 10-point scale). In addition, almost 30 percent of children worried about their families' financial difficulties, but just 18 percent of parents thought that was a source of worry for their children.

The findings are troubling because chronic stress left untreated can contribute to psychological problems as well as physical conditions, says Katherine Nordal, PhD, APA's executive director for professional practice. She says parents need to make themselves available and let their children know it's OK to approach them if they're worried about something.

"Parents need to be intentional about setting aside time to be available to their children," she says. "If parents aren't receptive, kids may feel like they're being an additional burden on their parents by talking about their problems."

The online survey, conducted by Harris Interactive for the third consecutive year for the Practice Directorate's ongoing Mind/Body Health public education campaign, polled a nationally representative sample of 1,568 adults in July and August. Results for children age 8 to 17 were drawn from a YouthQuery survey of 1,206 young people conducted online by Harris in August.

## Women Still More Stressed

The findings for adults are also troubling:

- Stress levels are high, with 42 percent of adults indicating their stress worsened in the past year. A total of 24 percent said they had an extreme level of stress (8, 9 or 10 on a 10-point scale) over the past month, and 51 percent report moderate stress levels (4 to 7 on a 10-point scale).

- About two-thirds of respondents said they've been diagnosed by a physician with a chronic condition, most commonly high blood pressure or high cholesterol. Seventy percent said a health-care provider recommended lifestyle or behavior changes. That data also show that adults who were advised to make lifestyle changes may not have received enough support from their physicians to do so. In fact, fewer than half were told by their physicians why the changes were important; only 35 percent were given tips or shown techniques for making changes; and only 5 percent to 10 percent were referred to another health-care provider for follow-up.

- Similar to last year's results, women report having experienced more stress symptoms than men, such as irritability or anger, fatigue and depression.

- Among parents of 8- to 17-year-olds, mothers reported higher levels of stress than fathers. On a scale of 1 to 10 (with 10 being the highest level), 15 percent of moms rated their stress as a 10, compared with only 3 percent of dads. Mothers were also more likely to report lying awake at night, eating unhealthy foods, overeating or skipping a meal because of stress.

Such findings underscore the need for psychologists to work within the nation's health-care system to help people make needed lifestyle and behavioral changes, Nordal says.

"The key in managing stress effectively for both physical and mental well-being is having effective coping strategies, a combination of relaxation strategies along with exercise, combined with good sleep habits and good eating habits," she says.

## Sources of Stress by Age

| | Total N=235 | Parents 8–12 101 | 13–17 134 | Total 1,206 | Youth 8–12 536 | 13–17 670 |
|---|---|---|---|---|---|---|
| **Managing school pressures/responsibilities/ homework/grades/**Doing well in school | 34% | 31% | 36% | 44% | 44% | 43% |
| **Relationships with siblings/**Getting along with my brother(s) or sister(s) | 17% | 17% | 16% | 8% | 14% | 2% |
| **Relationships with peers/**Getting along with my friends | 20% | 20% | 20% | 16% | 22% | 11% |
| **Your family's financial difficulties/**My family having enough money | 18% | 20% | 17% | 30% | 28% | 31% |
| **His/her physical appearance/weight/**The way I look/my weight | 17% | 17% | 17% | 22% | 17% | 26% |
| **Your relationship with your spouse/partner/**My parent(s)/ guardian or other family members arguing or fighting more | 12% | 16% | 9% | 10% | 14% | 7% |
| **Pressure managing extracurricular commitments (e.g. sports, hobbies)/**Managing activities such as sports, music, clubs, etc. | 12% | 12% | 12% | 10% | 7% | 12% |
| **Peer pressure to engage in risky behaviors (e.g., smoking, drinking, drugs, sex, etc.)/**Pressure from friends who want me to try smoking, drinking, drugs, sex, etc. | 6% | 1% | 10% | 2% | - | 3% |
| **Getting into a good college/determining future/**Getting into a good college/Deciding what to do after high school | 3% | 1% | 5% | 17% | 5% | 29% |
| Non-financial pressures on family members (e.g., health, job frustrations, getting along with extended family, etc.) | 3% | 3% | 4% | N/A | N/A | N/A |
| Getting along with my boyfriend or girlfriend | N/A | N/A | N/A | 3% | 1% | 4% |
| My parent(s)/guardian losing their jobs | N/A | N/A | N/A | 6% | 7% | 6% |
| Other | 8% | 10% | 6% | 10% | 12% | 8% |

This is particularly important for women who often face a "second shift" of caring for children and running a household when they get home from work, says Helen Coons, PhD, a Philadelphia-based clinical health psychologist who works primarily with women. "The reality is, so many women are just too tired. They're running on empty."

That calls for change at several levels to support women, says Coons. Workplaces should offer better access to day care and more flexibility to allow women time for medical checkups and exercise breaks. Spouses or partners need to watch the kids while mom goes out for a run or a brisk walk, and neighborhood families can rotate babysitting to give parents more flexibility.

"There's that African saying, it takes a village to raise a child. I think it takes a community to support women and families" for healthier lifestyles, she says.

## Mile-High Stress

This year's survey also took snapshots of how Americans are faring with stress in eight metropolitan areas—Atlanta, Chicago, Denver, Detroit, Los Angeles, New York, Seattle and Washington, D.C.—comparing results with national findings.

## Getting the Results Out

APA presented the results of the Stress in America survey on Nov. 3 at a New York press conference. Nationally, the research was featured on cable and broadcast news programs, newspapers, radio programs, news and health Websites, and blogs with local psychologists from the Practice Directorate's Public Education Campaign reaching out to local reporters. Coverage of the results reached almost 28 million people.

Outlets that featured articles and discussion of APA's stress survey included:

- NBC, ABC and FOX local affiliates.
- NBC's "Today Show."
- CNN en Espanol.
- "Dr. Nancy" on MSNBC.
- *Wall Street Journal's* The Juggle blog.
- *USA Today.*
- *The New York Times'* Motherlode blog.
- Newsweek.com's "Her Body" column.
- *The Washington Post Express.*

Faring the worst was Denver, where more than 75 percent of residents report that work and money are significant sources of stress, and 35 percent rated their stress as extreme over the prior month.

That distress sounds familiar to Stephanie Smith, PsyD, public education coordinator for the Colorado Psychological Association and a Denver-based practitioner. Although the city's unemployment rate isn't as high as the national average, many of her clients tell her they feel trapped at their jobs. They're working harder for less money because of layoffs and pay cuts, but they're unable to find better jobs and frightened of losing their health insurance.

Smith works with her clients to identify things they can do to relieve stress, such as spending more quality time with family and exercising. "We talk about the things you can control in your life," she says.

In Los Angeles, 71 percent of respondents said they've been told by a health provider they have a chronic condition, compared with 66 percent nationally.

"To me, that's absolutely frightening, because we know the role stress plays in wearing our bodies down," says Michael Ritz, PhD, co-chair of the California Psychological Association's public education steering committee.

Psychologists can help people manage their stress and live healthier lifestyles, Ritz says.

"That underscores so much why psychologists need to be part of our health-care team," he says.

*To read more about the 2009 results, go online to www.apa.org/news/press/releases/2009/11/stress.aspx.*

## Critical Thinking

1. To what extent do parents realize that their children experience stress? Why is this issue important for helping children learn to cope with stress?
2. How do men and women tend to differ in their experiencing of stress?
3. How can a person deal with stress effectively or learn to cope with stress?

# The Recession's Toll on Children

Low-income children are more likely to develop cognitive deficits, undermining their chances for successful lives. New psychological interventions could help protect them.

AMY NOVOTNEY

More than one in five American children now live in poverty, the highest rate in two decades, and one that surpasses that of most other industrialized nations, according to a June report from the non-profit Foundation for Child Development. Since 1975, the organization has tracked children's overall quality of life with 28 well-being indicators, including infant mortality, preschool enrollment and children's health insurance coverage.

The foundation predicts that the number of children living in poverty will rise to 15.6 million this year, an increase of more than 3 million children in four years. As many as half a million children could become homeless this year, up from 330,000 in 2007.

Perhaps most alarming is that even though the economy is likely to recover in the next few years, a generation of disadvantaged children may not. Today's poorer children could be haunted by the devastating effects of the recession for years to come, as they face an increased risk of engaging in violent crime and illegal drug use, and of experiencing chronic health problems such as obesity.

"Research shows that children who slip into poverty, even for a short time, suffer long-term setbacks even when their families regain their economic footing," says psychologist Ruby Takanishi, PhD, the foundation's president.

These setbacks are especially true for children under 10, she adds. In addition to negative health outcomes—such as a higher susceptibility to asthma, anemia and other health problems—research also shows that children raised in poverty are more likely to experience negative educational and cognitive outcomes, often as a result of less mental stimulation and increased stress in their living situations. Some research even shows that the brains of poor children may be unable to process information in the same way as the brains of kids in higher-income families.

With the economic downturn forcing more families into poverty, psychologists are using their expertise in child development and cognition to develop evidence-based early-childhood interventions to help improve the prospects for low-income children. They're also advocating for more resources for these children, including better educational and social support, says Martha Farah, PhD, director of Center for Neuroscience and Society at the University of Pennsylvania.

"Our ultimate goal is to understand the complex web of social, psychological and physiological influences that act upon children in low-socioeconomic families and to use that understanding to help them achieve their true potential," Farah says.

> "Our ultimate goal is to understand the complex web of social, psychological and physiological influences that act upon children in low-socioeconomic families and to use that understanding to help them achieve their true potential."
>
> —Martha Farah, University of Pennsylvania

## Poverty and the brain

In a classic 1995 study published in the book "Meaningful Differences in the Everyday Experiences of Young American Children" (Brookes Publishing, 1995), University of Kansas psychologists Betty Hart, PhD, and Todd Risley, PhD, found that the average vocabulary of 3-year-old children from "professional" families was more than twice as large as that of 3-year-olds on welfare. Since then, a steady stream of research by psychologists and other scientists has highlighted the gulf between poor and well-off children's performance on almost every measure of cognitive development, including working memory, impulse regulation and language skills. (See "Further Reading, Resources" for more on how poverty affects the brain.)

Last year, researchers at the University of California, Berkeley, presented even more definitive findings on developmental differences between low- and high-income kids: When presented with novel stimuli, EEG readings of 9- and 10-year-olds from poorer homes showed less brain activity in the prefrontal cortex than the brains of children from more well-off families (*Journal of Cognitive Neuroscience,* Vol. 21, No. 6).

"These kids have no neural damage, no prenatal exposure to drugs and alcohol," says cognitive psychologist Mark Kishiyama, PhD, one of the study's authors, who now works at the VA hospital in Martinez, Calif. "Yet the prefrontal cortex is not functioning as efficiently as it should be. This difference may manifest itself in problem-solving and school performance."

Research led by Carleton University psychologist Amadeo D'Angiulli, PhD, provides further evidence of poorer children's deficits in a key ability harbored in the brain's prefrontal cortex—selective attention. In a 2008 study in *Neuropsychology* (Vol. 22, No. 3), D'Angiulli monitored the brain activity of 28 children from grades six to nine while they listened to a random series of four tones. Researchers asked the children to press a button every time they heard two of those tones. The results of the study showed that the brains of the children from lower-socioeconomic backgrounds used more energy when listening to the "other tones" than those from higher-income homes.

A 2009 study in *Developmental Science* (Vol. 12, No. 4), conducted by Helen Neville, PhD, a professor of psychology and neuroscience at the University of Oregon, replicates D'Angiulli's findings. In the study, 32 children listened to two stories simultaneously, one in each ear, and were asked to filter out one. All of the children remembered the story, but the children from disadvantaged homes had more trouble shutting out the distracting stimuli of the other story. Their brains, researchers say, have to work harder to perform the same task, a difficulty that could make it tougher for them to focus on teacher instructions or class assignments.

What's to blame for these disparities? Many researchers suspect it's the stressful home environments and lack of parental education in many low-income homes. "There are, not surprisingly, big differences in the amount of cognitive and linguistic stimulation that children receive in the home," Farah says.

For example, only 36 percent of low-income parents read to their kindergarten-age children every day, compared with 62 percent of upper-income parents, according to a 2002 study by researchers at the nonprofit Educational Testing Service. And in a study co-authored by Farah this year, published in *NeuroImage* (Vol. 49, No. 1), researchers found a direct correlation between hippocampal volume—which is related to memory ability—and the amount of parental nurturance a young child receives; for example, how often a parent holds a child close.

Regardless of the cause, if these cognitive and social performance lags are left unaddressed, they will persist throughout a child's development, says Linda Mayes, MD, a professor of child psychiatry, pediatrics and psychology at the Yale Child Study Center. Her team, which includes Yale child psychologists Michael Crowley, PhD, and James C. McPartland, PhD, is five years into a six-year National Institute of Child Health and Human Development grant to study how economic adversity affects emerging executive control functions in 360 young children in New Haven, Conn.

"It appears that the issue for children from poorer environments is not only a slower start, but rather a slower progression in skill acquisition, so that they stay behind their peers," Mayes says.

## Promising Interventions

The good news is that a brain that is vulnerable to the adverse environmental effects of poverty is equally susceptible to the positive effects of rich, balanced learning environments and caring relationships, many psychologists say. While there's clearly no one solution to offset the grave challenges faced by disadvantaged children, evidence-based educational interventions can help poor children achieve cognitive and academic success, research suggests.

One of the most promising programs is the Tools of the Mind curriculum, developed by Metropolitan State College at Denver educational psychologists Deborah Leong, PhD, and Elena Bodrova, PhD. The yearlong program, based on the work of Russian psychologist Lev Vygotsky, helps children build their ability to control their behavior and resist impulses—skills psychologists say are critical for success in school and life. The program's 40 core activities focus on improving executive function through tasks such as "buddy reading," in which students pair up and take turns telling and listening to stories from a picture book. To help the children fight the urge to talk while the other student is telling a story, teachers pass out paper mouths and ears, and remind students that only mouths talk—ears don't.

"With that concrete reminder in front of them, they're able to exercise self-control and listen," says Adele Diamond, PhD, a professor of developmental cognitive neuroscience at the University of British Columbia, who has been testing the program with low-income preschoolers in the Northeastern United States. In her 2007 study published in *Science* (Vol. 318, No. 5,855), Diamond found that Tools students consistently scored higher on tests that require executive function than students enrolled in the school district's long-running curriculum addressing the same academic content. Tools of the Mind is now being used to teach 18,000 prekindergarten and kindergarten students in 12 states around the country.

The Tools program is different from most early education programs, Diamond says, because it encourages children to use executive functioning, while other programs often assume young children can't use those skills. Or, she says, educators in other programs may expect the children to exercise self-control, but don't support them in doing so, leading to failure and criticism. "Instead of getting yelled at for being a poor listener, here the child develops pride in being a good listener," Diamond says.

The Tools program also emphasizes the importance of imaginative, dramatic play, but requires the children to develop a plan for what character they would like to act out—say, an astronaut going to the moon—and holds them to it.

Neville, at the University of Oregon, is also testing an early-child intervention that trains children and their parents about the importance of impulse management and sustained concentration. "If you have control of your selective attention, you can do anything," she says. "You can learn soccer, you can learn to play the cello, you can learn to crochet, you can learn math—it's domain-general."

In the program, Parents and Children Making Connections–Highlighting Attention, parents and their preschoolers attend eight weekly, two-hour evening or weekend attention-training classes. The kids learn to be more aware of their bodies, attention and emotions, as well as how to focus on one thing at a time. In one task, for example, they practice figure-tracing, which requires a moderate amount of concentration, while other students in the room play with balloons, in an effort to challenge the concentration of the figure-tracers. Parents learn to use positive language with their children and remain patient. They also learn strategies to help their children develop their attention control—by pointing out small details on a walk, playing board games and reading books that require them to focus for long periods of time.

In an as-yet-unpublished study, Neville and her team found that children who completed the training improved

their IQ, message comprehension and social skills. Parents reported reduced stress and more positive interactions in response to children's crying and temper tantrums.

Overall, Neville says she predicts that programs that include extensive parent training may result in larger gains for children than programs that primarily focus on children. The intervention's initial success also points to the importance of the home environment and the parent-child relationship to children's cognitive development—links that often go unrecognized, she says.

## Speaking Out for Kids

But to ensure that low-income children have access to these interventions and others, psychologists must be among those raising awareness of these children's plight, as well as the research that shows there are solutions, Takanishi says.

"Investment during the first decade of life is crucial for the country's well-being, as well as for individual potential," she says. "In the United States, education is the only possibility for escaping from poverty. Thus, the recession's impact on declining availability of prekindergarten programs is very damaging for children in poverty."

Last year, Neville and her team developed a DVD for parents, teachers and policymakers, available at www.changingbrains.org, that explores brain development in children and provides simple techniques caregivers can use to help children reach their full potential.

Takanishi recommends that psychologists contribute newspaper op-eds highlighting research on the effects of poverty. Psychologists might also consider promoting dual-generation programs that focus on increasing literacy among low-income parents—and particularly immigrants—as a way to boost economic status and improve outcomes for children.

"Help other people think more broadly about how to address the issue of children in poverty," Takanishi says. "It's that kind of feeding of ideas and working with other sectors in society that will really help us move toward social change."

## Further Reading, Resources

National Center for Children in Poverty: www.nccp.org

Foundation for Child Development: www.fedus.org

Spotlight on Poverty and Opportunity: www.spotlightonpoverty.com

APA Office of Socioeconomic Status. www.apa.org/pi/ses/index.aspx

Hackman, D.A., & Farah, M.J. (2009). Socioeconomic status and the developing brain. *Trends in Cognitive Science, 13,* 65–73.

Jensen, E. (2009). Teaching With Poverty in Mind: What Being Poor Does to Kids' Brains and What Schools Can Do about It. Alexandria, Va.: Association for Supervision & Curriculum Development.

Lipina, S.J., & Colombo, J.A. (2009). Poverty and Brain Development During Childhood: An Approach From Cognitive Psychology and Neuroscience. Washington, DC: APA.

Raizada, R.D., & Kishiyama, M.M. (2010). Effects of socioeconomic status on brain development, and how cognitive neuroscience may contribute to leveling the playing field. *Frontiers in Human Neuroscience, 5,* 1–18.

## Critical Thinking

1. How does poverty affect children's intellectual development?

2. Describe the ways that parent training might be used to combat the negative effects of poverty on children's intellectual development.

# Stigma: Alive and Well

**Despite decades of anti-stigma campaigns, people may be more fearful of those with mental illness than ever. New research, however, is pointing the way toward real progress.**

SADIE F. DINGFELDER

"Julie" managed to keep her chronic depression at bay for two years, despite the stress of attending a prestigious law school. But when she got into a car accident during her third year, she experienced a brutal resurgence of anxiety, sadness and insomnia. In search of sleeping pills, Julie went to a doctor. He recommended she see a therapist, but she refused.

"I was afraid that I might have to disclose my medical records for bar admission," she says.

Julie's worries were warranted: All 50 states' bar associations ask about applicants' mental health histories, and there are several cases of people being denied admittance on the basis of mental health problems—even if they've been successfully treated.

Now a successful lawyer, Julie still keeps her depression from her co-workers for fear of how they'd react.

That's an all-too-common situation, says Bernice Pescosolido, PhD, a stigma researcher at Indiana University.

"She had a good reason to worry," says Pescosolido, principal investigator for several major National Institutes of Health-funded stigma studies. "The two areas where Americans are most stigmatizing are marriage into the family and work."

Despite decades of public information campaigns costing tens of millions of dollars, Americans may be as suspicious of people with mental illness as ever. New research by Pescosolido, published in the *Journal of Health and Social Behavior* (Vol. 41, No. 2), finds that 68 percent of Americans do not want someone with a mental illness marrying into their family and 58 percent do not want people with mental illness in their workplaces.

Some attitudes have gotten worse over time: For instance, people are twice as likely today than they were in 1950 to believe that mentally ill people tend to be violent.

Of course, the vast majority of people with mental illness are not violent—though they are 2.5 times more likely to be victims of violence than members of the general population, according to a study published in 2001 in the *International Journal of Law and Psychiatry* (Vol. 24, No. 6). And a new study, published in February in the *Archives of General Psychiatry* (Vol. 66, No. 2) finds that mental illness alone does not increase the chances that a person will become violent.

Since that fear of violence is not based in fact, it may stem from media portrayals of mental illness—particularly in the news, says Patrick Corrigan, PsyD, a psychology professor at the Illinois Institute of Technology and head of the Chicago Consortium for Stigma Research.

"Every time something really bad happens, people think it must be because of mental illness," says Corrigan. "If a woman drowns her children, people speculate—the news media speculates—that she must be off her medication."

In addition to being inaccurate and unfair, such beliefs come at a major cost to society, Pescosolido notes. An estimated one in four adults has a diagnosable mental illness, according to the National Institute of Mental Health. That's about 76 million Americans who live with the fear that others may find out about their disorder and think less of them or even keep them from getting jobs or promotions, she says. And people like Julie often avoid treatment due to the all-too-reasonable worry they'll be found out and discriminated against, Pescosolido says.

The good news: After decades of well-meaning but largely ineffective efforts to change public opinion, researchers are now working to understand the underpinnings of stigma and are even beginning to turn the tide of public opinion in America and abroad.

## An Insidious Effect

The toxic effects of stigma are well-documented, says Corrigan. People with mental illness often internalize society's beliefs about them—that they are incompetent, irrational and untrustworthy—and that can lead to distress that's sometimes worse than the mental illness itself, he says.

About half of people with schizophrenia believe that former psychiatric patients are less trustworthy than others, finds a study by psychologist Birgit Kleim, PhD, of Kings College in London, Corrigan, and colleagues. The patients who believed this tended to isolate themselves from social support, a course

# Parents Face a Treatment Dilemma

It's a story that's gained traction in the national media: Rather than tolerating the normal rambunctiousness of children, parents are turning to counseling and medication. However, new NIMH-funded research suggests that just the opposite may be true—parents fear that diagnoses such as depression or ADHD will stigmatize their children, and they may avoid treatment as a result, says Bernice Pescosolido, PhD, head of the National Stigma Study—Children and a sociology professor at Indiana University.

"I don't know one parent who had to make this decision who didn't struggle mightily with it," she says.

Specifically, the nationally representative survey of Americans, published in *Psychiatric Services* (Vol. 58, No. 5) found that:

- 45 percent believe mental health treatment makes children an outsider at school.
- 43 percent say children suffer as adults if others learn about their past mental health treatment.
- 57 doubt that confidentiality protections work to keep community members from finding out about children's mental health treatment.
- 81 percent report that childhood depression is the parents' fault.

Overall, the results suggest that people are less stigmatizing of children with mental health problems than they are of adults, but that parents fear a diagnosis may follow children throughout their life, limiting their opportunities, says study co-author Jane McLeod, PhD, a sociology professor at Indiana University.

Their concerns are well-founded, she says.

"Whether because of the symptoms of the disorders themselves, or because of the stigmatizing responses of others, children with emotional and behavioral problems have a lot of trouble as they transition into adulthood," says McLeod.

—S. Dingfelder

"Medication-induced stigma is regarded as one of the principal barriers to compliance," Tsang notes.

Even high-functioning college students fall prey to the effects of stigma, according to a study by Diane Quinn, PhD, a psychology professor at the University of Connecticut. In the study, published in *Personality and Social Psychology Bulletin* (Vol. 30, No. 7), Quinn and her colleagues asked college students to take a portion of the GRE Analytic Test, a difficult test of logic and reasoning. At the top of the test were several demographic questions, and, for half of the participants, a question about whether they had any history of mental illness.

Simply answering "yes" to that question caused some students' performance to plummet. Of the students who had a history of mental illness, those who had to disclose it before taking the test did about half as well as those who were allowed to keep quiet.

"It's really surprising that something as subtle as answering a question can effect people's performance," says Quinn.

The result, she notes, is similar to one that's found when students are asked to identify their race or gender before a test. Identifying oneself as part of a stigmatized group activates a fear of being stereotyped, and students must devote brainpower to pushing that out of their minds, which results in poorer test performance.

In addition to test performance, stigma can harm the physical health of people with mental illness, finds a study by Quinn, in press in the *Journal of Personality and Social Psychology*. In it, she surveyed 235 people who kept some parts of their identities secret to avoid stigma, including people with mental illness, rape victims and people with criminal histories. The more stigmatized their secret identities, the more likely people were to report symptoms of physical illness, Quinn found.

"Stigma is a day-to-day stressor," she says. "Little things happen every day to make people feel devalued, and that can add up and affect people's health."

# When Information Leads to Fear

Such findings underscore the importance of changing society's views of the mentally ill—especially those beliefs that the mentally ill are incompetent. However, most anti-stigma campaigns convey the message that mental illness is a disease like any other, says Pescosolido. Specifically, they explain the biological causes of depression and other disorders, emphasizing that people can't just "snap out of it," she says.

That was the case for the National Institute of Mental Health campaign, "Real Men, Real Depression," which focused on how common depression is, and gave men information to help them recognize it in themselves. Such information may encourage people to seek treatment, but the campaign's emphasis on

---

of action that can increase the severity of psychotic symptoms, according to the study published in the *Journal of Mental Health* (Vol. 17, No. 5).

"We know that social support of people with psychosis, for instance by friends or family, is crucial for their recovery," says Kleim.

Stigma can also keep people from taking their medications, finds a study by Hector Tsang, PhD, a psychology professor at Hong Kong Polytechnic University, published in the *Journal of Behavior Therapy and Experimental Psychiatry,* (Vol. 40, No. 1). That's in part because antipsychotic medication often has visible side-effects, such as tongue smacking and grimacing, which can mark one as mentally ill.

## International Attitudes Percent of Newspaper Articles on Mental Illness

| | United States | Iceland | Germany |
|---|---|---|---|
| Mentioning violence | 50% | 32% | 18% |
| Mentioning criminals | 34% | 14% | 18% |

Source: Olafsdottir, S. (2008). Medicalizing mental health: A comparative view of the public, private and professional construction of mental illness. Dissertation Abstracts International Section A: Humanities and Social Sciences, 68(9), 4100A.

how many people have a mental disorder may have reinforced fear in the general population, says Corrigan.

"Mental illness's impact is huge and omnipresent," he says. "Everyone's family in America has a person with serious mental illness, and that spooks us."

Canadian anti-stigma campaigns also tend to focus on the prevalence and symptoms of mental illness, says University of Calgary stigma-researcher JianLi Wang, PhD.

In one sense, these efforts work: In a study by Wang, published in the *Canadian Journal of Psychiatry* (Vol. 52, No. 7), 75 percent of Canadians correctly diagnosed a depressed person as described in a story, and they agreed with statements about the biochemical underpinnings the disorder. However, more than 45 percent of people Wang surveyed in a follow-up study said they believed that depressed people are unpredictable, and 20 percent said that depressed people tend to be dangerous.

"You can hold the belief that mental illness is a real disease and still be afraid of people with it," Wang says.

Such campaigns may even increase stigma, says Pescosolido. In particular, the idea that mental illness has genetic causes may make disorders seem incurable, she says.

"The 'disease-like-any-other' message was not an effective strategy, and it's what we used in the vast majority of anti-stigma campaigns," Pescosolido says.

A recent campaign in Scotland called "See Me" tried a different strategy. It educated reporters and editors about the harmfulness and inaccuracy of the stereotype that people with schizophrenia are prone to violence.

The campaign succeeded in reducing the number of news stories linking violence and mental illness, but had some unintended consequences, according to research published in February in the *International Journal of Health Promotion* (Vol. 10, No. 1). An analysis of five years of newspaper articles showed that, over the life of the anti-stigma campaign, coverage of people with mental illness became more negative—with stories frequently depicting people with mental illness as objects of pity, for example.

Perhaps even more concerning was that newspaper coverage of mental illness decreased overall, says study author Neil Quinn, PhD, a lecturer at the Glasgow School of Social Work.

## Stigma by the Numbers Percentage of Americans Reporting They Are Definitely or Probably Unwilling to Have a Person with Mental Illness

| | |
|---|---|
| Move next door | 38% |
| Spend an evening socializing with you | 56% |
| Make friends with you | 33% |
| Work closely with you | 58% |
| Marry into your family | 68% |

Source: Martin, J.K., Pescosolido, B.A., & Tuch, S.A. (2000). Of fear and loathing: The role of "disturbing behavior," labels, and causal attributions in shaping public attitudes toward people with mental illness. *Journal of Health and Social Behavior, 41,* 208–223.

"One of our conclusions was that journalists became afraid to report about schizophrenia full stop, because reporting did go down significantly," Quinn says.

## A New Tack

A lesson of the Scotland campaign, says study co-author Lee Knifton, is that anti-stigma campaigns can't just focus on eradicating negative depictions of people with mental illness. They need to tell positive stories as well, he says.

To that end, Knifton launched the Scottish Mental Health Arts and Film Festival, which highlights the contributions that people with mental illness make to society by showcasing music, film, comedy, literature and theater by people with mental illness. The festival, which began in 2007, also sponsors a contest for films that depict people with mental illness in realistic, holistic ways, says Knifton.

Last October, the festival drew 12,000 attendees and sparked 120 newspaper articles that emphasized the fact that people with mental illness are generally active, useful members of society, he says.

Such anti-stigma campaigns are more likely to work than the "disease like any other" campaigns of the past, says Pescosolido.

"If you focus on the competence of people with mental illness, that tends to lead to greater tolerance," she says.

That's also the goal of a new Canadian anti-stigma campaign, which tells the stories of people with mental illness—stories like that of Candace Watson, who was diagnosed as bipolar after an unsettling manic episode. She's since been successfully treated and now works as a nurse.

"I know I'm a competent person and I have things to offer," she says in a video that the campaign has disseminated through public service announcements and a website.

The Canadian campaign is based on research by Corrigan showing that contact with people who have mental illness tends to decrease stigma. For instance, one study by Corrigan, published in 2002 in *Psychiatric Rehabilitation Skills* (Vol. 6, No. 2), found that meeting people who have mental illness weakens people's tendency to link mental illness and violence.

It's also important to stress the normalcy of many people who have mental illness, he says.

"When the population gets a better sense of how many people with mental illness are actually successful—if more people come out of the closet—perhaps the stigma of mental illness will finally decline," he says.

## Further Readings

Burt, R.A. (2001). Promises to keep, miles to go: Mental health law since 1972. In Frost, Lynda E. (Ed); Bonnie, Richard J. (Ed.), *The evolution of mental health law.* (pp. 11–30). Washington, D.C.: APA.

Corrigan, P.W. (2005). *On the stigma of mental illness: Practical strategies for research and social change.* Washington, D.C.: APA.

Pescosolido, B.A., Jensen, P.S., Martin, J.K., Perry, B.L., Olafsdottir, S., & Fettes, D. (2008). Public knowledge and assessment of child mental health problems: Findings from the National Stigma Study—Children. *Journal of the American Academy of Child & Adolescent Psychiatry, 47,* 339–349.

## Critical Thinking

1. What leads people to stigmatize individuals who suffer from mental disorders?

2. What suggestions do psychologists have for reducing the stigma associated with mental disorders?

---

**Editor's note**—Julie is a pseudonym.

# ADHD among Preschoolers

Identifying and treating attention-deficit hyperactivity disorder in very young children requires a different approach.

Brendan L. Smith

Preschoolers can be inattentive or hyperactive even on the best of days, so it can be difficult to accurately diagnose attention-deficit hyperactivity disorder. But a growing body of research has shown that early treatment can help struggling children and frazzled parents.

The diagnosis of young children with ADHD is "very contentious" since there is a blurry line between common developmental changes and symptoms of the mental disorder, says ADHD researcher Stephen Hinshaw, PhD, chair of the psychology department at the University of California at Berkeley. "The symptoms for ADHD are very ubiquitous and very age-relevant," he says. "It's hard to know if you're seeing the signs of a disorder or just the signs of a young kid."

Hinshaw and some other researchers believe ADHD can be reliably diagnosed in children as young as 3 after thorough evaluations. In one study of school-age children, mothers reported that symptoms of ADHD appeared at or before age 4 in two-thirds of the children (*Journal of Developmental & Behavioral Pediatrics,* Vol. 23, No. 1).

Researchers disagree about whether ADHD is overdiagnosed, which may lead to unnecessary medication of healthy children. There is a tendency to overdiagnose young children with ADHD because of a lack of understanding about normative development in toddlerhood and the early preschool years, says Susan Campbell, PhD, a psychology professor at the University of Pittsburgh who has researched ADHD for more than three decades. "The only reason to diagnose a young child is to access appropriate services to help the child and family," she says. "Sometimes the earlier the better."

Overall, more children of all ages are being diagnosed with ADHD since there is greater awareness of the disorder and improvements in treatment, says Russell Barkley, PhD, a psychologist and professor at the Medical University of South Carolina who studies ADHD. Some inaccurate media reports have fueled a public misperception that ADHD is overdiagnosed, Barkley says. But only 20 percent of children with ADHD received any treatment in the 1960s and '70s, compared with roughly 70 percent to 80 percent today, he says.

"The rise in diagnosis is not bad news. It's good news," Barkley says. "Frankly, we were doing an awful job 20 or 30 years ago."

## Medication Issues

Often the first line of treatment for ADHD in school-age children is medication with stimulants, which have been found to be generally safe and effective. But drugs have less positive results for preschoolers. "I'm very opposed to the use of medication with young children because we don't really know the implications for brain development," Campbell says.

Approximately 4 million children—or 8 percent of all minors in the United States—have been diagnosed with ADHD, and more than half of them take prescription drugs. Methylphenidate hydrochloride (Ritalin) is the most commonly prescribed medication, but its use in children under 6 years old hasn't been approved by the Food and Drug Administration, which cites a lack of research for this age group. As a result, doctors are prescribing methylphenidate off label for preschoolers with ADHD.

The most comprehensive study on medication of preschoolers with ADHD showed mixed results for 3- to 5-year-old children. Funded by the National Institute of Mental Health, the multisite Preschool ADHD Treatment Study enrolled 303 preschoolers and their parents in a 10-week behavioral therapy course. Children with severe symptoms who didn't respond to therapy were given low doses of methylphenidate or a placebo. The medicated children showed a marked reduction in symptoms compared with the placebo group, according to the study results published in 2006.

> **"It's crazy to me that we use the same criteria for a 3-year-old as we do for a 35-year-old."**
>
> —George Dupaul, Lehigh University

More troublesome, though, was the fact that almost a third of parents reported that their medicated children experienced moderate to severe side effects, including weight loss, insomnia, loss of appetite, emotional outbursts and anxiety. Eleven percent of the preschoolers dropped out of the study because of their reactions to methylphenidate. During the study, the medicated children also grew about half an inch less in height and weighed about three pounds less than expected based on average growth rates (*Journal of the American Academy of Child & Adolescent Psychiatry,* Vol. 45, No. 11).

"The bottom line to me is for this age group, I don't believe stimulant medication is a first-line treatment," says George DuPaul, PhD, a professor of school psychology at Lehigh University who studies ADHD.

## Embracing Other Methods

Parental training and school-based interventions can be effective in treating preschoolers with ADHD, DuPaul says. His book, "Young Children With ADHD: Early Identification and Intervention" (APA, 2011), co-written with Lehigh University colleague Lee Kern, PhD, describes one of their studies of nondrug interventions with 135 preschoolers with ADHD.

Parents were given 20 training sessions on behavior problems, basic math and language skills, and child safety since children with ADHD often suffer accidental injuries because of their hyperactivity and impulsivity. One group of children also received individual assessments in the home and at preschool or day care. Both groups of children showed marked improvements in ADHD symptoms, although there was no significant advantage for the children with individual assessments (*School Psychology Review,* Vol. 36, No. 2). One limitation of the study was the lack of a control group because of ethical considerations about providing no treatment.

While older children can sometimes be taught to manage their ADHD symptoms, the training of preschool children has been more difficult, in part because cognitive-behavioral therapy doesn't work, Barkley says. Preschoolers with ADHD are delayed in communication skills, and language hasn't been internalized yet, so they can't use mental instructions or self-monitoring to change their behavior.

"It failed so we abandoned that after multiple studies found it had little or no influence," Barkley says.

But some behavioral management techniques are effective, including a token reward system and praise to provide extra motivation for preschoolers with ADHD, Barkley says. Teachers can seat children with ADHD near the teacher's desk and provide detailed explanations of class rules and disciplinary procedures, such as time-out or loss of tokens. Frequent class breaks and shorter work assignments also can help maintain children's attention and reduce outbursts.

Symptoms of ADHD can be exacerbated in children by impulsive parents who also have ADHD, Campbell says. Parents who are quick to anger and who frequently use physical punishment also can be detrimental. "There is going to be an interaction between the genetic risk and the support or lack of parental support the child has," she says.

## Looking Ahead

As the diagnosis of preschoolers with ADHD has increased, so have questions about the lack of age-specific symptoms in the Diagnostic and Statistical Manual of Mental Disorders, Fourth Edition. "It's crazy to me that we use the same criteria for a 3-year-old as we do for a 35-year-old," DuPaul says.

Scheduled for publication in 2013, the fifth DSM edition should require a greater number of symptoms for diagnosing young children with ADHD and more age-specific symptoms instead of generic descriptions such as fidgeting or running around and climbing, DuPaul says. "How do we apply that to a 17-year-old kid in a high school classroom?" he says. "They don't run about and climb on things."

Despite the risks, early identification and treatment of ADHD can provide substantial benefits for children and their families, Campbell says. "It can help so that when the child gets to the first grade, he isn't the only child no one else wants to play with and no teachers want in their class," she says.

## Critical Thinking

1. What is attention-deficit hyperactivity disorder (ADHD)?
2. Describe the alternatives to using drug therapy as an intervention in the treatment of ADHD in young children.

# UNIT 11

# Psychological Treatments

## Unit Selections

## Learning Outcomes

*After reading this Unit, you should be able to:*

- Explain how psychologists approach the treatment of post-traumatic stress disorder.

- Summarize the effectiveness of various methods of treating post-traumatic stress disorder.

- Discuss the effectiveness of psychotherapy and drug therapy in the treatment of psychological disorders.

- Evaluate the effectiveness of psychotherapy and drug therapy in successfully treating mental disorders.

- Explain the advantages of patient-centered home care as an alternative for traditional treatment of psychological problems.

## Student Website

www.mhhe.com/cls

## Internet References

**Abraham A. Brill Library**
    www.psychoanalysis.org/resources-library.html
**The C.G. Jung Page**
    www.cgjungpage.org
**Knowledge Exchange Network (KEN)**
    mentalhealth.about.com/library/2010/inf/blrc9.htm
**NetPsychology**
    netpsych.com/index.htm
**Sigmund Freud and the Freud Archives**
    http://users.rcn.com/brill/freudarc.html

Have you ever had the nightmare of being trapped in a dark, dismal place? No one lets you out. Your pleas for freedom go unanswered and, in fact, are suppressed or ignored by domineering authority figures around you. You keep begging for mercy but to no avail. You are fortunate to awake to the normal realities of your daily life. For the mentally ill, the nightmare of institutionalization, where individuals can be held against their will in what are sometimes terribly dreary, restrictive surroundings, is a reality. Have you ever wondered what would happen if we took perfectly normal individuals and institutionalized them in such a place? In one well-known and remarkable study, that is exactly what happened.

In 1973, eight people, including a pediatrician, a psychiatrist, and some psychologists, presented themselves to psychiatric hospitals. Each claimed that he or she was hearing voices. The voices, they reported, seemed unclear but appeared to be saying "empty" or "thud." Each of these individuals was admitted to a mental hospital, and most were diagnosed as being schizophrenic. After admission to the hospital, the "pseudopatients" or fake patients gave truthful information and thereafter acted like their usual, normal selves.

Their hospital stays lasted anywhere from 7 to 52 days. The nurses, doctors, psychologists, and other staff members treated them as if they were schizophrenic and never saw through their trickery. Some of the real patients in the hospital, however, recognized that the pseudopatients were perfectly normal. After their discharge, almost all of the pseudopatients received the diagnosis of "schizophrenic in remission," meaning that they were still clearly defined as schizophrenic; they just weren't exhibiting any of the symptoms at the time of release.

What does this study demonstrate about the diagnosis and treatment of mental illness? Is genuine mental illness always readily detectable? If we can't always pinpoint mental disorders, how can we treat them appropriately? What treatments are available, and which treatments work better for various diagnoses? The treatment of mental disorders is certainly challenging.

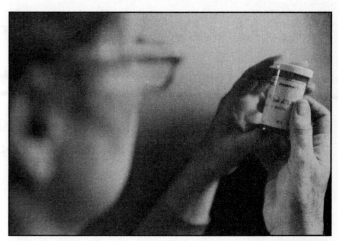

© Ingram Publishing

As you probably know, not all individuals diagnosed as having a mental disorder are institutionalized. In fact, these days, only a relatively small percentage of people suffering from one or more psychological disorders is confined to a mental institution. The most common treatments for mental disorders involve psychotherapy or counseling, medication, or some combination of both. Depending on the individual and the severity of his or her symptoms, the course of treatment may be relatively short (less than a year) or quite long (several years or more).

If truth be told, the array of available treatments is ever increasing and can be downright bewildering—and not just to the patient or client! Psychotherapists, clinical psychologists, and psychiatrists must weave their way through a complicated sets of symptoms, offer up their best diagnosis, and then suggest a course of treatment that seems best to address the client's problems. In order to demystify and simplify your understanding of treatments and interventions for mental disorders, we will look at them in this unit.

# PTSD Treatments Grow in Evidence, Effectiveness

**Several psychological interventions help to significantly reduce post-traumatic stress disorder symptoms, say new guidelines.**

Tori DeAngelis

I t's a bittersweet fact: Traumatic events such as the Sept. 11 attacks, Hurricane Katrina, and the wars in Iraq and Afghanistan have enabled researchers to learn a lot more about how best to treat post-traumatic stress disorder (PTSD).

"The advances made have been nothing short of outstanding," says Boston University psychologist Terence M. Keane, PhD, director of the behavioral science division of the National Center for Post-Traumatic Stress Disorder and a contributor to the original PTSD diagnosis. "These are very important times in the treatment of PTSD."

In perhaps the most important news, in November, the International Society for Traumatic Stress Studies (ISTSS), a professional society that promotes knowledge on severe stress and trauma, issued new PTSD practice guidelines. Using a grading system from "A" to "E," the guidelines label several PTSD treatments as "A" treatments based on their high degree of empirical support, says Keane, one of the volume's editors. The guidelines—the first since 2000—update and generally confirm recommendations of other major practice-related bodies, including the U.S. Department of Veterans Affairs (VA), the Department of Defense, the American Psychiatric Association, and Great Britain's and Australia's national health-care guidelines, he says.

In other PTSD-treatment advances, researchers are adding medications and virtual-reality simulations to proven treatments to beef up their effectiveness. Clinical investigators are also exploring ways to treat PTSD when other psychological and medical conditions are present, and they are studying specific populations such as those affected by the Sept. 11 attacks.

Though exciting, these breakthroughs are somewhat colored by an October Institute of Medicine (IoM) report that concludes there is still not enough evidence to say which PTSD treatments are effective, except for exposure therapies. Many experts, however, disagree with that conclusion, noting

that a number of factors specific to the condition, such as high dropout rates, can lead to what may seem like imperfect study designs.

## Treatments That Make a Difference

The fact that several treatments made the "A" list is great news for psychologists, says Keane. "Having this many evidence-based treatments allows therapists to use what they're comfortable with from their own background and training, and at the same time to select treatments for use with patients with different characteristics," he says.

Moreover, many of these treatments were developed by psychologists, he notes.

They include:

- **Prolonged-exposure therapy,** developed for use in PTSD by Keane, University of Pennsylvania psychologist Edna Foa, PhD, and Emory University psychologist Barbara O. Rothbaum, PhD. In this type of treatment, a therapist guides the client to recall traumatic memories in a controlled fashion so that clients eventually regain mastery of their thoughts and feelings around the incident. While exposing people to the very events that caused their trauma may seem counterintuitive, Rothbaum emphasizes that it's done in a gradual, controlled and repeated manner, until the person can evaluate their circumstances realistically and understand they can safely return to the activities in their current lives that they had been avoiding. Drawing from PTSD best practices, the APA-initiated Center for Deployment Psychology includes exposure therapy in the training of psychologists and

Percentage of soldiers reporting mental health problems during screenings

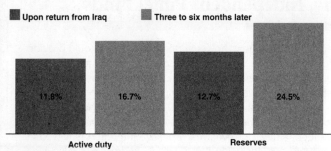

- ■ Upon return from Iraq
- ■ Three to six months later

11.8%  16.7%  12.7%  24.5%

Active duty          Reserves

**Delayed reaction.** When troops returning from Iraq are screened a second time, the proportion who report mental health problem rises.

Source: Journal of the American Medical Association

other health professionals who are or will be treating returning Iraq and Afghanistan service personnel.

- **Cognitive-processing therapy,** a form of cognitive behavioral therapy, or CBT, developed by Boston University psychologist Patricia A. Resick, PhD, director of the women's health sciences division of the National Center for PTSD, to treat rape victims and later applied to PTSD. This treatment includes an exposure component but places greater emphasis on cognitive strategies to help people alter erroneous thinking that has emerged because of the event. Practitioners may work with clients on false beliefs that the world is no longer safe, for example, or that they are incompetent because they have "let" a terrible event happen to them.
- **Stress-inoculation training,** another form of CBT, where practitioners teach clients techniques to manage and reduce anxiety, such as breathing, muscle relaxation and positive self-talk.
- **Other forms of cognitive therapy,** including cognitive restructuring and cognitive therapy.
- **Eye-movement desensitization and reprocessing,** or EMDR, where the therapist guides clients to make eye movements or follow hand taps, for instance, at the same time they are recounting traumatic events. It's not clear how EMDR works, and, for that reason, it's somewhat controversial, though the therapy is supported by research, notes Dartmouth University psychologist Paula P. Schnurr, PhD, deputy executive director of the National Center for PTSD.
- **Medications,** specifically selective serotonin reuptake inhibitors. Two in particular—paroxetine (Paxil) and sertaline (Zoloft)—have been approved by the Food and Drug Administration for use in PTSD. Other medications may be useful in treating PTSD as well, particularly when the person has additional disorders such as depression, anxiety or psychosis, the guidelines note.

## Spreading the Word

So promising does the VA consider two of the "A" treatments—prolonged exposure therapy and cognitive-processing therapy—that it is doing national rollouts of them within the VA, notes psychologist Antonette Zeiss, PhD, deputy chief consultant for mental health at the agency.

"Enhancing our ability to provide veterans with the psychotherapies for PTSD that have the strongest evidence base is one of our highest priorities," Zeiss says. In fact, the VA began training psychologists to provide the two approaches more than a year before the Institute of Medicine released its report of successful treatments, she says. "We're pleased that the report confirms our emphasis on this training."

The VA system's structure and philosophy make it possible to test the results of treatments in large, realistic samples—a clinical researcher's dream, notes Schnurr, who has conducted a number of such studies, most recently in a study of female veterans that led to the rollout out of prolonged exposure therapy. That study was reported in the Feb. 28, 2007, issue of *The Journal of the American Medical Association* (Vol. 297, No. 8, pages 820–830).

"The VA was able to support the science, so the research didn't just sit around in a journal and get discussed," Zeiss says. "They put money toward it, and they asked us to help them do a major rollout of the treatment."

## Boosting Effectiveness

Meanwhile, other researchers are experimenting with add-ons to these proven treatments to increase their effectiveness. Some are looking at how virtual reality might enhance the effects of prolonged-exposure therapy. By adding virtual reality, whereby clients experience 3-D imagery, sounds and sometimes smells that correspond with a traumatic event, "we think it might be a good alternative for people who are too avoidant to do standard exposure therapy, because it puts them right there," says Emory University's Rothbaum.

Other researchers are adding a small dose of an old tuberculosis drug, D-cycloserine, or DCS, to treatment to see if it can mitigate people's fear reactions. Rothbaum's team, which includes psychologist Mike Davis, PhD, and psychiatrist Kerry Ressler, MD, PhD, have recently shown that the drug helps to extinguish fear in animals, so they're hoping for a similar effect in people.

In one study with veterans of the current Iraq war, Rothbaum's team is giving all participants a type of virtual reality that simulates combat conditions in Iraq, then randomizing them into a drug condition where they get DCS, a placebo, or the anti-anxiety drug alprazolam (Xanax).

In a similar vein, researchers at the Program for Anxiety and Traumatic Stress Studies at Weill Cornell Medical College are using virtual reality and DCS to treat those directly affected by the 2001 World Trade Center attacks, including civilians who were in the towers or nearby buildings, witnesses, and firefighters and police officers who were first responders.

# PTSD Treatments Demand More Study, Independent Panel Finds

Inserting a cautionary note in the enthusiasm about effective treatments for post-traumatic stress disorders (PTSD), an Institute of Medicine (IoM) panel concluded in October that only exposure therapies such as prolonged exposure and cognitive-processing therapy have enough evidence to recommend them for treatment. The independent review was requested by the Department of Veterans Affairs (VA).

"At this time, we can make no judgment about the effectiveness of most psychotherapies or about any medications in helping patients with PTSD," states Alfred O. Berg, MD, the University of Washington professor of family medicine who chaired the IoM committee. "These therapies may or may not be effective—we just don't know in the absence of good data."

In a review of 53 drug studies and 37 psychotherapy studies, the seven-member panel concluded that many PTSD studies are flawed in terms of design and high dropout rates, which limit their generalizablity. Moreover, most drug studies were funded by pharmaceutical companies, and many psychotherapy studies were conducted by people who developed the techniques or by their close collaborators, the report finds.

Besides listing a number of drugs that need more independent investigation, the panel asserted that the following psychotherapies need better evaluation:

• Eye-movement desensitization and reprocessing.
• Cognitive restructuring.
• Coping-skills training.
• Group psychotherapy.

This said, the findings shouldn't be interpreted to mean that exposure therapies are the only treatments that should be used to treat the condition, the report adds. The reports' authors do suggest, however, that Congress should provide resources to the VA and other federal agencies to fund high-quality PTSD research that includes veterans and other affected groups in research planning.

Psychologists expert in PTSD commended the committee for its critical review and the VA for commissioning the independent study. However, many believe the report is flawed in several ways, including that it fails to address the difficulties in conducting PTSD research and to take into account existing reviews and guidelines conducted by other independent bodies.

"I think [the IoM panel] raised the bar too high and they're not realistic about what PTSD is and how hard it is to study and to keep people in treatment," says PTSD expert Barbara O. Rothbaum, PhD, director of the Trauma and Anxiety Recovery Program at Emory University. "High dropout is endemic in PTSD."

Dartmouth Medical School psychologist Paula P. Schnurr, PhD, well-known for her rigorous, large-scale studies of PTSD populations, says that in her view, the literature "differs from the conclusions of the report, in that there's good evidence that a wider range of cognitive behavioral therapies are effective."

In addition, the panel's findings are at odds with many reviews already done in the field, Rothbaum says. As one example, the committee did not support the evidence base on any drug at all, even though the Food and Drug Administration has approved the selective serotonin reuptake inhibitors paroxetine (Paxil) and sertaline (Zoloft) to treat PTSD. "There have been a number of reviews out there, and none has concluded that only one intervention works," she says.

—T. DeAngelis

---

Participants receive standard cognitive behavioral treatment enhanced with virtual reality, where they see graded versions of a Twin Towers scenario, starting with simple images of the buildings on a sunny day, and progressing gradually to include the horrific sights and sounds of that day. They also randomly receive either a small dose of DCS or a placebo pill before each session.

While neither study is complete, the researchers say the treatments appear to significantly reduce participants' PTSD symptoms. Rothbaum has recently submitted a grant proposal for a study where she plans to compare traditional and virtual-reality exposure therapies—which hasn't yet been done—in combination with DCS or a placebo.

## Addressing Comorbidity

Other psychologists are starting to think about ways to treat PTSD when it is accompanied by other psychiatric and health conditions. Psychologist John Otis, PhD, of Boston University and VA Boston, for instance, is testing an integrated treatment that aims to alleviate symptoms of both PTSD and chronic pain in Vietnam veterans and veterans of Operation Iraqi Freedom and Operation Enduring Freedom. The treatment combines aspects of cognitive processing therapy for trauma and cognitive behavioral therapy for chronic pain.

"We think these two conditions may interact in some [psychological] way that makes them more severe and challenging to treat," Otis says. In particular, he and others posit that "anxiety sensitivity"—fear of experiencing one's anxiety-related symptoms—may increase the odds that certain PTSD sufferers have more problems than others.

Again, while the study is not yet finished, results are encouraging, reports Otis. "Many of the veterans who are getting the integrated treatment are experiencing partial or complete remission of both kinds of symptoms," he says.

On a broader scale, the National Center for PTSD's Keane believes that much more research is needed on treating PTSD and psychiatric comorbidities such as depression, anxiety, substance abuse, personality disorders and psychosis—a common situation that escalates the more severe a person's PTSD symptoms are, he says.

He, for one, would like to examine possible applications to PTSD of the concept of a "unified protocol," a theory and methodology being developed by Boston University psychotherapy researcher David Barlow, PhD, to treat concurrent problems such as panic attacks, anxiety and phobias.

That said, the recent advances promise to help many more people suffering from a condition they did not bring on themselves, says Zeiss.

"While there is still more to learn, we have taken significant steps in developing treatments that have been shown to be effective and that will be increasingly provided both in VA and other mental health care settings," says Zeiss. "Those affected by combat stress and other traumas will be able to reach out for care without feeling ashamed or hopeless."

## Critical Thinking

1. How do psychologists effectively treat individuals with post-traumatic stress disorder?

---

**TORI DEANGELIS** is a writer in Syracuse, N.Y.

# When Do Meds Make the Difference?

**For most nonpsychotic conditions, empirically supported
therapies and medications yield similarly good results, but
therapy is better over the long haul, research finds.**

TORI DEANGELIS

As new psychotropic drugs enter the marketplace, and more psychologists gain the ability to prescribe, an inevitable question arises: Are drugs, therapy or a combination the best form of treatment?

Research shows fairly consistent results: For most non-psychotic disorders, behavioral interventions are just as effective as medications, and they hold up better over time.

"When researchers have directly compared empirically supported therapies with drugs in nonpsychotic populations, they hold their own very nicely," says Vanderbilt University depression expert Steven D. Hollon, PhD. Such therapies are also stronger in terms of enduring effects, he says. "People come away from treatment not only having their symptoms relieved, but learning something they can use the next time," he notes.

The British government, for one, is taking strong action with such findings: The United Kingdom's National Health Service is investing millions of dollars over the next few years to train more psychologists in evidence-based practices, making these interventions the treatment of choice over medications.

Meanwhile, research is continuing on combining drugs and therapy in treatment, and there, results are more mixed, says David H. Barlow, PhD, director of Boston University's Center for Anxiety and Related Disorders. In some cases, one treatment may boost the other. In other cases, there is no effect. Other times, combining the two may undermine an effective treatment. In addition, combination studies have been hobbled by theory and design problems, but research is improving and eventually should lead to clearer outcomes, Barlow says.

As the research continues to unfold, practicing psychologists—whether they prescribe themselves or collaborate with physicians—should educate themselves on psychopharmacological findings, says Jeff Matranga, PhD, one of two psychologists at the group practice Health Psych Maine who has completed postdoctoral psychopharmacology training.

"It is critically important that we gain information about the relative merits of medications, psychotherapy, a combination or a sequence for a given clinical problem," says Matranga, who lectures frequently on the topic. "Thankfully, this type of research has been increasing, and it is quite valuable for the treating clinician to help guide treatment choices."

## The Word on Depression

Research on depression shows that medications and empirically supported therapies such as cognitive behavioral therapy (CBT) and interpersonal therapy are equally effective, with each modality helping about 60 percent of clients, notes Hollon. Combined treatments produce even better results: In a literature review in the April 2005 *Journal of Clinical Psychiatry* (Vol. 66, No. 4, pages 455–468), Hollon and colleagues found that, in general, combining medication and therapy raised treatment effectiveness to as much as 75 percent.

"While that's not a huge increment in terms of the likelihood that someone will get better, you get a faster, more complete and more enduring response when you put drugs and therapy together," Hollon says.

One subgroup of depressed clients seems particularly amenable to combined treatment: severely and chronically depressed adults. One large multisite study was reported in the May 2000 *New England Journal of Medicine* (Vol. 342, No. 20, pages 1462–1470), and conducted by Brown University psychiatrist Martin B. Keller, MD, Virginia Commonwealth University psychologist James P. McCullough Jr., PhD, Stony Brook University psychologist Daniel Klein, PhD, and colleagues. In the study, researchers randomized patients with major depression either to a depression-focused CBT developed by McCullough, or to the antidepressant Serzone (nefazodone).

"The combination of the two was whoppingly more effective than either one alone," says Klein. About three-quarters responded to the combination, compared with about 48 percent for each individual condition. "People suffering from chronic depression often have longstanding interpersonal difficulties, and the virtue of combined treatment in this case may be that it simultaneously targets both depressive symptoms and social functioning," he says.

# Weighing in on Anxiety Disorders

Likewise, large-scale studies on anxiety disorders find that people do equally well with medication or CBT, but that fewer people relapse with CBT than with medication, says Barlow, a lead researcher in the area. Unlike with depression, however, combined treatments don't seem to confer extra benefits, he notes.

---

**"The ultimate positive circumstance is to have as many tools as you can."**

—Richard G. Heimberg , Temple University

---

The same pattern holds true for social phobia, says Temple University's Richard G. Heimberg, PhD, who has conducted a number of studies in the area. "You might get a bigger short-term burst from medication, but CBT is about as effective, and it's also associated with better protection against relapse," he says.

A long-standing line of research on obsessive-compulsive disorder (OCD) that has tested therapy and medication interventions has yielded what is considered a "best practice" for the disorder: a cognitive behavioral treatment for OCD combining exposure and ritual prevention, known as EX/RP. In this line of research, University of Pennsylvania researcher Edna Foa, PhD, and colleagues have conducted systematic studies to identify the active ingredients of EX/RP. In one set of studies, the team compared separate components of EX/RP and found that exposure only and ritual prevention only were not as effective as the combination of the two. In another line of research, they compared the efficacy of the trycyclic antidepressant clomipramine with EX/RP. They found that EX/RP reduced symptoms more than clomipramine and that EX/RP improved the effects of clomipramine, but the reverse was not the case.

The results of these studies "show that EX/RP is the treatment of choice for OCD, both as a treatment by itself and as an augmentation to medication," says Foa. She has found similar results with children and adolescents, though a related study on young people at Duke University did find an optimal effect by combining the selective serotonin reuptake inhibitor (SSRI) Zoloft (sertraline) and EX/RP, she notes.

Foa and her colleagues are now looking at how to improve OCD treatment further. In a current study, for instance, they're exploring how adding different conditions and more time might influence outcome. In the first part of the study, they're examining what happens when they give OCD sufferers not responding well to an SSRI an additional treatment of either EX/RP or the antipsychotic medication risperidone. In the second part, they're extending the length of each additional treatment for those still not experiencing much symptom relief.

# Real-World Considerations

Transporting such findings into the real world can, of course, be challenging. Unlike the relative purity of the lab, the treatment

## Combined-Treatment Research Gains Sophistication

Results of combined-treatment studies can be varied and confusing, as a result of methodology, researcher bias and patient characteristics, experts say. In fact, even the order in which you give treatments may make a difference, as may patients' treatment preference, notes Stony Brook University psychologist and depression researcher Daniel Klein, PhD.

Fortunately, research on combined treatments is becoming more sophisticated in design, theory and potential application, says David H. Barlow, PhD, director of Boston University's Center for Anxiety and Related Disorders. This evolution bodes well both for research and treatment, he believes.

The original studies on combined treatments tested drugs and therapy at the same time. The problem with this approach was a lack of theoretical rationale and hence a conflicting record of results. "No one provided a really good reason as to why these treatments might do better than one treatment alone," Barlow says.

A more sensible strategy that's being increasingly used examines "sequential" treatments, where researchers start with one treatment and either add or substitute a second one if the first isn't producing adequate results. This methodology promises to help tailor treatments and save money, Barlow says.

Now, researchers are launching what Barlow thinks may be the most effective research design yet: combining therapy with drugs developed specifically to work with a given psychological treatment—so-called "synergistic" treatments. For example, scientists are adding D-cycloserine—an old tuberculosis antibiotic recently shown to help extinguish fear in animals—as a complement to psychological treatments for conditions such as obsessive-compulsive disorder and post-traumatic stress disorder (PTSD). (See the January *Monitor* for its application to PTSD.)

Likewise, they're looking into possible applications of the hormone oxytocin to treat people with social anxiety, Barlow says. Traditionally used to stimulate labor and breastfeeding in women, oxytocin also helps to promote trust and bonding, which could help people with social anxiety overcome their fears, he notes.

—T. DeAngelis

world is a teeming bazaar of providers—many of whom do not have the credentials or training of psychologists—turf issues, cost concerns and varying patient inclinations and needs, experts say.

In the provider domain, practitioners both in psychology and medicine often are not as up to date on empirically tested treatments as researchers, Hollon says. "There's a large discussion in the literature about how few people in the real world tend to practice therapies with empirical support, and the same thing is true with pharmacotherapy," he notes.

And, of course, not everyone has access to mental health care. Even if they do, says Foa, "It's not easy for people to find this treatment, because there aren't a lot of experts in the area."

Meanwhile, cost issues can prevent the most effective treatments from being used, those involved say. For instance, therapy may be more expensive up front, though studies show it is often more cost-effective over the long run, Matranga notes.

Insurers are sometimes more willing to pay for medications than for therapy, and some primary-care physicians are more likely to prescribe medications before therapy for a range of psychological conditions, he says, particularly if they don't have easy access to someone trained in these therapies.

Patient variables present a mystery in need of greater understanding as well, says Heimberg: Some people don't believe that "talking" can help, others are too anxious to try medications on one side or therapy on the other, and still others can't tolerate medication side effects, for example.

**"There's a large discussion in the literature about how few people in the real world tend to practice therapies with empirical support, and the same thing is true with pharmacotherapy."**

—Steven D. Hollon, Vanderbilt University

Likewise, research is beginning to show that clients' preferences make a huge difference in outcome, says Klein. "They're more willing to stick with and invest in something they believe will work," he notes.

Finally, drugs and therapy each carry pros and cons that need to be assessed when finding the right treatment for someone, Hollon says. With therapy, there's a learning curve; with drugs, there are side effects, he says.

Given that we're moving into an era where pharmacological and behavioral strategies will be increasingly used and blended, it's wise to be as informed as possible, Heimberg emphasizes.

"The ultimate positive circumstance," he says, "is to have as many tools as you can."

## Critical Thinking

1. Is psychotherapy effective in treating psychological disorders? How does its effectiveness compare to the use of drugs in treating psychological disorders?

TORI DEANGELIS is a writer in Syracuse, N.Y.

# Placing the Patient Front and Center

The patient-centered "health home" promises to revitalize primary care and provide integrated, cost-effective treatment. How can psychologists get in the door?

Tori DeAngelis

Imagine a diabetes patient going to her primary-care physician with health concerns related to her condition. Instead of getting an initial assessment and being referred out, an interdisciplinary team immediately starts working on her case, involving her throughout the process. As part of that team, a psychologist assesses her level of depression, knowing that it often goes hand in hand with diabetes. The psychologist might also devise behavioral strategies to control her blood glucose levels.

That dream scenario would be commonplace in a patient-centered medical home, also referred to as a "health home." First conceived in 1967 by pediatricians as a way to coordinate care for children with developmental disabilities, the concept is regaining steam as a way to make primary care more robust, comprehensive and cost-effective. Versions of the concept—which is a central part of the 2010 health-care reform law—are already being adopted at the Mayo Clinic, the Department of Veterans Affairs and in pilot projects nationwide.

"The patient-centered health home is what primary care will be revitalized into," predicts James H. Bray, PhD, 2009 APA president and a primary-care psychologist at Baylor College of Medicine in Houston.

Psychologists could be key players in both shaping and implementing this concept, but experts inside and outside the field say they aren't moving fast enough.

"Psychology has an unprecedented opportunity in the medical home movement to integrate ourselves into the redesign of primary care," says Benjamin Miller, PsyD, assistant professor of family medicine at the University of Colorado School of Medicine in Aurora and co-founder of the Collaborative Care Research Network or CCRN (www.aafp.org/nrn/ccrn). "But if we don't decide which direction to go as a profession, other mental health professionals will step up and fill the roles we are not filling."

## Opportunities Ahead

One reason psychologists will be attracted to the patient-centered home model is its ability to increase access to mental health care for all patients. Research shows that up to two-thirds of people who need mental health or substance abuse treatment are first seen in general medical settings, yet only 12.7 percent receive even minimally adequate treatment there, according to data compiled by the independent actuarial firm Milliman Inc.

Moreover, between 30 percent and 50 percent of people referred to mental health services don't make their first appointment, according to studies in the *Archives of Internal Medicine* (Vol. 6, No. 4) and the *Journal of the American Medical Association* (Vol. 295, No. 9).

"There's a huge set of patients who, if they got a referral from their physicians into the community, would never show up," says Rodger Kessler, PhD, a clinical and primary-care psychologist at the University of Vermont College of Medicine in Burlington who has helped get behavioral health integrated into primary-care practices and in patient-centered health home pilot projects throughout Vermont.

Because care is better coordinated in a health home than in traditional medical settings, psychologists on these teams can improve the quality of both medical and mental health care, adds Katherine Nordal, PhD, APA's executive director for professional practice. And by normalizing what psychologists do, psychologists' integration into teams is likely to reduce stigma, as well, she says.

"Psychologists in this model are seen as just another doctor on the team—they're not necessarily even identified explicitly as a psychologist or health-care provider," she says.

At the same time, primary-care physicians are finally understanding the importance of incorporating a behavioral and psychological perspective in medical care, says Paul Grundy, MD, president of the Patient Centered Primary Care Collaborative (see www.pcpcc.net/behavioral-health), a consortium of Fortune 500 companies that played a key role in incorporating the health home concept in health-care reform legislation and that embraces behavioral health as part of its model.

"Many of us are beginning to grasp that the kinds of services and training and leadership that [psychologists] have been talking about for years is what is needed to address people's presenting complaints," Grundy says. "If you just peel back the onion a little bit, you'll find that for many people, multiple mental health and behavioral issues are the norm."

But to become permanent members of patient-centered teams, psychologists might benefit from more evidence demonstrating that their interventions make a positive difference in primary care. The research that does exist suggests definite benefits: A meta-analysis published online in *BMC Medicine* on June 25 indicates that brief psychotherapy in primary-care settings to treat anxiety and depression helps to reduce both mental and physical health problems. Meanwhile, studies show that one of the largest evidence-based treatment trials for depression to date, IMPACT (http://impact-uw.org/) shows that the model—which provides collaborative, integrated and supportive care using a team of health and mental health providers—significantly reduces depression, improves functioning and quality of life, and reduces health-care costs. The program, run out of the University of Washington and funded by the John A. Hartford Foundation and others, randomized 1,801 depressed, older adults to IMPACT or treatment as usual at 18 diverse primary-care sites across the country.

Further research now under way could bolster the evidence that integrating psychology can improve care in patient-centered health homes. With a grant from the Agency for Healthcare Research and Quality, for instance, Miller will be able to combine his CCRN network with another large national federated network called the Distributed Ambulatory Research and Therapeutics Network (DARTNet) to examine the aggregated electronic health records of thousands of patients. Analyses will allow him to compare outcomes of practices that integrate treatment for co-morbid mental and physical health conditions with those that do not.

"The data will let us go to policymakers and talk about the importance of addressing the whole person—not just mental health, not just physical health, but the two intertwined," he says.

# The Health Home on the Ground

While researchers are gathering evidence, other psychologists are already working on health home teams. Miller's network has enrolled 60 practices throughout the country that integrate mental health providers either in primary care or in patient-centered health homes.

Among such settings are the Salud Family Health Centers, nine clinics that serve low-income and immigrant patients in north-central Colorado. Salud is developing a health home model that involves a strong behavioral and mental health component, says clinical psychologist Andrea Auxier, PhD, Salud's director of integrated services and clinical training.

"Many of our patients have immigration-related stressors and limited financial resources, and they don't speak English or know how to navigate life in the United States," she says. "It was important for us to find a way to address their needs in a comprehensive way." As a result, patients receive both a full medical evaluation and a mental health screening by a psychology team made up of three postdoctoral fellows and seven practicum students. If psychological problems surface, the psychology team conducts further tests, working in tandem with the medical providers to ascertain how those issues might affect physical health issues, for example.

"All of our providers consider medical and mental health issues at the same time, using the same records and notes," she says.

Treatment looks different at Salud than it would in a traditional setting, too, Auxier adds. Patients with mental health issues have the option of seeing an in-house professional for treatment, rather than being referred out—and many take that option. Another feature: Patients, no matter what their condition, aren't kept waiting.

"Once someone comes in for help, we pretty much see them right away," she says.

Salud Medical Services Director Tillman Farley, MD, says he can't imagine good care being delivered without mental health professionals fully on board. "Not only do physicians not have a magical ability to spot mental health problems, but it is well-studied that they actually have a very *poor* ability to know who should be seen," says Farley, who spoke about Salud's version of integrated care at the APA 2009 Summit on the Future of Psychology Practice (www.performedia.com/apa/fpps09/gallery.shtml). "We rely on psychologists and other behavioral health professionals to provide that expertise."

Another setting that is adopting the medical home model is New York's University of Rochester Medical Center, where psychologist Susan McDaniel, PhD, has spent 28 years building a fully integrated care system. There, psychologists work on teams of medical professionals to provide comprehensive care that taps the wisdom of patients and their family members, McDaniel says.

"Because families are such an integral part of people's lives and health, the family systems approach has particular salience for primary care and the patient-centered medical home," says McDaniel, who also directs the medical school's Institute for the Family in Psychiatry.

To ensure that the model extends beyond the confines of her clinic, McDaniel also heads a two-year psychology fellowship program at the medical school that brings together psychology postdocs with medical residents. These budding professionals learn a family systems approach to care and how to work effectively with one another.

"It demystifies who we are for them, and it demystifies them for us, too," says Ann Cornell, PsyD, a second-year fellow in the program. Besides learning how physicians think, she has been able to share her perspective on the biopsychosocial challenges faced by older adults with medical residents doing geriatrics rotations, for example.

Psychologists have a wealth of other roles to play in health homes, as well. They're well-equipped to design and lead patient-centered care programs, evaluate systems, and measure quality-improvement outcomes, says APA's Nordal. "These are areas where psychology can shine," she says.

In addition, psychologists can serve as team facilitators, a skill that will be increasingly necessary as team-based care becomes more common, McDaniel says.

"Research shows it takes people at the top of their scope of practice and who are part of a cohesive, well-functioning team for the medical home concept to actually provide better care," she says.

Students who want to get involved in this movement can seek internships, postdocs or fellowships in settings that are adopting patient-centered health home models, including at the VA (see article on page 45), at federally qualified health centers such as Salud and at other leading-edge primary-care settings, such as the Mayo Clinic and the medical centers at the University of Rochester, University of Vermont and University of Colorado. In addition, the Graduate Psychology Education Program, a federally funded grant program initiated by APA, supports the development of and training in integrated-care teams at a number of sites across the country (see www.apa.org/about/gr/issues/gpe/grants-list.aspx for a current list of funded sites).

> **"Psychology has an unprecedented opportunity in the medical home movement to integrate ourselves into the redesign of primary care. But if we don't decide which direction to go as a profession, other mental health professionals will step up and fill the roles we are not filling."**
>
> —Benjamin Miller, University of Colorado School of Medicine

Practicing psychologists who are interested in the area should consider taking continuing-education courses in primary-care psychology, behavioral medicine and family systems psychology, says Bray. They can also consider gaining practical experience in primary-care settings, for example through programs such as the Certificate Program in Primary Care Behavioral Health at the University of Massachusetts (see www.umassmed.edu/pcbh.aspx).

Practicing psychologists can strengthen existing relationships with physicians and hospitals by keeping in contact with them and attending team meetings at hospitals to discuss shared patients, if possible, McDaniel adds. It also helps to highlight your ability to address problems that may be eluding physicians, such as lurking depression that is inhibiting a person's ability to heal, she says.

If psychologists become full players in the health home movement, they're likely to achieve an incredibly satisfying result: helping to develop a system that provides the kind of health care we'd all like to receive, McDaniel adds.

"Ninety-nine percent of the time, patients who receive this kind of care can't believe how lucky they are," says McDaniel. "To be able to come to the same place and get all of your care, and for people to work together on your behalf, is a great feeling."

## Further Readings

Frank, R.G., McDaniel, S.H., Bray, J. H. & Heldring, M. (Eds.). (2003). *Primary care psychology.* Washington, DC: American Psychological Association.

Gatchel, R.J. & Oordt, M.S. (2003). *Clinical health psychology and primary care: Practical advice and clinical guidance for successful collaboration.* Washington, DC: American Psychological Association.

James, L.C. & Folen, R.A. (Eds.). (2005). *The primary care consultant: The next frontier for psychologists in hospitals and clinics.* Washington, DC: American Psychological Association.

Hunter, C.L., Goodie, J.L., Oordt, M.S. & Dobmeyer, A.C. (2009). *Integrated behavioral health in primary care: Step-by-step guidance for assessment and intervention.* Washington, DC: American Psychological Association.

McDaniel, S.H. & Fogarty, C.T. (2009). What primary care psychology has to offer the patient-centered medical home. *Professional Psychology: Research and Practice, 40* (5), 483–492.

APA's Blueprint for Change: Integrated Health Care for an Aging Population, www.apa.org/pi/aging/programs/integrated/index.aspx. This report addresses the hallmarks of medical home and patient-centered integrated care models for older adults, as well as related fact sheets for consumers and policymakers.

## Critical Thinking

1. What is patient-centered home care?
2. Detail its advantages over traditional forms of psychotherapy.

# Test-Your-Knowledge Form

We encourage you to photocopy and use this page as a tool to assess how the articles in *Annual Editions* expand on the information in your textbook. By reflecting on the articles you will gain enhanced text information. You can also access this useful form on a product's book support website at www.mhhe.com/cls.

NAME:                                                                                    DATE:

_____

TITLE AND NUMBER OF ARTICLE:

_____

BRIEFLY STATE THE MAIN IDEA OF THIS ARTICLE:

_____

LIST THREE IMPORTANT FACTS THAT THE AUTHOR USES TO SUPPORT THE MAIN IDEA:

_____

WHAT INFORMATION OR IDEAS DISCUSSED IN THIS ARTICLE ARE ALSO DISCUSSED IN YOUR TEXTBOOK OR OTHER READINGS THAT YOU HAVE DONE? LIST THE TEXTBOOK CHAPTERS AND PAGE NUMBERS:

_____

LIST ANY EXAMPLES OF BIAS OR FAULTY REASONING THAT YOU FOUND IN THE ARTICLE:

_____

LIST ANY NEW TERMS/CONCEPTS THAT WERE DISCUSSED IN THE ARTICLE, AND WRITE A SHORT DEFINITION:

# NOTES

# NOTES

# NOTES

# NOTES

# NOTES

# NOTES